A. D. LIVINGSTON'S
BIG BOOK OF MEAT

Other Cookbooks by A. D. Livingston

Jerky

Sausage

Cold-Smoking & Salt-Curing Meat, Fish & Game

Cast-Iron Cooking

The Curmudgeon's Book of Skillet Cooking

Complete Fish & Game Cookbook

The Freshwater Fish Cookbook

Venison Cookbook

The Whole Grain Cookbook

A. D. LIVINGSTON'S
BIG BOOK
OF
MEAT

HOME SMOKING, SALT CURING, JERKY, AND SAUSAGE

Guilford, Connecticut

An imprint of Globe Pequot

Distributed by NATIONAL BOOK NETWORK

Content from *Jerky* copyright © 2001, 2011, 2018 by A. D. Livingston

Content from *Sausage* copyright © 1998, 2011, 2018 by A. D. Livingston
Illustrations by Jonathan Milo

Cold-Smoking & Salt-Curing Meat, Fish & Game copyright © 1995, 2011, 2018 by A. D. Livingston
Illustrations copyright © 1995 by Manuel F. Cheo

Specific acknowledgments to individuals, other books, and authors are made in the text as appropriate. A few of the recipes and a little of the text were used, in slightly altered form, in the author's column for *Gray's Sporting Journal*.

British Library Cataloguing in Publication Information Available
Library of Congress Cataloging-in-Publication Data Available

ISBN 978-1-4930-2602-9 (paperback)
ISBN 978-1-4930-3452-9 (e-book)

∞™ The paper used in this publication meets the minimum requirements of American National Standard for Information Sciences—Permanence of Paper for Printed Library Materials, ANSI/NISO Z39.48-1992.

Printed in China

CONTENTS

INTRODUCTION

Jerky is simply raw meat that has been slowly dried at a low temperature. As the water is removed, the meat loses both weight and volume. What it doesn't lose, however, is flavor. In fact, the flavor of the meat is greatly concentrated, which might explain why just about everybody with good teeth loves jerky.

These days jerky is popular as a snack, and it also comes in handy as a high-energy food for backpackers, dogsledders, trail walkers, hunters, anglers, boaters, and other people who spend lots of time outdoors. For long-distance runners and sports competitors, jerky can deliver a burst of energy all out of proportion to its compact size and light weight. For campers, jerky is easy to pack and store. On an auto trip, jerky is great for the kids and doesn't make a mess in the car, and, of course, it's perfect for snacking during the football game or television shows—and for sneaking into movie theaters that don't allow their patrons to bring their own popcorn. Family dogs savor the stuff, too, if my Nosher is a good representative.

Indeed, modern man eats jerky by the ton, piece by savory piece. It's available these days in supermarkets and outfitter shops and through mail-order catalogs and online retailers—and even in corner convenience stores. In other parts of the world, freshly made jerky is often sold at wayside stands and by street vendors. More and more people are making it at home these days, in this country and abroad, and packets of jerky seasoning mixes are sold in sausage and jerky supply catalogs and at the meat counters of large supermarkets.

These days deer hunters are perhaps America's greatest jerky makers, in terms of volume, because they sometimes have large amounts of meat to preserve and because jerky seems to be a popular chew among this group. Also, a lot of dehydrated-food buffs—many of whom have purchased expensive food dehydrators and vacuum-pack systems for home use—are especially interested in making their own jerky.

Historically, jerky making is usually attributed to the American Indian, who made good use of it to store buffalo and other meats for future use and for journey food. But jerky really wasn't first invented in the Americas. It has been made around the world since the time of the caveman, and records of its use date back as far as the ancient Egyptians. Before the invention of canning and refrigeration, drying was the only way to preserve meat.

Jerky is still a practical way of preserving meat for future use. Yet modern man, for the most part, has taken to jerky for a more epicurean reason: Jerky simply tastes good and lasts longer, as a chew, than other foods or snacks. And since jerky is made from low-fat cuts of meat, it is also healthier than most junk food.

As a practitioner, I believe that the very best jerky is made at a low temperature over a long period of time. There are, however, other opinions and practical considerations in this matter. If truth be told, there's simply more than one way to jerk meat. Recipes abound, and techniques vary. Experts set forth conflicting information in books and magazine articles. Practitioners argue hotly, head to head. In truth, just about every jackleg jerky maker has something to share, as well as secrets to keep, and I hope the variety of recipes and methods in this book, old and new, will prove to be interesting and helpful. These variations will be discussed in more detail in the chapters that follow, along with suitable recipes. Meanwhile, here is some information that applies to all jerky making.

The Shape of Jerky

Most jerky these days is cut into thin strips. True, some commercial jerky is made in rather jagged pieces, but most of it is made in a more uniform size. Pressed jerky, which is made from ground or chopped meat, is almost always quite uniform. The strips of meat usually run 5 to 6 inches long by 1 inch wide, and often less than ¼ inch thick; when the strips of meat are dried, the dimensions shrink considerably. In any case, the length and width of the strips aren't nearly as important as the thickness, which greatly influences how long the jerky should be dried and how it will be eaten. Thick jerky tends to make a better chew and lasts longer, but thin requires less drying time and is easier to chew for quick consumption.

Cutting the Meat

A sharp knife is the jerky maker's best friend. I always prefer blades made of carbon steel, because they can easily be sharpened with the aid of a good Arkansas whetstone. Modern stainless-steel knives and various sharpening devices fall into the gadget category. If you don't believe me, talk with some professional butchers who don't sell cutlery.

An electric meat saw comes in handy for making jerky, especially if you are a stickler for uniform thicknesses. There are also some other aids for cutting jerky in uniform thicknesses. Check the mail-order and Internet sources listed at the end of this book. Meanwhile, keep your knife sharp.

It's almost always best to partially freeze the meat before attempting to slice it thinly. How thin should it be? Most practitioners want ¼ inch thick or less. Not only does the thickness help determine the time required to dry the meat, but it also has a bearing on the texture of the finished jerky. The texture is also influenced greatly by the grain of the meat and how it is cut. If the jerky is cut with the grain, lengthwise, it will be stringy and tough, which is what most people want for a good chew. If it is cut across the grain, it tends to be crumbly and easier to chew up and swallow. Jerky that will be used in pemmican (see chapter 11, page 80) or in recipes (see chapter 12, page 87) works best if it is cut across the grain.

When drying a batch of jerky, there is no rule stating that all your pieces must be of the same thickness or overall shape. It is, however, best to keep thick separated from thin, on separate trays. That way, you can dry the thicker strips longer without having to judge each piece in the whole batch.

This might come as a cultural shock to some people, but jerky does not have to be made in narrow strips. Chapter 4, Jerky Every Which Way (page 32), sets forth recipes for jerky nuggets, chunks, and slabs. So, if you are inept at carving meat with a knife, jerk it all and enjoy the variety.

One other thing: You should wash your hands and utensils before and after cutting meat. This precaution is especially important before handling meat that is to be cut into chunks and then ground for making burger jerky.

Drying Jerky

Modern practitioners are fortunate enough to have kitchen ovens and electric dehydrators suitable for making jerky. These are convenient, yes, but good jerky has been made for centuries without them. The idea, of course, is to remove the moisture from the meat at a low temperature. Several ways to accomplish this are detailed in the first five chapters of part one, including how-to texts on drying jerky in kitchen ovens, in electric dehydrators made especially for drying foods, in the open air, in patio smokers, and so on.

The weight of the finished jerky as compared to the weight of the fresh meat is a pretty good indication of dryness. For the best overall results, 5 pounds of beef should be dried down to at least 2 to 2½ pounds of jerky. For long storage, however, it can go down to about 1 pound—but this jerky will be very hard and will lose some flavor. A good deal depends on the meat, however. Some venison, for example, will be considerably drier than most beef.

Most people don't bother to weigh the meat before and after jerking it in order to determine dryness. Instead, experience usually prevails. Properly prepared jerky feels dry to the touch; strips of jerky will bend without snapping but at the same time will show cracks and breaks in the bend.

Clearly, drying jerky at home is not an exact science. There are too many variables, such as temperature, air circulation, humidity of the ambient air, drying time, thickness of the meat, and so on. The "cure" that the practitioner uses also affects the process.

The trend of minimizing salt in modern jerky recipes or techniques is not recommended by this writer—but some excellent-tasting recipes do just that. I argue that the salt is very important, partially because it stimulates the taste buds, but mainly because it helps preserve the meat directly and helps draw out the moisture. Most bacteria simply can't thrive without adequate moisture.

Storing Jerky

There are several approaches to and some conflicting opinions about the best way to store jerky. Some practitioners put it into an airtight jar or other container, whereas others want to store it in a cloth bag so that it can breathe. Some people tell you to keep it in a brown bag; others say not to do so under any circumstances. Some of the recipes and methods throughout this book will reflect some of these opinions, which in turn often apply to the jerky made by a certain procedure and under certain conditions.

If I had to be pinned down to one method of storing jerky, I would wiggle a little, but in the end I would surely choose wide-mouthed Mason jars sealed with the new vacuum-pack systems, now available for the home kitchen. In some cases, vacuum-packed plastic bags work better than Mason jars.

Much depends on the temperature and humidity of the air. In cool, dry climates, jerky stores satisfactorily without refrigeration, and the storage method isn't very

important. In hot, humid climes, it's best to store the jerky in the refrigerator (which will usually be low in both humidity and temperature) or in a freezer. If the jerky is to be kept outside the refrigerator, I prefer to either vacuum-seal it or keep it in a breathable container. Often I'll wrap the strips in paper towels, which tend to wick away any moisture the jerky might contain or absorb on a humid day. Jerky wrapped, a few strips at a time, in paper towels and stored in a pillowcase will keep for a very long time, if it is properly dried to start.

Sometimes jerky that wasn't quite dry enough for storage will develop a mold on the surface. This can be wiped off with a cloth dipped in vinegar, but most people find that the mold quells their appetite for that particular batch of jerky.

Keep in mind that jerky taken from an oven or a dehydrator will become harder as it cools. Also remember that such jerky will continue to dry out during storage if the humidity is low. So, air can work in two ways: Moist air adds moisture to the jerky; dry air draws moisture out of the jerky. Using a vacuum-pack system will minimize either action simply by removing the air. Consequently, I highly recommend the vacuum-pack systems for storing jerky, as well as fish and fresh meats, in the refrigerator or freezer. These machines are very easy to use. Just follow the manufacturer's instructions, making sure that you have the proper kind of bags and new lid seals for the jars.

One other tip: Always allow the jerky to cool down before storing it in an airtight container. Hot jerky tends to sweat.

Using Jerky

Jerky isn't limited to snacks; it can be eaten in other ways or cooked for a meal. Chapter 11 (page 80) sets forth recipes and techniques for making and using pemmican—an American Indian mixture of powdered jerky and animal fat, which is storable and easy to eat. Chapter 12 (page 87) contains some recipes for using jerky in complete one-pot dishes, such as chili. Anyone who puts up lots of jerky, perhaps as a means of preserving the meat from a moose or elk taken on the hunt, may want to cook these dishes fairly often, and, of course, culinary adventurers will want a taste of the old ways of doing things.

Why Make Your Own Jerky?

Jerky is expensive if you buy it ready-made and neatly packaged in small units. But it's really inexpensive—or can be—if you make your own in bulk and don't go overboard on spices and herbs. At $3.00 per pound for the meat, homemade jerky will figure out at about $7.50 per pound. You'd pay that for an ounce or two of gourmet jerky ordered from a catalog. The price can be even lower if you buy and jerk a big chunk of meat, such as a beef hindquarter from a meat-processing plant or even a large roast from your favorite butcher. Put the pencil to it.

Jerky tastes better fresh than it does after long storage, and jerky is at its very best when eaten directly from the oven or dehydrator, still warm and not as hard as it will become on cooling. Trouble is, warm jerky is just a little *too* good. More than one batch (never mind whose) has been entirely consumed by the "testing" while it was still drying in the oven. Warm jerky is addictive, really, and my mouth starts to water just to think of it as I write these words. You can taste it, too. Lean back in your easy chair, close your eyes, and whiff the aroma gently wafting from the kitchen oven.

The following chapters set forth several methods and a number of recipes for making jerky in the kitchen, on the patio, and in remote camps. Most of the recipes and techniques call for a lean red meat or some commonly understood cut such as flank steak. These recipes can be adapted quite readily to venison, lean beef, and other good red meats—with some emphasis on "lean." Specific meats such as beef, venison, and ostrich are also discussed, along with recipes for jerking them.

CHAPTER 1

KITCHEN OVEN JERKY

The ordinary kitchen oven permits the home cook to make excellent jerky without any specialized equipment or start-up costs. Usually, jerky strips are simply placed on the crosspieces of the oven racks, possibly with a drip pan at the bottom. A few people may prefer to hang the jerky vertically from the racks. To accomplish this, it's easy to skewer the end of each strip with a toothpick and hang it, but the process is time-consuming. Multiple strips can be threaded onto bamboo skewers and properly spaced to hang between the metal rods. Draping the strips of meat directly over the metal rods isn't recommended, however—except possibly for very thin jerky—but long strips can be folded over two rods for better air circulation. Also, drying the meat on trays with a solid bottom isn't ideal, because the bottom of the jerky isn't exposed to air.

One problem with a tightly closed oven is that the moisture from the jerky can't escape, which slows the drying process. Leaving the door slightly ajar helps but will alter the temperature of the oven. It's best to check the oven temperature with a thermometer instead of relying on the thermostat.

Of course, one oven may not be quite as good as another for making jerky, and each type will have advantages or disadvantages. Here's my take:

Electric Ovens. The electric kitchen oven can be credited with bringing about the recent renaissance in homemade jerky. As a general rule, the door should be left slightly ajar, letting the water vapor escape from the oven. Most kitchen ovens come with two racks, which can be used in several positions. Additional racks can be obtained for some models, either at retail outlets, from the manufacturer, or perhaps from flea markets and junk stores. For best results, test the temperature of your own oven with a thermometer placed in the center. Make the test after the oven has been turned on for an hour, with the door ajar. In other words, test the oven under the conditions that will be used for making jerky. If the oven thermostat is not accurate, you can usually compensate. Also make sure that only the bottom heating element is in use. This will normally be the bake mode. The broil mode heats from the top element. Some oven preheat modes use both top and bottom. In any case, if your oven uses both the top and bottom elements for regular baking, it's best to unplug the top element before making jerky.

Auxiliary Toaster Ovens. These small ovens come in handy for making a small batch of jerky, starting with about a pound of meat. Remember that with most of these small ovens you'll have only one rack, which should be in the center position. Also remember to use the bake mode, not the broil. Put the thermostat on the lowest setting, which will usually be marked WARM. Then turn it up if needed, testing the actual temperature in the middle with an oven thermometer. Leave the door cracked open (slightly) to let the moisture escape.

Convection Ovens. Basically, these are regular ovens with fans to circulate the air. They range in size from countertop to full-size kitchen ovens, such as the Jenn-Air. Some have regular dehydrating modes, and some have a space for water vapor to escape—a very good feature for drying jerky. In general, they heat evenly and do a good job of making jerky. It's best to follow the manufacturer's instructions for these ovens. They are more expensive than dehydrators, but the larger ranges are really useful appliances to have for regular cooking as well as for drying foods. They also operate as a regular oven, convection oven, broiler, and dehydrator, as well as having a stove-top grill and burners on top. Moreover, some of these ovens hold up to ten racks. In any case, the manufacturers of convection ovens publish instruction books and even cookbooks, which cover dehydrating.

I don't recommend buying a convection oven for making jerky. But if you already own one, or plan to add one to your kitchen for regular cooking, then by all means take advantage of its dehydrating capability. The forced-air-circulation feature is great for drying jerky, as compared to regular ovens, but note that merely circulating the same air in the oven in a closed loop will not help remove the moisture from the system. Read the manufacturer's instructions—and remember that dry air is the key to making good jerky, always.

Gas Ovens. Most of these are not ideal for jerky simply because they get too hot. After all, the idea is to dry the meat, not cook or toast it. Before attempting a batch of jerky in a gas oven, turn the thermostat to the lowest setting and put a thermometer inside close to the center. To be suitable for jerky, it should read 150°F or lower. If the oven has a pilot light, try making jerky without turning on the main burner. This will usually take considerably longer, however, depending on the internal temperature, but it will make the jerky at a low temperature.

Woodstove Ovens. These old-time ovens can be used for making jerky if the temperature is held low enough. The better way would be to start the jerky in the oven for a few minutes, then hang it over the stove. The air will naturally rise from the stove, bringing heat to the jerky and taking away any water vapor. See also chapter 3, Camp and Old-Time Jerky (page 21).

• • •

The rest of this chapter sets forth recipes for making jerky in a large electric kitchen oven. Adjustments can be made as necessary for other types of ovens. Bear in mind that these recipes can also be used to make jerky in a dehydrator (see chapter 2, page 15). The measures of the meat in these recipes are suited for making jerky on two large racks. For larger batches of jerky, see the recipes in the next chapter.

SMOKY JOE

Here's a jerky with a smoke flavor—without the smoke. It is especially good with top-quality lean beef, such as top round steak, thinly sliced. Cut it against the grain for normal use, or with the grain if you want a chew.

| 2 pounds lean red-meat steaks | liquid smoke |
| salt and black pepper | |

Partially freeze the steaks; this makes them easier to cut. Trim off all the fat, then slice the meat into strips about ¼ inch thick. Place the meat into a nonmetallic container, making a layer ½ inch thick. Sprinkle with salt, pepper, and liquid smoke. Add another layer of meat, another sprinkling, and so on, ending with the seasonings. Weight the meat with a plate or some such object. Cover and place in the refrigerator for 8 hours or so. Arrange the strips on a rack in a shallow baking pan or dish. Put into the oven at 140°F for 6 to 8 hours, or until dry. Cool the jerky and store it in airtight containers, preferably in the refrigerator or a cool place.

TERIYAKI JERKY

This jerky can be made with a commercial teriyaki sauce, or you can mix your own with this recipe.

2 pounds lean red meat

½ cup soy sauce

¼ cup brown sugar

2 cloves garlic, crushed

1 tablespoon salt

1 tablespoon freshly grated gingerroot

½ teaspoon freshly ground black pepper

Cut the meat into strips ¼ inch thick. In a nonmetallic container, mix the rest of the ingredients and stir well. Add the meat, a few strips at a time, tossing about to coat all sides with the teriyaki sauce. Cover and marinate in the refrigerator for 8 to 10 hours. Drain and dry in a kitchen oven at 140°F for 6 to 8 hours, or until dry.

A small batch of this jerky will probably be eaten right away—and in my house, it is half gone before the drying process is complete. So, storage isn't a problem. For large batches that will be stored for a long time, vacuum-packed jars work best for me.

BARBECUE SAUCE JERKY

This jerky can be made with the aid of your favorite barbecue sauce, or you can use the recipe below.

4 pounds lean red meat

1 cup catsup

½ cup red wine vinegar

¼ cup brown sugar

2 tablespoons Worcestershire sauce

2 tablespoons salt

1 tablespoon dry mustard

½ tablespoon onion powder

1 teaspoon freshly ground black pepper

⅛ teaspoon Tabasco sauce

Trim the fat and tissue off the meat, then cut it into strips ½ inch thick. Mix all the other ingredients in a nonmetallic container. Add the meat, toss it about to coat all sides, and refrigerate for 10 hours or so. Drain the meat and place the strips on racks in a kitchen oven. Dry at 145°F for about 8 to 10 hours, or until the jerky is hardened to your liking. Store in sealed jars, preferably in the refrigerator, or in vacuum-packed containers.

Note: Some people call this "barbecued jerky." It isn't. A barbecued meat is juicy and soft and tender; jerky is dry and hard and tough, or very chewy.

HONEY JERKY

The combination of honey, soy sauce, and lemon juice is not entirely lost in jerky. Be sure to try it, using regular soy sauce (with lots of salt). Also remember that honey is a natural food preservative.

2 pounds lean red meat	¼ cup fresh lemon juice
½ cup dark soy sauce	2 cloves garlic, minced
½ cup honey	1 teaspoon finely ground black pepper

Trim the meat and cut it into strips ¼ inch thick. Mix the rest of the ingredients in a nonmetallic container. Dip the meat strips into the marinade mixture. Cover and marinate for several hours in the refrigerator. Place the slices on a rack over a drip pan and dry at 150°F for 8 hours, or until the jerky is as dry as you like it. Store like ordinary jerky—but this won't last long.

DIANE'S CHOICE

My niece passed this recipe on to the rest of the family, saying that her children really love it. Well, uncles love it, too, and so does my dog Nosher. I don't have exact measures to offer. Just sprinkle on each ingredient, using what you think you need. Don't skimp on the salt, however.

2 red-meat flank steaks	sugar
seasoned salt	Ac'cent
garlic salt	liquid smoke
black pepper	

Slice the meat bacon-thin on a slant while it is partially frozen. Sprinkle both sides with seasoned salt, garlic salt, black pepper, sugar, and Ac'cent. Brush with liquid smoke. Marinate in a glass container for 24 hours. Drain the meat and drape the strips over the oven racks. Dry for 15 minutes at the lowest setting. Turn off the oven, leaving the door closed, for 1 hour. Repeat the procedure two more times. Enjoy.

MORTONIZED JERKY

The Morton Salt Division of Morton Thiokol Inc. markets a line of meat-curing salts and seasonings. The Tender Quick mix used in this recipe is widely available, usually sold in the canning section of supermarkets or from mail-order sources. The mix contains mostly salt, with small amounts of sodium nitrate, sodium nitrite, and other ingredients. In addition to curing the meat (mostly with the salt), the mix helps retain the color of red meat such as beef or venison. For more on curing salts, see glossary, page 369.

2 pounds lean red meat

1 tablespoon Morton Tender Quick cure mix

2 teaspoons sugar

1 teaspoon black pepper

1 teaspoon garlic powder

Trim the meat and slice it with the grain into strips about 1½ inches wide and ½ inch thick. (Partially freezing the meat will make the slicing easier.) In a bowl, mix the other ingredients. Rub the slices of meat on all sides with the cure and spice mix, using all of it. Place the strips in a plastic bag and seal. Refrigerate for 1 hour. Rinse the strips in cold water and pat dry with paper towels. Place the strips on greased racks in shallow baking pans. Do not allow the meat to overlap or touch. Place the pans in the oven and set the temperature as low as you can get it—120°F to 150°F. Dry for 8 hours or longer with the oven door cracked open. Cool and place the jerky into airtight jars or bags. Store in a cool place or freeze until needed.

LOW-SALT PEPPER JERKY

Here's a tasty jerky for people who feel a need to avoid salty fare. Be sure to use low-salt soy sauce, because most regular soy sauce is very high in salt. The measures below are for a modest amount of jerky, intended to be eaten right away. I don't recommend long storage under less-than-ideal conditions for low-salt jerky.

2 pounds lean red meat

¼ cup liquid smoke

1 cup low-salt soy sauce

freshly ground black pepper

Cut the meat into strips ⅜ inch thick. Mix the liquid smoke and low-salt soy sauce in a large plastic bag. Add the meat, shaking it a little to coat all sides. Marinate for several hours in the refrigerator. Arrange the meat on oven racks. Sprinkle with freshly ground black pepper to taste; turn each strip and sprinkle the other side. Dry at 155°F for 6 hours or longer, depending on how hard you want the jerky.

SESAME SEED JERKY

Here's an Asian-style jerky made with sesame seeds. I especially like it while it is still warm from the oven.

½ cup soy sauce

½ cup sake, sherry, or dry vermouth

1 tablespoon brown sugar

1 tablespoon salt

½ teaspoon finely ground black pepper

2 pounds red-meat flank steak

¼ cup sesame seeds

Mix all the ingredients except the meat and sesame seeds in a nonmetallic container; stir well. Cut the meat into strips about ¼ inch thick or a little thinner. Put the meat into the container, tossing it about to coat all sides. Cover the container and marinate overnight in the refrigerator, stirring a time or two. Drain the meat and arrange the strips on racks. Sprinkle the strips with the sesame seeds and dry for 6 hours or so, or until dry to your liking.

HAWAIIAN JERKY

Pineapple juice helps this island recipe along. For a variation, use a can or two of chunk pineapple instead of juice. Pour off the juice for use in the jerky. Marinate and dry the chunks of pineapple right along with the meat.

½ cup pineapple juice

½ cup soy sauce

2 cloves garlic, crushed

2 tablespoons brown sugar

1 tablespoon grated fresh gingerroot

1 tablespoon salt

1 teaspoon black pepper

½ teaspoon cayenne pepper

2 pounds lean red meat

Mix all the ingredients except the meat in a nonmetallic container. Slice the meat into strips about ¼ inch thick. Add the meat to the container, tossing to coat all sides. Marinate in the refrigerator overnight. Dry the strips in the oven at 140°F for 8 to 10 hours, or until the jerky is ready to your liking.

CHINESE JERKY

Jerky is enjoyed as noshing fare in China, where it is often made on the sweet side, as in this recipe. Try it for a change.

2-pound, red-meat flank steak

1 cup sugar

½ cup soy sauce

¼ cup catsup

¼ cup hoisin sauce

¼ cup oyster sauce

¼ cup honey

¼ cup sake, sherry, or dry vermouth

2 tablespoons salt

Slice the meat thinly—about ⅛ inch thick. Mix the rest of the ingredients in a nonmetallic container. Add the beef strips, tossing to coat all sides. Marinate for 24 hours or longer in the refrigerator. Rig for drying in an oven at 250°F. Place the beef strips on drying trays. Dry for 45 minutes to 1 hour. It's best to eat this jerky warm, or save it for a few days. The recipe is not designed for long storage.

DRIED-HERB JERKY

If you like the flavors of mixed herbs, try this recipe. It works best with finely powdered dried herbs.

2 pounds lean red meat

1 tablespoon salt

1 teaspoon onion salt

½ teaspoon garlic salt

½ teaspoon lemon-pepper seasoning salt

½ teaspoon dried oregano

½ teaspoon dried basil

½ teaspoon dried marjoram

½ teaspoon dried thyme

Trim the meat and cut it into strips about ³⁄₁₆ inch thick. Thoroughly mix all the dry ingredients and sprinkle onto one side of each beef strip, using about half of the mixture. Pound the strips with a meat tenderizer, working in the spices. Turn the strips and sprinkle with the rest of the dry mix. Arrange the strips on racks and dry in the oven at 140°F, with the door ajar, for about 4 hours. Turn the strips and dry for another 4 to 6 hours, until the jerky bends the way you want it. Wrap each piece in paper towels and store in a jar.

FLANK STEAK JERKY

The flank of beef and other large animals makes an excellent jerky and can be prepared without actually cutting the meat with a knife—the way of some primitive peoples. According to Linda West Eckhardt's The Only Texas Cookbook *(the source of this recipe), some Mexican cooks use this method. The idea is to tear off strips of meat with the grain, and, of course, flank steak is ideal for this method. Note also that this method keeps the heat at about 200°F, which is higher than most practitioners recommend.*

flank steak	salt and black pepper
minced garlic	

Put the flank steak into the freezer until it is partially frozen but still pliable. Tear off small strips with your hands. Pound each meat strip slightly with a wooden spoon or wooden spatula, flattening it. Rub each piece of meat with minced garlic (use about 1 clove of garlic to each pound of meat). Sprinkle the meat lightly on both sides with salt and pepper. Place the flattened strips on a rack in a baking pan. Place the pan in the center of the 200°F oven. Bake 5 to 6 hours, turning once, or until each piece is dry to the touch but still pliable. Place the cooled jerky in jars, cover, and store in a dark place.

CHAPTER 2

ELECTRIC DEHYDRATOR JERKY

Modern electric dehydrators, made primarily for drying slices of fruits and vegetables, have proved to be ideal for making jerky. They look small when compared to kitchen ovens, but the tightly spaced trays hold lots of jerky strips. The dehydrators are fitted with thermostats that control the temperatures to jerky-making and fruit-drying ranges, usually from 80°F to 150°F. In other words, they don't get too hot. Most dehydrators provide a constant flow of fan-forced air around the jerky, which helps promote even heating and exhaust the moisture from the unit.

The trays are a big part of the convenience, and anyone who sets out to build a wooden-box-type cold-smoker or dehydrator should look into the possibility of using store-bought trays designed for dehydrators. Most of the units are made of a tough plastic, although stainless-steel dehydrator trays are also available. In either case, the trays have a mesh bottom that allows the air to contact both sides of the meat.

All in all, the units are very easy to use—almost foolproof. Moreover, they operate at about 500 watts, a little more or less, which makes them inexpensive. It's about like burning five 100-watt lightbulbs.

There are two basic types of electric dehydrators, with two shapes of trays.

Round. These units feature round trays that stack atop each other. Usually they come with four or five trays, but additional trays can be purchased for some models. I'm acquainted with one unit that permits the use of up to fifteen trays— which will make lots of jerky. The total capacity, however, also depends on the diameter of the trays. These round dehydrators are widely available, and the cheaper models can be purchased in most discount stores. One potential problem with some of these units is that the airflow is from bottom to top, which means there may be a difference in temperature and humidity from one tray to another. Rotating the trays during drying helps.

Rectangular. Usually more expensive than the round dehydrators, these units feature a box with close-fitting, removable, drawer-like trays. The rectangular shape works a little better for loading strips of jerky, for the same reason that a square skillet works better than a round one for frying bacon. Several sizes are available, varying in the number and size of the trays. Usually the trays are plastic, but one large model has metal mesh trays. One disadvantage of the design is that more trays can't be added once the unit is full. On the other hand, trays can be removed to make enough headspace to hold thick chunks of meat. In most of these units, the heat flows from the side, across the trays, rather than from the bottom up. This promotes even heating and drying, with no need to rotate the trays, which works a little better for unattended jerky making. The more expensive models come with a timer as well as a thermostat.

• • •

All of the recipes in the previous chapter can be made in a dehydrator instead of a kitchen oven. It's easier, really, partly because the trays are so perfect for jerky. The recipes in the first chapter are designed for making small batches. The ones that follow, however, are for making larger amounts of jerky, partly because the larger dehydrators process more meat at a time. As a rule, any of the jerky recipes in this book can be scaled up or down, depending on the meat at hand and the equipment available. In some cases—usually when jerking large batches of meat—it may be desirable to choose recipes that work both with and without marinades or rubs. In other words, start using the dehydrator immediately to make a batch of jerky while part of the meat is being marinated.

EASY BIG-BATCH JERKY

Here's a big-batch recipe that's really hard to beat. Note that most of the salt used in the recipe comes from soy sauce. Do not use low-salt soy.

2 cups soy sauce	10 pounds lean meat, cut into strips ¼ inch thick
1 cup Worcestershire sauce	
¼ cup liquid smoke	salt and black pepper to taste

Mix all the liquid ingredients in a nonmetallic container. Add the meat, tossing about to coat all sides, cover, and refrigerate overnight. Drain the meat and arrange it on dehydrator trays. Salt and pepper the strips lightly and dry at 140°F for 30 minutes or so. Turn, sprinkle lightly with salt and pepper, and dry for 6 to 8 hours, or until dry to your taste and needs.

SMOKY JERKY

Here's a good basic recipe for people who want a smoky flavor from dehydrator jerky.

2 cups liquid smoke

2 cups Worcestershire sauce

2 cups soy sauce

¼ cup salt

2 tablespoons garlic powder

1 tablespoon black pepper

10 pounds lean red meat, thinly sliced

Mix all the ingredients except the meat in a nonmetallic container. Add the meat, tossing about to coat all sides. Marinate in the refrigerator overnight. Drain the jerky, blot dry with paper towels, and arrange the strips on dehydrator trays. Dry at 140°F for 6 to 8 hours, or until done to your liking. Cool and store in glass Mason jars or airtight plastic bags, preferably using a vacuum-pack system.

CURING-SALT JERKY

Commercial curing mixes usually contain small amounts of sodium nitrate and sodium nitrite, both of which will impart a reddish color to the meat. The color isn't as important in jerky as it is in corned beef or cured ham, but some people want it.

10 pounds lean red meat

⅔ cup Morton Tender Quick cure mix

¼ cup sugar

2 tablespoons black pepper

1 tablespoon garlic powder

Cut the meat into slices ¼ inch thick. Thoroughly mix the dry ingredients. Rub the mix into the meat slices, covering all surfaces. Place the meat in a nonmetallic container and refrigerate for 1 hour. Rinse the meat under running water and let it dry. Place the strips over dehydrator racks. Dry at 145°F for 8 hours or longer, depending on how hard you want the jerky.

SWEET PICKLE JERKY

A good many brine cures (or pickles) call for granulated or brown sugar. Often sugar-cured jerky is smoked, but it can also be made in a dehydrator.

10 pounds lean red meat	1 cup brown sugar
2 gallons hot water	¼ cup black pepper
2 cups salt	1 tablespoon freshly ground allspice berries

Cut the meat into strips about ¼ inch thick. Mix the other ingredients in a nonmetallic container and let cool. Add the meat, swishing it around to coat all sides. Keep in a cool place overnight. Rinse the strips under running water and drain. Place the strips over racks and dry at 140°F for 10 hours, or until dry to your liking. Store in airtight containers, preferably vacuum-packed, until needed.

CHILI POWDER JERKY

This recipe for 10 pounds of meat can be doubled as needed, or it can be reduced. The chili powder can be purchased in the spice section of the supermarket. One 8-ounce or two 4-ounce cans will yield about 1 cup. This jerky makes a nice chew, and don't forget to try it cooked in a stew with pinto beans if you like chili with beans. (See chapter 12, Cooking with Jerky, page 87, for recipes.)

1 cup prepared chili powder	1 tablespoon garlic powder
½ cup salt	½ tablespoon cayenne pepper
1 tablespoon freshly ground black pepper	10 pounds lean red meat
1 tablespoon freshly ground cumin seeds	

Mix all the dry ingredients. Trim the meat and cut it into strips about ⅜ inch thick and 1 inch wide, cutting with the grain if you want a chewy jerky, or across the grain for pemmican. Blot the moisture from the meat with paper towels. Rub the spice mix into the meat on all sides. Place in a nonmetallic container, cover, and refrigerate overnight. The next day, pat with paper towels to remove any surface moisture. Process the meat in a dehydrator (or kitchen oven) at 145°F for 4 hours. Lower the heat to 120°F and dry for another 4 hours or longer, until the meat is hard but not brittle. Vacuum-pack for long storage.

HOT WOOSTER JERKY

Here's an easy recipe that makes use of Worcestershire sauce and soy sauce. These staples can be purchased from big box stores and other warehouse outfits in gallon bottles at considerable savings.

10 pounds lean red meat,
cut into strips ¼ inch thick

3 cups soy sauce

2 cups Worcestershire sauce

½ cup liquid smoke

¼ cup freshly ground black pepper

Put the meat into a nonmetallic container. Add the rest of the ingredients, mixing thoroughly. Refrigerate for several hours, or overnight, tossing or turning a time or two. Dry at 140°F for about 8 hours, or until done to your liking.

Note: I don't recommend low-salt soy sauce for this recipe. If you do, add some salt.

NO-FUSS JERKY WITH BARBECUE SAUCE

This is a jerky that requires no complicated soaks or rubs. You don't even have to measure the ingredients if you have a little experience with cooking or jerky making. It's best to use a tomato-based barbecue sauce, available in any supermarket these days. Some markets carry it in gallon jugs, which usually makes it quite economical. Please, however, don't call the results of this recipe "barbecued jerky." All true barbecue is moist and succulent; all true jerky, dry and chewy. For best results, cut the meat into strips about 1/16 inch thick, but thicker jerky will also work.

thinly sliced red-meat strips

barbecue sauce

garlic salt

onion salt

Arrange the strips of meat on the drying trays without overlapping. Brush each strip lightly with the barbecue sauce and sprinkle with garlic and onion salts. Dry at 140°F for 3 to 4 hours. Turn the strips and brush lightly with more sauce. Dry for another 3 to 4 hours, or until dry to your liking. This jerky will keep for several days, preferably in the refrigerator.

BIG-BATCH HAWAIIAN JERKY

Here's a nice mild jerky for sweet chewing.

10 pounds lean red meat

2½ cups pineapple juice

2½ cups soy sauce

¼ cup brown sugar

¼ cup grated fresh gingerroot

10 cloves garlic, crushed

3 tablespoons salt

3 tablespoons ground ginger (dry)

1 tablespoon black pepper

½ tablespoon cayenne pepper

Cut the meat into strips ¼ inch thick, or a little thinner. Mix together all the ingredients except the meat, stirring well. Put the meat into a nonmetallic container. Pour the marinade over the meat, tossing the mixture about with your hands to coat all sides. Cover and marinate overnight in the refrigerator, stirring a time or two if convenient. Drain the strips and arrange them in dehydrator trays. Dry at 140°F for 6 to 8 hours, or until done to your liking. Store in an airtight container in the refrigerator for a few days. Freeze for longer storage.

Note: Kids love this jerky recipe—and I do, too.

CHAPTER 3

CAMP AND OLD-TIME JERKY

You don't have to use a kitchen oven or an electric dehydrator to make jerky. In fact, the best jerky might well be made out in the sun or in a dry, breezy open-air place. Open-air jerky, made without the aid of a little heat of some sort, works best when the humidity is quite low. So choose a dry climate, or watch your local weather report for the proper conditions, which will usually be during periods of high pressure.

I might add that most writers on the subject do not recommend the old ways of making jerky under any circumstances. I won't go that far, but there are some precautions. First, do not hang jerky out in the open if flies are a problem. Second, do not attempt to air-dry jerky when the humidity is high. Third, proceed only with very, very fresh and uncontaminated meat. Fourth, use lots of salt. Fifth, hang the jerky in a breezy place, if possible. Sixth, do not allow the jerky to get wet during the drying process.

In addition to open-air drying, the complete outdoor cook may want to use large covered grills or various smokers to make jerky. Essentially, these are more or less closed systems, not unlike ovens or dehydrators in principle. Often a little smoke is used to flavor the jerky. In general, the big problem is keeping the temperature hot enough to generate smoke but low enough to prevent the jerky from cooking. Another problem is getting the water vapor from the meat out of the smoker or closed grill. Further instruction is provided in the recipes below.

INDIAN JERKY

If you want a long strip of jerky, making it easier to hang, you might try an old American Indian trick. Place a partially frozen round steak of buffalo or beef about ¾ inch thick on a flat surface. Start your cut around the edge of the meat. Cut carefully, working in a spiral, until you get to the center. This will give you a continuous strip of meat—easily hung from a clothesline. Dry in the sun for several days, depending on the heat and humidity. Take it into the tepee at night or during a rain, hanging it high above the fire.

8TH VIRGINIA JERKY

I found this recipe in a booklet called Confederate Camp Cooking, *by Patricia B. Mitchell. It calls for smoking the jerky for 6 hours in a covered grill, which I doubt was standard camp equipment. It also calls for a "dash" of liquid smoke, but I'm not sure that this stuff would have been readily available to a Confederate soldier. In any case, I don't see the point in using both liquid smoke and real smoke. My guess is that a Confederate soldier would simply suspend the meat well above the campfire, using the heat to dry the meat and counting on the smoke to keep the insects away. On the other hand, maybe the seasoned Reb wouldn't want to risk much of a fire, lest the smoke draw Yankees.*

1 pound lean red meat

1 tablespoon salt

1 teaspoon red pepper

1 teaspoon black pepper

1 teaspoon garlic powder

⅛ teaspoon liquid smoke

1 cup water

Trim the meat of fat and cut it into thin strips, then put these into a nonmetallic container. Mix the rest of the ingredients and pour over the meat. Toss about to coat all sides. Marinate in a cool place overnight. Smoke for 6 hours or longer "in a covered grill." Modern practitioners can use a large covered grill, putting the fire and wood chips in one end and the meat in the other. Choke off the airflow, thereby reducing the heat.

VIETNAMESE GRILLED SUN-DRIED JERKY

Fresh lemongrass is becoming more readily available in American supermarkets as well as in Asian stores, and it can be grown in the home herb garden in mild climates. The outer leaves of the stalk should be peeled away, down to the inner core, about ½ inch in diameter. This core is then thinly sliced and will impart a lemony flavor to food. The red meat (usually beef) for this recipe should be sliced very thin into pieces about 3 inches wide and 3 inches long, more or less.

2 small red chili peppers, seeded and minced

2 tablespoons brown sugar

1 pound lean red meat

2 stalks fresh lemongrass, thinly sliced

3 tablespoons light soy sauce

1 tablespoon Vietnamese fish sauce

1 pound lean red meat, sliced as described above

Using a mortar and pestle, pound together the red chili peppers and brown sugar. Add the lemongrass, soy sauce, and fish sauce, mixing well. Spread the paste over both sides of the meat slices. Marinate for 30 minutes. Spread the slices on drying racks and place in the sun for about 10 hours, until both sides are dry. Cover at night or during a rain. (I put my jerky on dehydrator trays and dry in the sun, or start in the sun and finish in the dehydrator on a low temperature, if necessary.) When dry, grill the strips of meat over charcoal for a few minutes, until nicely crisp. Serve as a snack with sticky rice. The grilled jerky can be stored for a week or two in the refrigerator.

SOUTH AFRICAN *BILTONG*

This is the jerky of South Africa, made commercially as well as in the home, especially in rural areas. Biltong is eaten as a snack, sold at refreshment stands in movie theaters and at soccer games and wayside stands; it is also sometimes used as a flavoring or ingredient in recipes for home cooking. Coriander seeds, freshly ground, give it a special flavor. Note that the meat is cured in a cool, dry place, not in a warm oven. The ingredients list calls for beef or venison, but other meats can also be used. According to Best of Regional African Cooking, *"You can buy biltong of beef or springbok (a South African antelope) or even ostrich. The latter, South Africans will tell you, is the best."*

10 pounds lean red meat	3 tablespoons freshly ground coriander seeds
1 pound coarse salt	2 tablespoons freshly ground black pepper
1 ounce saltpeter	brine

Cut the meat with the grain into strips about ⅜ inch thick. Thoroughly mix the coarse salt, saltpeter, coriander, and black pepper, making sure that the saltpeter is evenly distributed. Rub most of the spice mixture into the strips of meat. Layer the strips in a crock or nonmetallic container and sprinkle the top with the rest of the spice mix. Refrigerate or keep in a cool place for 48 hours or longer. Mix a strong brine, using enough salt to float an egg. Rinse the meat in the brine and hang it in a cool, well-ventilated place until it dries thoroughly. This makes a superb chew.

EAST AFRICAN *BILTONG*

Although South Africa is the biltong capital, the stuff is also widely eaten in most of eastern Africa, where it is sold by street vendors along with fruits and other snacks and delicacies, such as roasted termites. This recipe produces a thicker jerky than the South African version.

10 pounds lean red meat	1 ounce saltpeter
1 pound salt	dried red chili peppers, ground finely, to taste
2 ounces sugar	vinegar

Trim the fat off the meat and cut it into strips about 1 inch thick. Mix the rest of the ingredients thoroughly. Rub the mixture into the meat, covering all sides, and put it into a nonmetallic container. Sprinkle any leftover rub over the meat. Marinate for 2 days in a cool place, tossing the strips a time or two. Dip a clean cloth in vinegar, wring out the excess, and wipe the meat strips. Hang the strips in a cool, airy, dry place for several days, until the jerky is dry. In case rainy weather develops, this jerky can be finished in a kitchen oven on very low heat or in a dehydrator.

SURVIVAL JERKY ACCORDING TO HERTER

Knowing how to make this jerky might save the day in case of an atomic bomb attack, says George Leonard Herter in the book Bull Cook and Authentic Historical Recipes and Practices, *at which time our electric freezers and meat dehydrators wouldn't help.*

Rig for smoke-drying by building a log tower, Herter says, about 3 feet square and open at the top. Form a rack by placing 1-inch-diameter green branches over the top. Cut the meat into strips ½ inch thick, 1 inch wide, and 10 to 12 inches long. Place these strips on the rack. Keep a slow, smoldering fire going in the bottom, preferably using hickory, mesquite, or maple wood. Smoke for about 12 hours, or until the meat is dry. (If a log tower isn't practical, Herter says use a hole in the ground with a rack on top.)

Before eating, soak the jerky in water for 4 to 5 hours, or, better, simmer the jerky in a stew along with vegetables. If no vegetables are available, Herter advises, use wild grape leaves, aspen leaves, laurel leaves, or the bark from small pine trees. (I might add that the inner bark of a pine tree is by far better than the outer scale.) Further recipes for using the jerky are found in chapter 11, Pemmican (page 80), and chapter 12, Cooking with Jerky (page 87).

ALASKAN CABIN JERKY

Woodstoves are still being used for heat and cooking, especially in remote areas. The heat of the stove causes the air to rise, creating a sort of open dehydrator for making jerky and drying the long johns.

2 pounds lean red meat

¾ cup water

3 tablespoons salt

½ tablespoon onion powder

¼ tablespoon garlic powder

¼ tablespoon black pepper

1 teaspoon cayenne pepper

Trim the meat and cut it into slices about ³⁄₁₆ inch thick. Mix the rest of the ingredients in a jar, shaking well. Put the meat into a nonmetallic container and pour the contents of the jar over it, tossing about to coat all sides. Let sit in a cool place for several hours. Dry the meat strips with paper towels and place them on racks in the oven on low heat for 30 minutes or so. The purpose of the stay in the oven is to dry the meat a little to reduce the drip; do not cook the meat in a hot oven. Hang the meat strips on the clothesline above the stove for a day or two. If there's any jerky left hanging after 2 days, store it in a jar or a clean pillowcase.

WEST TEXAS PORCH JERKY

Many ranch houses have screened porches on the front or back, or both. Some even have porches all the way around. In dry climates with a good wind, these screened porches can be used to make excellent jerky. String some barbed wire across the top and hang the strips of meat from the barbs. In some parts of the West, small wild peppers are free for the picking. Any dried hot red chili pepper can be used, ground to a powder. Cayenne from the supermarket also will do, or use a commercial chili powder, if you like the taste of cumin and other spices.

5 pounds lean red meat

salt

wild chili peppers, dried and powdered

Trim the meat and cut it into strips about ¼ inch thick. Sprinkle the meat strips liberally with salt and sparsely with powdered chili peppers, put them into a nonmetallic container, and keep in a cool place overnight, tossing a time or two if convenient. Drain the meat, pat the strips dry, and impale each strip by the end on the barbs of the wire. Let it hang for 2 to 3 days, or longer, depending on the heat, wind, and humidity. Good stuff, weather permitting.

CLOTHESLINE JERKY

If you have a suitable climate—dry, warm, and breezy—you can make jerky by simply hanging it on the clothesline. It's best to punch a hole in the end of each jerky strip, insert a short length of cotton twine, and tie each strip to the main line with a loop. To separate one strip from another, the loop can be kept in place with a clothespin. If you don't have any string at hand, use strips of fiber from the blades of bear grass or other suitable yucca. You can also string the jerky strips onto strong line, such as the fine-diameter Kevlar thread used in fly tying, with the aid of a large needle. Still another possibility is to string up sticker vines (such as catbrier) in a suitable place, open to the sun and a light wind, and merely hang the strips on the spurs. Don't be tempted to hang the jerky strips on fishhooks, as when setting a trotline. If you do, you might catch a neighborhood dog.

long meat strips, ³⁄₁₆ inch thick and 1 inch wide	hickory-smoked salt (or regular salt) black pepper

Sprinkle both sides of the meat heavily with hickory-smoked salt and black pepper. Hang on the line as described above for 2 days or longer, depending on the climate and how dry you want the jerky. Lots of pepper will discourage flies and insects. Transfer the strips to a dry place during rain and at night.

BRINE-CURED SMOKED JERKY WITH RUB

Here's a good recipe for making smoked jerky, using both a brine and a rub.

5 pounds lean red meat

THE BRINE

2 quarts spring water

1 cup salt

½ cup unsulfured molasses

¼ cup freshly ground black pepper

1 teaspoon bottled garlic juice

THE RUB

½ cup fine sea salt

1 tablespoon dried lemon zest, powdered

½ tablespoon cayenne pepper

Trim and cut the meat into strips about ⅜ inch thick. Mix the brine ingredients in a nonmetallic container. Add the meat strips, tossing about to coat all sides. Cover and refrigerate for 8 hours or longer. Rinse the meat and pat it dry with absorbent paper. Air-dry the meat for about an hour.

While waiting, mix all the rub ingredients and then rub into both sides of the jerky strips. Arrange the strips in a smoker. Smoke the meat for an hour or so at 140°F or less. Continue drying without smoke until the strips are stiff but bendable. Cool and store until needed.

WATER SMOKER JERKY

Several kinds of water smokers, some shaped like a small silo, can be used to make jerky. These are usually rigged with a wood-chip pan above a heat source (gas, charcoal, or electric) and a pan for holding water or other liquid. Most of these have two circular trays spaced far apart, which limits the amount of jerky that can be handled at one time. The temperature inside the smoker can also be a problem. The best jerky will be produced with the temperature at 140°F or lower. Also remember to keep any top vents open to promote airflow across the jerky.

2 pounds lean red meat	hardwood chips
salt	black pepper

Cut the meat into strips about ¼ inch thick. Sprinkle the strips heavily on both sides with salt. Put into a nonmetallic container overnight, tossing a time or two. Rinse the strips in running water to remove some of the salt. Rig for smoking, heating some hardwood chips. Dry the meat strips with paper towels, sprinkle lightly with black pepper, and arrange on the racks. Smoke for several hours, then finish without smoke until the jerky is dry to your liking.

ELECTRIC SMOKER JERKY

Portable electric smokers will make good jerky if they are well ventilated to encourage a fresh airflow from the bottom to the top, along with the smoke. Temperature can be a problem. Check it with an oven thermometer, shooting for about 140°F or less. Most of these units have two pullout racks for holding large chunks of meat, which limits their capacity. Check for availability of additional racks, or perhaps hang the jerky from the top by using toothpicks or some other method.

hardwood chunks	salt
2 pounds lean red meat	freshly ground black pepper
bacon drippings (optional)	or cayenne pepper

Rig for smoking, putting the hardwood chunks into the pan. Cut the meat into strips about ³⁄₁₆ inch thick. Brush the strips lightly with bacon drippings, then sprinkle with salt and lightly with black pepper or very lightly with cayenne. Place the strips over the racks, or hang them from the top rack. Smoke for several hours, then finish drying without adding more wood to the tray.

Note: Don't go too heavy on the bacon drippings, especially if the strips are to be hung. The purpose of the drippings is to help the beef take on a smoke flavor. They can be omitted, however.

COLD-SMOKED CURED JERKY

Very good jerky can be made in a cold-smoker at 100°F or even lower. The problem here is getting enough heat for a fire to generate smoke while at the same time keeping the smoke chamber cool. Often the smoke chamber is removed from the fire, as in the familiar barrel placed uphill from a small fire and connected by a conduit of some sort. Several designs, as well as advice on woods and techniques for smoking, have been set forth in part three, Cold-Smoking and Salt-Curing Meat. In any case, for cold-smoking I insist that the meat be salt-cured in one way or another. The recipe below has been adapted from an old Scottish recipe for corned beef. You can, in fact, use the chunks of meat for corned beef (simmered in fresh water for 5 to 6 hours, or until tender), or you can cut the meat, after curing, into strips, rinse them in fresh water, and cold-smoke them for a couple of days, until dry to your liking. You can also cut the meat into strips before curing, in which case the curing time would be shortened to 8 hours or so, or overnight.

Many of the old-time recipes call for saltpeter, which is no longer used in commercially cured meats such as sausage. It is, however, still available over the counter in some pharmacies.

1 gallon spring water	½ ounce saltpeter
1 pound salt	lean red-meat roast, about 5 pounds
⅓ pound brown sugar	

Put all the ingredients except the meat into a large pot. Bring to a boil and simmer for 5 minutes. Strain the brine into a crock or other suitable nonmetallic container. Let cool. Trim the roast nicely and add it to the crock. Weight the roast with a clean block of wood or plate to keep it submerged. Cover the crock and put it in a cool place for 2 weeks. Turn the meat every day or two.

After 2 weeks, rinse the roast in cold water and soak it in fresh water for several hours. (To cook it like corned beef, put the meat into a pot, cover with cold water, and bring to a boil. Reduce the heat and simmer for about 40 minutes per pound, or until tender. The emphasis is on a simmer, not a hard boil. Serve the corned meat hot or cold, or use it in recipes that call for corned beef. When slicing the roast, it's best to cut against the grain.)

For jerky, rinse the roast in cold water, cut it into strips about ³⁄₁₆ inch thick, rinse the strips in fresh water, pat dry, and arrange on the trays of a cold-smoker, or hang if necessary. Cold-smoke until the strips are dry to your liking. The exact time will, of course, depend on the temperature, the humidity, and the thickness of the meat. Note also that the smoke doesn't have to be continuous during the drying process, unless perhaps insects would be a problem without the smoke.

Variations: Many recipes call for adding a long list of spices to the brine. I prefer to leave them out, but anyone who feels the need to alter the flavor might want to add 2 tablespoons mixed pickling spices, available in the spice or canning sections of supermarkets, and perhaps 1 tablespoon black pepper. About 2 heaping tablespoons allspice berries and a few bay leaves also work.

BIG-BATCH COLD-SMOKING FOR BIG GAME

If you like the flavor of the jerky or corned beef made by the recipe above, remember that the process is quite suitable for larger quantities of meat and won't require quite as much brine per pound. Corning and smoking are good ways to deal with the sheer bulk of a steer, moose, or elk when your freezer is already full. The biggest problem with corning a big batch of meat will be finding a large crock and having a cool place to keep it. A clean wooden barrel can be used, if you have one.

100 pounds lean meat	8 pounds salt
5 gallons clean water	2 ounces saltpeter
2 pounds brown sugar or honey	

Bone the meat and cut it into rather large chunks about 5 pounds each. Boil the water. Add all the ingredients except the meat and bring to a new boil. Turn off the heat and let the water cool to 40°F or lower. Pack the meat loosely in the crock. Pour the brine into the crock and top the meat with a clean wooden block or platter, weighted with a clean stone (preferably flint) if necessary. The idea is to keep all the meat submerged. After several days, repack the meat, reversing the order; repeat this step every few days. Cure for about 2 weeks for 5-pound chunks of meat. Smaller pieces will require less time and should be eaten first. As a general rule, judge each piece of meat separately, allowing at least 3 days for each pound.

The fully corned meat will keep for a couple of months in the brine, depending partly on the storage temperature, but the brine should perhaps be drained off after about 20 days and replaced with a freshly made solution. For jerky, the meat can be cut into strips and cold-smoked or air-dried after the cure is complete, using the technique on page 30 for the small batch. Start jerking the smaller pieces of meat first, leaving the large chunks in the brine longer.

CHAPTER 4

JERKY EVERY WHICH WAY

Jerky doesn't have to be made in thin strips like bacon. As a practical matter, slabs and chunks are often easier to cut than thin strips. Time spent in cutting the meat can be a factor, especially if you are working on a large volume, such as an elk or a beef hindquarter, without the help of an electric meat slicer or other professional tools. As a rule, however, large chunks of meat will take lots of time to dry.

Smaller chunks, like stew meat, can also be made into jerky and are much easier to chew. These can be made from round steak or other supermarket cuts, or they can be made from the trimmings left from cutting larger cuts of meat into thin jerky strips.

In any case, be sure to try these recipes and methods. The directions are for using a dehydrator, but a kitchen oven will also work.

A. D.'S JERKY NUGGETS

Small chunks of jerky are perfect for eating while you are driving a car or on the trail, and for people who have trouble biting off a chew from a strip of tough jerky. The trick here is to simply plop a nugget into your mouth and roll it around with your tongue until it is soft enough to chew. I like to make this jerky from a large chunk of meat, such as a bottom round beef roast, but it can also be made quite easily by using a steak about 1 inch thick. Round steak will do, if nicely trimmed of fat and sinew.

5 pounds lean red meat	½ cup brown sugar
1 cup salt	1 tablespoon freshly ground black pepper

Dice the meat into 1-inch cubes, putting them into a nonmetallic tray or other suitable container. Mix the dry ingredients and sprinkle evenly over the meat. Toss the meat about to coat all sides. Cover and refrigerate for 48 hours, turning the meat a time or two each day. Rinse the meat, pat it dry, and arrange it on dehydrator trays. Dry at 120°F for 24 hours or longer, or until the meat is dry on the outside but still pliable inside. Store in an airtight container, preferably in the refrigerator.

STEW-MEAT JERKY

These are similar to jerky nuggets, but the pieces can be more irregular. I make them from trimmings left from large chunks of meat, but very fresh supermarket stew meat (beef) can also be used. The pieces, however, should be rather uniform in thickness and should not be too large. If you use several sizes, it's best to sort them and put them on separate trays. The larger chunks will require more drying. If you purchase supermarket stew meat, make sure it is quite fresh, and be prepared to trim off any fat and sinew.

I don't normally use spices and seasonings in this jerky, partly because these can be added when making the stew. Of course, this jerky can also be used as a snack, in which case spices and flavorings may be added to taste.

stew-cut lean red meat	black pepper
salt	

Put the meat in layers into a nonmetallic container, sprinkling each layer liberally with salt and sparsely with black pepper. Cover and put into the refrigerator for 24 hours. Rinse in clean water, pat dry with paper towels, and arrange on dehydrator racks. Dry at 120°F for a day or longer, until the meat is dry to your liking. For longer storage without refrigeration, the jerky should also be dry inside.

See chapter 12, page 87, for suitable recipes for cooking with this jerky.

JERKY PLUGS

At one time, country boys liked to keep a plug of tobacco in the bib pocket of their overalls. To take a chew, they simply sliced off a piece of tobacco from the end of the plug with the small blade of their pocketknife. The same technique can be used for jerky, and, boy, is it tasty. For meat, any good slab of low-fat red meat of suitable size will do. I sometimes use "breakfast steaks" as sold at my local supermarket. These are simply small steaks cut from eye of round. Larger plugs can be cut from other parts of the hind leg of beef. I like the thickness to be about 1 inch. Thinner slices will dry into plugs that are too thin. If properly prepared, these make a truly great jerky that seems to have more flavor than strips. At least, they come to flavor more quickly, owing to the freshly cut surfaces.

small steaks or cutlets of lean red meat

soy sauce

liquid smoke

salt

black pepper

Place the meat onto a nonmetallic tray or other suitable container. Sprinkle both sides with soy sauce, liquid smoke, salt, and black pepper to taste. Cover and keep in a cool place for about 8 hours, or perhaps overnight, turning the steaks from time to time. Pat the steaks dry and place on dehydrator trays for 12 hours at 140°F, or until done to your liking. Wrap each piece separately with paper towels and store in an airtight container until needed.

Note: These plugs can also be used for cooking some of the recipes in chapter 12, page 87.

FOXFIRE JERKY

Several people contributed to the section on dried beef in the book Foxfire 11. *This account relies heavily on the method reported by Garnet Lovell, who used rather large chunks of meat from the hindquarter. "And you'd never cut it into strips," he said, because they don't "have the flavor."*

beef or other lean red meat in chunks of about
5 pounds each

plenty of salt

Sprinkle the chunks of meat on all sides with plenty of salt. Put the meat in a dry place for about 2 days, or until it stops sweating. (If the weather is humid, the process will take a week or so, in which case the practicality of using the method should be questioned.) After the meat has "taken the salt," as they say in *Foxfire* country, cut a hole in the small end and slide in a sweet birch stick to use for hanging it. Hang it about 6 feet above a fireplace for about 4 weeks, or longer for larger pieces. When the meat dries, put it in cloth bags (clean flour sacks or pillowcases will do) and hang it in a dry place.

Another *Foxfire* contributor said to wrap the meat in cheesecloth, then hang it over the woodstove in the kitchen to dry.

CHAPTER 5

GROUND-MEAT JERKY

Although jerky is traditionally made from solid strips, ground meat offers a way to use scraps and odd cuts. Moreover, burger jerky, if properly made, is of uniform size and shape. It is also quite tasty—and easier to chew than solid strips. There is a thin line here between jerky and small dried sausage such as Slim Jims. Of course, if the meat is stuffed into a natural (gut) or artificial casing, it becomes a sausage. As a rule, jerky is flat, not round.

The first step toward acceptable burger jerky is to obtain good low-fat ground meat. Forget off-the-shelf supermarket ground meat, which almost always contains quite a bit of fat and sometimes, if we may believe newspaper accounts, *E. coli* and other bacteria. It is almost always safer and better to grind your own meat. Start with a large chunk of meat that is relatively fat-free, such as roasts cut from the hind leg of beef.

After you obtain a large chunk of good red meat, rig your meat grinder. I use an ordinary hand-cranked sausage mill with a $\frac{3}{16}$- or $\frac{1}{8}$-inch wheel. Electric meat grinders

will do just fine. In either case, sterilize the grinder parts with boiling water. With clean rubber gloves on your hands, cut the meat with a sharp knife into chunks suitable for feeding into the hopper of the grinder. Spread the meat chunks out on a clean surface and sprinkle them evenly with the seasonings. Then grind the chunks slowly, letting the meat fall into a sterilized container as it comes out. Note that the meat is not touched by hand during the grinding process.

Of course, smaller cuts of supermarket meat, such as round beef steaks or even stew meat, can be used—but with added risk. Market-ground meat can be relatively safe to eat, if you know and trust the butcher. But meat ground in one location in large batches, packaged, and shipped around the country should be avoided. The larger the batch, the more likely it is that the meat will be contaminated, for the same reason that it's better to keep your apples in several small baskets than to put them into a large barrel.

I prefer to proceed with meat fresh from the farm or, better, from the hunt, but many people consider this unsafe because the meat hasn't been "inspected" by the US Department of Agriculture (USDA). I might add, however, that government experts and meat processors will be quick to point out that wild meat may be tainted. Suit yourself. Just remember that most jerky is not really cooked.

Anyhow, after you obtain good ground meat, you'll have to form it into thin strips or perhaps nuggets. There are several ways of doing this:

Jerky Shooters. These handy gadgets are available commercially for extruding ground meat from a cylinder onto drying trays. Basically, they work like caulking guns. The meat is loaded into a cylinder. A plunger operated with a ratchet trigger forces the meat through a flattened tip, causing the meat to ooze out in a thin ribbon of uniform thickness and width. These strips can be squeezed out directly onto dehydrator trays. Some oven racks, however, may be spaced too widely for easy use, in which case a finer-mesh rack or even a solid sheet must be used. It's best to avoid, if possible, having to transfer the strips from one surface to another, because they come apart easily.

Most of the jerky guns have interchangeable tips, from wide and thin to small and round (Slim Jim–style). Most of these tips can be used for jerky, but, of course, those thin strips are more conventional and are easier to dry.

In addition to handheld guns, several commercial extruders are available, some of which fit directly onto the grinding machine. At the other extreme, some home cooks may already have pastry bags with ribbon tips, and these may do the trick if the ground meat is of the right consistency.

In any case, the texture of the meat has a bearing on how nicely it extrudes. Sometimes grinding the meat with a smaller wheel, or grinding it a second time with a regular wheel, will make it easier to use—but don't make it mushy enough to lose its shape after being extruded. Much depends on the grind, the extruder, and the kind of meat.

Rolling Pins. Many people roll a mound of ground meat out into a sheet, like pizza dough. The thickness of the meat can be controlled almost exactly by putting one thin strip of wood on each side of the meat; the wood, of course, prevents the rolling pin from going too deep. (Try strips of ¼- or ⅜-inch plywood or paneling.) After being rolled out, the meat sheet is cut into strips with a knife or cutting wheel. Usually, the meat is rolled out on waxed paper, then transferred to a cookie pan or some other surface for drying. The big problem is keeping the strips together, for they stick to the surface and tear easily.

In one method, put the meat between two sheets of waxed paper and roll until it is about ¼ inch thick. Place the rolled-out meat and both sheets onto a cookie pan and carefully remove the top paper. Put the cookie pan into the oven on low heat—120°F—and leave it for about 2 hours. Place a second cookie pan on top, flip the whole thing over, and remove the first pan and waxed paper. The drying continues for another hour or so. When the meat is firm and pliable, cut it into strips with kitchen shears. The strips are then dried—preferably on racks—at 140°F until done to your liking. Blot any grease off the jerky, cool, and store in a cool place in glass jars, preferably vacuum-packed.

Press Method. Several jerky presses are available commercially. Typically, these simply squeeze a ball or blob of ground meat down to a flat sheet, which in turn is cut into jerky strips. If you have a tortilla press, use it to make small wheels. You can also press the meat between sheets of waxed paper, using a flat surface and a flat pan or other suitable moveable object. The difficulty with the press method is that the jerky sheets tend to stick to the surfaces of the press.

Finger Method. If you want chunk jerky, simply shape the meat into small balls and place them onto dehydrator trays or fine-mesh oven trays. These can be flattened somewhat before being placed on the trays, if you want patties. Also try rolling a little jerky by hand into small logs.

Most good jerky recipes can be adapted in one way or another to ground meat. Marinades and long-standing rubs should be applied to the meat, perhaps in chunks, prior to grinding. Also try your favorite sausage recipes for jerky, perhaps making both from the same grind. Here are a few other recipes to try.

SHOOTER JERKY

The measures for this recipe can easily be adapted for larger batches of meat. For 10 pounds of meat, simply multiply everything by 5.

2 pounds ground lean red meat	½ teaspoon onion powder
6 tablespoons soy sauce	¼ teaspoon garlic powder
2 tablespoons Worcestershire sauce	¼ teaspoon freshly ground nutmeg
½ teaspoon freshly ground black pepper	¼ teaspoon ground ginger

Cut the meat into cubes suitable for feeding into a sausage mill. Place the cubes in a nonmetallic container, pour in the soy sauce and Worcestershire, toss about to cover all sides, cover, and marinate overnight in the refrigerator, turning a time or two. The next day, spread the meat cubes out over a clean surface. Mix all the dry ingredients and sprinkle evenly over the meat cubes. Grind the meat, using a ³⁄₁₆- or ⅛-inch wheel. Stuff some of the meat into a jerky gun with a wide nozzle attached. Extrude the meat in strips directly onto dehydrator trays. Dry at 140°F for 6 to 8 hours or longer, depending partly on how long you plan to keep the jerky.

Note: This recipe also works with the rolling-pin method.

GROUND-MEAT JERKY

Use only very fresh or frozen lean meat for this recipe. Partially thaw the frozen meat before proceeding.

4 pounds lean red meat
1 tablespoon freshly ground black pepper
1 tablespoon garlic powder
1 cup soy sauce

¼ cup Worcestershire sauce
1 tablespoon Tabasco sauce
1 tablespoon liquid smoke (optional)

Trim the meat closely, cut it into chunks, and spread it out, tightly packed, on a clean surface. Sprinkle the black pepper and garlic powder over the meat. Mix all the liquid ingredients, then drizzle them evenly over the meat. Grind the meat with a ³⁄₁₆- or ⅛-inch wheel. Put the ground meat into a clean bowl, cover, and refrigerate for 12 hours.

When you are ready to proceed, divide the meat into 2 equal loaves. Put each loaf on a flat cookie pan and roll it out into a ½- to ¼-inch-thick sheet. Cut the sheet with a knife, but do not separate it at this point. Place the cookie pans into the center of the oven and dry at 150°F for 4 hours or longer, depending on the thickness of the strips. Cut the strips again to separate them. If need be, turn the strips over and dry a little longer. Store in an airtight container in the refrigerator or freezer.

Note: If using a large dehydrator with rectangular plastic trays, you can place the cookie pans on the trays. With round units, you'll have to work something out.

SAUSAGE MIX JERKY

Here's a spice mix that I like in country sausage and jerky. Try other sausage spice mixes, but note that the jerky meat should be quite lean, whereas most really good sausage meats contain some fat.

10 pounds lean red meat
6 tablespoons salt
1 tablespoon freshly ground black pepper

1 tablespoon ground cayenne pepper
½ tablespoon dried sage

Cut the meat into cubes, spreading them out over a clean work surface. Mix the dry ingredients and sprinkle evenly over the meat. Grind the meat in a sausage mill. Load into a jerky gun and lay some thin ribbons onto dehydrator trays. Dry at 140°F for 6 to 8 hours, or until dry to your liking. This recipe can also be made with the rolling-pin method.

HERBED JERKY

The herbs in this recipe can be changed to suit your taste, but I think it's best to avoid spices like cloves or allspice.

2 pounds red meat

1 teaspoon salt

1 teaspoon onion salt

½ teaspoon garlic salt

½ teaspoon lemon-pepper seasoning salt

½ teaspoon dried thyme

½ teaspoon dried oregano

½ teaspoon dried marjoram

½ teaspoon dried basil

Cut the meat into chunks suitable for feeding into the meat grinder and spread them out over a flat surface. Thoroughly mix the rest of the ingredients and sprinkle them evenly on the beef chunks. Grind the beef with a ³⁄₁₆- or ⅛-inch wheel. Using a jerky shooter, lay the ground beef out in ribbons onto dehydrator trays. Dry at 140°F for 6 to 8 hours, or until dry to your liking.

BEEF, VENISON, AND OTHER MEATS FOR JERKY

Although most of America's jerky is made from beef these days, many other meats can be used. Some of these are local favorites here and there around the globe. In Tibet, yak jerky is almost a part of the daily diet. In South Africa, both springbok (a large antelope) and ostrich are highly esteemed. In Australia, crocodile jerky is just the ticket. In Europe, reindeer from the north country can be a more-than-worthy substitute for beef.

In any case, the remaining chapters in part one set forth a variety of recipes for culinary sports and jerky aficionados to try, and hopefully the text contains something for everybody. Most of the recipes can be made either in the kitchen oven or in a dehydrator, as well as in the open air, with readily available beef or other good red meat. Before drying a batch, a review of the methods and techniques for using kitchen ovens and dehydrators may be helpful. Also remember that many of the previous recipes can also be made with game or other meat as well as with beef. In general, however, venison and other game require less drying time simply because they are leaner and drier meats—just perfect for jerking! Still, many people may find it easier to start with more familiar fare.

CHAPTER 6

BEEF: IT'S FOR JERKY

There's no question about it: In spite of modern concerns about its animal fat content, beef is still the favorite meat for jerky in many parts of the world—especially North America, South America, and Australia—partly because it is so readily available. The best or most expensive cuts of beef, however, are not ideal for jerky, simply because they contain lots of fat marbled in the tissue of the meat. (The fat is harder to dry and sometimes reduces storage times.) These expensive cuts come from along the backbone. The front part of the animal, especially the chuck and brisket, is also rather fatty and should be avoided for making jerky if another cut is available. To be sure, fatty beef will make jerky of excellent flavor, but the fat may cause storage problems—and many people today are trying to cut back on fat. Note also that range-fed animals are not normally as fat as those fed in feedlots, fattened on purpose for the market.

In any case, the best beef for making jerky is lean and contains very little fat marbled in the tissue. For the most part, this meat comes from the hindquarter and the belly or flank. Here's my take:

Flank Steak. Often called London broil, the flank steak is thin, rather like a slab of bacon. It is really the belly muscle of the animal. When trimmed, it weighs about 2½ pounds. The flank steak is quite lean and is rather easily cut into jerky strips, either with the grain or across the grain. Often the flank is cut into smaller steaks and packaged for the meat counter. Ask your butcher for the whole flank, but be warned that some butchers buy beef that has been robbed of the flank steak.

Skirt Steak. This strip of meat—actually diaphragm muscles that control breathing—is a very good choice for making jerky, but these are not always available in supermarkets, because they are sold off to the restaurant trade. Ask your butcher.

Chuck and Brisket. The meat from the chuck or forequarter is usually quite fatty. It can be used for jerky if it is carefully trimmed, but I do not recommend it. In some books, the brisket is recommended for jerky and billed as low in fat. This has not been my experience, and I usually avoid it.

Rib and Loin Meat. The most expensive part of the beef is along the backbone. The meat has a little too much fat marbled in the flesh, making it a poor choice for jerky. If you buy a whole cow, or perhaps a baron, use the loin and tenderloin, as well as the rib eye, for steaks.

Hindquarter. Excellent jerky meat—and lots of it—comes from the hindquarter of the animal. Often the hind leg, or part of it, is cut into round steaks. These have a section of bone in the middle, surrounded by four distinct sections of meat attached by membranes. These sections follow the natural division of the muscles in the leg. Anyone who buys a whole leg or hindquarter of beef, which is what I recommend for those who want to make lots of jerky, can easily reduce it to roasts simply by cutting the meat along the divisions. These roasts can then be cut with the grain into strips, or across the grain into steaks. Invariably there will be odd-shaped chunks and pieces left over. These can be used for stews (along with the bones), sausage, or ground-meat dishes, or you can use them for jerky nuggets and burger jerky, as discussed in chapter 4, Jerky Every Which Way (page 32), and chapter 5, Ground-Meat Jerky (page 37). In any case, here are some cuts of meat taken from the hindquarter:

- **Top round** is the larger of the leg muscles and weighs in at more than 20 pounds. It is lean and has a fine grain—great for jerky.

- **Bottom round** weighs about 14 pounds. It contains more tough fibers than top round and requires more trimming if you want perfect jerky strips.

- **Tip sirloin,** known as the silver tip, also weighs about 14 pounds. The meat has a fine texture and makes good jerky, but be warned that the word *sirloin* is often misleading, simply because it is attached as a marketing term to several cuts of meat.

- **Eye of round** is the smallest muscle in the hind leg and usually the toughest. It can be cut with the grain into strips or across the grain into small steaks, which in turn can be cut into strips.

Ground Beef. The best meat for grinding comes from the hindquarter, such as top round. The chuck and even the brisket can be used, however, if the meat is carefully trimmed before grinding. Your best bet, if you want to make lots of jerky, is to buy a whole leg or perhaps a whole top round; part of it can be cut into strips or slabs, and the trimmings can be used for grinding.

The beginner, and some old hands, will probably want to proceed with packaged steaks and other cuts selected from the supermarket. Cut into steaks or cutlets of uniform size and thickness, most of these are certainly easier to cut into strips. Sometimes small steaks are marketed as "breakfast steaks" or some such term. Most of these can be used for making jerky; I have even used packages of stir-fry meat that looked fresh. When making a selection from the packaged meat counter, look for lean red meat, which will not contain specks and spiderwebs of fat. Compare round steak to chuck steak, and you'll see the difference.

It's best, always, to buy freshly butchered meats for jerky. Precut packaged meats will have dates on the package, and freshly cut beef will usually have a bright color.

In any case, all of the previous jerky recipes will work with good lean beef. If you like the flavor of beef as much as I do, however, you may want to try a couple of basic recipes, made without a long list of spices and flavorings.

CAVEMAN JERKY

In his book NeanderThin, *Ray Audette sets forth a simple method of making jerky, which could have been made from aurochs, the wild cattle of the day. Simply cut the meat into strips ¼ inch thick and dry it in the sun for a day or two. Audette allows that the oven of a kitchen stove can be used, but adds that a dehydrator is preferable. Use no salt, sugar, or other ingredients.*

10 pounds fresh beef

Put the strips of meat onto the dehydrator trays and dry at 90°F to 100°F for a day or two, or to your liking. Since the jerky contains no salt or other preservatives, it may not keep indefinitely. If practical, store it in a freezer until needed.

A. D.'S CAVEMAN VARIATION

I have tried Caveman Jerky more than once, and I like it. I do, however, feel a little safer if salt is sprinkled over the meat prior to drying. Besides, salt improves the flavor, costs very little, and gets the mouth's juices flowing.

10 pounds beef   1 cup salt

Cut the beef into strips about ¼ inch thick. Sprinkle the strips with salt in a nonmetallic container. Toss the meat to coat all sides. Place the strips over the racks of an oven or dehydrator and dry at 140°F for 6 to 8 hours, or until dry to your liking.

Note: To compare this to the no-salt recipe above, separate the meat into two batches, follow each recipe's directions, and keep it separate for tasting and storage.

A. D.'S EASY SOY BEEF JERKY

I've always been fond of meats marinated in a little soy sauce and black pepper. The combination is especially good in jerky. Note, however, that the operative ingredient in soy sauce is salt. I do not recommend the so-called low-salt soy sauce for making jerky unless additional salt is added. Exact measures aren't necessary, but use enough soy sauce to coat or wet all sides of the meat; usually ½ cup per pound of meat will be about right. Pepper to taste.

| beef strips, ⅛ to ¼ inch thick | freshly ground black pepper |
| soy sauce | |

Place the beef strips into a nonmetallic container. Pour in a little soy sauce and sprinkle liberally with black pepper. Toss about to coat all sides. Refrigerate overnight. Place the meat strips on a rack in your kitchen oven or dehydrator. Dry at 140°F for 6 to 8 hours, or until the jerky is barely pliable, depending on the exact temperature, humidity, and thickness of the meat. Store in jars, properly sealed, in a cool, dark place, or, better, vacuum-pack in jars or plastic bags. This jerky is especially good when cooked in rice; the soy sauce gives it a Chinese flavor. It also makes a good chew.

Variation: Use red pepper flakes instead of black pepper. Also, try this recipe with half soy sauce and half rice wine or perhaps dry vermouth left over from martinis.

THAI FRIED JERKY

The Thai are fond of a fried beef jerky as a snack or as part of a complete meal.

3 tablespoons whole coriander seeds

1 tablespoon whole cumin seeds

2 pounds beef

¼ cup soy sauce

1½ tablespoons brown sugar

1 cup peanut oil

Toast the coriander and cumin seeds in a cast-iron skillet, bringing out their fragrance. Cool the seeds and grind them with a mortar and pestle. Cut the beef into strips ¼ inch thick, 2 inches wide, and 3 inches long, trimming away any fat as you go. Mix the soy sauce, ground toasted seeds, and brown sugar in a nonmetallic container. Add the beef strips and toss to coat all sides. Marinate for an hour or longer. Drain and dry in a kitchen oven or dehydrator at 140°F for 6 hours, or until the beef is dry to the touch.

Heat the peanut oil in a skillet on medium. Fry the jerky pieces a few at a time until crispy around the edges, adding more oil if necessary. Drain on brown bags or absorbent paper. Store in an airtight container at room temperature. Serve alone as a snack or with sticky rice as part of a meal.

OLD-TIME DRIED BEEF

If you want a different jerky, try this old recipe from the American National Cow Belles Association. Like many old-time recipes, it calls for saltpeter, which can be omitted entirely, or you can substitute an equal amount of sodium nitrate, available from pharmacists. Note that the recipe calls for large chunks of meat—roasts from 5 to 10 pounds—for a total of 20 pounds. I quote the recipe here mainly for historical interest. Personally, I wouldn't want to try it unless I had a cool, dry place to hang the meat.

"Mix 1 pint of salt, 1 teaspoon saltpeter, and ¼ pound brown sugar. Divide into three parts. Rub into meat for three successive days. Turn beef in the juice formed for 1 week, once each day. Hang in a dry cool place to dry until finished. Put a little extra salt in the holes cut for the cord to hang by. Chunks of beef could be from five to ten pounds in weight. If you like a smoked flavor, smoke the meat after it has quit dripping, then dry. Slice thin when serving."

CHAPTER 7

VENISON JERKY

Deer of one sort or another have been hunted for ages. Today, more than thirty species roam wild over much of the world. Almost all species of deer make excellent venison and superior jerky—if they are properly handled. Here's a brief rundown:

White-Tailed Deer. Native to North America, Central America, and parts of South America, the whitetail is currently our most popular big-game animal. In some areas, the population has exploded, causing these animals to be considered pests in many suburban areas and farmlands. In most places, a hunter can take more than one whitetail during the season, buck or doe, in which case the home freezer might well be too full to hold more meat. Jerky is the ideal solution. Note also that frozen venison can be removed from the freezer, thawed, and made into jerky if you need to make room for bumper catches of fish in spring and summer.

Mule Deer. Several subspecies of these animals are native to North and Central America. They make excellent jerky.

Moose. These large animals are called elk in Europe. They also live in Siberia, Mongolia, and Manchuria, as well as in the northern parts of North America. By whatever name, moose make excellent meat and lots of it, as a grown male can weigh up to 1,750 pounds. Jerky strips can be obtained from the saddle, hindquarter, and flank meat.

Elk. This large deer, called *wapiti* by the Native Americans and second in size only to the moose, is a popular game animal in some of the Rocky Mountain states. It also inhabits Asia and is raised on farms in Siberia and elsewhere. Weighing in at 1,000 pounds, elk makes excellent jerky and sports very impressive antlers.

Caribou. Also called reindeer, tundra deer, and a dozen other names, these large animals range over the treeless tundra and boreal forests of northern Canada and much of Alaska. The meat—tasty, tender, and very lean—makes excellent jerky. Many of the northernmost Native Americans depend partly on the caribou for sustenance, just as the Lapps do in northern Europe, where the reindeer is more or less domesticated. The meat is available in some American markets and by mail order.

Other Deer. Most other species of deer from around the world also make good jerky, and some, such as the fallow deer from Europe and Asia Minor, are ranched commercially and available in some markets. Some of the world's deer, however, are quite small as compared to the moose or elk. The pudu deer of the Andes, for example, weighs only about 15 pounds. Antelope and other venison-like animals are covered in the next chapter.

• • •

Regardless of the species of deer, the best venison for jerky comes from the loin and the hind leg, saving the shoulders and other parts for boned roasts and stew or burger meat. The loins and tenderloins are relatively easy to reduce to strips or thin slices, cutting the meat with the grain, or cutting it across the grain into medallions, if that shape is acceptable to you. The hind leg, which will have the most meat, is made up of distinct muscles, connected by tissue. If you don't have a meat saw, your best bet is to separate the leg into parts, following the natural division of the meat; then each piece can be reduced to slabs and strips, or perhaps cut across the grain into cutlets of about ½-inch thickness.

If you have a meat saw or use a commercial butcher, another approach would be to cut the whole leg crosswise into thin round steaks. Then remove the center bone and cut the steak into jerky strips. The American Indians had a way of cutting a single strip from around the outside of the steak, making a spiral; see Indian Jerky, page 22. Having a continuous long strip makes the jerky easy to hang.

Good fresh venison can be jerked to perfection, and the meat doesn't necessarily have to be aged. By "good venison," I mean meat from a deer that was dropped with a well-placed shot instead of being run all over the country—and from a deer that was promptly field-dressed. Such meat has no gamy flavor, unless perhaps it is taken during the rut. If the meat does have a gamy flavor, complicated marinades with a dozen ingredients and secret rubs won't help very much. In any case, a clean kill and prompt field dressing are necessary for good meat, and these essential steps are the hunter's responsibility. I might add that a boar hog or a steer that has been chased all over the country by dogs, shot, slung across the hood of a pickup truck, driven through town for show, and taken to the local meat processor many hours after the kill would probably taste quite gamy.

Essentially, the field dressing removes the innards from the animal, but it's not the innards as such that cause the so-called gamy flavor. It's the body heat they contain. Thus, field dressing removes much of the total body heat and allows air to circulate in the cavity. Of course, the heat should be removed as soon as possible. (The one exception may be in extremely cold weather.) Removing the heat, and cooling the meat, also makes the venison safer to eat simply because bacteria and such grow best at warm temperature. In this regard, note that the USDA has warned that fecal matter can cause *E. coli* contamination in venison. This would probably come from an animal that was not properly field-dressed or was badly gut shot—or, most likely, both. In any event, I don't think the problem is as frequent as regulators would have us believe. If given a choice, I'll take my chances with properly handled venison every time over USDA-inspected chickens or ground meat.

Of course, venison can be purchased in specialized markets these days, as well as by mail or over the Internet. Usually, this meat will be in good shape and will not be gamy. However, beware of venison given away by local hunters. It may be good meat, but the chances are that the hunter is merely passing the buck.

In any case, deer hunters are often people of firm opinion, and many of them have their own ways of jerking venison. Here are a few of my favorites. See also the next chapter on other large game and exotic meats.

VENISON JERKY ACCORDING TO MEL MARSHALL

Texans are never short on opinions, food related or otherwise. If Mel Marshall was not a Texan, then he lived in that place long enough to disallow beans in anything called chili. After saying that sun-dried jerky can be made only in places with long, warm summer days and nights and pure, unpolluted air, he added, "Sadly, there is no place today on the North American continent that provides both these conditions." Then he set forth his recipe and alternative method for making it in an oven, pretty much as follows.

lean venison	hickory-smoked salt
garlic powder	

Cut the venison into strips about ½ inch thick. Sprinkle the meat with garlic powder and hickory-smoked salt. Arrange the strips on a pan and put into an oven set at its lowest possible temperature (usually 125°F). Dry for 3 to 6 hours (maybe 8 or 10 hours in some ovens), depending on the meat and on the individual oven. Use the jerky as noshing fare, or cook it in soups and stews.

Note that Marshall cuts his meat a little thicker than most experts. This makes it a good chew.

VENISON JERKY ACCORDING TO SAM GOOLSBY

I found this method in The Great Southern Wild Game Cookbook, *by Sam Goolsby, billed on the dust jacket as hunter, outdoor writer, and wild-game expert, and pictured in black tie and with shotgun at ready, standing by a white table setting. His recipe for venison jerky requires no oven or dehydrator. He tells us to cut the venison into strips less than ½ inch wide, and I presume that it should be the same thickness or thinner.*

about 2 pounds venison	1 cup salt
1 gallon boiling water	black pepper and spices of your choice

Keep the water at a rolling boil. String the venison strips up on a wire and dip them into the boiling water. As soon as the meat loses its red color, lift it from the water. Drain (but do not rinse) and sprinkle with salt, pepper, and other spices, if desired. Hang the venison in the sun until dry, usually about 2 days. It should be covered during rain and at night. More pepper will help keep the flies away, Goolsby says, if they are a problem. The meat can also be hung in a screened enclosure, but this slows down the drying process, he allows.

JERKED VENISON ACCORDING TO STURDIVANT

All you need for delicious jerky, sayeth E. N. Sturdivant, coauthor of *Game Cookery*, is fresh venison, salt, pepper, and a sharp knife. Slice the meat with the grain into slabs. Place these on a board and trim away all the fat. Salt and pepper both sides of the meat. Hang the meat on a string or put it on well-ventilated racks, preferably on a screened porch or otherwise protected from flies and insects. With low humidity and a temperature between 55°F and 70°F, the jerky will be ready in about 2 full days. Remove the jerky and put it into a porous cloth bag. Hang until you are ready to use the jerky.

If you prefer to smoke the jerky, Sturdivant goes on, use a hardwood for smoke, preferably from a nut tree such as hickory or pecan. Build a smoldering fire, with just enough heat to keep the smoke coming. Getting the jerky too hot will make it brittle instead of chewy, he says. After 4 to 6 hours in a smoker, hang the meat as described to finish the job. "You will find this a highly flavorsome jerky, and quite unlike the kind for sale in stores and delicatessens," he declares. Indeed.

VENISON JERKY ACCORDING TO DR. LONGLEY

Here's a recipe from Dr. Andrew Longley of Cundy's Harbor, Maine, pretty much as published in *The Maine Way*, a collection of fish and game recipes. It calls for cold-smoking, preferably at 80°F, for 12 hours. This recommendation rules out the method for some of us, except in winter, but remember that the 80°F mark is what Dr. Longley considered ideal. (That's a long way from the 160°F recommended by the USDA!)

First, cut the venison into strips as thin as possible, Dr. Longley advises. Lay the strips flat and press them with the flat side of a knife blade until paper thin. Sprinkle the strips lightly on both sides with salt, then place them in a smoker for 12 hours at 80°F. After smoking, complete the drying by placing the strips uncovered in a frost-free refrigerator. Once dried, the jerky does not have to be refrigerated, he adds.

20 GAUGE VENISON JERKY

I asked Chef Myron Becker, a culinary sport who brews and markets the 20 Gauge Wild Game Sauce, whether he had a jerky recipe for me to try. He replied that his friend and fishing buddy, Don Chapin of Cape Cod, has made copious amounts of venison jerky using 20 Gauge in a marinade application. "He just tossed the strips in a ziplock bag with a bit more than enough 20 Gauge to coat them well, squeezed out all of the air, zipped it up, and let them sit overnight in the refrigerator. The next morning he put the strips into a drying oven. He also tried just a salt-and-pepper cure and then brushed the 20 Gauge onto the strips while in the drying oven. I thought the marinated version was better. Sometimes he finished the jerky in a smoker with a light applewood- or grapevine-smoked finish."

DEER JERKY ACCORDING TO DON BANGS

A hunter from St. Louis sent this recipe to the Missouri Conservationist *in 1954. It eventually found its way into Cy Littlebee's* Guide to Cooking Fish & Game, *published by the Missouri Department of Conservation, on which this account was based. The curing mix is made ahead of the hunt and will be enough to jerk a hindquarter.*

THE CURE MIX

½ cup black peppercorns

¼ cup whole allspice berries

3 pounds salt

Grind the peppercorns and allspice berries, using a spice mill or perhaps mortar and pestle. Mix together with the salt. Set aside or store in a jar until needed.

THE JERKY

Dress the deer as soon as possible after the kill. Debone the hind leg, separating the muscles by their natural division. Trim off the membranes. Ideally, the pieces should be 4 inches thick, 6 to 8 inches wide, and no more than 12 inches long. (Trimmings can be used for stew meat.) Rub the curing powder onto the surface of the meat, evenly and thoroughly. Attach a string to the small end of each piece of meat and hang it in the wind. If the sun is hot, hang the meat in the shade. (In the north, Bangs adds, the sun helps the process.) If the weather is rainy, hang the meat near the campfire, but do not expose it to more smoke than necessary. Cover the meat with canvas at night and during a rain. "Meat prepared like this is not at its best until it's about a month old. After that, no hunter or trapper can get enough," he says.

I recommend using the meat in soups and stews that will be simmered for several hours.

ALASKAN VENISON JERKY

Here's a good jerky recipe that I used in my book Complete Fish & Game Cookbook, *as adapted from an article by Karen Cantillion in* Alaska Fish & Game *magazine. The venison should be cut into strips about 1 inch wide and ¼ inch thick. For a brittle texture, cut the meat across the grain; for a chewy texture, cut the meat with the grain. I normally use the muscles from the hind leg. The meat should be fat-free and well trimmed. Make sure that the soy sauce is not salt-free; if it is, add some salt to the recipe.*

½ cup Worcestershire sauce

½ cup soy sauce

1 tablespoon liquid smoke

1 tablespoon onion powder

1 tablespoon garlic powder

1 tablespoon black pepper

red pepper flakes to taste

Tabasco sauce to taste

3 pounds venison strips

Mix all the ingredients except the meat. Put the meat into a nonmetallic container and pour the marinade over it, tossing well to cover all surfaces of the meat. Marinate in the refrigerator for 8 to 12 hours. Drain the meat and put it on racks in your oven, placing a shallow baking pan at the bottom to catch any drippings. Turn the oven to 150°F for 6 to 8 hours, or until the meat is dry. Leave the oven door ajar so that the moisture can escape. (A dehydrator can also be used.) Store the jerky in tightly covered containers. Refrigeration isn't necessary.

HICKORY-SMOKED WHITETAIL JERKY

This recipe was submitted by J. Oscar Sullivan to The South Carolina Wildlife Cookbook, *first published in rather scant detail by the South Carolina Wildlife and Marine Resources Department.*

venison

salt and pepper

hickory chips

Cut the venison into strips from ¼ to ⅜ inch thick. Rub both sides with salt and pepper. Hang the strips in a cool place until they are dry and stiff. Then smoke with hickory chips. Store in a jar. "This always used to be in the pantry and was our 'candy' in the old days," Sullivan said.

A. D.'S SEA SALT JERKY

I like this jerky made with sea salt. Ordinary table salt can also be used.

1 cup sea salt
½ gallon spring water

2 pounds venison

Dissolve the salt in the water in a nonmetallic container. Cut the venison into strips about ¼ inch thick. Place the venison strips in the brine and stir about with a wooden spoon. Cover and refrigerate overnight. Drain the strips and arrange them on the racks of your oven or dehydrator trays. Dry at 145°F for 6 to 8 hours, or until dry to your liking. Cool the strips and store in a cloth bag or in vacuum-packed Mason jars, depending partly on how long you intend to keep the jerky.

SYLVIA BASHLINE'S SPICY VENISON JERKY

Here's a good venison jerky recipe adapted from The Bounty of the Earth Cookbook, *by Sylvia Bashline. She says the jerky will store for many months but warns that it will surely be gobbled up before it has a chance to get cold! I agree.*

1½ pounds venison round steak
¼ cup soy sauce
3 tablespoons steak sauce
1 teaspoon onion powder

1 teaspoon celery seeds
1 teaspoon seasoned salt
¼ teaspoon black pepper

Partially freeze the venison steak, then cut it into thin strips. Thoroughly mix the rest of the ingredients. Put the meat into a plastic bag, pour in the marinade, and place in the refrigerator overnight, turning the bag a time or two. Drain the venison strips on paper towels. Dry on oven racks at 150°F until the moisture is gone. Store in a covered container.

WYOMING JERKED ELK

Many of the old-time recipes call for a small amount of saltpeter. The stuff can be purchased at the pharmacy, or it can be omitted. If you use it in this recipe, mix it thoroughly into the brown sugar solution. If you follow the drying procedure for this one, you'll need cotton twine and dry weather.

4 pounds lean elk

1 cup salt

1 cup brown sugar

water

½ tablespoon saltpeter

1 tablespoon crushed allspice

½ tablespoon red pepper flakes

Cut the meat into slices ¼ inch thick. Make a layer in a nonmetallic container. Sprinkle with salt. Repeat until all the meat is layered, using all the salt. Dissolve the brown sugar in water. Stir in the saltpeter, allspice, and red pepper. Mix thoroughly. Pour the mixture over the layered meat. Marinate for 36 hours. Using a darning needle, tie a loop of cotton twine on the end of each strip of meat. Hang the strips on a wire or clothesline, using clothespins to secure the twine to the main line. The jerky will dry in a few days, depending on the weather. It's best to bring it inside at night or during a rain.

HONEY-MUSTARD JERKY

This recipe works with any good lean meat. Try it with elk or other game. Cut the meat into strips about 1 inch wide, 6 inches long, and ¼ inch thick, with or against the grain, depending on how the jerky will be used. Try some both ways.

2½ cups soy sauce

½ cup honey

2 tablespoons prepared mustard

2 tablespoons onion juice

1 tablespoon salt

5 pounds lean venison

Mix the liquid ingredients and salt. Put the meat into a nonmetallic container, cover with the liquid mixture, and toss to cover all sides. Marinate for several hours. Drain and dry in the oven or in a dehydrator at 145°F for about 6 to 8 hours, or until done to your liking.

MOOSE JERKY

Here's a good recipe for moose, which, according to some culinary sports, makes the best possible jerky. The meat should be from the hind leg, trimmed and cut into strips about ¼ inch thick or a little thinner.

2 cups soy sauce

¼ cup honey

1 tablespoon prepared mustard

1 teaspoon onion salt

1 teaspoon garlic salt

2 pounds moose meat

Mix all the ingredients except the meat in a nonmetallic container. Add the meat, tossing about to coat all sides. Cover the container and refrigerate for 8 hours or overnight, turning the meat a time or two. Drain the meat and arrange the strips on dehydrator trays or oven racks. Dry at 140°F for 6 to 8 hours, or until dry to your liking.

TWO-PEPPER MOOSE JERKY

This recipe makes a rather hot jerky from moose or other good lean meat. Increase or decrease the pepper measures to taste.

1 cup soy sauce

1 cup beer

1 tablespoon red pepper flakes

1 tablespoon freshly ground black pepper

1 tablespoon garlic salt

1 teaspoon liquid smoke

2 pounds moose, cut into strips ¼ inch thick

Mix all the ingredients except the meat in a nonmetallic container. Add the meat strips, toss about to coat all sides, cover, and refrigerate overnight. Drain the jerky and dry the strips at 140°F for 6 to 8 hours, or longer.

LEMON-PEPPER MULE DEER JERKY

Mule deer makes excellent jerky. It's best to use meat from the hind leg, either cut into steaks or separated into roasts. Cut the meat into strips about ¼ inch thick.

2 pounds mule deer	garlic powder
1 cup soy sauce	lemon-pepper seasoning salt

Put the meat strips into a nonmetallic container and pour the soy sauce over them. Toss the meat about to coat all sides. Remove and drain the meat, discarding any remaining soy sauce. Sprinkle both sides of the meat with garlic powder and lemon-pepper seasoning salt. Place the strips on oven racks and dry at 140°F for 6 to 8 hours or longer, depending on how dry you want the jerky. Cool and store in an airtight container, preferably vacuum-packed.

CHAPTER 8

OTHER DOMESTIC, GAME, AND EXOTIC MEAT JERKY

Most big-game species make excellent jerky if they are properly field-dressed, and several large animals are now ranched commercially for either meat or hunting, or both. Sometimes this is merely a matter of managing wild herds, and sometimes it involves stocking exotic species from another land.

Almost all of these farmed or managed animals have been hunted at one time or another in the wild. The giraffe, for instance, has excellent meat and can weigh up to 2 tons. They were once pursued on horseback in Africa for sport as well as for meat. Today the giraffe fits a niche on some small farms and pasturelands that have a few shade trees suitable for long-necked animals (up to 18 feet high) to browse on. Giraffe meat is highly esteemed, and the bone marrow is considered a delicacy in Africa. Other examples include the capybara, a wetland rodent (weighing up to 140 pounds) that is actually hunted and rounded up on horseback in Venezuela.

Some of these meats are readily available in specialized markets and by Internet or mail order. The bison or American buffalo is surely among the best of these meats—and might well be better than beef (see the Buffalo Jerky recipe later in this chapter). The farm-raised ostrich and emu are also gaining in popularity, along with the smaller rhea, but these are covered in chapter 9 (page 66) on birds.

If you dress your own game or exotics from the farm, be warned that proper handling is necessary. This includes prompt field dressing, as discussed in chapter 7, Venison Jerky (page 47). Notes on the various meats are set forth under the headings below and in the recipes that appear later in this chapter.

Before getting into exotics, however, we'll take a quick look at more common fare.

Pork. Since pork can carry the parasite that causes trichinosis in humans, it is not a good choice for making jerky. Note that most jerky is not really cooked, and tons of it are made at marginal temperatures that are not carefully controlled. In short, I don't feel good about eating pork jerky, and I am not going to recommend it to others. Some people maintain that freezing the meat at 0°F or lower for twenty-one days will kill the parasites, but it doesn't completely eliminate the idea, at least not in my mind. Still, fresh pork can make excellent jerky, at least in taste. If you want to try it, choose the loin or meat from the hind leg, which won't be as fatty as the typical shoulder (which includes the picnic ham and Boston butt).

Sheep and Lamb. Sheep and lamb are very important in some parts of the world, and they make excellent jerky. It's best to buy a hind leg and reduce it to pieces, following the natural division of the muscles. These can then be cut into long strips. Or have your butcher cut the leg into 1-inch steaks. These can then be easily sliced into strips.

Antelope. There are several kinds of wild antelope, and some are ranched more or less commercially. In South Africa, springbok jerky, or biltong, is highly esteemed.

In general, follow the directions for deer in chapter 7.

Bison and Buffalo. The American bison, commonly called buffalo, might well be the best of all red meats. Lean, red, and sweet, it makes purely excellent jerky. The bison was hunted almost to extinction during the country's westward expansion, but these days it is ranched commercially, and limited hunting may be available. The real buffalo of Africa and Asia also produces good meat suitable for jerky; studies have been made on the feasibility of raising these animals commercially in the swampy lands of Florida and other places.

Wild Boar and Pigs. These are not recommended for jerky because, like domestic hogs and bears, they carry the parasite that causes trichinosis in humans. I think they are safer than supermarket pork, but many other people and government officials in charge of inspecting the nation's meats will disagree.

Mountain Goat and Sheep. These animals have surprisingly mild meat, for the most part, but old ones are likely to be quite tough. Strips of jerky can be cut out of the hind leg quarter, and any of the meat can be cut into jerky nuggets or ground for use with a jerky gun.

Bear. Although the flesh of a young but fully grown bear is one of the very best of meats, and although bear fat is used in some areas for pastry making and frying foods, it should not be used for jerky. The culprit is the parasite that causes trichinosis. Bear meat should be cooked well done—to an internal temperature of 165°F to 170°F. In Russia, however, where the meat is highly prized, bear hams are often dry-cured and eaten raw, thinly sliced like prosciutto.

Lion, Bobcats, Lynx, and Other Cats. Ernest Hemingway gives us a recipe for grilled loin of African lion, which he and his wife Mary sampled raw during the field-dressing operation. ("We both thought the clean pink flesh delicious, steak tartare without the capers," Mary later recounted.) Mountain lion or cougar also has lean, mild, white meat, and the smaller wild cats, such as lynx, were highly prized by Native Americans and early settlers. Check the game laws, however, before shooting any of these big cats. Wild-food guru Euell Gibbons once ate a bobcat, reporting that the "bob" part was quite tasty but the "cat" part was hard to swallow. I feel pretty much the same way about jerky made from anything with *cat* in the name, except, of course, for catfish.

Beaver. In many areas, beavers are so plentiful that some consider them to be pests, free for the taking. The meat is very good, and sometimes trappers will have it in great plenty. Jerky strips can be cut from the hind leg and loin, and the rest provides ground meat or jerky nuggets.

Rabbit and Hare. These small-game animals are often available to the hunter, and some states have very liberal game laws for them. In Florida, for example, there is no closed season or limit restrictions on rabbits, which include the cottontail, the large swamp rabbit (a hare), and the smaller marsh rabbit. Most of these are small and difficult to cut into jerky strips, except possibly for the backstrap (loin) that runs along either side of the backbone, but the meat can be cut into nuggets or ground. The snowshoe hare weighs 3 pounds or better, and the much larger tundra hare can weigh in at 15 pounds. All rabbits should be field-dressed promptly. If properly handled, the meat is mild and lean. Of course, domestic rabbits raised for food can also be used for jerky.

Kangaroo and Other Bush Meats. Several animals from Australia make good jerky. Some imported animals, such as the rabbit, the buffalo, and the camel, are also available as bush meat. Some of these meats, as well as prepared jerky, can be purchased by mail order and over the Internet.

Alligator and Crocodile. Once considered endangered, the alligator has made a remarkable comeback in some of the lower southern states, a few of which offer limited hunting. The meat is also available from alligator farms and dealers who traffic in exotic meats. Here in Florida where I live, I can buy all I want from legal sources: They process animals taken by licensed hunters who go after nuisance 'gators, which sometimes take a liking to backyard pools and golf course ponds. The American crocodile, which lives in the brackish waters on the fringes of the Everglades, is still endangered and highly protected. Crocodile meat and prepared jerky are available from Australia and perhaps other countries. Also, several cousins of alligators and crocodiles grow in various parts of the world, mostly tropical. All make good eating. See the recipe on page 63.

• • •

Clearly, most edible animals make good jerky, if they are properly handled. Here are some favorite recipes.

BUFFALO JERKY

The American Plains Indians depended on jerky made from buffalo. It was the only way they had to preserve the meat; jerking the meat also made it much easier to transport from one camp to another. As a rule, they merely hung the meat out in the sun to dry, or perhaps strung it inside the tepee during rainy weather. A smoky fire was used if necessary to help dry the jerky and to keep away the bugs—but often the fuel (buffalo chips) did not much improve the flavor. Actually, the flavor of rich sweet meat from a prime animal properly dressed needs no enhancement, but I do insist on a little salt, partly for flavor, partly to help draw out the moisture, and partly to help preserve the meat.

The best meat for jerky comes from the hindquarter, with the cuts being similar to beef.

buffalo meat, cut into ¼-inch strips   **salt**

Sprinkle the buffalo strips heavily with salt and keep in a nonmetallic container overnight, turning them a time or two. Rinse the meat in fresh water, pat dry with paper towels, and arrange the strips on oven or dehydrator trays. Dry at 140°F for 6 to 8 hours, or longer.

Note: If you have good sun in a dry climate without many flies swarming about, try hanging the strips out during the day, exposed to the sunlight. If need be, finish the job in a dehydrator after sunset.

VARMINT JERKY

Here's a recipe from the great state of Louisiana, where nutria have become something of a pest in some wetlands. The recipe is said to work with both muskrat and nutria, as well as beef and venison. I have used it with large swamp rabbit, and I wouldn't hesitate to try it with woodchuck. It's best to slice the meat to a thickness of ¼ inch, adjusting the width and length to the size and shape of the meat. If you end up with odd chunks of meat, save them for a stew or perhaps jerk them for use as stew meat. Trim away any fat and gristle. Make sure that the soy sauce is not the low-salt kind; if it is, add some salt.

1 cup brown sugar	1 tablespoon onion powder
1 cup soy sauce	1 tablespoon garlic powder
⅔ cup Worcestershire sauce	1 teaspoon black pepper
6 tablespoons liquid smoke	3 pounds nutria, cut into ¼-inch strips

Mix all the ingredients except the meat in a nonmetallic container. Add the meat, tossing about to coat all sides. Cover and refrigerate overnight, stirring a time or two with a wooden spoon. The next morning, pat the meat dry with paper towels, then distribute the strips on dehydrator trays. Dry at 250°F for several hours, or until the jerky is dry to your liking.

Note: I would prefer my jerky to be prepared at 140°F or lower, but 250°F is what this recipe recommends. Suit yourself.

ALLIGATOR AND CROCODILE JERKY

Both alligator and crocodile make excellent jerky. In spite of the popularity of the term alligator tail steaks, *some of the best meat comes from the front and hind legs and from along the backbone. The leg meat, however, is difficult to cut into long strips. Your best bet is to use a segment of the loin or tenderloin, or make chunk jerky from the legs.*

Any good jerky recipe can be used for these meats, but I would suggest a marinade that won't greatly discolor the nice white meat, as in the following.

2 pounds alligator meat, cut into ¼-inch strips	½ cup sea salt
1 quart spring water	½ cup lemon juice

Mix all the ingredients in a nonmetallic bowl. Refrigerate overnight. Drain the meat and arrange the strips on trays for the dehydrator or kitchen oven. Dry at 140°F for 6 to 7 hours or so. Most of this will be eaten right away. If you want to save some for future use, dry it a little longer and store it in airtight jars, preferably vacuum-packed.

ALASKAN BIG-BATCH WILD-GAME JERKY

Here's a recipe for jerking large batches of meat from moose, elk, caribou, or other game when freezing the meat might be a problem, either because of remote location or because the home freezer is full. You'll need some large crockery pickle vats to hold the salt cure and the meat, but plastic containers will do, if necessary. Do not use metal.

6 gallons spring water

2 gallons soy sauce

3 pounds brown sugar

1½ pounds chopped fresh garlic or wild onions

4 ounces black pepper

8 ounces saltpeter

50 pounds meat, cut into strips
¼–½ inch thick

Heat the water and add all the ingredients except the meat. Let the brine cool. Add the meat, cover, and let cure for 5 to 6 days in a cool place, stirring with a wooden paddle a time or two daily. Rinse the meat in fresh water. Air-dry the meat strips for an hour or so, then arrange them on dehydrator trays. Dry for 6 to 8 hours at 140°F. If you can't dry the whole batch at one time, start drying it after 4 days in the cure. Process in batches until you finish. Dry this jerky thoroughly and store in vacuum-packed bags or Mason jars until needed.

JAMAICAN GOAT JERKY

Goats are popular in parts of the West Indies, Mexico, and points south, and jerky from the goats of Jamaica, dried in the mountain air, was once an important food for way-stopping mariners. Here's a recipe calling for jerk seasoning, which is popular in Jamaica in both dry and wet form. There are many formulas, but all good jerk contains lots of allspice berries (native to the island), very hot bird or habanero peppers, garlic, onions, and salt. Dry jerk seasoning is available in most spice markets, in some supermarkets, and by mail order. Most jerk seasoning is quite hot, so use it sparingly in your first batch of Jamaican jerky.

Goat meat is available in some places, and often farmers will sell one on the hoof. It's best to use a young one. The meat can be cut into neat strips, small chunks, and various pieces, every which way.

I have always wanted to explore the etymological connection, if any, between jerky and jerk seasoning—but I promise not to do so here.

goat meat, cut into thin strips	jerk seasoning
dark rum	freshly ground sea salt and black pepper

Roll the meat in a little rum and set it aside for 30 minutes or so. Then sprinkle it with the jerk seasoning, along with a little freshly ground sea salt and black pepper. Dry in a slow oven or dehydrator.

CHAPTER 9

BIRD JERKY

Most edible birds make good jerky, but the meat on the smaller birds doesn't lend itself to long strips. Usually the breast is your best bet for most bird jerky—but this isn't always the case. Some of the very large birds, such as the ostrich, have better meat in the thigh. In any case, these large birds are the easiest to use. For variety and flavor, however, the hunter has the best choices, partly because a wild turkey is better than a domesticated bird. The next best choice is enjoyed by the farmer or those who raise their own chickens and turkeys and other birds for the table. The worst choice comes from the modern poultry "farm" and the supermarket, owing partly to salmonella problems associated with mass production, mass distribution, and mass marketing.

Big Flightless Birds

Several species of large flightless birds have evolved down through the ages. The ones that have survived modern hunters are swift runners, and even these are no match for the modern long-range rifle rigged with telescopic sights. Among the survivors are the ostrich of Africa, the emu of Australia, and the rhea of South America—all of which were once hunted for food and sport, and are now being raised commercially on farms in North America and other parts of the world. At present, the meat is more expensive than beef or pork, at least in this country, but the price may come down as it becomes more widely available. The meat is currently sold in specialty meat markets, by mail order, and in a few upscale supermarkets.

In any case, these are large flightless birds with lean, dark cherry-red meat. In taste, the meat compares readily to beef, but it is sweeter. The meat has much less fat and cholesterol than beef, and it is lower in calories than chicken or turkey. The birds do have fat, but it is not marbled in the grain of the meat.

The ostrich is the largest ratite, weighing as much as 400 pounds. The emu is much smaller, about 140 pounds, and the rhea weighs in at less than 100 pounds. The best meat on all of these birds is on the thigh, not the breast, which is rather flat. Market forms include steaks (usually thigh meat), fillets, roasts, ground meat, and so on. Some firms that specialize in these birds may have whole birds or halves for sale, or perhaps leg and thigh quarters.

AUSSIE BUSH JERKY

The emu still grows wild in Australia, where it was once hunted with boomerangs, but it is also raised commercially in the United States and Canada. Be sure to try it.

3 pounds emu thigh meat	3 cloves garlic, crushed
1 cup pineapple juice	2 tablespoons finely grated fresh gingerroot
¾ cup soy sauce	1 tablespoon black pepper
¼ cup salt	½ teaspoon cayenne pepper
¼ cup brown sugar	

Cut the emu meat into strips about ⅜ inch thick. Mix the rest of the ingredients in a nonmetallic container, stirring well. Add the meat strips, toss about to coat all sides, and marinate for 8 hours. Drain the meat and pat it dry with paper towels or a cloth. Arrange the strips on dehydrator trays (or oven racks) and dry it at 145°F for 2 hours. Reduce the heat to 130°F for about 6 hours, or until the jerky is as dry as you want it.

Note: This recipe can also be used with ostrich, rhea, and other good red meats.

BUSH *BILTONG*

Ostrich meat was highly esteemed by the ancient Roman epicures, and wild ostrich was once hunted extensively in Africa. Since they have very keen eyesight and can run 40 miles per hour, they were worthy game for the bushman armed with primitive weapons. Now farmed commercially in Africa, North America, France, and other parts of the world, the ostrich makes a very good jerky. Most of the recipes for red meat can be used for ostrich, but here's the real biltong, made with rather thick strips of meat. Don't try this one unless you have a cool, dry climate.

ostrich thigh meat	vinegar
salt	

Cut the meat into strips about 2 inches wide and 1 inch thick. Sprinkle both sides with salt, rubbing it in well. Put the meat into a nonmetallic container and refrigerate overnight. Then dip a clean rag in vinegar, wring it out, and wipe off the strips of meat. Hang the strips in a cool, dry, airy place until dry.

Variation: Use a dehydrator on the lowest heat setting, in which case drying may take 2 days or longer. If you are in a hurry, use thinner strips and dry it in a dehydrator at 140°F for 6 to 8 hours, or until dry to your liking.

RHEA JERKY

Once hunted with the bola, these birds still roam the grassy plains of Argentina. They are also farmed commercially in North America and abroad. As compared to most peoples of South America, the Argentines don't spice their food highly. The strips of meat are best cut from "round" steaks taken from the thigh.

sea salt   2 pounds rhea thigh meat, cut into thin strips

Salt the strips of meat heavily on both sides. Put the strips into a nonmetallic container, cover, and refrigerate overnight, turning a time or two if convenient. Rinse the strips, pat dry, and arrange on dehydrator or oven trays. Dry at 140°F for 6 to 8 hours, or until it is done to your liking. This jerky can be eaten as is, or it can be used in cooking, as is the custom in much of South America.

See also *charqui*, page 94.

Turkey, Chicken, and Guinea Fowl

Turkey breast is usually your best bet for jerky, simply because there's lots of it. When partially frozen, the meat can be cut lengthwise into strips or across the grain for medallions. It's best, of course, to bone the meat before jerking.

Chicken is much smaller, but the principle is the same. One possibility is to use frozen "chicken tender" pieces, those choice strips of meat found in the innermost part of the breast. These are available in 10-pound bags from wholesale outfits that sell food in fairly large lots.

Guinea fowl, also called guinea hens and African pheasants, are game birds in West Africa and are raised commercially in some parts of the world. In the American South, they are a popular barnyard bird. The meat is lean and quite tasty.

Geese and Ducks

Both geese and domestic ducks have lots of fat, but most of it is under the skin. The meat itself is lean and tasty. Wild ducks and wild geese may or may not have lots of fat, depending on what they have been eating. The diet also determines the taste. In general, fish-eating ducks have a strong flavor and are not recommended for jerky, unless, perchance, you have a taste for Thai fish sauce.

In both ducks and geese, the easiest and best jerky comes from the breast, which is simply filleted on both sides, leaving a slab of meat. The whole slab can be dried, or it can be cut into strips for regular jerky. In either case, the fine-grained lean meat makes an excellent chew. If you want to use the whole bird, trim away the fat and cut it into chunks for jerky nuggets or grind it for ground-meat jerky. Personally, I prefer to jerk the breast and use the rest of the bird for duck soup.

DUCK BREAST JERKY

Make this jerky with whole duck breast fillets, skinned and trimmed—but not sliced. Use either wild ducks, large or small, or domestic birds, but adjust the drying times as necessary. The recommendations below are for mallard-size birds.

hickory-smoked salt	salt and pepper
brown sugar	duck breasts, boned and skinned

Mix the hickory-smoked salt, brown sugar, salt, and black pepper. Sprinkle it liberally on both sides of the duck breast fillets and layer in a nonmetallic container. Cover and chill for 2 days, turning several times. Pat the fillets dry with absorbent paper and place them in a single layer on a baking sheet or dehydrator tray. Sprinkle again with the seasoning mix. Dry at 140°F for 6 to 8 hours, or until dry but still bendable without breaking. Cool and slice either across the grain or with the grain, depending on whether you want to chew the jerky as is or use it in recipes.

Upland Game Birds

Most game birds, such as quail and dove, are too small to be practical for making jerky. The pheasant has lean, white meat and can be used to advantage. The real prize, at least in North America, is the wild turkey. It can be used like domestic turkey—and really is better meat. Some other birds, such as sandhill crane, can be hunted on a limited basis in some areas.

PHEASANT BREAST JERKY

Almost any good jerky recipe can be used for pheasant breast, but I think a teriyaki marinade works just right. Do not use a no-salt mixture, however, unless you add some salt to the marinade.

pheasant breasts, cut into strips about ⅜ inch thick	commercial teriyaki sauce
	sake, sherry, or dry vermouth

Put the pheasant strips into a nonmetallic container. Add a little teriyaki sauce and sake. Toss about to coat all sides. Marinate in the refrigerator for several hours. Arrange the strips on dehydrator trays and dry at 140°F for 6 hours, or until done to your liking.

CHAPTER 10

FISH JERKY

Tasty jerky can be made from a variety of fresh- and saltwater fish. As a rule, those fish with firm, white, low-fat flesh will dry and store better (or longer) than fatty species. Some rather fatty species, such as salmon, can be used, however, and are, in fact, often recommended for jerky, possibly because the fillets are boneless, easy to slice into strips, and readily available in fish markets.

Personally, I put more stock in freshness than in species, and I really do prefer to catch and dress my own fish for jerking. Fresh fish can be purchased at the market, if you have a trained eye and a good nose or trust your fishmonger. Look for fish with bright eyes.

There is nothing wrong with making jerky from properly frozen fish—if they were frozen while very fresh. I like frozen grouper fillets, for example, from the Gulf of Mexico. People who catch their own fish should gut them and put them on ice as soon as possible. The larger the fish, as a rule, the more important this becomes. A shark, for example, might well have dozens of pounds of excellent meat if it is gutted and iced as soon as it is caught. Within minutes in the hot sunlight, however, the flesh of some sharks develops uric acid and smells like ammonia.

I am reluctant to set forth a list of fish suitable for making jerky, partly because there is so much confusion in the fish trade and in sportfishermen's lingo. *Catfish*, for example, can refer to many things, ranging from a barely edible bullhead to a choice channel cat from a clean river, so that recommending catfish in general would be very misleading, or could be. There are dozens if not hundreds of other problem fish. *Bass* can mean many things. Or *perch*. The perch that some writers and chefs have in mind is the ocean perch, a fish that is quite fatty, whereas the perch that some freshwater anglers have in mind is the white perch or yellow perch, both of which have lean flesh. Also note that some so-called trash fish make excellent jerky.

In general, however, I will say that fillets from large fish work better than those from small ones, simply because they are easier to cut into jerky strips. Also, the bellies of large fish often provide convenient jerky meat, because they are rather flat and of a uniform thickness, making them easy to slice, just as bacon is sliced from a slab of sow belly.

SALMON JERKY

Native Americans, the Japanese Ainu, and other peoples just below the fringes of the Arctic Circle have enjoyed salmon in great plenty during the spring spawning run upstream. Drying the fish was the best way to preserve it for consumption throughout the year. If we reduce the salmon to boneless strips of meat before drying it, we've got jerky. The strips, of course, are easily obtained by cutting the boneless fillets crosswise or perhaps on a diagonal to a uniform width. I prefer to leave the skin on, but skinless fillets can also be used. In any case, this simple jerky can be prepared in a small electric smoker on the patio.

5 pounds boneless salmon fillets	1 gallon spring water
1 cup fine sea salt	green wood for smoking

Cut the fillets into strips from ½ to ¾ inch thick. Dissolve the salt in the water in a nonmetallic container. Mix in the salmon strips. Place a clean plate on top to hold all the salmon strips under the water. Refrigerate for 12 hours or longer. Remove the strips and rinse in fresh water, preferably running, for about an hour to remove the excess salt. Place the strips on racks and allow to air-dry for 3 to 4 hours. They will dry quicker if placed in a breeze or under a fan.

Rig for smoking at 145°F. Place some green-wood chips around the coals or heat. Place the strips in the smoker for 6 to 8 hours, more or less, depending on the heat and the thickness of the meat. When ready, the jerky will be dry and firm to the touch but will not crumble. Take a test bite. It should be chewy. Cool the jerky and then store it in airtight containers. I prefer to vacuum-pack mine in Mason jars. Store in a cool place for up to 3 months.

Variation: Try this recipe without the smoke, using a dehydrator or kitchen oven.

CHEYENNE'S MARINATED SALMON JERKY

Here's a good recipe that I received from Cheyenne West, who once published a magazine about cooking fish and game and wild stuff. The combination of honey, rum, and lemon juice goes nicely with salmon. Note that the recipe does not contain much salt or such salty ingredients as soy sauce. Hence, I don't recommend the recipe for long storage. Not to worry, though: It's so good that a pound won't last very long.

1-pound salmon fillet	5 whole cloves
¼ cup honey	5 crushed peppercorns
¼ cup rum	1 teaspoon garlic salt
juice of 1 lemon	½ teaspoon dried parsley
5 allspice berries	1 bay leaf

Slice the fillet into strips about ⅜ inch thick. Mix all the ingredients except the fish in a nonmetallic container. Let sit for 15 minutes or longer. Add the salmon strips one at a time. Cover and refrigerate for 1 hour, turning the strips a few times as convenient. Arrange the strips on trays or racks and dry for 6 to 8 hours at 140°F, or until dry to your liking. Store each strip separately in a ziplock bag, Cheyenne says.

SHARK JERKY

This jerky recipe is based on information distributed by the California Sea Grant, the University of California, and the US Department of Agriculture. The Sea Grant people recommend using blue shark, but any good shark will work. There are dozens of edible species—blacktip, spinner, soupfin, mako, lemon, leopard, and so on—but in many cases the fish must be gutted and iced down as soon as it is boated or landed.

The procedure that follows, adapted from my *Saltwater Fish Cookbook*, is for making the jerky in a kitchen oven. It works just as well using a commercial dehydrator.

Start with about 3 pounds of shark fillets. Cut the fillets into strips of convenient length, ½ to ¾ inch thick and 2 inches wide. You can cut with or against the grain, thereby producing a different texture in the final product. Cutting with the grain will produce a chewier jerky. Note that partially frozen shark is much easier to slice.

Prepare a sauce with ⅛ cup teriyaki sauce, ⅛ cup liquid smoke, and 6 drops Tabasco sauce.

Place the shark strips on racks. Sprinkle moderately with onion salt, garlic salt, and table salt. Turn the strips and sprinkle the other side.

Mix the shark strips and the sauce thoroughly in a large plastic bag. Expel the air from the bag and seal. (Use a vacuum-seal system if available.)

Marinate for 12 hours in the refrigerator, turning the bag a time or two.

Remove the shark strips and place them on the oven racks.

Turn the oven to 140°F. Leave the door ajar. Start checking the jerky after 2 to 3 hours, but leave it in the oven until firm, dry, and tough—but not crumbly. It should be rather rubbery. The curing time will vary and may take as long as 12 hours. A good deal depends on the thickness of the meat, individual ovens (and thermostatic controls), and sometimes on the species of shark.

Store the strips in airtight jars in a cool place. Enjoy.

HALIBUT POPCORN

Here's an interesting recipe adapted from the excellent book Cooking Alaskan. *To make it, you will need a long, thin, very sharp knife. The recipe calls for halibut fillet, which can be quite a chunk of meat from a large fish.*

halibut fillet	salt in a large shaker

Skin the fillet and slice it very thin—thin enough to see the knife blade through the fish flesh. Salt each strip heavily on both sides and hang to air-dry. The dried strips will taste "quite a bit like popcorn," the book says—but they really don't.

SPICY FISH JERKY

Use this recipe with boneless fillets of any mild fish, preferably low in fat content. The strips can be cut across the grain, on a bias, or lengthwise.

½ cup tomato sauce	1 tablespoon freshly ground black pepper
2 tablespoons minced onion	1 tablespoon dried thyme
1 tablespoon minced garlic	1 tablespoon dried basil
1 tablespoon salt	1 tablespoon liquid smoke
1 tablespoon cayenne pepper	2 pounds fish strips

Mix all the ingredients except the fish in a nonmetallic container. Let stand for 15 minutes. Add the fish, one strip at a time, gently tossing about to coat all sides. Marinate for an hour or two, turning once or twice. Drain the fish strips and place on a dehydrator tray or fine-mesh oven rack. Dry at 140°F for 6 to 8 hours, or until done to your liking. This jerky can be stored for a few days in an airtight container, preferably vacuum-packed.

CATFISH JERKY

Some catfish make an excellent jerky, but there are so many edible species and so much prejudice and misunderstanding about the genre that it's difficult to hold this text to a reasonable length. In general, the better the meat, the better the jerky. In general, the whiter the meat, the better it is. The angler will quickly realize that this truism rules out several species of bullhead. Perhaps I should add that there is no such thing as a mudcat, although several species are called that—some of which, such as the bowfin, aren't even catfish. In any case, here is my list, based on common North American species. Other parts of the world, such as the Amazon Basin, produce some cats of excellent culinary quality.

Channel Catfish from running water. (Pond-raised fish are not quite as good.) These grow to a large size, making the fillets and belly ideal for cutting into jerky strips.

Blue Catfish. These are also excellent eating and grow quite large—up to 100 pounds or better.

Flathead Catfish. Excellent eating, these large catfish are from the Mississippi River, but they have been introduced in Florida, Georgia, and no doubt other states. These prefer live food, such as hand-size bluegills, and are not scavengers. Flatheads grow to a very large size; 30- to 40-pounders are not uncommon.

White Catfish. These are excellent for the table, but they do not get as large as the channel, blue, and flathead catfish, making them harder to use for jerky. Good, though.

Farmed Catfish. These are better than no catfish at all, but the meat is usually softer than river-run fish. The fish scientists keep "improving" on these by making them grow faster. They don't necessarily taste better, however.

In any case, this recipe is for large flathead. These have a thick belly flap, rather like a slab of bacon, that is easy to slice into pieces of uniform size. I recommend ⅜- to ½-inch thickness. It's best to partially freeze the slab before slicing.

flathead strips	**Tabasco sauce**
sea salt	

Sprinkle the strips generously with salt and lightly with Tabasco. Put the strips into a nonmetallic container and toss about to coat all sides with salt and Tabasco. Arrange on racks in a dehydrator or kitchen oven. Dry at 140°F for 6 hours or longer. For long storage (as might be the case if you jerk a 40-pound flathead), get the meat quite dry and store it in vacuum-packed bags or Mason jars.

TSUKEYAKI JERKY

I make this jerky with Chef Myron's Tsukeyaki sauce, a mixture of soy sauce, ginger, and other ingredients made especially for fish. If Myron's mix is unavailable, use any good commercial teriyaki sauce. Note that large, thick fillets can easily be cut across the grain into fingers or lengthwise into longer strips.

1 cup Tsukeyaki or teriyaki sauce (more if needed)

1 cup beer (more if needed)

2 pounds fish fillets, about ½ inch thick

Mix the sauce and beer in a nonmetallic container. Add the fish. If the liquid doesn't cover the fish, add some more. (Much will depend on the shape of the container.) Cover and refrigerate for 24 hours. Rig for smoking at about 150°F. Add some applewood or alderwood for smoke, or use any good hardwood. Smoke for 8 hours or longer, depending on the thickness of the fillets. Cool the strips on the smoking racks, then wrap in paper towels and store in a brown bag in the refrigerator until needed.

Note: Also try this one with hard apple cider instead of beer.

ALASKAN BIG-BATCH FISH JERKY

This recipe from Alaska works with sockeye, king, chinook, and other salmon, as well as with steelhead and other trout. Fillet the fish, leaving the skin intact. Then cut the fillets crosswise or on a diagonal into strips about ⅝ inch thick. If you prefer, cut the strips lengthwise, maintaining the same thickness. The mixture below works for 10 to 15 pounds of fillets. Double or reduce the measures as required.

2 gallons boiling water	1 tablespoon onion powder
2 cups salt	1 tablespoon garlic salt
2 cups soy sauce	1 tablespoon freshly ground black pepper
2 cups teriyaki sauce	10–15 pounds trout fillets
5 pounds brown sugar	

In a crock or other nonmetallic container of suitable size, mix all the ingredients except the fish. Stir with a wooden paddle to dissolve all the ingredients. Let the mixture cool, then mix in the fish strips. Marinate in a cool place for about 30 hours. Drain and quickly rinse the fish. Let dry to the touch in an airy place. While waiting, rig for smoking with alder or other good hardwood. Place the fish strips on racks and smoke heavily for a few hours at 140°F to 150°F. Discontinue the smoke and dry for several hours, until the jerky is dry but pliable. Store the jerky in jars or vacuum bags until needed. For long storage, dry the strips longer, until rather brittle.

MIPKU

The Eskimos and Native Americans of Alaska and Canada made good use of available whale meat along the seacoasts and in Hudson Bay. (Of course, the whale is a mammal, not a fish, but it seems more fitting in this chapter.) Apparently the Native Americans can still hunt some species of whale as a source of food and fuel oil, although sport and commercial hunting is forbidden. According to *Northern Cookbook*, on which this text is based, whale meat is boneless, very dark, and fine grained. The meat is usually soaked in salt water, which is said to remove some of the blood.

To make whale jerky, called *mipku*, "cut black whale meat into thin strips, about 8 inches wide by 2½ inches long by ½ inch thick. Hang the strips over poles to dry in the sun, or cure the strips over a driftwood fire in a log smoke house. When the meat is ready, it is hard and brittle. Break it off in small pieces and chew well. You must have strong teeth."

JONESPORT TAFFY

At one time, tons and tons of dried fish and salt fish, mostly cod, were shipped from New England to various parts of the world. The trade has diminished in recent years, but fish are still dried for home consumption in some coastal areas. According to James R. Babb—author, editor of Gray's Sporting Journal, *angler, and jackleg chef who lives in Maine—one of the best fish for salting is the pollack, about 18 inches long. These aren't much good for cooking fresh and don't freeze well, he says, but, when properly dried, they make the best imaginable fish chowders. Besides, he says, the local people have a good supply of pollack because the fish have a habit of nosing their way into lobster traps. If fresh cod or pollack aren't readily available, use any good lean white-fleshed fish.*

pollack or cod   salt

Split and butterfly the fish. Place a layer skin side down in a nonmetallic container. Sprinkle generously with salt. Add another layer and more salt. Repeat until all the fish are used. When a brine forms, rinse the fish and hang them on the clothesline until dry. (Take them inside in case of rain.) The dried fillets can be stored and used as needed in chowders and other recipes. For a chew of Jonesport Taffy, simply cut off a strip with a pocketknife and have at it.

MAKING USE OF JERKY

These days, most jerky is consumed as a tasty snack between meals or as an energy boost on the trail. It is especially welcome as a campfire chew and as an easy-to-take, no-mess journey snack. People with very good teeth and most large family dogs simply chew it up and swallow it, but this is not the best way. For maximum flavor, simply hold the jerky in your mouth for a while without actually chewing on it. At first, it is relatively tasteless, but soon the taste buds start to work and the saliva flows. After a while, the jerky will become soft enough to chew rather easily, releasing its flavor over a long period of time. Eventually it can be chewed up and swallowed, but the enjoyment should last for several minutes. That is the gustatory magic of jerky.

Although jerky has been eaten in this manner from the beginning, it was once even more important in the daily diet of the American Indians, early settlers, and other peoples the world over. It can be cooked in many soups and stews, or used in other recipes set forth in chapter 12, Cooking with Jerky (page 87). It can be mixed with fat and dried fruits to make pemmican (next chapter), which in turn can be eaten as is or mixed with other ingredients. Jerky can even be powdered and sprinkled over other foods, or used as a soup base like bouillon cubes.

So, don't forget the old ways for camp cookery, for sea journeys, for emergency home eating, and possibly for new culinary experiences. Hunters, anglers, sustenance farmers, and survival freaks will find that making jerky and pemmican is an inexpensive way to preserve food for future use.

CHAPTER 11

PEMMICAN

One of the greatest of the high-energy trail foods, pemmican was first made by the Native Americans. The word itself probably came from the Cree Nation, but pemmican of one kind or another was common over most of North America. It always contained powdered or ground venison or bison jerky and animal fat, and often dried fruits or berries were mixed in. The wild berries could be dried blueberries or huckleberries, cranberries, buffalo berries, and so on. Sometimes wild nuts or sunflower seeds, along with such nutritious wild edibles as powdered mesquite beans, were used in the pemmican, making it even more nutritious. Often the dried fruits and nuts were treated separately and added to the pemmican shortly before the time of consumption.

Usually, the Indians sun-dried both the jerky and the berries, and not necessarily at the same time or place. The modern practitioner, outfitted with an electric food dehydrator, will find it much easier to make relatively foolproof jerky and dried fruits. The use of seedless raisins from the supermarket as well as dried figs, blueberries, and other fruits from health food stores and trail mix outfits also simplifies the process.

These days, pemmican is usually shaped into finger foods for convenience. But convenience wasn't behind the development of pemmican. It was a means of storing food, and often relatively large slabs of pemmican were made in rawhide bags the size of a modern pillowcase. The slabs weighed 80 to 90 pounds. To make these, the Indians filled a rawhide bag with the powdered jerky, poured in melted fat, sewed the end of the bag shut—and then walked on it to mix and flatten the contents. These slabs could be stacked one atop the other for storage in large caches, sometimes underground, and, if properly made, would keep for many years. After the Europeans arrived, the Indians sold pemmican to the white trappers and settlers, as well as to the military. Each tribe made it a little differently, depending in part on what kind of game was available, and each bragged that it made the best.

Although such vegetable products as Crisco can be used more or less successfully, it's really hard to beat beef suet, because it hardens to a tallow. Sheep fat is also good, and the Indians made very good use of fat from bears, moose, caribou, buffalo, and other big game; from sea mammals such as seals and manatees; from ducks, geese, and other fowl; and from smaller animals such as opossums and armadillos. Also, bone marrow was used. Hog lard, still available in some supermarkets, is a great preservative, but it is a little too soft to be ideal for pemmican.

If you want to use animal fat and don't have big game at hand, ask your butcher for some beef suet, the best of which comes from around the kidneys. Cut the suet into ½-inch cubes. Put these into a cast-iron pot and cook on medium heat, stirring from time to time. The fat will cook out, and what's left of the cubes will float to the top. When the cubes are quite brown, they can be strained off, drained, and used as cracklings for breads and for sprinkling over salads or baked potatoes. The rendered fat should be simmered a while longer to make sure all the water is driven out, which is quite important for long storage. While still warm, rendered fat can be poured over powdered jerky, or it can be chilled and stored for later use, in which case it will have to be reheated for proper mixing with the jerky.

Most good jerky will do for making pemmican, but I think a basic recipe without all manner of spices works best. (If desired, the spices can be added to the pemmican mix.) A dry (but not cooked) jerky cut against the grain works better simply because it is easier to reduce to a powder. Ground-meat jerky is also good. For using large batches of jerky, try cutting it into pieces with kitchen shears and then grinding it in a sausage mill or food processor. Small batches can be pounded on a heavy block of wood with a hammer. A large mortar and pestle can also be used but is not ideal. Also try a handheld grater to help reduce the jerky to small pieces, which can then be ground to a fine powder. Again, the ease of preparation depends in large part on the texture and thickness of the jerky. Anyone who wants to make a large batch of pemmican should prepare the jerky especially for grinding to a powder; that is, the meat should be cut across the grain in thin slices, then dried until it crumbles easily. I might add that powdered jerky stores well in a jar, and some people use it to season soups and stews as well as salads, sprinkling it on like salt and pepper, as discussed briefly in chapter 12, Cooking with Jerky (page 87). Thus, the American Eskimos powdered jerky made from moose and caribou; South Africans, ostrich and springbok; Tibetans, yak.

Most pemmican is used as a trail food or snack these days, but it can also be an ingredient for cooking a complete meal, as reflected in a few of the recipes in this chapter.

For storage, some people shape the pemmican into fingers and wrap it in plastic wrap. Others even dip the fingers into melted paraffin, which will ensure long storage, if the pemmican has been properly made. Cakes and other shapes can be stored in airtight containers, and, of course, the modern vacuum-pack systems are ideal for storing either pemmican fingers or cakes. It should be stored in a cool place; a refrigerator is ideal.

HAPPY CAMPER PEMMICAN

All you need for basic pemmican is ground jerky and melted fat. Mix the melted fat into the pulverized jerky until you have a thick doughlike consistency. Add in some minced or ground dried fruit—blueberries, apricots, peaches, and so on. Shape the mixture into small loaves and wrap in cheesecloth. These loaves will keep for some time and can be taken on camping trips or journeys without refrigeration if need be. They can be eaten without cooking, giving a burst of energy, or they can be used in soups and stews.

For longer storage, wrap the loaves in cheesecloth and dip in melted paraffin. Or, better, seal the pemmican with a vacuum-pack system, if the equipment is available.

ROCKY MOUNTAIN PEMMICAN

Here's a Rocky Mountain recipe, made with the aid of melted bone marrow. Use marrow bones from buffalo, elk, moose, caribou, or beef. To get the marrow, saw the bones off at both ends and push it out with a dowel pin. This is good stuff, and some of the Eskimos call it caribou butter.

6 cups ground jerky	approximately ½ cup melted bone marrow
4 cups dried currants, chopped	melted beeswax (optional)

Mix the jerky and currants, then add the melted marrow slowly until the mixture sticks together. Shape into small balls or cigars. Store in a cool, dry place for a few days. For longer storage and travel, dip the balls or logs into melted beeswax, or seal in plastic bags with a vacuum-pack system.

NEW ENGLAND PEMMICAN

This jerky calls for maple sugar, but light brown sugar can also be used. The dried fruit can also be varied, depending on what's available. If you want another variation on Rocky Mountain Pemmican (page 82), for example, try dried wild buffalo berries instead of cranberries.

2 pounds jerky

¼ pound seedless raisins

¼ pound dried cranberries

1¼ cups maple sugar or brown sugar

1 pound beef suet or other good fat

Grind the jerky in a food mill. In a nonstick, loaf-shaped pan, mix the ground jerky, dried cranberries, raisins, and maple or brown sugar. Melt the fat and stir it into the mixture. Cool and remove the pemmican from the pan. Vacuum-pack in a plastic bag (or dip into melted paraffin) and store in a cool place until needed.

HONEY NUT PEMMICAN

Honey, being a natural preservative, fits right in with the making of pemmican and can be used instead of suet or other fat. After making the pemmican, it's best to store it in the refrigerator— and do not depend on a shelf life longer than a few months. This one is closer to candy, however, than to a true pemmican. Be warned that black walnuts (most of which are harvested from the wild) are a little too strong for most tastes. For a wild mix, try ½ cup black walnuts and 2 cups hickory nuts.

2½ cups chopped walnuts
or other suitable nuts

2½ cups seedless raisins or (better)
chopped dates

4 cups powdered jerky

approximately 2½ cups honey

In a food mill, grind the nuts and raisins or chopped dates. Mix in the powdered jerky. Gradually stir in enough honey to hold the mix together. Pour into suitable mold to a depth of ¼ inch. Chill and cut into bars. Wrap each bar in foil, or, better, seal individually in vacuum-packed bags.

RAY'S PEMMICAN

Here's a very good recipe adapted from Internet material by Ray Audette, author of NeanderThin: A Caveman's Guide to Nutrition. *He uses beef eye of round to make the jerky, but venison or any good red meat will do. The jerky should be dry but not cooked. (Cooking the jerky, Ray says, makes the pemmican gritty like sand.) Pound the jerky with rocks or use a food processor.*

1 pound beef suet (or ⅔ pound previously rendered tallow)

1 pound powdered jerky

handful of chopped dried cherries

Chop the suet into cubes and fry it in a cast-iron pot or large skillet. When the cracklings float to the surface, remove them and continue heating the grease to drive out all the water. Remove from the heat. When the fat is cool enough to touch (but before it turns too hard), mix it with the powdered jerky and dried cherries. Pack the mixture into cupcake forms or pie tins (or perhaps breadstick pans) and let harden. Store in a dry place.

Note: In his book, Audette seems to favor pemmican made without dried fruit. If properly made, it will keep for a very long time—up to one hundred years, he says. If dried berries are needed for a recipe, add them as needed. In other words, the pemmican will keep longer without the fruit. Also see the Caveman Jerky recipe (page 44).

ZUÑI CANDY

The sunflower might well have been the first plant cultivated by the North American Indians, and, of course, the peanut is a Native American contribution to the world's foods, as is the chili pepper. In the Southwest, cactus pear or Indian fig is a popular wild fruit, and, at one time, the honey from the replete ant was considered a delicacy. Of course, substitutions are permitted in this recipe.

1 cup powdered venison or beef jerky

1 cup sunflower seeds

1 cup chopped dried cactus pears, fruit, or berries

⅔ cup animal fat or vegetable shortening

1 tablespoon wild honey

½ teaspoon ground red pepper (cayenne will do)

Mix all the ingredients and mold in a shallow baking pan. Cut into bars, wrap in plastic wrap, and store in a cool place.

HERTER'S ATOMIC AGE PEMMICAN AND CHILI CON CARNE

George Leonard Herter, coauthor of Bull Cook and Authentic Historical Recipes and Practices, *was somewhat haunted with fears of the atomic bomb. Many of his recipes and practices reflect this. (See also his Survival Jerky recipe on page 25.)*

2 pounds ground or powdered jerky	**¼ cup sugar**
¼ pound ground dried fruit	**10 ounces melted suet**

Mix the powdered jerky, dried fruit, and sugar, then stir in the melted suet. Form the mixture into solid blocks. Store in cans or glass jars.

Variations: Chili powder from the grocery store, Herter goes on, helps turn a cake of pemmican into a wilderness chili con carne. Simply place the pemmican into a little boiling water. Add a little chili powder to taste, along with more water if needed. Dried beans can also be added, along with plenty of water, but they must be cooked for several hours. Presoaking the beans will help them cook quicker. Personally, I want my beans cooked separately, then put into the serving bowls as desired, along with some chopped onions and maybe some crumbled hardtack.

SOURDOUGH'S PEMMICAN

Here's a rather unusual recipe for a cooked pemmican submitted by Mrs. Aline Strutz and adapted here from the book Cooking Alaskan. *She says the pemmican can be eaten as is, fried like a steak, or used in a stew.*

1½ cups beef suet or bear fat

¾ cup cranberry jam or wild currant jelly

½ cup soup stock or beef stock

4 cups powdered jerky

½ cup brown sugar

½ cup finely ground dried blueberries, raisins, or currants

1 teaspoon minced dried wild chives

¾ teaspoon freshly ground black pepper

½ teaspoon dried savory

½ teaspoon freshly ground allspice

½ teaspoon garlic powder

½ teaspoon onion powder

Preheat the oven to 300°F. Melt the suet or bear fat in an oven-safe pot. Add the jam or jelly. Bring to a simmer. In a separate bowl, mix the stock and powdered jerky, then add the rest of the ingredients; gradually stir this mixture into the pot with the suet. Cover the pot and bake for 3½ hours. Pour a little of the mixture into a pie pan or muffin tin. If it seems too thick, add a little more stock. Then pour the mixture and let cool. Wrap each cake individually in foil. Store in a cold, dry place until needed.

CHAPTER 12

COOKING WITH JERKY

In modern times, jerky has become popular mostly as noshing fare and trail food for hikers. Its historical use, however, was much broader, and modern practitioners can make more extensive use of it. Once the idea of reconstituting the dried meat in water is understood, the creative cook can come up with hundreds of dishes, depending in part on available ingredients and personal preference. When properly reconstituted, jerky can be used in many recipes that call for corned beef, and sliced thinly, it can be fried like bacon.

Jerky is especially useful in camp, travel trailer, and boat cookery where the use of refrigeration or bulky canned goods might be limited. Jerky is easy to pack, light in weight, and quite durable.

In any case, here are some recipes for openers, starting with an old cowboy favorite and ending with an excellent Mexican recipe to be used "the morning after."

JOWLER WITH SADDLEBAG JERKY

Here's a recipe for cowboys who are tired of chewing on jerky or who have bad teeth, or both. Any kind of good homemade jerky will work, but I like it marinated in soy sauce and cold-smoked until dry. It's best to use meat that has been cut with the grain. Any good chili pepper can be used, but a cowboy in the Southwest might well use a small wild bird pepper (so named because the birds feed on them and spread the seeds). These are very hot, so you might want to remove the seeds and inner pith. (The pith contains most of the heat.) Or try half a smoke-dried habanero if you've got one and aren't afraid of it.

jerky	water
diced bird pepper or red pepper flakes	flour
salt	rice (cooked separately)

Put the jerky, pepper, and salt in a skillet with water and simmer until the jerky is reconstituted and tender. This may take 2 hours or longer, so you'll have to add a little water from time to time. When the jerky is done to your liking, remove it from the skillet. You should have about a cup of liquid left in the skillet; if not, add some water. In another bowl, make a paste with a little water and flour; stir slowly into the skillet liquid and heat, stirring as you go, until you have a nice gravy. Put the jerky back into the skillet and simmer for a few minutes. Serve hot over rice.

CARACAS

If you've got a Martha Stewart in camp, you may need a recipe with a few more ingredients than cowboy jowler, but without beans if you're tenting. Here's an old southwestern dish that cooks easily and might fill the bill in camp or at home. It is very good, especially for brunch or perhaps a hearty breakfast.

1½ cups chopped jerky	½–1 teaspoon ground cayenne pepper
water	½ teaspoon ground cumin
2 tablespoons butter	1 cup grated Monterey Jack cheese
1 cup chopped tomatoes	3 chicken eggs, lightly beaten
1 teaspoon salt	toasted tortillas or toast

Freshen the jerky by soaking it in water until softened, usually overnight. Heat the butter in a skillet. Drain the jerky, then add it to the skillet along with the tomatoes, salt, cayenne, and cumin. Cook for a few minutes, then stir in the cheese. Whisk the eggs and stir them in. Cook, stirring as you go, until you have a mixture not unlike scrambled eggs. Serve hot on toasted tortillas or toast. Feeds 2 to 4.

JERKY AND GARBANZO BEANS

Garbanzo beans—often called chickpeas—are widely available these days in supermarkets and specialty shops. I have enjoyed them for many years as a major ingredient in soup, to which they add a delightful crunch. It was not difficult, then, for me to come up with the following recipe. It is very good, ideal for canoe or camp cookery, where the grub is light and nonperishable. I like to top this dish with a little bottled tomato-based salsa, if I have some at hand. If not, a little catsup or chili sauce will do.

1 cup dry garbanzo beans	salt
1 cup chopped jerky	water
red pepper flakes	salsa (if available)

Using separate nonmetallic containers, soak the garbanzo beans and the jerky, in water, preferably overnight. Drain them, put them into a cooking pot, and sprinkle on a few red pepper flakes and a little salt. Cover with water, bring to a boil, reduce the heat, cover tightly, and simmer for an hour, adding more water if needed. Serve hot in soup bowls, topped with a little mild, medium, or hot salsa, if available.

ZAMBIAN STEW

Central Africa makes good use of peanuts, sometimes called groundnuts, in its cuisine. Other groundnuts (such as chufas) are also used, but peanuts, imported from South America, have become standard. Ground peanuts can be used, but it's easier to use chunky peanut butter. Any good game or beef jerky can be used. The seasonings are optional, but I like some red chili pepper in mine.

1 pound jerky	2 tablespoons chunky peanut butter
water	salt (if needed)
1 large onion, chopped	flaked red pepper to taste (optional)

Soak the jerky in water for several hours and then simmer it in fresh water until almost tender. Add the onion, peanut butter, salt, and red pepper flakes. Simmer for another 20 minutes. Serve hot.

CREAMED JERKY

Here's a recipe that makes a wonderful (but very rich) cabin brunch or lunch on a cold winter day. It works best with a smoked jerky chopped into a fine dice or ground coarsely in a food mill. The jerky works a little better if the strips have been cut against the grain, but chewy jerky can also be used.

1 cup minced jerky	2 cups half-and-half or light cream
water	salt and pepper to taste
¼ cup butter	toasted bread or English muffins
¼ cup flour	

Soak the minced jerky in a little water for several hours, or simmer it for 30 minutes over very low heat, to soften it. Drain. Heat the butter in a large skillet, slowly stirring in the flour as you go. Take the skillet off the fire and stir in the half-and-half. Add the softened jerky, salt, and pepper; simmer for about 10 minutes, stirring constantly. Serve hot, spooning the mixture over toast. I also like creamed jerky served over English muffin halves, which hold lots of gravy for their size, or over sourdough biscuit halves.

NEW MEXICO MEAT LOAF

Here's a recipe from New Mexico. Use it with sun-dried beef, buffalo, or venison jerky, ground in a food mill.

1 pound red-meat jerky	1 cup raisins
1 cup sugar	1 tablespoon freshly ground allspice
3 cups boiling water	

Soak the jerky in water overnight, drain it, then grind it in a sausage mill or chop it in a food processor. Brown the sugar in a stove-top dutch oven or other suitable pot. Stir in 3 cups of boiling water, mixing well with a wooden spoon. Stir in the raisins, allspice, and ground jerky. Put the mixture in the middle of a square of cheesecloth. Bring the ends up, forming a bag. Place a block of wood on top and drain until the liquid stops running. Slice and serve like meat loaf.

BHUTANESE YAK JERKY CURRY

Dried beef and sometimes yak, along with lamb, are favorite ingredients in the Himalayan cookery of Bhutan. The meat is cut into long, thin strips about an inch wide and hung in the sun for several days. Any good red-meat jerky can be used, but note that the Bhutanese version is not salted or otherwise seasoned prior to drying. Highly seasoned jerky can be used in this recipe if necessary, but it will alter the flavor of the dish. The dish is made with lots of hot chili peppers in Bhutan, but you can adjust the heat, depending on your taste and the kind of peppers at hand. For more on Bhutanese cookery, see Indian & Chinese Cooking from the Himalayan Rim, *by Copeland Marks, the excellent work from which this recipe has been adapted.*

½ pound yak or beef jerky	10 dried red chili peppers (or to taste), seeded
water	½ pound string beans, split
¼ cup peanut oil	3 cloves garlic, sliced
salt to taste	cooked rice

Simmer the jerky in about 2 cups of water for half an hour. Add the oil, salt, chili peppers, and beans. Cover the pot and simmer for a few minutes. Stir in the garlic and cook for another half an hour, or until the jerky is tender and most of the water has cooked off. (Add more water if necessary.) Serve hot with rice.

PERUVIAN HORSE JERKY STEW

Because it is hard to find horsemeat in North American markets, feel free to substitute any good red-meat jerky in this recipe. Calvin W. Schwabe's excellent book Unmentionable Cuisine, *from which this recipe has been rather freely adapted, points out that donkey meat "is more flavorful than horsemeat and is highly valued in several cuisines." Historically, however (the book goes on), the pre-Columbian version would have been made with jerked llama or guinea pig. The modern Peruvian recipe calls for calves' feet, but I have listed pig's trotters because they are more widely available in most modern supermarkets north of the border. But use calves' feet if you have them. The other meat ingredient, tripe, is also available in some supermarkets either fresh or frozen. Peruvians have a number of hot chili peppers to choose from, but most of us will have to settle for what's available in local markets and home gardens. How many you use depends on your taste and the variety. For openers, use only a few red chili peppers. If you want the stew hotter, sneak in some red pepper flakes toward the end.*

dried red chili peppers to taste	2 pig's trotters, cleaned and split
salt	1 rib celery with tops, chopped
water	4–5 pounds potatoes
2 pounds red-meat jerky	2 large onions
2 pounds tripe	1 cup cooking oil
1 handful fresh parsley, chopped	chopped hard-boiled eggs

Seed the chili peppers and soak them overnight in salted water. Bake the jerky in a 350°F oven until browned, then simmer it in salted water until tender. In another pot, simmer the tripe and parsley until tender. In a third pot, simmer the trotters and chopped celery until the meat is ready to fall away from the bones. When tender, cool and chop all of the meats. Combine the pot liquors and boil gently until reduced by half.

Meanwhile, boil and mash enough potatoes to approximately equal the weight of the meats. In a stove-top dutch oven or other suitable pot, cook the onions and drained chili peppers in 2 cups of water until all the water evaporates and the onions start to char. Add about 1 cup of oil and stir with a wooden spoon to keep the onions and chili peppers from sticking to the pan. Simmer for several minutes, then drain off and reserve the oil. Add all of the meats and mashed potatoes. Stir in some of the reduced pot liquor. Cook on low until you have a thick, smooth mixture. Just before serving, stir in a little of the reserved chili oil and garnish with chopped hard-boiled eggs. Enjoy.

JERKY AND RICE

This recipe makes a good dish for camp cookery, partly because the ingredients are so easy to transport and store. You can even carry the jerky inside the rice container, remembering that Chinese peasants store dry sausage for long periods of time in the family rice crock.

½ pound jerky   2 cups uncooked rice

water   soy sauce

Soak the jerky overnight in water. Bring 4 cups of clean water to a boil in a pot. Add the rice. Place the jerky strips atop the rice, bring to a new boil, cover tightly, lower the heat, and simmer for 20 minutes without peeking. Remove the pot from the heat, stir in a little soy sauce to taste, and let cool for a few minutes.

CAMP STEW

Here's a basic recipe that can be easily modified, depending on the vegetables you have on hand. Dried stew-beef chunks work fine, or you can cut strips of jerky with shears. Also cut the vegetables into pieces before measuring them. If you are going on a camping trip, the ingredients, except for the rice, can be measured and put into a jar or plastic bag, preferably vacuum-packed. The forager may want to add some fresh catbrier sprouts, fiddleheads, Jerusalem artichokes, and perhaps spring beauty bulbs, as available.

½ pound beef jerky chunks   ½ tablespoon dried garlic bits

1 cup dried potato pieces   ½ tablespoon dried parsley

1 cup dried tomato pieces   salt and pepper to taste

½ cup dried carrot   1 quart water

1 tablespoon dried bell pepper pieces   rice (cooked separately)

1 tablespoon dried onion bits

Put all the dry ingredients except the rice into a pot. Add the water and set aside for about 30 minutes. Put the pot over the heat. Bring to a boil, reduce the heat, cover tightly, and simmer for an hour or so. Serve hot over rice.

JERKY CHILI

This chili can be made with any good red-meat jerky. If you use highly seasoned jerky, however, you might want to modify the ingredients accordingly.

½ pound basic jerky

¼ cup cooking oil

¼ cup prepared chili powder

1 tablespoon red pepper flakes (or to taste)

1 tablespoon dried onion flakes

1 teaspoon garlic powder

1 teaspoon cumin seeds, crushed

water

flour (if needed)

Cut the strips of jerky into ½-inch pieces. Heat the oil in a cast-iron pot. Add the jerky pieces and stir for a few minutes. Add the chili powder and stir until well mixed. Stir in the rest of the seasonings and cover with water. Bring to a boil, reduce the heat to simmer, and cook for 3 hours, stirring from time to time and adding more water as needed. Cool the chili, then reheat it for serving. Thicken with a little paste made with flour and water, if needed. Serve hot in bowls, adding pinto beans, chopped onions, and other toppings, if wanted. Corn pone or rolled tortillas go nicely with chili, but saltines will do. Feeds 2 to 4.

EASY *CHARQUI* CHILI

In Argentina, dried meat, made from beef, rhea, or guanaco is called charqui. *It was, and still is, an important part of the nation's cookery. Various stews are made, often with several different kinds of charqui, and most of them are rather complicated. Here's an easy one, mixed to taste.*

beef jerky, cut into small pieces

water

tomato paste

chili powder

salt

Simmer the jerky pieces in water until tender, adding more water as needed. Stir in some tomato paste, chili powder, and salt, a little at a time, tasting as you go. Cook until you have a thick chili. Serve on plates, along with rice, chopped onions, and black beans. It is permissible to mix it all together as you eat.

JERKY BACON

Thinly sliced jerky can be fried in cooking oil and used like bacon. I prefer to use jerky plugs and slice them thinly, against the grain, just prior to cooking, but thin strips of jerky can also be used. Use from ½ to ¾ inch of oil in a skillet, and get it quite hot. Cook the jerky, a few strips at a time, until the strips are crispy. Overcooking will give the jerky a burned taste. Drain the jerky on absorbent paper and serve hot or warm, preferably for breakfast along with chicken eggs and toast or perhaps grits.

SNOEKSMOOR

Here's an old dish from the southern part of Africa, where dried fish is an important part of the cuisine.

1 pound plain fish jerky	2 medium to large onions, diced
water	4 medium to large potatoes, peeled and diced
2 tablespoons cooking oil	2 fresh chili peppers (jalapeños will do), chopped

Freshen the fish for several hours in cool water. Drain and dice. Heat the oil in a deep skillet or suitable pot, preferably cast iron. Sauté the onions until they are lightly brown. Add the potatoes and chili peppers and sauté until the potatoes are done. Add the diced fish and cook for 5 to 6 minutes over medium heat, stirring a time or two and adding a little water if needed to prevent scorching. Serve hot with rice and lots of sliced tomatoes.

Note: For better color, use 1 green chili and 1 fresh red chili, if available.

STEWED *PAPA*

According to Harva Hachten's book Best of Regional African Cooking, *on which this recipe is based, dried shark is called* papa *in East Africa and is available in Asian markets. (The coconut milk required for the recipe is also available in Asian markets and sometimes in our supermarkets; do not use the highly sweetened piña colada mixes.) Jerky made from a shark's belly is ideal.*

water	1 large onion, sliced
½ pound shark jerky or papa	1 teaspoon curry powder
2 cups coconut milk	1 teaspoon red chili pepper flakes
2 large tomatoes, sliced	salt (if needed)

Bring some water to a boil in a pot. Add the shark jerky and let stand for 10 minutes. Drain the jerky and cut it into bite-size pieces using kitchen shears. Discard the water from the pot and add the coconut milk, tomatoes, onion, curry powder, and chili pepper flakes. Bring to a boil, then reduce the heat and simmer until the liquid begins to thicken and the onions are tender. Add the shark jerky and cook for about 15 minutes. Add a little salt if needed. Serve hot with a good flatbread, hardtack, or perhaps saltines.

JERKY SEASONING

Powdered or chopped jerky is used in South Africa and several other countries as a tasty and nutritious seasoning ingredient for soups and stews. In Alaska, crumbled jerky is sprinkled over scrambled eggs, salads, clam chowders, and so on. When making jerky for use as a seasoning, it's best to cut the meat thickly and across the grain so that it will be easier to crumble. The jerky pieces can be run through a food mill, or ground with a mortar and pestle. I think a plain jerky made with only salt and perhaps a little pepper works better as a seasoning than one flavored with a dozen herbs and spices.

Also see the previous chapter on making pemmican.

CALDILLO DE CARNE SECA

Here's a good recipe from George C. Booth, author of The Food and Drink of Mexico. *Booth's version called for two pickled wax peppers or a drop or two of Tabasco sauce. I have substituted fresh red cayenne peppers, which add a little color as well as fire. Any hot pepper will do, used with restraint. I have also taken liberties with the amount of jerky used, reducing the measure by half.*

¼ pound jerky

water

1 medium onion, finely chopped

2 cloves garlic, peeled and minced

½ bell pepper, finely chopped

2–3 fresh red cayenne peppers,
seeded and minced

1 large tomato, chopped

1 tablespoon cornstarch

1 teaspoon cooking oil

salt and pepper

thyme

Soak the jerky in water for several hours, drain, then chop or grind it. In a saucepan, sauté the jerky, onion, garlic, and peppers for 5 minutes. Add the tomato. Mix the cornstarch into a little water. Add to the pot, along with 2½ cups of water. Cook for 10 minutes, seasoning to taste with a little salt, pepper, and thyme. Serve hot with toasted tortillas. According to Booth, this soup is a favorite with cowboys, sportsmen on the morning after, and honeymooners. "It alters the stomach, steadies the pulse, and puts new light in the eyes," he says. Enjoy.

PART TWO | SAUSAGE

INTRODUCTION

Tasty sausage can be made with an expensive hand-cranked meat grinder, a chunk of fresh pork, and a few readily available spices. Because the process is so easy, I decided to start part two of this book by actually making and cooking sausage in the first chapter, hopefully whetting the appetite instead of bogging down for a hundred pages in techniques and meat-curing formulae.

In subsequent chapters, we'll be stuffing good country sausage into casings, smoking and drying the links, and globe-trotting for recipes, sampling surprisingly modern sausages from ancient Rome as well as tantalizing new flavors from Thailand along the way.

Most of the recipes in this book are designed for using a total of 10 pounds of meat. It's easy to scale the recipe up or down, but remember that the setup and cleanup time required to grind and stuff the meat will be the same for 1 pound or 10 pounds. Besides, homemade sausage is so good that

10 pounds goes pretty fast. Also, many homes have an extra freezer these days, making the large batch even more practical.

The "servings" recommended by most modern cookbooks have always bothered me. I suppose that some guidance is needed, but far too many people have been left hungry by some recipes and serving recommendations in modern cookbooks and magazines. How much sausage you eat depends on you and your requirements, tastes, and capacity, as well as, I think, on the occasion. However, sausage is highly spiced and quite filling, so that those people who like half a pound of meat will probably find that a quarter pound of sausage will do. In this book, the recipes for the various sausages do not offer advice on the number of servings. Recipes for various dishes that call for sausage as an ingredient, or for cooking sausage in some special way, may or may not offer serving sizes.

CHAPTER 1

EASY SAUSAGES

Good sausage starts with good meat. It's true that sausage is traditionally made with scraps from the butchering process, but they should at least be good scraps, Of course, you can also use prime cuts of meat in sausage, provided that the fat content is adjusted, and I've known rural practitioners who bragged about using entire hams or even the whole hog for sausages. If you make your own, the choice is yours. You also have more control of the fat content and chemical additives.

Of course, the complete sausage maker will want to grind his own meats. This process is discussed later in this chapter, along with equipment and meat-grinding tips. Right now, let's put together a simple sausage and cook some recipes just to show how easy it is.

SIMPLE SAUSAGE

The ingredient list for this recipe calls for ground lean pork and ground pork fat. Anyone who isn't proficient in the fundamentals of meat grinding should read the chapter through first, or perhaps get a butcher to grind the meat.

7 pounds ground lean pork

3 pounds ground pork fat

4 tablespoons salt

2 tablespoons crushed dried sage

2 tablespoons freshly ground black pepper

1 tablespoon red pepper flakes

Thoroughly mix the ground meat, fat, and seasonings. Shape a thin patty and fry it in a hot skillet. Taste for seasonings. Add a little more sage, black pepper, and/or red pepper flakes to the mix if you want to make it hotter or change the flavor. Either cook the meat right away, refrigerate it for a day or two, or freeze it. Don't forget that sausage patties are easy to cook on a griddle or in a skillet, and don't require cooking oil because some of the fat in the mix will cook out. These patties can be served for breakfast with eggs and toast and perhaps sliced tomatoes. Also, a great American classic requires nothing but a sausage patty sandwiched in biscuit halves. No mayonnaise or gravy or other condiments are needed.

Storing Bulk Sausage

Bulk sausage should be cooked right away or frozen. If properly made from good meat, it will keep for several days in the refrigerator, but freezing it is the better choice.

Freezing Patties. I often make sausage patties from bulk sausage, wrap them with plastic film, and freeze them for future use. The sausage should also be labeled so that you'll know what they are and when they were made. Instead of labeling individually, I write the information on a freezer-proof plastic container and pack the patties in it for storage. This method helps keep things straight, and helps you find the small patties a month or two later.

The patties can be unwrapped and cooked in a skillet or on a griddle without prior thawing.

Freezing by the Pound. In addition to patties, I freeze bulk sausage in 1-pound units. These are wrapped in plastic film, wrapped again in freezer paper or aluminum foil, and labeled. I also freeze them in small, freezer-proof plastic boxes that hold 1 cup each, packed tightly and capped with a little water. These are easy to thaw out in a microwave.

Larding Sausage Patties. Before the days of mechanical refrigeration, sausage patties were fried in lard on hog-killing day. The lard, of course, was rendered on the scene from pork fat. (Frying chunks of fat yielded lard and a delicacy known as cracklings, which, contrary to some modern cookbooks, are not merely fried pork skins.) The sausage patties were fried in the bubbling lard and packed into stone crocks. Then hot lard was poured in, completely covering the patties. As it cooled, the lard turned to a paste. The patties were dug out and reheated as needed. These patties are delicious. The crock must be kept in a cool place, such as in an old-time springhouse or a modern refrigerator.

Cooking Bulk Sausage

In addition to being shaped into patties and cooked for breakfast in a skillet or on a griddle, bulk sausage can be used in meatballs, spaghetti sauce, pizza toppings, and so on, as well as in a variety of other recipes. Here are some of my favorites.

EASY SAUSAGE CASSEROLE

1½ pounds bulk sausage

8 hard-boiled chicken eggs, sliced

1 (10¾-ounce) can condensed mushroom soup

2 cups grated cheddar

½ cup bread crumbs

salt and pepper to taste

Brown the sausage in a skillet, cooking until done, and drain. Place the sliced eggs into a large buttered casserole dish. Distribute the sausage evenly over the eggs, then cover with the soup. Mix cheese and bread crumbs together; sprinkle over the dish. Bake at 350°F long enough to heat the casserole through, then brown it under the broiler. Season with salt and pepper to taste.

MISSISSIPPI CASSEROLE

This old Mississippi dish calls for a combination of oysters and bulk sausage. It's hard to beat for texture and flavor, especially if you can gather your own fresh oysters. I cook it from time to time when I go oystering, or when I purchase a bag of fresh Apalachicola oysters.

3 cups uncooked brown rice

2 pounds bulk sausage

2 cups chopped onion

2 cups chopped celery with tops

1 cup chopped fresh parsley or cilantro (divided)

2 pints freshly shucked oysters, drained

Cook the rice following the directions on the package. Preheat the oven to 350°F. Brown the sausage in a skillet, then pour the drippings into a saucepan or another skillet. Sauté the onion and celery in the sausage drippings for 10 minutes. In a bowl, mix the cooked rice, sausage, onion, celery, ½ cup of the parsley, and all the oysters. Turn the mixture into a casserole dish and sprinkle with the rest of the parsley. Bake for 30 minutes. Feeds 6 to 10.

SAUSAGE 'N' TWO-SOUP CASSEROLE

This dish, like many other American casseroles, makes easy use of canned soups. It's very good. I like it with hot country sausage, made with plenty of red pepper flakes.

1 pound highly seasoned bulk sausage

1 (10¾-ounce) can cream of chicken soup

1 (10¾-ounce) can cream of mushroom soup

1 cup uncooked long-grain rice

1 (8-ounce) can bamboo shoots

1 (8-ounce) can water chestnuts

½ cup chopped red bell pepper

¼ cup chopped onion

¼ cup chopped celery with tops

salt

Preheat the oven to 350°F. Grease a casserole dish suitable for serving. Mix all the ingredients, spread in the dish, cover, and cook for 45 minutes. Feeds 4 as a main dish or 8 as a side.

SAUSAGE FINGERS

Here's an easy way to make finger food from bulk sausage. It's best to grate your own cheese instead of buying packaged shredded cheese. I think these are especially good when made with a rather hot sausage.

2 pounds bulk sausage

4 cups biscuit mix

10 ounces grated sharp cheddar

Preheat the oven to 350°F. Mix the ingredients together, shape into fingers, place on a rack in a baking pan, and cook for 15 to 20 minutes. Serve warm.

CROWN ROAST WITH SAUSAGE STUFFING

This beautiful and tasty dish requires a crown roast of pork. Your butcher can prepare this for you. The chine bone should be removed, making the roast easy to carve at the table, and the roast should be joined at the ends for a round presentation.

SAUSAGE STUFFING

1 tablespoon cooking oil	½ cup chopped walnuts
1 pound bulk sausage	1½ cups chicken stock or broth (divided)
1 cup chopped onion	4 cups French bread cubes
1 cup chopped celery	

Heat the oil in a large skillet. Sauté the sausage meat until lightly browned, then stir in the onion, celery, and walnuts. Cook for a few minutes. Stir in ½ cup of the chicken stock. Simmer for 15 minutes, stirring and adding a little more stock as needed. Place the meat mixture into a large bowl, then mix in the bread cubes and the remaining chicken stock. The stuffing can be refrigerated for a few hours, but it's best to use it immediately.

THE ROAST

1 crown roast, 7–12 pounds	salt to taste
½ teaspoon granulated garlic	juice of 1 lemon
1 teaspoon freshly ground black pepper	

Record the weight of the roast. Preheat the oven to 350°F. Place the roast into a well-greased shallow roasting pan. Mix the garlic, pepper, and salt into the lemon juice. Brush the juice mixture over the roast. Stuff the roast with the sausage mixture. Place a strip of aluminum foil over the stuffed roast, being sure to cover the exposed bones at the top. Bake for 25 minutes per pound of meat, or until done. (If in doubt, cut into the roast; when done, the juices will not be bloody. Or use a meat thermometer, which should read at least 150°F.) Remove the roast to a heated serving platter and let it cook a little longer from its own heat while you prepare the gravy.

THE GRAVY

pan drippings from roast

2 tablespoons flour

4 cups water

salt and pepper to taste

Remove the rack from the roasting pan. Measure 2 tablespoons of the pan drippings, putting it into a saucepan or skillet. Heat the drippings and slowly stir in the flour, cooking and stirring over low heat for 15 minutes or longer; set aside. Pour off most of the remaining grease from the roast pan, then place the pan over two stove burners and stir in the water along with some salt and pepper. Bring to a light boil, scraping up the pan dredgings with a spatula. Using pot holders, carefully tip the roasting pan and pour about ½ cup of the liquid into the flour mixture. (If you prefer, remove the hot liquid with a large spoon.) Turn up the heat on the saucepan and pour in a little more liquid, stirring as you go. Pour and stir until all the pan drippings have been blended into the saucepan. You should now have a nice gravy. Thin with a little more water if needed. Place the gravy into a serving dish.

Serve the gravy with the roast and stuffing, along with boiled or steamed cauliflower, snap beans, pickled crab apples, and plenty of French bread.

Pork for Sausage

In spite of the direction of contemporary winds, pork has always been and still is, from a purely culinary viewpoint, the best all-around meat for sausage. Since the fat is not marbled in the flesh (as it is in beef), pork can be very lean, if properly chosen and well trimmed. On the other hand, sausage needs some fat. It really does. This fact makes fatty scraps of pork, trimmed out during the butchering process, a good choice for making sausage. Of course, such scraps were traditionally used for making sausages at home during hog-killing time, usually during the first cool snap in autumn. If you butcher your own hogs, then by all means use scraps. But hog-killing day is for the most part a thing of the past, and these days even those people who raise their own pork usually take it on the hoof to a meat processor. Modern farmers and farm wives don't want to get their hands in it, and even some hog farmers and chicken farmers call themselves "producers."

The amount of fat in many sausage recipes is as high as 50 percent, and my guess is that most commercial sausages contain 50 percent or more. The home practitioner can cut back considerably, making a sausage that doesn't shrink drastically when cooked. The stickler for exact numbers can separate the fat and lean, then mix by weight as desired. It's easier, however, to use such cuts as the pork shoulder, which will contain about 25 to 30 percent fat. The fat content of these cuts will vary from pig to pig, and the trend these days is toward a leaner meat. In any case, using all the fat and lean meat from a shoulder will usually give a pleasing ratio of lean to fat. Of course, hams or hindquarters can also be used, but these will often be more expensive.

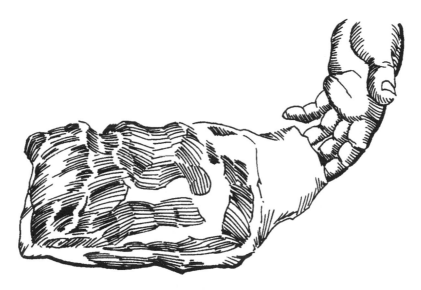

Picnic and Boston butt

The pork shoulder is sometimes butchered and sold as one chunk, but it is usually divided into two main pieces, plus the shank and trotter. The butt, or Boston butt, is the big end and is often marketed boned or semi-boned. I buy them bone-in because I like to make soup and provide a treat for my dog Nosher. The picnic looks like a small ham. A little meat can be trimmed from the shank, but I like to save this piece for soups and stews, used along with the bones from the butt and picnic.

In addition to the shoulder, other parts of the pig can be used—even the very lean and more expensive loin and tenderloin cuts. It's fun, I think, to purchase a whole pig and reduce it to sausage. The term *whole-hog sausage* implies a superior product, giving you at least a psychological edge when serving sausage to your family and friends. Good meat really does help.

If you don't raise your own pigs or purchase them on the hoof from a farmer, your best bet is to gain the confidence of a good butcher. Tell him what you want and why. Some large supermarkets will provide good fresh meat because the turnover is high, but in many cases, the personal touch and consumer confidence are missing, at least with this customer. Moreover, my experience with frozen meats purchased from supermarkets has been unpleasant. I don't want meat that has been displayed until the date of sale expires, then wrapped (or rewrapped) and frozen. If such meats were thawed, cooked, and eaten right away, they might be all right. Not ideal, but all right. But when made into a large batch of sausage, it might well be stored in the refrigerator for several more days or even longer if cased and cured.

Most sausages are made with fresh pork instead of cured hams or other cured parts. The meat may be cured (salted down) during the sausage-making process, but it almost always starts out as fresh pork or fresh frozen pork. The fresher the better, I think. Of course, any fresh pork can carry the parasitic roundworm known as trichina, which is the culprit of trichinosis. This parasite can be killed by heating the pork to an internal temperature of 140°F or thereabouts during the cooking process. It can also be destroyed in raw pork by freezing it at 5°F or less for thirty days. Freezing at colder temperatures shortens the time requirement, but most sausage makers working with home freezers will probably want to stick to the thirty days—and use a reliable thermometer.

Pork that has been properly frozen for the required length of time is said to be certified. Certified pork may also be purchased from your butcher. If readily available from a reliable source, it can save you some time. I hate to repeat this term in every pork recipe in this book, but I like to use it in any sausage that calls for pork. Sausages that are made and cooked or frozen right away can be made with uncertified pork, but they should be cooked thoroughly. Any sausage that is cured, smoked, or dried should be made with certified pork.

Salmonella is always a threat, especially with poultry and meats that have been run through a batch process. It can be controlled by cleanliness, proper refrigeration, and thorough cooking. Other problems—mainly bacterial toxin buildup—come about during curing and smoking and are discussed in subsequent chapters.

Other Sausage Meats

Although pork is the traditional sausage meat, until modern times the pig wasn't widely eaten outside Europe and China. Nomadic peoples—the Arabs, the Mongols, the Lapps, the American Plains Indians—really didn't care much for pork and might well have used other animals, such as camels or yaks or reindeer or aardvarks, for making sausage. The Mongols considered a fondness of pork to be a sure sign of "going Chinese," and they, or perhaps the ancient Scythians, might well have been the source of *kazy*, a modern-day Russian sausage made with horsemeat. Also, the Scythians are known (if we may trust Herodotus) to have stuffed horsemeat into a stomach, like Scotland's sheep haggis (page 191), and cooked it over a low-smoke campfire made or perhaps sustained with the aid of horse bones.

Of course, the Germans also love pork (even more than the French do), and today the *wurstmachers* offer more than 1,500 kinds of sausage. Whether for domestic use or export, the German *wurst* must be made with pure meat—no fillers or extenders, chemical additives, or colorings. Don't ask what's in an American-made supermarket frankfurter these days.

In any case, pork isn't the only meat that can be used in sausages. Other chapters offer recipes and tips for working with chicken, turkey, beef, veal, lamb, game of all sorts, variety meats such as liver, and even fish.

Often, the use of other meats instead of pork won't really alter the taste of the final product very much, especially with such highly seasoned sausages as chorizo (page 142). But often the texture and the color will be altered considerably.

Preparing the Meat

Here are a few steps and tips that will make it easier to grind sausage meat and hamburger.

1. Chilling or freezing the meats. Cold or partially frozen meats are easier to cut and grind—and they are safer to use because bacterial growth is greatly retarded at temperatures below 40°F.

2. Trimming the meats. Trimming the meats of sinews prior to grinding can be very, very important. Tough, stringy tissue clogs up the meat grinder, making frequent cleaning necessary. Some of the tissue can be cut out in sheets while you trim the meat. A small, sharp fillet knife works well. Thorough trimming should be part of cutting the meat into large segments and then into smaller chunks suitable for grinding.

3. Cutting the meat into chunks. Use a sharp knife to reduce the meat to chunks suitable for feeding into a sausage mill. I like mine about 1 inch square. Some people use strips of meat, but I cut mine across the grain to minimize the tissue problem. In other words, it's always best to cut the meat so that the tissue is not fed into the grinder in long strings.

   Usually, when cutting fatty pork such as Boston butts, I chunk the fat right along with the meat, trying to give a good mix. (Exceptions to this practice are pointed out in a few recipes in subsequent chapters.)

   It's best to keep the chunks of meat cold. If you are a slow worker or have lots of meat to cut, devise some way to keep the meat on ice. I use a large plastic tray with ice spread over the bottom, then I put the meat into a similar tray and nest it on top.

4. Mixing the meat. If using more than one kind of meat, or with a meat and fat ground separately, I usually mix them equally on a work surface within easy reach of the meat grinder, or in a large plastic tray. The tray is especially useful when the meat (or meats) is to be cured in the refrigerator before grinding, and the maximum size of the tray should be determined by the width and depth of your refrigerator interior.

5. Mixing the spices. Normally, I mix all the dry spices and salts, then sprinkle them evenly over the chunks of meat prior to grinding. It is important that the spices be evenly mixed and evenly distributed. This is especially important if the spices contain a cure such as saltpeter or sodium nitrite. (These cures are discussed in chapter 3, Stuffing Sausages, page 121.)

   In some recipes, other ingredients, such as bread crumbs or diced onions, are added at this point. In other recipes, these ingredients are mixed in after the meat has been ground.

6. Grinding the meat. Grind the meats while they are still very cold. If the meats have been properly cleaned, the grinding operation should go smoothly and quickly, although the plate and knife of the grinder may have to be cleaned along the way. To make sure all is well, keep an eye on the meat being extruded from the plate. If things clog up inside, you will notice a reduced "flow." If you keep on grinding, the meat will be mashed and pulverized instead of cut, and it will start to back up along the rotor. With a little practice, you'll be able to spot trouble early. A lot depends on your equipment, which is discussed below.

7. Adding other ingredients. Recipes vary, but liquids such as water and wine along with minced fresh onions and perhaps bread crumbs are usually mixed in after the meat has been ground. Use your hands.

After grinding, the mixture is usually stuffed into casings (see chapter 3, page 121) or treated as bulk sausage. In a few recipes, the ground meat is put into the refrigerator for a day or two to "cure" or to blend the flavors.

The Meat Grinder

Any good meat grinder or mincer can be used to make sausage, but a grinder equipped with fine, medium, and coarse plates is highly desirable. Most of these grinders also have several plates and sausage-stuffing tubes available as accessories. Never buy a sausage mill unless such accessories and spare parts are available.

Several mechanical and electric meat grinders are marketed. I use the old-fashioned kind.

Hand-Cranked Meat Grinders

Usually made of plated cast iron, these grinders are available in several sizes. The small size will be satisfactory and may even be preferable for home kitchen production, owing to the simple mounting system, as explained below.

Mounting. Some sausage mills attach to the table or countertop with a suction cup, but these are not stable enough to be satisfactory. Others are mounted with four bolts. While this is indeed a superior mounting system, remember that the four bolts require four holes in your table or countertop. Never buy one of these unless you want to drill holes in your work surface.

The clamp-on meat grinder, which attaches to a flat surface with a hand screw and pressure plate, is better suited for easy use in most kitchens. Even so, this device won't fit without trouble on some countertops or tables.

Clearly, the prospective sausage maker should consider the mounting systems before purchasing a meat grinder.

Mechanical meat grinder

The Handle and the Auger. On a mechanical grinder, the handle turns an auger inside a cylinder in the housing. As it turns, the auger forces meat chunks from the hopper toward the knife and plate.

The Knife. The knife, usually with four blades, fits onto the end of the auger shaft and turns as the handle turns the auger. The knife fits flush against the circular plate. When the auger forces meat against the plate and into the holes in the plate, the knife cuts the meat and forces it into the holes.

Obviously, the knife should be kept sharp. Your sausage supply dealer may sharpen the knives for you, or perhaps refer you to some such service. I sharpen my own with the aid of a large whetstone. The knife is placed flush against the stone and worked in a figure-eight motion. (There may be better sharpening schemes, but I think it's a mistake to start filing on the blade at an angle. Remember that the blade should fit flush against the plate.) When you purchase your grinder, you may want to order an extra blade or two.

The Plate. The plate, round and about ⅛ inch thick, fits into the grinder housing in contact with the cutting edges of the knife. The plate has geometrically spaced holes, through which the sausage meat passes. The size of the holes determines whether the meat is ground fine, medium, or coarse. Of course, the smaller holes are more numerous. For most sausages, a plate with ³⁄₁₆-inch holes will be all you need, but it's nice to have other sizes as well.

As a rule, the smaller the diameter of the holes, the more often the plate will have to be cleaned, because stringy tissues clog it up. For this reason, it's sometimes prudent to grind a meat with a ¼- or ⅜-inch plate and then grind it again with a ³⁄₁₆- or ⅛-inch plate. In any case, cutting the meat into small chunks helps reduce the clogging problem. Properly trimming and cutting the meat will take more time but will save lots of cleaning during the grinding process.

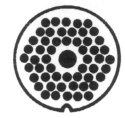

Cutting plates

Before purchasing your grinder, make sure that you can obtain plates of various sizes. The manufacturer may sell these plates directly to users through a customer service department, or they may be available through dealers and mail-order outfits. Each manufacturer of sausage grinders may offer different-size plates, sometimes measured in centimeters. Here's my own classification according to the diameter of the holes:

⅛ inch	=	extra fine
³⁄₁₆ inch	=	medium fine
¼ inch	=	medium
⅜ inch	=	coarse
½ inch	=	extra coarse

I recommend that the sausage maker have ⅛-, ³⁄₁₆-, and ¼-inch plates. If you are limited to a single plate, go with the ³⁄₁₆ inch. If expense isn't important, get two or three of the ³⁄₁₆-inch plates so that you can change them during the grinding process instead of interrupting the process to clean a plate. (To clean the smaller sizes, by the way, I hold them under running water and poke out the holes one by one with the wooden end of a kitchen match or some such object. Clearly, this is a time-consuming process.)

Be warned that the plate must not turn inside the housing. It is, or should be, held in place by a notch on the perimeter of the plate and a protuberance on the grinder housing. If the plate is not properly installed, the meat tends to mush instead of grind.

Retaining Ring. This large threaded ring fits over the end of the grinder and holds the plate in place. It should be tight but not tight enough to make the handle difficult to turn.

Capacity and the Hopper. As a rule, the larger the grinder, the larger the auger, knife, and plate, and the more meat the unit will grind per unit of time. The capacity listed by the manufacturer is not without value, but it doesn't really account for cleanup, cleaning clogged plates, and so on. Consequently, the smaller units are just about as good as the larger ones, at least for small sausage-making operations. And, as stated earlier, the smaller units are more likely easier to mount.

I would, however, like to see a larger hopper on the smaller units. The idea would be not so much to hold more meat but to keep the meat from falling to the floor. In other words, a wide hopper, within reason, is easier to load.

Sterilization. It's best to sterilize the grinder and all its parts in boiling water before grinding meat. After sterilization, the parts should be chilled before proceeding. Note that harmful bacteria are everywhere. The trick is not to avoid them entirely, which is impossible, but to minimize their growth. They do not thrive at temperatures below 40°F or above 140°F. Several kinds of potentially harmful bacteria are discussed in chapter 3, Stuffing Sausage (page 121), and in the glossary. The parasitic worm that causes trichinosis is discussed earlier in this chapter.

Electric Grinders

Some people prefer electric meat grinders, and I certainly have no objection to them, provided that they operate with a knife and plate. Most of the electric grinders are freestanding and therefore don't present mounting problems.

Prices of electric grinders vary, ranging up to hundreds of dollars for a commercial unit. Before buying, make sure that you can get extra parts and sausage-stuffing attachments.

Food Processors

I don't recommend food processors and various high-speed zappers for grinding meat because it's difficult to control the consistency and it's too easy to mush the meat. Some practitioners recommend this type of machine, however, for emulsifying meats for use in frankfurters, bologna, and other such sausages and sandwich meats, making them more like commercial fare. I don't recommend the practice, but suit yourself.

One other consideration is that most food processors on the market don't have sausage-stuffing attachments (discussed in chapter 3, page 121).

Seasonings, Additives, and Spices

All sorts of spices are used in sausage recipes. Some of these give a certain sausage its characteristic flavor, such as the use of fennel in some mild Italian sausages.

Most spices tend to lose flavor and aroma with long storage. It's best to keep them in a dry, cool, dark place. It's preferable, if possible, to purchase or store whole spices, then grind or crush them as needed.

Salt. Historically, salt is the most important seasoning ingredient in a sausage. It still is, especially in sausages that will be hung to smoke or dry for some time. Ordinary table salt will be satisfactory for most sausage making. Sea salt is a little better, at least to me, but it is rather expensive these days.

Black Pepper. Buy whole peppercorns in bulk, then grind or crush your own as needed for making sausage, for cooking, and for table use. To me, the aroma of freshly ground pepper is one of the great small pleasures of cooking and eating.

White Pepper. White pepper is the same as black pepper, only it is harvested earlier. It is not as strong as black pepper.

Paprika. This powdered red pepper is often used as a spice for seasoning, but it is really more important, in its mild form, as a coloring agent. Most of the paprika sold in American supermarkets is mild, and much of it is made from the common Anaheim pepper or something similar. Although Hungarian paprika is perhaps the best known, the best paprika comes from Spain, where it is a major ingredient in some famous sausages, paella, and other national dishes. It is made from sun-ripened peppers hung and smoke-dried for fifteen days over an oak-wood fire. Then the peppers are ground in a stone mill. This pepper is available by mail order in either sweet, bittersweet, or hot.

Red Pepper. Crushed dried chili peppers are often used in sausage making, especially country sausages from the American South, and Spanish or Latin American sausages. Crushed or flaked red pepper, including the hot seeds, is available at most spice markets. Some outlets that specialize in spices market pepper flakes, or whole peppers, in varying degrees of hotness. I prefer to go this route, often selecting a somewhat mild pepper. These milder peppers can be used in recipes in greater bulk, giving more color and flavor without the hotness.

I prefer to buy mild pepper flakes in bulk. For hot red pepper flakes, I usually buy off-the-shelf name brands from my local supermarket, and sometimes I use dried Tabasco peppers from my own garden. Be warned: Wear gloves when seeding hot peppers, and also remove the inner pith as well as the seeds. Do not touch the seeds and pith with your hands and then touch your eyes or tender parts. Pepper burns can be serious.

Additives and Cures. Commercial sausage makers add all manner of extenders and fillers to sausages, such as "corn syrup solids." Some of these are discussed briefly in the glossary, but most of the recipes in this book do not call for such ingredients. Meat is cured primarily by more or less natural salt, some of which may have some of the minerals removed. Sometimes saltpeter, sodium nitrite, and sodium nitrate are mixed in with the salt. A few of the recipes for cured and dried sausages (see chapter 3, page 121) call for such chemicals and cure mixes, but for the most part, I omit them.

Spice Mixes for Sausages

Anyone who makes lots of one kind of sausage may want to purchase a spice mix, or, better, might make their own mix. Such a mix can save money and time. Mixes for specific sausages, such chorizo or bratwurst, are marketed by firms that sell such stuff; see Sources of Materials and Supplies (page 373). My own rather basic mix recipe is set forth below, and it can be modified to suit your taste and fancy.

A. D.'S BASIC SAUSAGE MIX

Here's a seasoning for fresh pork sausage that I like to make, using plenty of rather mild red pepper flakes. The mix is enough for 100 pounds of fresh pork. By calculation, the entire batch weighs about 40 ounces, depending on how much pepper you use. To make only 10 pounds of sausage, use 4 ounces of the mix. This amount can be weighed with the aid of a home or office postal scale or a kitchen scale, if you have one.

2 pounds regular table salt	1–4 ounces red pepper flakes
2–4 ounces ground sage	1 ounce ground coriander
3–4 ounces freshly ground black pepper	

Thoroughly mix all the spices and store in sealed jars. Although the mix will last for several years, it's best to use it within a year or so.

Cleanup

Dismantle and wash your sausage mill with soap and hot water as soon as practical after grinding meat or stuffing sausage. Thoroughly dry the knife, plate, and other parts. Store the knife and plate (usually made of carbon steel, which is not stainless) in a plastic bag, and put them into a box along with the rest of the parts.

I use the original packing box for storage. In any case, keep all the parts together. A meat grinder isn't of much use if you can't locate the knife or plate when needed.

During the cleanup and dismantling, you'll find some good sausage meat around the auger inside the housing. While this meat can be taken out at the end of the grinding (and stuffing), I usually leave it in until cleanup time. Then, after washing and storing the sausage mill, I shape the meat into a patty or two, fry it in a skillet, and make myself a sausage patty sandwich with lots of mayonnaise.

CHAPTER 2

SAUSAGE LOAVES

Some of the best sausage meats are made in molds or unusual casings. For the most part, the following recipes are quite old and are neglected by modern cookbooks. One excellent recipe of this sort—haggis—is a specialty of Scotland and is covered in chapter 8, British Isle Sausages (page 184).

BOSTON COOKING SCHOOL SAUSAGE

Here's a recipe and stuffing technique from Mrs. D. A. Lincoln's *Boston Cooking School Cook Book*. "Of sweet fresh pork take one third fat and two thirds lean, and chop fine, or have it ground by your butcher. Season highly with salt, pepper, and sage (use whole sage; dry, pound, and sift it). Mix thoroughly. Make cotton bags, one yard long and four inches wide. Dip them in strong salt and water, and dry before filling. Crowd the meat into the bags closely, pressing it with a pestle or potato-masher. Tie the bag tightly and keep in a cool place. When wanted for use, turn the end of the bag back, and cut off the meat in half-inch slices, and cook it in a frying pan until brown. Core and quarter several apples, and fry them in the hot fat and serve with the sausages.

"A safe rule in seasoning sausage meat is one even tablespoonful of salt, one teaspoonful of sifted sage, and a scant half-teaspoon of white pepper to each pound of meat."

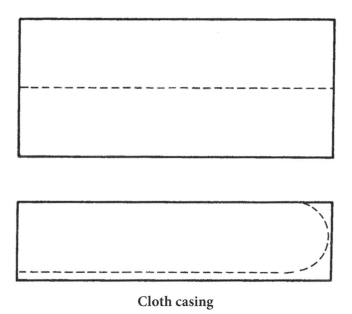

Cloth casing

CORN SHUCK SAUSAGE

This unusual recipe was adapted from *The Foxfire Book*. Into 10 pounds of lean pork chunks, thoroughly mix ¼ cup salt, ½ cup brown sugar, 2 tablespoons sage, 2 teaspoons black pepper, and 2 teaspoons red pepper flakes. Grind the mixture with a sausage mill. Remove the ears from some corn shucks, pack the sausage inside, tie the end of the shuck closed, and hang in a smokehouse.

The Foxfire Book was short on details, but when I tried this method, I smoked the sausages for 2 hours on one side of a large grill, then put them directly over the coals for a few minutes, turning from time to time. The corn shucks, as many Native Americans knew, added something unique to the flavor. I like to think that this method was suggested to the settlers by Cherokee cookery.

PENNSYLVANIA PONHAWS

Here's an old recipe that I have adapted from *Butchering, Processing and Preservation of Meat* by Frank G. Ashbrook.

Clean a pig's head, split it, and remove the tongue, eyes, and brains. Put the head halves and tongue into a pot, cover with 4 to 5 quarts of water, bring to a boil, reduce the heat, and simmer for 2 to 3 hours, or until the meat falls from the bones. Turn off the heat, letting the pot cool until the grease rises to the top. Skim off the top. Remove and finely chop the meat. Discard the cleaned bones and strain the stock to remove any bits of gristle or bone. Save a little of the stock (to be used later) and put the rest back into the pot.

Add the chopped meat. Bring to a new boil and lower the heat to a simmer. Mix a little yellow cornmeal with some of the reserved stock, forming a paste. Mix the paste slowly into the pot, simmering and stirring with a wooden spatula until the mixture thickens almost into a soft mush. Be sure to scrape the bottom as you go to prevent sticking and scorching. Be patient. When the mixture is almost to the mush stage, stir in 1 teaspoon of powdered sage, along with some salt and pepper to taste. Pour the mixture into shallow well-greased pans and chill as quickly as possible.

When the ponhaws set, slice and fry until nicely browned. If you prefer, the slices can be dusted with flour before frying. Ponhaws can be refrigerated for several days or frozen for longer storage.

PHILADELPHIA SCRAPPLE CROQUETTES

I, a hopeless scrapple buff, opened my edition of *Pennsylvania Dutch Cook Book*, a work first published back in 1935, with great expectation. The index listed nine recipes. Going to the first one, I opened to a chapter called "Ways with Philadelphia Scrapple." Interesting stuff—but there wasn't a single recipe for actually making scrapple. Most people, I surmised, purchased it ready-made at the market.

The author of the book also had high praise for Pennsylvania Dutch sausage but failed to give a single sausage recipe. An essay at the end of the book called "Around the Food Season with my Grandmother at the Farm" did contain some good information:

"With meat grinders, large mixing bowls, and sausage stuffing machines, my grandparents would produce, before my astounded young eyes, a wide variety of foods, fresh pork sausage, smoked beef and beef sausages, Lebanon style bologna, highly spiced, liverwurst, and half a dozen other wursts. These Pennsylvania Dutch women did not flinch at their job of handling freshly killed animals; they had centuries of experience from childhood. They made meat jellies and pigs-feet jelly (a most delightful dish).

"Only in Pennsylvania Dutch territory have I even eaten the fresh pork sausages in the style they made, or the smoked beef sausages. The Lebanon bologna, 5 inches in diameter, is probably over-spiced for most tastes, but it surely is appetizing."

Well . . . my mouth waters as I long for the recipes for the sausages and scrapple. In any case, here's one of the recipes for cooking with scrapple, either made at home or purchased at market.

1 cup minced scrapple	salt and pepper to taste
2 hard-boiled chicken eggs, finely chopped	1 chicken egg, whisked
1 cup cooked white rice or mashed potatoes	½ cup cracker or bread crumbs
1 teaspoon minced parsley	cooking oil or fat

Mix the minced scrapple, hard-boiled eggs, rice or potatoes, parsley, salt, and pepper. Shape the mixture into croquettes, dip in whisked egg, roll in bread crumbs, and fry in hot oil, turning to brown all sides. Serve hot with horseradish sauce or green fried tomatoes, which is, somewhat surprisingly, another Pennsylvania Dutch specialty.

EASY SCRAPPLE

You don't have to butcher hogs or deal with hog heads, feet, and innards to enjoy scrapple.

10 pounds pork butt	2 tablespoons salt
salted water	freshly ground black pepper to taste
10 cups white stone-ground cornmeal	1½ tablespoons crushed dried sage

Chop the pork into ½-inch dice. Put it into a pot, cover with salted water, and simmer for 1 hour or so. Drain the meat. Measure the broth, adding enough water (if needed) to make 20 cups. Put the 20 cups of broth back into the pot. Mince the meat or run it through your sausage grinder with a ¼-inch plate. Stir the meat, cornmeal, salt, pepper, and sage into the pot. Bring to a boil and cook, stirring as you go with a wooden spoon, for 5 minutes, or until the mixture thickens. Put the mixture into greased loaf pans. Chill. Unmold and cook, refrigerate, or freeze. To cook, slice the scrapple into ½-inch slices, then panfry in a little oil until brown on both sides, turning once. Serve warm for breakfast.

Recipes for Making Old-Time Souse and Head Cheese

These two loaf products are similar. Both are made from the head (including the ears and snout) and feet of hogs. Typically, chunks of these parts are embedded in the loaf. When the loaf is sliced, these bits appear as half-moons and other interesting shapes. There are thousands of recipes. The two used below are quoted from the *Boston Cooking School Cook Book*, cited earlier in this chapter. In this work, the author said, "Though seldom seen on modern tables, these dishes when carefully prepared are very acceptable to many who have pleasant recollections of them served at 'grandmother's table.'" In more modern times, I remember one of my aunts making souse and, I assure you, the results were more than acceptable!

SOUSE

"Take the gristly part of the pig's head, but not the fat; also the ears and feet. Remove the hard part from the feet. Scald or singe the hairs, soak in warm water, and scrape thoroughly. Let them remain in salt and water for 10 hours. Scrape, and clean again, and put them a second time in freshly salted water. With proper care they will be perfectly clean. Put them in a kettle and cover with cold water; skim when it begins to boil; set back and let it simmer till the bones slip out easily. Skim out the meat, and remove the hard gristle, bones, and any superfluous fat. When hard, cut in slices, and brown in the oven."

HEAD CHEESE

"Prepare the same as souse and season with sage. Put into a strainer cloth, and press out the fat. Pack it in jars or moulds. Serve cold, or brown slightly in a frying-pan."

My aunt used a similar recipe, but she left the head cheese in the bag and hung it up to drip—that is, the bag was hung over a syrup bucket, which caught the fatty liquid that dripped out. From time to time, she would twist the bag, helping the process along. After a few days, the head cheese was sliced and eaten as sandwich fare. I liked to cut it into chunks and eat it on crackers. I still like it that way.

I might add that the Swedes are great champions of head cheese. In fact, they serve it at a traditional Christmas Eve supper along with pickled beets. When preparing the pig's head, they singe off any hair or bristle, cut off the ears, and brush the teeth. After long boiling, the broth left from the head is strained and served as a soup.

Although the pig's head is the highlight in most recipes, don't be tempted to leave out the trotters. These provide a natural gelatin that helps firm up the head cheese, making it easier to slice and serve atop good ol' American saltines or other crackers or with Swedish pickled red beets.

MOBILE PAN HAM

Here's an old scrapple recipe, quoted from *Gulf City Cook Book*. This work, published back in 1878, was probably the first "committee" fund-raising cookbook put together in the United States, the committee being formed by the Ladies of the St. Francis Street Methodist Episcopal Church, South, in Mobile, Alabama.

"Take a hog's head and feet; boil them until the meat falls from the bones; withdraw them from the liquor, which strain and return to the vessel. Chop the meat very fine; season with pepper, salt, spice, onions chopped fine, thyme, sage, and parsley. Add all to the liquor, adding a sufficient quantity of cornmeal to make a stiff mush. Let it boil 10 minutes, stirring all the time. Pour into a deep pan; when cold, cut in thin slices and fry."

"FRENCH" SAUSAGE

The *Gulf City Cook Book*, quoted above, also contained a recipe for "French" sausage, made up of minced chicken or turkey stuffed in the skin of chicken necks. It's very good, but these days it may be difficult to get enough skin-on necks. Talk to your butcher, or save up some necks if you raise your own fryers.

"Chop very fine, or pound in a mortar, equal parts of cold fowls, cream, dried bread crumbs, and boiled onions; season them with salt, pepper, and nutmeg to taste; put them into the neck—skins of poultry—tying the ends, and fry them as you would fry sausages."

UBALDI JACK'S SPICY SOUTHERN SAUSAGE

I understand that Lee Iacocca, past president of Chrysler Corporation, once took a managerial auto sales job in the southern United States. Figuring that his name wouldn't help his cause in this part of the country, he changed it to Iacocca Lee—with great success. I have used the same trick with this recipe because "Ubaldi's Southern Sausage" simply didn't play. In any case, it's good stuff made with the aid of aluminum foil. I have adapted the recipe from Jack Ubaldi's Meat Book.

3 pounds pork shoulder

½ cup cold water

1 ounce salt

¾ teaspoon freshly ground black pepper

¾ teaspoon hot red pepper flakes

½ teaspoon rubbed sage

¼ teaspoon ground allspice

¼ teaspoon ground nutmeg

⅛ teaspoon ground clove

aluminum foil

Cut the meat into chunks and grind it with a ⅜-inch plate. Grind it again with a ⅛-inch plate. Mix in the water and seasonings. Shape the mix into a long roll and wrap it in aluminum foil. Refrigerate overnight. For breakfast, slice off some ½- to ¾-inch rounds and panfry or broil for about 20 minutes.

Note: I must point out that hog casings, not aluminum foil, were Ubaldi's first choice for stuffing this mix. If you like the recipe but want the real thing, go directly to the next chapter to read all about sausage casings.

CHAPTER 3

STUFFING SAUSAGES

Sausages are usually stuffed into casings and formed into links of convenient measure. Traditionally, the casings are animal intestines, stripped, turned, and washed. In times past, the casings were prepared during the butchering process, and the sausages were stuffed on the spot. If you butcher your own hogs, you might ask your wife to strip and rinse the casings several times while you salt down the hams.

These days, however, the sausage maker usually purchases casings from meat supply houses. These commercial casings are packed in salt and will last for many months in the refrigerator or even longer in the freezer. I purchase mine in 3-pound hanks by mail order. A hank will make about 100 pounds of sausage. To make a small batch of sausage, I merely cut off what I think I'll need. With regular hog casings, 25 feet will be about right for 10 pounds, allowing a foot or two for waste. (Double the length if you are using sheep casings.) Then I refrigerate the rest until needed again. It would be better, perhaps, to separate the casing into

25-foot lengths, then freeze each strip separately in small ziplock bags. Maybe I'll do it that way one day.

Choosing the Right Casing

In most of the stuffed sausage recipes in this book, I specify the recommended casing in the list of ingredients. The size of the casing (the diameter when full) can be very important, as it determines the correct cooking and drying times. Adjustments can be made in most cases, but it's best to use the recommended casing if feasible.

Hog Casings. These are by far the most popular casings, partly because pork itself is so popular for making sausages. Prepared hog casings come in several sizes, often defined in millimeters. In round numbers, it takes 25 mm to equal 1 inch. The Sausage Maker catalog (see Sources of Materials and Supplies, page 373) lists four sizes: 29 to 32 mm, 32 to 35 mm, 35 to 38 mm, and 38 to 42 mm. For most sausages, a 32 to 35 mm will do. After all, most of us don't want to inventory dozens of different casings.

Sheep Casings. These are smaller than hog casings. They are, of course, used for stuffing the smaller-size sausages such as the French chipolata (page 194). I understand that goat casings can be used instead of sheep. Who would know? Sheep casings can be purchased in specific sizes, but they average a little less than 1 inch. I like the smaller kind—about ¾ inch—for stuffing finger sausages, but these are difficult to load onto some stuffing tubes.

Beef Casings. These are larger than hog or sheep casings. They are also thicker and tougher, so that drying times for the sausages are longer. When needed in this book for specific recipes for large sausages, beef casings are specified in the list of ingredients. They are subdivided into rounds, middles, and bungs, depending on which part of the intestine is used. The rounds, about 1½ inches in diameter, aren't much larger than hog casings; they are sometimes used for kielbasa and other sausages. Middles are about 2½ inches in diameter; they are used for some bologna and liverwurst sausages. Bungs are about 4 inches in diameter or larger; they are used in large bologna and cooked salami.

Collagen Casings. These days most of the commercial sausages made in the United States are stuffed into collagen casings. Collagen is a protein material contained in the connective tissue and bones of animals. After processing, the material is made into casings.

They are available from the larger suppliers in a variety of kinds and sizes, some made very thin for fresh sausages and some made thicker (and stronger) for sausages that are to be cold-smoked or dried, or both.

Synthetic Casings. A dozen types of synthetic casings can be purchased from sausage and meat supply houses. Some of these are quite specialized, made for a certain kind of sausage. For example, there is a mahogany-colored synthetic casing that is designed for stuffing sausage meat that contains liquid smoke; the idea, of course, is to give the color and flavor of smoke without actually smoking the sausage. I prefer the real thing, but suit yourself. If synthetic casings appeal to you (or, perhaps, if natural casings don't), your best bet is to get catalogs from the sausage supply houses or perhaps check with local meat-processing plants.

Some of the synthetic casings are lined with fiber to make them stronger. Others are lined with protein, which in turn causes the casing to adhere the meat as it shrinks in the drying process.

Clearly, the home sausage maker operating on a budget shouldn't try to buy large quantities of all these natural and synthetic casings. Assortment kits are available, but I think that the beginner should start with a hank of medium hog casings, then add a hank of sheep casings for franks and finger sausages. Others can be added later.

Sausage-Stuffing Devices and Attachments

Meat Grinder Attachments. Most of the hand-cranked sausage mills can be fitted with a sausage tube. This is a slightly conical metal or plastic tube that is flared on the big end, as shown in the drawing below. To use the tube, remove the cutting plate and knife from the sausage mill. Stick the tube through the retaining ring, seat the flared part into the retaining ring, and attach to the sausage mill. Set the knife and plate aside, as they are not normally used in the stuffing operation.

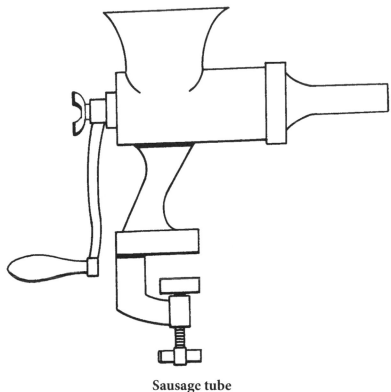

Sausage tube

Sausage tubes can also be used on many electric meat grinders, but most food processors and other machines that cut meat with a high-speed blade aren't designed for such attachments.

Stuffing Machines. Several stuffing machines are marketed by meat and sausage supply houses. These are nice to have, but they really aren't needed for making small batches of sausage, provided that you have a grinder that works with a stuffing attachment or tube. Available in a number of sizes, the stuffing machines usually work on a screw principle or a lever-operated plunger.

Other Stuffers. Plastic bottles, funnels, and pastry tubes can sometimes be modified and used to stuff sausages. It is important that the tube end fit snugly inside the casing, and that the casing can be gathered onto the tube, accordion-fashion, as discussed below. Sometimes, the home sausage maker will use these makeshift stuffers when the regular attachment is too large for small sheep casings.

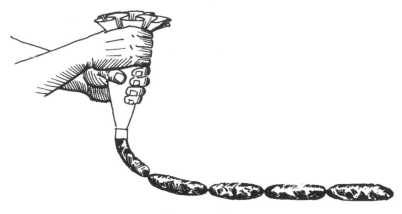

Pastry tube

Stuffing the Sausage

Regardless of the type of stuffer you use, note that the sausage meat isn't forced through the casing from one end to the other. To force the sausage meat through the casing would either pack the meat much too tightly or burst the skin, or both. When properly gathered onto the tube and fed out, the casing merely slips off the tube as the sausage grows in length. This principle is very important with any sausage-stuffing device, whether it be a $500 commercial machine or a devised handheld tube.

The text below is for a tube attachment used with a hand-cranked meat grinder, which I consider to be the more common arrangement by far. If you use other stuffers, it's easy to modify the procedure as necessary.

Match the Tube and Casing. Many kinds of sausages have an ideal size, or diameter, which means that a certain kind and size of casing should be used for stuffing. But note that a small sheep casing simply won't work properly on a tube designed for medium or large hog casings. The casing will be difficult to thread and feed—and it will probably split at the tube. (Most animal casings are quite strong lengthwise, and in the past have been used for fishing line and other applications. But their strength against bursting is relatively poor.) If your casing doesn't go onto the tube easily, either rig your stuffer with a smaller tube or use a larger casing. All this should, of course, be worked out before you grind the meat. If you have a problem at grinding time, try to keep the sausage meat cold until you work something out.

Get the Casing Ready. If using natural casings, cut them into convenient strips of about 12 feet. Rinse the casings inside and out. The inside can be flushed by running water through the casing, using a hose or faucet. If the casing has been salted for storage, it's best to soak it in cool water overnight, then rinse and flush it. If the casing isn't properly soaked, it may not slip over the tube easily and without splitting.

Loading the Tube. After you have ground all the meat, quickly remove the plate and knife from your sausage mill. Attach the sausage-stuffing tube, tightening it with the threaded retaining ring. Lubricate the tube with a little of the fat from the ground meat. Also, make sure there is a little water inside the casing. Fit one end of the casing over the end of the tube. With your fingers, work most of the casing onto the tube, accordion-style. Leave a few inches loose so that surplus air can escape. The end will be knotted or twisted later.

Casing gathered over tube

Other types of stuffer tubes are loaded by the same method. To my way of thinking, the tube is more important than the mechanism, and some expensive machines might well come with tubes that are a little too large.

Stuffing the Casing. After you get the casing gathered onto the tube, load the hopper with ground and ready sausage meat; then turn the crank or otherwise force the meat into the casing. Go slowly. It's best to hold the end of the tube with your left hand, making sure that the casing feeds correctly off the tube, while turning the crank with your right hand. Don't force the meat. Packing the casing too tightly can burst the casing during the stuffing operation, during the linking process, or while cooking. Also, avoid making air pockets in the casing if possible.

Linking. When the length of casing that you threaded onto the tube has been stuffed, inspect the sausage visually for air pockets. Prick the skin of the casing as needed to release the air. Twist the far end of the casing. Then, using both hands, shape a link of suitable size; hold the sausage with both hands and twirl the link, twisting the ends several times. Repeat this process until the entire length has been linked. The exact length of the links isn't too important, although some sausages are traditionally stuffed in standard sizes. You might want to stuff a particular sausage to yield a serving per link.

When the stuffed and linked sausage dries to the touch, the ends will hold together when cut. Usually, the sausages are left joined for hanging or storing. If you don't trust the twisted links to hold, you can always tie the sausage off with cotton string. As a general rule, I twist small sausages but tie larger ones, such as bologna.

Making links

Making and Cooking Fresh Sausages

Fresh sausages are not cured and can be cooked right away. They can be kept in the refrigerator for a day or two, which will sometimes help the flavors blend, but for longer storage they should be frozen. Usually, fresh sausages are made with fresh pork and should be cooked thoroughly. The short recipe below, although used mainly as an example, should not be taken lightly! The procedure assumes that you are using a hand-cranked sausage mill that has a suitable stuffing attachment. I have gone into detail on the grinding and stuffing operations that were described above and in chapter 1, Easy Sausages (page 99). Sometimes a little repetition isn't a bad thing.

small to medium hog casings	2 tablespoons crushed dried sage
10 pounds fatty Boston butt	2 tablespoons freshly ground black pepper
4 tablespoons salt	1–2 tablespoons finely crushed red pepper

Soak some hog casings overnight in cold water. Rinse the casings and run some water through them, using a water hose or faucet. Sterilize your sausage mill and its parts in boiling water. Cool and assemble the mill. Cut the meat (partially frozen, if feasible) into chunks suitable for grinding, trimming off sinew and tough tissue. Spread the chunks over your work surface. Mix all the spices and sprinkle them evenly over the meat. Grind with a $\frac{3}{16}$-inch plate.

Quickly remove the sausage knife and plate, placing them in the sink for washing later; don't waste time by washing them now. Quickly install the stuffing tube, securing it with the retaining ring. Carefully start the end of the casing over the end of the tube. Gather the casing around the tube. This should go smoothly; if not, add a little water to the inside of the casing for lubrication. I usually thread on 10 or 12 feet of casing, but the exact amount isn't too important. When you have gathered the casing around the tube, fill the hopper with ground meat and turn the crank, adding more meat to get it coming out the tube. Go slowly, helping the tube along with your left hand. Don't stuff the casing too tight; remembering that you'll have to link it later. Stuff all the casing, or a good part of it, then go over it with your hands, smoothing out any lumps. Using a large sterilized needle, prick the skin to eliminate any large air bubbles. Twist the far end of the sausage, then twist it closed. Holding the end with one hand, squeeze into the sausage with your right hand, separating the stuffing. Then, using both hands, sling the link over and over, as when jumping rope, thereby twisting the casing a number of times. When all the sausage has been stuffed into casings and linked, dry the sausage to the touch. At this time, the links can be cut and separated in the twisted part, but usually, it's best to leave two or more links connected.

Now you have a complete fresh sausage. It should be cooked right away, refrigerated for a day or two, or frozen for longer storage. For frying a fat sausage, most experts agree that the links should be pricked with a fork and simmered in a little water or stock for 15 to 20 minutes. Then they are dried with paper towels and sautéed in a skillet until nicely browned on all sides. I endorse this practice, but I sometimes like to panfry the sausages without the poaching process. Cutting slightly dried sausages in half lengthwise helps them cook through, and I also slice them into wheels before cooking. The diameter of the sausage should also be considered, and the small finger sausages made in sheep casings, as in the next recipe, are much easier to cook.

Note: You can also cold-smoke these sausages for an hour or so before storing or cooking. See the instructions later in this chapter.

SMALL BREAKFAST SAUSAGE

For this recipe, you'll need sheep casings. The sausage links should be about the size of a finger. These small sausages, or a similar recipe, are often sautéed and served for breakfast or as a finger food. In either case, an electric skillet will work. They can also be used in kebabs, preferably grilled over charcoal or wood coals, or cooked in soups and stews. Pork butt is specified in the ingredients, but any rather fatty pork will do. The fat content should be about 30 percent, so you can use 7 pounds of lean pork and 3 pounds of pork fat, or thereabouts. Note that the pork will cut and grind easier if it is partially frozen.

10 pounds pork butt	1 teaspoon dried sage
4 tablespoons salt	1 teaspoon dried marjoram
2 teaspoons freshly ground black pepper	4 cups cold water
1 teaspoon grated nutmeg	sheep casings

Cut the pork butt into chunks suitable for grinding. Spread them out on your work surface. Thoroughly mix the salt , spices, and herbs, then sprinkle the mix evenly over the pork chunks. Grind the chunks with a ⅛-inch plate, or grind twice with a ³⁄₁₆-inch plate. Using your hands, mix in the cold water. Stuff into sheep casings. These sausages can be cooked immediately, refrigerated for a few days, or frozen for longer storage.

To cook, sauté, broil, or grill the sausages, making sure that the pork is well done, which isn't much of a problem with sausages of small diameter.

Note: You can also cold-smoke these sausages for an hour or so. See the instructions later in this chapter.

Recipes for Cooking Fresh Link Sausages

Links of sausage are often fried in a skillet, broiled, or grilled. They are very good when cooked over charcoal, especially if they contain quite a bit of fat. The fat, of course, keeps the sausage from drying out too much—but it also tends to cause fires in the grill, so that cooking sausage is a full-time job. No recipes are needed for cooking stuffed fresh sausages, but here are a few that I highly recommend. Other recipes are scattered throughout the book.

SHAKER SAUSAGE WITH APPLE RINGS

The Shakers, perhaps the best American cooks, believed that the Kingdom of God can be achieved right here on earth. This recipe, which I have adapted from the Heritage Cook Book, *comes pretty close. It can be made in an electric skillet.*

THE SAUSAGE AND SAUCE

¾ pound pork sausage	salt
¼ cup chopped onion	1 cup apple cider
1 tablespoon flour	1 tablespoon minced fresh parsley

Heat about ½ inch of water in a skillet. Simmer the sausage for 5 minutes, pricking it with a fork to release some of the fat. Drain the liquid from the skillet. Continue to cook the sausage until it browns, turning several times. Drain off all but 2 tablespoons of the fat that cooked out of the sausage. Set the sausage aside to drain. Sauté the onion for 5 or 6 minutes. Stir in the flour and a little salt, stirring with a wooden spoon. Add the cider; cook and stir until bubbly. Stir in the parsley. Put the sausage back in the skillet, cover, and heat through. Place the sausage on a heated serving platter. Put the sauce from the skillet into a serving container. Serve the sausage with the sauce and honeyed apple rings.

HONEYED APPLE RINGS

4 apples	salt to taste
½ cup honey	¼ teaspoon ground cinnamon
2 tablespoons apple cider vinegar	

Core but do not peel the apples. Slice crosswise into ½-inch wheels. In a wide saucepan, mix the honey, vinegar, and salt. Bring almost to a boil. Add the apple rings and cook, turning frequently, for about 12 minutes, sprinkling with cinnamon. Serve hot with the sausage and sauce.

HOPPIN' JOHN WITH SAUSAGE

Traditionally eaten on January 1 in the South for good luck during the year, this dish is usually made with dried black-eyed peas, sometimes called cowpeas. It can be made with spicy sausage or with smoked ham hocks, or, better, with both. Some recipes call for cooking the onions with the peas, but I think my way is preferable in flavor and texture.

1 pound dried black-eyed peas	1 pound hot and spicy pork sausage
water	1 tablespoon lard or cooking oil
½ pound smoked ham hocks	3 to 4 cups cooked long-grain rice
salt to taste	2 large, mild white onions, chopped
1 tablespoon red pepper flakes	

In a large dutch oven or other similar pot, cover the black-eyed peas with about a quart of water and add the ham hocks. Bring to a boil, reduce the heat, cover tightly, and simmer for 2 hours. Add more water if needed. Pull the meat from the ham hock, chop it, and add it back to the pot, along with salt and red pepper flakes. Cut the sausage into ¾- to 1-inch segments. Heat the lard or oil in a skillet and brown the sausage wheels. Pour off the grease and add the sausage to the black-eyed peas. Simmer for a few minutes while you chop the onions. You may need to add a little more water at this point; the black-eyed peas should have some juice. To serve, spoon a dollop of rice into a bowl, top with black-eyed peas (making sure everybody gets an equal share of sausage and chopped ham hock), and sprinkle liberally with chopped onions. Serve with corn pone.

Variation: If you have fresh vine-ripened tomatoes, chop 2 and serve sprinkled atop the hoppin' John, along with the chopped onions.

PENNSYLVANIA DUTCH FRIED SAUSAGE

The Pennsylvania Dutch were fond of pork sausages and cooked them in a number of ways. Here's an old favorite.

2 chicken eggs, whisked	salt to taste
½ cup flour	1 tablespoon cooking oil
1 cup bread crumbs	2 pounds fatty pork sausage links

Mix the eggs, flour, bread crumbs, and salt. Heat the oil in a skillet. Dip the sausages into the egg mixture, then fry them slowly until they have browned and cooked through. Serve with sauerkraut.

Note: If your sausages contain very little fat, increase the measure of cooking oil.

SAUSAGE IN POTATOES

For this recipe, use small pork sausages or franks. These should be fully precooked, preferably by steaming or simmering.

2 cups mashed potatoes	milk
1 large chicken egg (separated)	oil for deep frying
1½ tablespoons minced green onion with part of green tops	6 small pork sausages or hot dogs
salt to taste	bread crumbs

Mix the mashed potatoes, egg yolk, green onion, and salt. Whisk the egg white along with a little milk. Rig for deep-frying. When the oil is hot (about 350°F), coat the sausages with the mashed potato mixture. Roll the logs in bread crumbs, then in the egg white, and again in the bread crumbs. Fry the logs until nicely browned. Serve hot.

Making Cured-Meat Sausages

When making fully cured or dried sausages, the meat itself must be salt-cured before the casings are stuffed. The meat can be ground and then cured, but I always prefer to cure the meat in chunks before grinding it. Of course, the meat can be cured in large pieces, as in hams, but this way requires lots of time for salt penetration and equalization. When cut into 2-inch cubes, the meat can be cured in about 48 hours.

To cure the meat, cut it into chunks of a size suitable for grinding. Spread the meat out in a large plastic tray, sprinkle evenly with salt or a salt cure (according to the recipe you are using), toss to coat all sides, cover, and place in the refrigerator, or in a very cool place, for 48 hours.

As mentioned earlier, the trays work best for 10 pounds of meat if they are long, wide, and shallow. Heavy polyethylene trays made especially for food handling are ideal. These are usually about 25 inches long and 16 inches wide, which fits nicely into my refrigerator after I clean off a whole shelf. Measure, however, before you buy.

Salt is the ingredient that cures meat. There are, it is true, some additives that many people use and believe to be necessary, and several chemicals are used—in very small amounts, as the law allows—in commercially cured meats and meat products. Most of these chemicals give the meat a redder color, but how effective they are as curing agents has been questioned, and they are believed to cause cancer in animals. But the chemicals are probably harmless if used in moderation, and, in fact, they have been used in meat curing for two thousand years. These cures include sodium nitrite, sodium nitrate, saltpeter (potassium nitrate), ascorbic acid, and others. A few of the recipes in other chapters call for some of these chemicals, and they are also discussed in the glossary. Because popular and journalistic opinion as well as official guidance tends to change over time, anyone who is concerned about such additives in our meats should get in touch with the consumer affairs offices of the US Department of Agriculture and the federal Food and Drug Administration (FDA), both in Washington, DC.

To use these ingredients, it's always best to measure them carefully and mix them with a small amount of salt, making what is called a cure. The small amount of salt used in the cure is called a carrier; its purpose is to facilitate equal mixing with the meat and other ingredients. The cure is always mixed with lots of regular salt before it is used in the recipe.

There are several commercial cures suitable for making sausage. It is best to follow the manufacturer's instructions unless you have very good reason to deviate. A few cures are described below.

Prague Powder

Prague Powder is a meat-curing trade term for a mixture either of sodium nitrate and common salt or of sodium nitrite, sodium nitrate, and common salt. The recipes below are based on formulations set forth by Rytek Kutas in *Great Sausage Recipes and Meat Curing*. The author runs a mail-order house specializing in sausage making, and for some reason or another, the mixture is called Insta Cure.

PRAGUE POWDER 1, OR INSTA CURE 1

This mix is not normally used in fresh sausage. It can be used in "cured sausage" that is not fully dried. Recipes for several such sausages are set forth in this book, in which the meat is salted and cured for 2 to 3 days before the sausage is stuffed.

1 pound salt	1 ounce sodium nitrite

Thoroughly mix the salt and sodium nitrite. Uneven mixes will result in too much sodium nitrite in some parts of the sausage and not enough in others. For every 10 pounds of meat to be used in the sausage, add 2 teaspoons of Prague Powder 1. Unused Prague Powder 1 can be stored in a dry jar.

Note that the Prague Powder 1 dissipates after about 2 weeks, making it unsuitable (the theory goes) for long cures.

PRAGUE POWDER 2, OR INSTA CURE 2

This cure is intended to be used in sausage that is cured and dried, and can be eaten without cooking. The sodium nitrate in the formula breaks down, over time, into sodium nitrite, thereby giving the cure an extended working life. It is used in sausage that is cured and then dried for several weeks.

1 pound salt

0.64 ounce sodium nitrate

1 ounce sodium nitrite

Thoroughly mix all the ingredients. Add to chunks of meat just before the curing period. (In this book, the meat is cut into chunks, sprinkled with salt, and cured in the refrigerator before grinding.) Use exactly 2 teaspoons for every 10 pounds of meat to be ground. Unused Prague Powder 2 can be stored in a dry jar.

A SALTPETER CURE

Jack Ubaldi, coauthor of Jack Ubaldi's Meat Book, *champions the use of saltpeter in cured meats. The mix can be used for cured hams and other products, and it can be used in many of the recipes in this book simply by substituting the cure for the salt in the recipe. For example, if the recipe calls for 8 tablespoons of salt, simply use 8 tablespoons of the saltpeter cure.*

4 pounds salt

1¼ ounces saltpeter

1 pound sugar

Thoroughly mix the salt, sugar, and saltpeter. When properly stored in a jar, the mix will keep for several years.

Other Cures

Morton Salt company and other firms offer cures. These are marketed by mail order, meat outlets, and sometimes large supermarkets.

DRIED SAUSAGE

A cured and dried sausage is rather firm to the finger and chewy, like hard pepperoni. Often it is thinly sliced before serving or before using in recipes. Some highly spiced dried sausages, such as dried Spanish chorizo and Chinese sausages, work best in recipes that require steaming or long simmering. Several recipes for making and cooking with dried sausages are set forth in subsequent chapters. Meanwhile, here's a rather basic Italian-style dried sausage, without a long list of flavoring spices or herbs, that I recommend for openers. Note that this recipe has the following ingredients that discourage the growth of bacteria: salt, saltpeter, and wine. Some recipes for dried sausage even have vinegar and brandy along with red pepper. It is also important to note that the pork is certified (as discussed in chapter 1, Easy Sausages, page 99), that the meat is kept cold, and that it is hung in a dry place at a cool temperature. Also, don't underestimate the importance of "dry," which clearly implies the absence of moisture, without which bacteria can't thrive.

As a rule, dried sausages may contain a little less fat than a fresh sausage. In the recipe below, try a rather lean Boston butt or similar cut with about 20 percent fat. Measure out 8 pounds lean and 2 pounds fat if you prefer. Both the lean and the fat should be certified. Also, remember that it's best to start off with partially frozen meat; it cuts easier, it grinds better, and it's safer.

10 pounds rather lean pork butt (certified)

5 tablespoons regular table salt or sea salt

2 teaspoons Prague Powder 2 (optional)

2½ tablespoons freshly ground black pepper

5 cloves garlic, minced

1 cup dry red wine

hog casings (medium)

Trim and cut the meat and fat into chunks suitable for grinding. (Be sure to avoid long strings of sinew or tough tissue that can clog up your grinder's plate and knife.) Place the meat into a wide plastic tray (small enough to fit into your refrigerator). Thoroughly mix the salt and Prague Powder. Sprinkle the mix (now called a cure) evenly over the meat chunks, toss thoroughly with clean hands to coat all sides of the meat with the cure, cover, and place in the refrigerator for 48 hours. (If you have a cool place other than the refrigerator, fine. Just remember that it's best to keep the temperature under 50°F.) This will salt-cure the meat.

When you are ready to proceed, sterilize the meat grinder and its parts in boiling water. Cool, assemble the parts, and mount the grinder on a clean work surface. Remove the meat tray from the refrigerator and place the meat on a work surface near the sausage mill. Grind the meat with a ³⁄₁₆-inch plate, feeding it into a tray. (I like to place the ground meat as well as the meat chunks into a double tray unit with crushed ice in the bottom unit. This step isn't necessary if you can grind and stuff the sausages quickly. The point is that it's best to keep the meat cold at all times during cutting, curing, grinding, and stuffing.)

When the meat is ground, sprinkle it evenly with the black pepper, garlic, and wine. Mix thoroughly with your hands. Quickly rig for stuffing by removing the meat grinder's knife and plate, replacing them with a stuffing tube. Quickly thread the washed and rinsed casings over the tube. Stuff the sausages evenly, pricking the casing with a needle as needed to relieve any large air bubbles. When the stuffed casing grows long, twist the end and link every 4 to 6 inches. Cut the links in pairs (or perhaps by fours) and hang them to dry in your refrigerator or other cool, dry place. The temperature should be between 34°F and 40°F. An airy place is desirable, but too much airflow can dry the outside of the sausage before the inside ages properly. The humidity in the drying chamber will also have a bearing on how long it takes the sausage to dry, but usually the home sausage maker will have to make do with what he has—and usually the refrigerator is hard to beat. Also, the size of the casing as well as the temperature will have an influence on the drying times.

Hang the sausages for 6 to 8 weeks, or until they are hard to the touch. When properly dried, the sausages are fully cured and can be stored in or out of the refrigerator. I prefer to wrap mine in plastic film or aluminum foil (to prevent further drying) and then keep them in the refrigerator or freezer until needed.

A properly air-dried sausage made from certified pork can be eaten without cooking, but I prefer to cook mine by steaming or using them in soups and stews. Although thoroughly dried sausages can have a texture and flavor all their own, the main purpose of drying (especially from a historical viewpoint) is to preserve the meat. Often, such sausages are called summer sausage because they are cured in cool weather and last into summer.

Remember also that dried sausages, as well as fresh and semi-dried sausages (covered next), can be smoked for a while to enhance the flavor. But also remember that smoking adds very little to the preservation of the sausage.

Note that the recipe above calls for Prague Powder 2. This ingredient, discussed earlier, contains sodium nitrite and sodium nitrate, both of which experts think are necessary for making dried sausages. I can take it or leave it in the sausages that I make. If eating another person's sausage, frankly, I would prefer the use of a cure containing both sodium nitrate and sodium nitrite. Suit yourself. Before leaving dried sausages, let's make one without any such cure and without going into quite the detail used above. Then we'll move on to a semi-dried sausage—dried more for flavor than for preservation.

DRIED CERVELAT, OR FRENCH SUMMER SAUSAGE

For this recipe, we'll use a combination of lean beef, lean pork, and pork fat, along with white wine. You can also use veal instead of beef. It's best to start with partially frozen meats and fat.

4 pounds lean beef	10 cloves garlic, minced
4 pounds lean pork (certified)	1 large onion, grated
2 pounds fresh pork fat (certified)	2 cups dry white wine
6 tablespoons salt	hog casings
3 tablespoons freshly ground black pepper	

Cut the meats and fat into chunks suitable for grinding. Mix the meats in a plastic tray, sprinkle evenly with salt, cover, and refrigerate for 48 hours. Grind the meats with a ³⁄₁₆-inch plate. Using your hands, mix in the black pepper, garlic, onion, and wine. Stuff the mix into medium hog casings, link every 4 to 6 inches, and hang to dry for 4 weeks.

At the end of the 4-week period, mix the following in a small saucepan:

¼ cup dry white wine	½ teaspoon dried sage
½ teaspoon dried thyme	2 bay leaves, crushed

Bring the mixture to a boil and let cool. Rub or brush the sausages with the mixture, then hang them to dry for another 4 weeks, or until hard to the touch.

Semi-Dried Sausages

A few recipes call for partially drying a sausage, which, of course, produces a texture somewhere between soft fresh sausages and hard, dried cured sausages. Sometimes, hanging the sausage for a certain period of time ages it, allowing its flavors to develop, as in Lebanon bologna in chapter 14, American and Canadian Sausages (page 223).

Some of the sausages that are usually dried, such as pepperoni, can be semi-dried, giving a different texture suitable for topping pizza. How dry should it be? That's up to you. Just remember that a semi-dried sausage should be treated as though it were fresh. I have eaten sausages, fully cooked in such recipes as stews, at all stages of the drying process. This allows me to eat some of the sausage without having to wait 8 weeks, and it gives me experience with what happens during the drying process.

Semi-dried sausages can be wrapped and frozen.

Cold-Smoking Sausages

Cold-smoking can be a part of the curing process, usually done at the start of the drying time. But remember that smoke does very little to preserve the meat. Salt-curing and drying are the operative principles in curing meats and sausages suitable for long storage without refrigeration. Smoke does, however, add considerably to the flavor and color of meats and fish, and it can work wonders on pork sausages. Hot-smoking, as discussed next, merely adds some smoke while cooking the sausage. Cold-smoking at temperatures below 100°F—preferably below 70°F—does not cook the sausage and permits it to be smoked for relatively long periods of time.

Often, cold-smoking works with dry-curing sausage, in which case several hours or a day or so in a cold-smoker can be considered the first part of the overall drying time of 4 to 8 weeks or longer, depending on the size of the sausage and the kind of casing.

I discuss smokehouses and the cold-smoking process at some length in part three. In essence, however, all you need for cold-smoking is a smoke chamber and a smoke generator. The smoke generator, of course, requires heat, either from wood, charcoal, gas, or electricity. You don't want too much heat in the smoke chamber if you are trying to cold-smoke. Consequently, the smoke generator is often removed to some distance from the chamber, allowing the smoke to cool down. Obviously, the ambient temperature is very important for cold-smoking operations. It's difficult, for example, to cold-smoke when the outside temperature is 102°F. Normally, cold-smoking in most parts of the United States is easier to accomplish during the winter months.

The kind of wood used to make smoke isn't as important as people think, especially with highly seasoned sausages. I recommend using any good hardwood, either in chips, chunks, or sawdust. Further, I prefer to use freshly cut green wood instead of dry wood that has to be soaked in water.

If you smoke a lot of sausages, you might consider buying a commercial smoker with thermostats and other controls. The small electric smokers will do a good job (without using the water pan) if the temperature can be kept low enough. You can also build a walk-in smokehouse or rig some sort of barrel or box smoker with the heat source placed some distance away.

The key to any cold-smoking operation, of course, is the temperature inside the smoke chamber. A thermometer inside the chamber is the best guide to exactly what's going on. Once you have the smoke coming at the right temperature, it's really easy to smoke link sausages. They are simply hung vertically from rods or hooks. Large sausages such as bologna are hung by the end, sometimes with the aid of a string, but smaller link sausages are usually hung in pairs.

After cold-smoking for a day or so (sometimes depending partly on the recipe), the sausages are then hung in a cool place—34°F to 40°F—to dry or semi-dry, as discussed above and in some recipes in the subsequent chapters.

Of course, fresh sausages can be cold-smoked for a few hours for flavor, then cooked, refrigerated, or frozen. These are not cured and should therefore be thoroughly cooked, refrigerated, or frozen.

Hot-Smoked Sausages

Most fresh sausages can be cooked on a grill heated by charcoal, wood, gas, or electricity. Add some wood chips and you've got hot-smoked sausages. Some recipes, such as the Boerish sausage in chapter 12 (page 217), work especially well on a grill, but the truth is that most fresh sausages can be hot-smoked successfully.

I like sausages cooked directly over the heat, but the indirect method in a closed-hood grill will produce more smoke. That is, the heat is on one side of the grill and the sausages on the other. Wood chips are placed on or around the heat source, producing a dense smoke under the covered hood. To cook the sausages, the temperature under the hood should be about 200°F. The lower the temperature, the longer the cooking time and the stronger the smoke flavor. The complete outdoor chef, of course, will be adept at controlling the temperature with the amount of fuel and the airflow (oxygen). One good method is to smoke the sausages by the indirect method, then finish them off directly over the coals. Direct and indirect grilling can be accomplished best with large covered grills, whether the style be rectangular, kettle, or barrel.

For flavor, I think that freshly cut green wood is really better, and a good deal cheaper, than dry wood purchased in bags. Hickory, apple, pecan, oak, and so on will be just fine.

Those people who have a cooker/smoker can also cook sausages to perfection. Typically, these units have a heating element (or charcoal pan) in the bottom, on which the wood chips are piled. Over the heating element is a water pan, which provides moisture and helps keep the temperature low, owing to the latent heat of evaporation. I question whether using the water pan is always a good idea, but suit yourself and follow the manufacturer's instructions. Just make sure that you are cooking the sausages. Some "smokers" with electric heat may not get hot enough to cook the sausage when used in cold, windy weather—but they may get too hot for cold-smoking. If in doubt, rig a thermometer inside the smoker and check the temperature from time to time. It should be at least 150°F in order to cook the sausage, and 200°F will work better. Some of these cookers come with a temperature indicator, but they are not very reliable and often reflect only LOW, MEDIUM, or HOT instead of degrees Fahrenheit.

I like to cook sausages on a grill directly over wood coals, with a few wood chunks along the edge. Wood coals produce more smoke and are hotter than charcoal. Cooking over wood is a full-time job. This is especially true with pork sausage because the fat drips out, causing lots of smoke and sometimes fires. I like hot-smoked sausages prepared on a large grill, along with steaks, chops, and other meats or even fish, and perhaps some quartered pineapples. Typically, sausages grilled and hot-smoked by this method will be quite done on the outside, browning and crisping the casing, but juicy and tasty on the inside, bursting and squirting flavor when you bite into one. It's a gustatory experience like no other.

CHAPTER 4

IBERIAN AND LATIN AMERICAN SAUSAGES

Spain, for the most part, has a much warmer climate than the rest of Europe. As a result, foods tend to go bad quicker, and sausage is no exception. To help keep the meat palatable and safe to eat before the days of mechanical refrigeration, more spices were used, along with such preservatives as salt, vinegar, and booze.

Although both Spain and Portugal have a number of regional sausages, it is the highly spiced ones that have dominated the cuisine in the homelands as well as in Mexico and other Spanish and Portuguese parts of the New World.

FRESH CHORIZO

This classic Spanish sausage, also popular in Latin America, is distinguished by chili peppers, vinegar, and spices. For best results (in my opinion), use a lot of rather mild red peppers, well seeded, so that you get the flavor and color without all the heat. Since there is a good deal of difference between one pepper and another, experience is the best guide. If in doubt, fry a small patty and taste it before stuffing the whole batch into casings. Then you can add more meat if the mix is too hot. If it's not hot enough, mix in some cayenne. For the pork, I usually use fresh pork butts or shoulders that are about 25 percent fat. If in doubt, weigh the lean and fat separately, then use 8 pounds lean and 2 pounds fat. Of course, other cuts of pork can also be used, and the fat can be fatback.

1 ounce fried chili peppers	2 tablespoons Spanish hot paprika
2 cups water	10 pounds fresh pork butt or shoulder
½ cup red wine vinegar	cayenne pepper to taste (optional)
5 cloves garlic, minced	hog casings
4 tablespoons salt	

Cut the peppers in half lengthwise, then remove the seeds and membrane. (I use a spoon for this. After handling the chili peppers, be sure to wash your hands before you rub your eyes or touch sensitive parts of your body; some people wear rubber gloves when seeding peppers.) Bring 2 cups of water to a boil, add the seeded peppers, turn off the heat, and soak for an hour or two. Place the peppers in a food processor, along with the wine vinegar, garlic, salt, and paprika. Puree and hold.

Cut the meat into small chunks and grind with a rather coarse plate, say ¼ inch. Thoroughly mix the puree into the meat. Let stand for 1 hour or so, then take out a little bulk sausage to fry a few patties, if you want to enjoy some of your chorizo immediately. After tasting a patty, add the cayenne if you wish. Stuff the rest in hog casings. Hang in a cool, airy spot and dry for about 2 days. Cook, refrigerate for a few days, or freeze.

These sausages are best when simmered for a long while in such dishes as garbanzo bean soup or paella.

DRIED CHORIZO

In the past, chorizo has been dried for long storage without refrigeration. In many recipes, saltpeter or sodium nitrite or some such cure is used, but ordinary salt will do if you use enough of it. (If you want to use a cure, however, see the instructions in chapter 3, Stuffing Sausages, page 121.) When drying the sausage, it helps to have a cool, airy, and dry atmosphere. If you live in a mountain climate that stays at a relatively constant temperature—between 34°F and 40°F—great. If not, you've got a problem. I normally use a section of my refrigerator, as discussed in chapter 3.

10 pounds fresh pork butt or shoulder (certified)

1 cup salt

½ cup Hungarian paprika

2 tablespoons freshly ground black pepper

1–2 tablespoons red pepper flakes

1 tablespoon cayenne pepper

2 teaspoons crushed fennel seed

2 teaspoons crushed cumin seed

2 teaspoons dried oregano

20 cloves garlic, minced

1 cup red wine vinegar

1 cup brandy

hog casings

Cut the pork into chunks suitable for grinding. Put the chunks into a plastic tray, sprinkle with the salt, coating all sides, cover, and refrigerate for 2 days. When you are ready to proceed, thoroughly mix the dry seasonings into the salty meat. Grind with a ³⁄₁₆-inch plate. Mix in the garlic, wine vinegar, and brandy. Stuff into hog casings, tying off in 4-inch links. Hang in a cool place (34°F to 40°F) for 8 to 10 weeks. These sausages, if properly processed, will be thoroughly cured and can be hung without refrigeration. I like to wrap mine in plastic film, however, and refrigerate or freeze them.

Being hard and dried, these sausages are best when used in soups and stews so that they will be simmered for a long time. The flavor is on the strong side, but they are usually used in small quantities.

MEXICAN CHORIZO

Most recipes for chorizo call for hog fat, which, along with beef fat, or suet, is held to be a toxic substance in some quarters. Here's a modern recipe that calls for vegetable shortening. Although pork remains in the ingredients, note that lean pork does not contain fat marbled in the meat. The use of brandy in a Mexican recipe might raise some French eyebrows, but, according to my source for this recipe (George C. Booth's The Food and Drink of Mexico*), good brandy has been in production south of the border for 450 years.*

2 pounds lean pork

6 bay leaves, crushed

4 tablespoons salt

3 tablespoons chili powder

2 tablespoons Spanish hot paprika

1 teaspoon fresh coarsely ground black pepper

1 teaspoon dried oregano

1 teaspoon ground cumin

1 teaspoon dried thyme

½ teaspoon ground cinnamon

½ teaspoon ground clove

¼ teaspoon ground ginger

¼ teaspoon grated nutmeg

¼ teaspoon ground coriander seed

2 bell peppers, grated

8 cloves garlic, grated

1 pint red wine vinegar

½ cup 100-proof brandy

½ cup vegetable shortening

hog casings

Cut the meat into small chunks and spread it over your work surface. Mix all the herb and spice ingredients, then sprinkle them evenly over the meat along with the grated bell peppers and garlic. Grind the mixture, using a ⅛- or ³⁄₁₆-inch plate. Put the ground meat into a nonmetallic container; mix in the wine vinegar, brandy, and vegetable shortening; cover; and refrigerate for 24 hours. Stuff the mixture into medium hog casings, tie into 4-inch links, and hang in a cool, breezy place for 24 hours. Use immediately, refrigerate for several days, or freeze.

For a long time, chorizo has been a major ingredient in soups and stews. In the time of the Crusades, the Christians in Spain used chorizo—a pork product—to distinguish themselves from the Arabs. Hence, it became customary to use a little chorizo in just about every pot, in case unexpected company came by.

The tradition was continued in Spanish and Portuguese lands of the New World, where chorizo has become a part of several of what can only be described as national stews. Many of these are quite elaborate, calling for ten to twelve kinds of meats, variety meats (such as pig tails, ears, and snouts), birds, and, almost always, chorizo. The Spanish bean soup below is an example of this sort of stew.

GARBANZO BEAN SOUP

This filling soup is popular in the Tampa Bay area of Florida, where Cubans provided the labor for the cigar industry years ago. It's very, very good. To cook it, you'll need a large pot—preferably a cast-iron stove-top dutch oven. The dried garbanzo beans give a nice and quite surprising crunch to soups. Some people soak the beans overnight in water, perhaps with a little baking soda added, but I prefer to cook them right out of the package.

4 pig's feet, split	4 large onions, chopped
2 pounds smoked ham hocks	8 cloves garlic, chopped
1 pound chorizo sausage, sliced	½ green bell pepper, chopped
1 pound dried garbanzo beans	½ red bell pepper, chopped
3 bay leaves	1 small cabbage, shredded
water	salt and freshly ground black pepper to taste
4 medium potatoes, diced	½ teaspoon saffron

Put the pig's feet, ham hocks, chorizo, and garbanzo beans into a large pot, along with the bay leaves. Cover with water, bring to a boil, reduce the heat, and simmer for 1½ hours, or until tender, adding more water (boiling hot) from time to time if needed. Add the potatoes, onions, garlic, bell peppers, cabbage, saffron, salt, and pepper. Increase the heat until the soup boils, then lower the heat, cover, and simmer until the potatoes are done. Water may be needed all along, but remember that the soup should be quite thick. Serve hot along with plenty of crusty Cuban bread. I sometimes make a whole meal of this soup.

PAELLA

More and more, we see colorful seafood variations of this traditional Spanish dish. The essential ingredients, however, are chicken, rice, and chorizo. Although pimiento strips are traditionally used, they are mostly for garnish; I usually cook strips of red bell pepper in the dish. It is best cooked in a special paella pan or a large jambalaya skillet about 13 inches in diameter. A large electric skillet will also work nicely. Part of the pleasure of this dish is in seeing the whole thing. So, serve the dish at the table right out of the skillet or paella pan, letting diners help themselves.

Fish is an excellent addition to paella, provided that it is fresh and firm so that it holds its shape during cooking and serving. I like to use saltwater sheepshead, which is often used as a substitute for crabmeat. If readily available, I like to use stone crab claws, but other crab claws will work. Squid, eels, scallops, and other seafood can also be used. The shrimp in my recipe are not beheaded or peeled, partly because the "fat" in the head adds to the flavor. The peeling is done at the table, using the fingers. If you are serving squeamish folks, however, it will be best to behead, peel, and de-vein the shrimp before adding them to the pot.

The saffron used in the recipe is an expensive Mediterranean ingredient that adds color to the dish. Omit it if you are on a tight budget, or perhaps substitute the colorful annatto oil—an unsung ingredient that gives a nice color—if you have it on hand from culinary adventures in tropical American cooking.

1 dozen fresh mussels

2 dozen small clams

¾ cup olive oil

1 fryer chicken, cut into serving pieces

1 pound chorizo, cut into ½-inch wheels

1½ cups chopped onion

2 cups chopped fresh tomato

½ red bell pepper, cut into thin strips

½ green bell pepper, cut into thin strips

10 cloves garlic, minced

salt and freshly ground black pepper to taste

½ teaspoon Spanish hot paprika

3 cups uncooked white rice

boiling water

½ teaspoon saffron

1 pound stone crab claws, cracked

1 pound medium shrimp (whole)

½ pound firm fish fillets, cut into 1-inch chunks

2 dozen shucked oysters, medium size

Wash, trim, and steam the mussels and clams. (Discard any that do not open.) Set them in a pan or dish nested over hot water. Heat the olive oil in a skillet over medium-high heat. Fry the chicken pieces, turning from time to time, until they are lightly browned. Add the chorizo slices. Cook for another 3 to 4 minutes, stirring with a wooden spoon. Place the chicken and chorizo on a brown paper bag to drain. Sauté the onion in the remaining oil, stirring as you go, for 5 minutes. Add the tomatoes and turn the heat to high, cooking until much of the liquid has left the tomatoes. Add the red pepper, green pepper, garlic, salt, black pepper, and paprika. Cook for a few minutes, until the peppers are tender. Add the rice and cook for 5 minutes, stirring constantly, until it starts to turn brown. Put the chicken and chorizo pieces back into the pan. Add 4 cups of boiling water. Mix the saffron into a little boiling water, add it to the pan, and mix well.

When the liquid starts to boil nicely, add the stone crab claws. Stir in 3 more cups of boiling water. Cook for 3 or 4 minutes, then add the shrimp and fish chunks. Cook for 3 to 4 minutes, then add the oysters. Cook for another 3 to 4 minutes, or until the oysters start to curl around the edges. Fish out some of the red bell pepper strips. Garnish the paella with steamed mussels, clams, and red pepper strips. Place the paella pan on trivets in the middle of the table. Serve hot, spooning the paella directly onto preheated plates, along with plenty of crusty hot bread.

CHORIZO AND BARLEY

For this Andalusian dish, I owe thanks to Bert Greene, author of The Grains Cookbook, *who said he got it while on a tourist excursion out from Madrid. The dish has truly wonderful flavor.*

½–¾ pound chorizo, cut into wheels
1 tablespoon butter
1 medium or large onion, chopped
1 cup pearl barley
¼ teaspoon chopped fresh thyme

3 cups chicken stock or broth
½ cup sliced green olives
salt and freshly ground black pepper to taste
chopped fresh parsley to taste

In a saucepan or skillet over medium-low heat, sauté the chorizo until they are browned. (If they are fatty, no grease will be required.) Remove the sausages to drain. Add the butter and sauté the onion for a few minutes. Add the barley and thyme, tossing well. Add the chicken stock and browned chorizo. Bring to a boil, reduce the heat, and simmer for 30 to 40 minutes, or until the barley has absorbed all the liquid. The barley should be tender at this point. If it is too chewy, add a little more broth or water, cooking again until the liquid has been absorbed. If it is too wet, cook uncovered until the liquid had been absorbed. Stir in the olives, along with some salt and pepper to taste. Sprinkle with chopped parsley. Serve hot.

MENUDO

Tripe is popular in Mexico and is often cooked with the aid of chorizo, as in this recipe. If you can't find tripe in your meat market, talk to your butcher. I use whole chopped tomatoes in my menudo, but more persnickety cooks may choose to peel and seed them.

2 pounds tripe	2 cloves garlic, minced
salt	3 tomatoes, chopped
water	1 tablespoon chopped fresh cilantro
lard or cooking oil	1 teaspoon chopped fresh thyme
1 pound chorizo link sausage, sliced	1 teaspoon chopped fresh oregano
1 medium to large onion, chopped	pepper to taste

Put the tripe in a pot, cover with salted water (2 tablespoons salt per quart), bring to a boil, cover, reduce the heat, and simmer for 3 hours, or until the tripe is tender. Drain the tripe and cut it into cubes from 1 to 2 inches in size. Heat a little lard or oil in a skillet and sauté the sausage for about 20 minutes. Remove and drain the sausage, then sauté the onion and garlic for 5 to 6 minutes. Remove and drain the onion and garlic. Add more oil to the skillet if needed, then fry the tripe, turning, until it starts to brown.

Put all of the ingredients into a stove-top dutch oven, adding enough water to cover everything. Bring to a boil, reduce the heat, and simmer until the liquid thickens. Serve hot. Feeds 6.

MEXICAN MEAT LOAF

This wonderful dish may be of Arabic origin, going back to the time of the Moors. The Spanish name is albondigón, *but this version has a Mexican spin.*

1 whole chicken breast (both halves)	4 eggs
1 pound chorizo	3 pickled green peppers, minced
2 medium to large onions	¼ cup finely chopped cilantro
½ cup stone-ground white cornmeal	1 cup pitted black olives, chopped
salt and pepper to taste	2 cups vinegar
2 tablespoons chili powder	2 bay leaves
1 pound ground lean pork	

Skin the chicken breast and chorizo. Cut chicken breast, chorizo, and onions into chunks suitable for feeding into a sausage mill. Mix the chunks, spread them out, and sprinkle evenly with the cornmeal, salt, pepper, and chili powder. Grind the mix with a ³⁄₁₆- or ¼-inch plate. With your hands, mix in the ground pork, eggs, minced peppers, cilantro, and olives. Shape the mixture into a 10-inch loaf. Roll the loaf in a piece of cheesecloth, twisting the ends to make handles.

Heat some water in a pot or pan large enough to hold the loaf comfortably; there should be enough water to barely cover the loaf. Add 2 cups vinegar and the bay leaves. When the liquid boils vigorously, place the loaf in the pan. Simmer on low heat for 2 hours. Unwrap the loaf, slice, and serve hot with sliced tomatoes, sliced jícama, sliced avocado, salsa, and refried beans. A drop or two of lemon juice goes nicely on the jícama and avocado.

CHORIZO AND LENTILS

Here's a South American dish that is often cooked with very fatty sausages. If your chorizo is on the lean side, you'll need to add a little cooking oil or hog fat. If you have a choice, use fresh chorizo instead of dried.

1 pound chorizo

cooking oil (if needed)

1 cup cooked lentils

1 medium to large onion, sliced

1 green bell pepper, seeded and sliced

1 fresh hot chili pepper, seeded and minced

2 cloves garlic, minced

2 medium tomatoes, peeled and quartered

salt and pepper to taste

Cut the chorizo into short lengths and fry in a cast-iron skillet, Drain the chorizo and pour off all but about 2 tablespoons of the grease that cooked out of the sausages. If necessary, add a little oil. Heat the grease, then sauté the lentils, onion, peppers, and garlic for about 10 minutes, stirring with a wooden spoon. Add the tomatoes, browned chorizo, salt, and pepper. Cover and simmer for 10 or 15 minutes. Serve hot.

LINGUIÇA (HOT SMOKED)

Also known as longaniza, this Portuguese sausage is made with a dice of pork lean and fat. That's right. No grinding. It is, however, permissible to grind the fat and lean separately with a ¼- to ½-inch plate. Either way, be sure to try this one. Exact measures aren't necessary, but use 10 pounds total, mixed approximately 6 to 7 pounds lean to 3 to 4 pounds fat.

6–7 pounds lean pork

3–4 pounds fat pork

10 cloves garlic, minced

10 dried red chili peppers, crushed (or to taste)

3 tablespoons salt

3 tablespoons Spanish hot paprika

1 tablespoon freshly ground black pepper

1 tablespoon finely chopped fresh marjoram

¾ cup ice water

½ cup cold cider vinegar or wine vinegar

hog casings

Cut the fat and meat into a dice of ¼ to ½ inch. Thoroughly mix all the ingredients (except the casings) and place them into a plastic tray or other suitable container. Cover and refrigerate for 2 hours. Stuff the mixture into hog casings, tying off 12-inch links. Hang the links in a cool, breezy place until dry. Cold-smoke at 100°F or less for several hours, then hot-smoke (perhaps on a grill) until the sausage is cooked through and safe to eat. (If in doubt, use a meat thermometer inserted into the center of the sausage; it should read 150°F or more.) If you are not going to cook all the sausage right away, freeze it immediately after cold-smoking, then thoroughly cook it before eating. It can be cooked by poaching, grilling, or broiling.

MUSHROOMS STUFFED WITH LINGUIÇA

When you make your linguiça (or chorizo), save ½ pound of bulk sausage for this recipe. If you are working with stuffed sausage, remove the casing and crumble the mixture.

2 pounds large mushrooms	2 tablespoons chopped dark raisins
2 tablespoons olive oil	1½ tablespoons minced fresh cilantro
1 medium to large onion, finely chopped	1 teaspoon minced fresh oregano
½ cup soft bread crumbs	salt and pepper to taste
½ pound bulk linguiça (or chorizo)	1 cup chicken stock

Remove and chop the stems from the mushrooms. Heat the olive oil in a small skillet. Sauté the onion and mushroom stems for about 10 minutes. Mix the onion and mushroom stems in a bowl along with the bread crumbs, sausage, raisins, cilantro, oregano, salt, and pepper. Stuff the mushroom caps with the mixture.

Preheat the broiler. Arrange the mushroom caps on a baking sheet with the stuffed side up. Broil close to the heat for about 5 minutes, or until the tops are golden. Using tongs, arrange the mushrooms, stuffed side up, in a large skillet. (An electric skillet is ideal.) Pour the chicken stock around the mushrooms. Bring the stock to a boil, reduce the heat, cover, and simmer for 15 to 20 minutes. Place the mushrooms on a heated serving platter. Increase the heat to the skillet. Boil the stock until the volume is reduced by half, making a sauce. Pour the sauce over the mushrooms. Serve warm.

BOUDIN BARBADOS

The Caribbean area has several blood sausages. This unusual variation from Barbados (as adapted from The Complete Book of Caribbean Cooking, *by Elisabeth Lambert Ortiz) is made with sweet potatoes and pumpkin with a pig's-blood binding. The pumpkin is a West Indian sort called calabaza; Hubbard squash can be substituted. Any fresh chili pepper can be used, but vary the amount according to the heat. Be warned that a full tablespoon of minced bird peppers or habaneros will be hot indeed!*

3 pounds sweet potatoes

2 pounds calabaza

1 cup finely chopped shallots

1 tablespoon minced fresh thyme

1 tablespoon minced fresh marjoram

1 tablespoon minced fresh hot chili pepper (seeded)

1 teaspoon ground clove

salt to taste

1–2 cups pig's blood

hog casings

Peel the sweet potatoes and pumpkin. Either grate them or chop and run them through a food mill. Mix in the chopped shallots, thyme, marjoram, chili pepper, clove, and salt. Add the pig's blood, a little at a time, until the pudding has a soft consistency. Stuff the mix into medium hog casings, tying into 6-inch lengths.

Place a trivet in the bottom of a large pot, heat some salted water to a boil, add the sausage, and simmer for 20 minutes, or until no juice runs out when the lengths are pricked with a fork. Drain the lengths. Serve hot or refrigerate and reheat as needed.

According to Mrs. Ortiz, these blood sausages are served along with souse (page 118) for a Saturday night meal. They are also served for lunch and as appetizers.

ANNATTO SAUSAGE

To the European sausage-making traditions, America has contributed red peppers, potatoes, and allspice. Other spices were also used in the New World, and still are. Annatto seeds, for example, add flavor as well as color to various dishes of the Yucatán, Cuba, and the other islands of the Caribbean. The seeds, as well as annatto oil, can be purchased in some ethnic stores or by mail order. The list below calls for 10 red peppers. Be careful, however, that you have peppers of medium strength. If you used 10 bird peppers from the islands or habaneros from the Yucatán, they might eat up your sausage mill. A truly American sausage of this sort would not contain pork, which was introduced to the New World by the Europeans. But also remember that the Natives enjoyed fatty meats similar to pork, such as the guinea pig, opossum, armadillo, manatee, and peccary.

10 pounds pork shoulder

¼ cup salt

1 cup annatto seed, crushed

10 dried red peppers, crushed

1 tablespoon ground allspice

1 tablespoon crushed cumin

20 cloves garlic, minced

4 cups cold water

hog casings

Cut the meat into chunks suitable for grinding. Spread the meat out on your work surface, then sprinkle with the salt, spices, and garlic. Grind the meat, mix with the cold water, and stuff into hog casings. Poach these in hot water for 20 minutes, then dry and grill over charcoal or, better yet, wood coals. Serve with grilled fresh pineapple, another Central American product.

CHAPTER 5

CAJUN AND CREOLE AMERICAN SAUSAGES

If cooking is almost a religion in the lower half of Louisiana, my personal Old Testament is the second edition of *The Picayune Creole Cook Book*, first printed in 1901 and reprinted in an unabridged edition in 1971 by Dover Publications. (*The Picayune*, of course, refers to the famous New Orleans daily newspaper.) To this work, I stand head over heels in debt not only for the recipes and techniques in this chapter but also for some of the terminology. The *Picayune* recipes were intended for use by the housewife, who, the book says, "generally prepares a sufficient quantity to last several days." Although I have tried to stick to the old-time recipes as much as possible, I take the liberty of using a mechanical sausage grinder instead of "hashing" the meat with a knife.

ANDOUILLES AND ANDOUILLETTES

This popular Cajun sausage is made with the aid of chitterlings, a word that might not be recognized at first glance by the most enthusiastic andouille fan, who will know them as chitlins. These are the largest intestines of the hog—turned, washed, soaked in water, washed again, and cut into pieces. I can purchase them frozen in my supermarket, and they are available at most meat shops, although they might not be on display. I normally buy them frozen in 10-pound boxes. What I don't use in the andouilles are boiled (outside the house, my wife says) until tender. Then they are dusted with seasoned flour and deep-fried, or boiled and then frozen in small packages for frying at a later date. In any case, this is an excellent sausage. Be sure to try it.

4 pounds lean pork, partially frozen	2 tablespoons salt
4 pounds fat pork, partially frozen	2 tablespoons freshly ground black pepper
2 pounds chitterlings, partially frozen	1–2 teaspoons cayenne pepper
4 large onions, chopped	1 teaspoon ground mace
10 cloves garlic, chopped	1 teaspoon ground clove
2 tablespoons minced fresh parsley	1 teaspoon ground allspice
1 tablespoon minced fresh thyme	1 teaspoon ground or finely crushed bay leaf
1 tablespoon minced fresh sweet marjoram	hog casings

Chop the pork, fat pork, and chitterlings into chunks, then mix and spread them out on a work surface. Mix the onions, garlic, parsley, thyme, and marjoram; spread the mixture evenly over the meat. Mix all the remaining dry ingredients and sprinkle evenly over the meat. Grind the mixture in a sausage mill, using a ³⁄₁₆-inch wheel.

If you want andouilles, stuff the mixture into large hog casings. If you want andouillettes, stuff into small hog casings or perhaps sheep or goat casings. Try some of each.

Often, these sausages are simmered in a broth or poached in milk, then broiled, grilled, or baked. When freshly made, they will keep for a few days in the refrigerator, or they can be frozen. Also, they can be poached and then frozen.

Andouilles are often served with mashed potatoes. Try them grilled and served with boiled new potatoes (golf ball size) and steamed cabbage or perhaps sauerkraut.

Note that many modern Cajuns discreetly omit the chitterlings from the recipe—and some will even deny that this great sausage is in fact named (in French) for the pig's intestines. I disclosed this bit of culinary trivia one night while eating an excellent gumbo in a Florida eatery called The Bayou. The owner, a frisky jackleg cook, damn near threw me out.

DUCK AND ANDOUILLE GUMBO

Andouille or other sausage can be added to thousands of gumbo recipes, and there is some confusion about what's a gumbo and what's not. For the right texture, either okra (the word gumbo *derives from an African word meaning "okra") or filé powder is necessary. The recipe below calls for okra. (If you follow a filé recipe, remember to use it sparingly, at the very end of the cooking, as it can make a stringy mess. In fact, I recommend that filé not be added to the main pot. Instead, ladle hot gumbo into serving bowls. Then stir in the filé to taste. Add a dollop of cooked rice last. In this okra gumbo, however, it is permissible to add gumbo to the rice.)*

1 duckling, 4–5 pounds	5 cloves garlic, minced
3–4 tablespoons flour	hot water
3 medium onions, chopped	1 cup oyster liquor
½ cup chopped green onion tops or fresh chives	salt and pepper to taste
1 red bell pepper, chopped	1½ pounds andouille
1½ cups sliced fresh okra	1 large turnip root, peeled and diced
¼ cup chopped fresh parsley	½ pint freshly shucked oysters
3 bay leaves	rice (cooked separately)

Pluck, skin, and disjoint the duckling, trimming away any fat. Cut the skin and fat into small pieces, then render the oil in a cast-iron, stove-top dutch oven. When most of the oil has been cooked out, what's left of the pieces will be very crisp. These are cracklings. Drain them and set aside. Heat the duck oil to high. Brown and drain the duck pieces. Drain all but about ½ cup of oil from the skillet. Stir 3 to 4 tablespoons of flour into the duck fat. Cook on low, stirring constantly with a wooden spoon, for 30 minutes, or until the mixture (roux) is dark brown. The longer the cooking time, the better—within reason.

Add the chopped onions, green onion tops, bell pepper, okra, parsley, bay leaves, and garlic. Cook for a few minutes. Add the browned duck pieces, along with enough hot water to cover everything. Bring to a light boil, then reduce the heat. Stir in the oyster liquor, along with the salt and pepper. Cover tightly and simmer for 1 hour. In a skillet, brown the sausage pieces, then add them to the pot along with the diced turnip. Cover and simmer for 30 minutes. Add the oysters and simmer for 20 minutes. Serve the gumbo hot over rice, along with a crusty New Orleans sourdough or French bread. Enjoy.

ANDOUILLE À LA JEANNINE

Cajun chef Justin Wilson named this recipe for his wife in The Justin Wilson Gourmet and Gourmand Cookbook. *In fact, it was the first recipe in what I reckon to be the first chapter of the book, prefaced only by a one-pager on how to make a roux.*

2 pounds andouille	2 tablespoons honey
1 cup dry white wine	1 tablespoon Creole mustard

Slice the sausage into ¼- to ½-inch wheels. Place in a skillet. Mix the other ingredients and pour over the sausage. Cover and simmer over low heat for 15 to 20 minutes, or until the sausage is tender. Serve as an appetizer.

CHAURICE

Often used in jambalaya and to season various vegetable and bean dishes, chaurice is a hot, spicy pork sausage made with approximately 2 parts lean meat to 1 part fat. For convenience, I list 7 pounds lean and 3 pounds fat. Usually, however, I use 10 pounds of fatty pork butts without measuring the lean and fat.

7 pounds lean fresh pork, partially frozen

3 pounds pork fat, partially frozen

4 large onions, chopped

4 cloves fresh garlic, minced

1 tablespoon minced fresh parsley

½ tablespoon minced fresh thyme

3 tablespoons salt

1½ tablespoons freshly ground black pepper

1 tablespoon cayenne pepper (for a hot sausage)

1 tablespoon mild red pepper flakes (for color)

1 tablespoon ground allspice

1 teaspoon ground bay leaf

sheep or hog casings

Cut the meat and fat into small chunks, mix, and spread out over your work surface. Sprinkle the chopped onions, garlic, parsley, and thyme evenly over the meat. Mix the salt and all the spices, then sprinkle over the meat. Grind the meat with a ³⁄₁₆-inch wheel. Make a test patty and fry it in hot lard. Add more black pepper if you want a hotter sausage. If the seasoning suits your taste, stuff the mixture into sheep or hog casings. (Old-time New Orleans Creoles preferred sheep casings, but I usually use medium hog casings because I'm more likely to have them on hand.) Tie the sausages off in convenient lengths.

Use the chaurice in dishes of boiled vegetables, beans, gumbo, or jambalaya. Or eat it by itself if you like a hot, spicy sausage. For best results, deep-fry the links in very hot lard or other cooking oil. Drain and serve.

SAUSAGE AND OYSTER JAMBALAYA

The defining ingredients of a true jambalaya, a Spanish-Creole dish akin to the paella, are ham and rice. Since both of these are used in this recipe, I don't have a problem with the name. The sausage and oysters, however, make it special. For best results, use a 13-inch, cast-iron jambalaya skillet to cook this recipe. A large stove-top dutch oven will also do.

¼ cup butter	1½ cups long-grain white rice
1 cup diced baked cured ham (½-inch cubes)	3 cups beef stock
1 pound smoked pork sausage	1 tablespoon salt
1 cup diced fresh lean pork (½-inch cubes)	½ teaspoon freshly ground black pepper
4 cups chopped onion	½ teaspoon cayenne pepper
¼ cup chopped green onion tops	½ teaspoon dried thyme
½ cup chopped red bell pepper	½ teaspoon crushed bay leaf
½ cup chopped green bell pepper	1 pint freshly shucked oysters
4 cloves garlic, minced	oyster liquor as needed
¼ cup chopped fresh parsley	

Melt the butter in a large skillet or stove-top dutch oven over medium heat. Sauté the ham, sausage, and pork for 10 minutes or so. Add the onion, green onion tops, bell peppers, garlic, and parsley. Cook for 30 minutes, stirring from time to time with a wooden spoon. Add the rice. Cook for 5 minutes. Add the beef stock, salt, pepper, cayenne, thyme, and bay leaf. Increase the heat, bringing the liquid to a boil. Add the oysters. Cover and simmer for 1 hour over very low heat. Stir from time to time, being careful not to chop up the oysters. Add a little oyster liquid as needed to keep the dish from drying out. Remove the cover and simmer until the rice dries out a little, stirring gently with a wooden spoon. Serve hot in bowls, along with crusty French bread.

CHAURICE WITH CREOLE SAUCE

I included this recipe in the first draft of this chapter. Later, I took it out because I felt guilty about using too much material from The Picayune Creole Cook Book. *In the end, I put it back in because I owe it to my readers to publish what I consider to be the best sausage dishes. Besides, it's relatively short whereas most modern Cajun and Creole recipes contain a list of ingredients as long as your leg.*

½ teaspoon lard	2 pounds chaurice
1 large onion, chopped	1 teaspoon salt
1 clove garlic, minced	1 teaspoon freshly ground black pepper
3 tomatoes, peeled and chopped	½ cup boiling water

Heat the lard in a cast-iron skillet. Lightly brown the onion. Add the garlic and tomatoes, stirring with a wooden spoon. Prick the sausage links with a fork, then add them to the skillet, cover, and simmer for 5 minutes. Sprinkle with the salt and pepper. Add about ½ cup boiling water. Cover and simmer for 20 minutes. Serve hot for breakfast, along with scrambled eggs and fluffy biscuits.

Picayune Saucisses and Saucissons

According to *The Picayune Creole Cook Book*, saucisses are sausages made with a mixture of meats—beef, pork, veal, and pork fat. They are made with the same seasonings and technique used for chaurice (page 160). For a 10-pound batch, try 3 pounds lean pork, 3 pounds beef, 2 pounds veal, and 2 pounds pork fat. For breakfast, saucisses are sliced and deep-fried in fat.

Saucissons are made with beef, pork, and fat—using only the lean tenderloins of beef and pork. To make a 10-pound batch, use the same seasonings listed for chaurice, along with 4 pounds fresh beef fillet, 4 pounds fresh pork tenderloin, and 2 pounds pork fat. Use small sheep casings tied in lengths of 3 inches, making a sausage about the size of your little finger. Saucissons are usually fried whole.

Both saucisses and saucissons can be smoked for flavor and make a wonderful ingredient for soups, stews, and rice dishes.

RED BEANS, RICE, AND SAUSAGE

Traditionally, this dish is made with smoked sausage. In Louisiana, it is often cooked on Monday, the day for washing, and, at one time, the water from the rice was used to starch the clothes before they were ironed. But the dish is good any day of the week, if it is properly made. I like it on a cold day during winter.

1 pound dried red beans	2 pounds smoked ham hocks
water	2 pounds smoked sausage (in casings)
4 large onions, chopped	salt and pepper to taste
6 cloves garlic, minced	rice (cooked separately)

Rinse the beans, put them into a suitable pot (preferably a cast-iron dutch oven) with water, bring to a boil, and cook for 5 minutes. Then turn off the heat and let the beans sit for at least an hour. Pour the water off the beans. Add 3 quarts of fresh water to the beans, then add onions, garlic, and ham hocks. Bring to a boil, reduce heat, cover tightly, and simmer for an hour, or until the beans are tender. Remove the ham hocks and pull off the lean meat, which is put back into the pot. Cut the sausage into 3-inch lengths and add them to the pot. Add a little salt and pepper to taste. Simmer for 30 minutes, stirring from time to time and adding a little more water if needed. Serve the dish in bowls over rice.

Boudins

Although some modern recipes call for beef blood, a true boudin, sometimes called black pudding, is made with hog blood and fat. According to my old edition of *Larousse Gastronomique*, the addition of blood from other animals "amounts to a fraudulent act!" Moreover, a basic boudin does not call for any lean meat whatsoever, whereas some modern recipes allow fatty pork instead of pure fat. Suit yourself.

YOUR BASIC CREOLE BOUDIN

If you don't butcher your own animals, check with your friendly local meat processor for the availability of blood. Substitute beef blood if you must.

1 pound pork fat	½ teaspoon ground allspice
3 medium to large onions, minced	½ teaspoon ground mace
4 cloves garlic, minced	½ teaspoon ground clove
salt and freshly ground black pepper to taste	½ teaspoon ground nutmeg
cayenne pepper to taste	2 pints hog blood
1 teaspoon crushed dried parsley	hog casings
1 teaspoon crushed dried thyme	

Heat a little of the pork fat in a skillet, frying out some grease. Sauté the onions for 5 minutes, stirring often with a wooden spoon. Add the garlic and cook for another 2 to 3 minutes. Set aside. Mix the salt, pepper, cayenne, parsley, thyme, allspice, mace, clove, and nutmeg. Mince the remaining fat. In a suitable container, thoroughly mix the blood, minced fat, and spice mixture. Stuff the mixture into hog casings, making 3-inch links. Place the links in very hot water. Heat but do not boil until the boudins can be pricked without bleeding. Be warned that boiling the boudins will curdle the blood. Dry and cool the boudins, then cook as needed. Refrigerate for a day or two, or freeze for longer storage. Boudins are best when deep-fried in lard, but they can also be grilled or broiled.

JOHNSON'S BOUDIN BLANC

Adapted from Tony Chachere's Cajun Country Cookbook, *this recipe makes an excellent white boudin. Note that rice is an essential ingredient, helping to give the sausage a whitish color. Other recipes for boudin blanc (mostly French) call for cream—lots of cream—and chicken eggs as well as pork fat, making them very rich as well as high in fat.*

3 pounds lean fresh pork	2 cloves garlic, minced
1 pound pork fat	1 cup chopped green onion tops
1 pound pork liver	½ cup chopped fresh parsley
1 medium onion, chopped	Tony Chachere's Original Creole Seasoning
1 green bell pepper, chopped	cooked rice
2 stalks celery with tops, chopped	hog casings

Trim and dice the meats, and combine with the vegetables and parsley, spreading the mixture over your countertop or work surface. Sprinkle with the Creole seasoning. Grind the mixture in a sausage mill, using a ⅛-inch wheel. Measure the mixture, counting the cups. To each cup of the mixture, add 2 cups cooked rice. Mix well. If the mixture seems too dry, add a little water. Stuff the mixture into medium or large hog casings, linking every 6 to 8 inches. Bring a large pot of water to a rolling boil. Place the sausage into the water and boil gently for 30 minutes. Refrigerate until needed.

Variation for Leftovers: During my boyhood in the country, we always had a huge turkey and fresh pork for both Thanksgiving and Christmas. I also ate the same fare with relatives. In short, I was turned off by leftovers before the holiday season was over. Boudin blanc sausages make a good way out. Just substitute leftover turkey or cooked fresh ham, or both, for the fresh pork in the above recipe.

CHAPTER 6

GERMAN AND AUSTRIAN SAUSAGES

Being the home of the world-famous frankfurter should be enough to establish Germany's place in the history of food. Germans love sausage; in fact, they eat more pounds of sausage per year than any other people. They like not only quantity but also variety. From the Middle Ages to modern times, Germany has been the center of the commercial sausage industry. Over 1,500 different kinds of *wursts* have been developed in Germany, where in times past the local *wurstmacher*, usually with a secret recipe, often grew rich and powerful. Today sausage eating is a traditional part of the annual Oktoberfest, not only in Munich but also in the German communities in Texas and Wisconsin.

The popular frankfurter (also called wiener or hot dog) is covered in chapter 15, Deli Fare and Cold Cuts (page 227), leaving the wursts to be covered here. It's impossible to cover all these in a short book, but here are my favorites.

BRATWURST

This pale, mildly seasoned sausage is usually made with a combination of pork and veal; proportions vary, but 2 parts pork to 1 part veal is the norm. It is stuffed in medium hog casings and tied off in 6-inch links.

7 pounds pork butt or shoulder

3 pounds veal

2 tablespoons salt

1 tablespoon white pepper

2 teaspoons caraway seed

2 teaspoons dried marjoram

2 teaspoons ground allspice

1¾ cups ice water

medium hog casings

Cut the pork and veal into chunks. Mix and spread out over your work surface. Combine all the spices, mix well, and sprinkle evenly over the meats. Grind with a ³⁄₁₆- or ⅛-inch plate. Mix in the ice water with your hands. Stuff into hog casings. Dry the casing surface and refrigerate.

Typically, links of bratwurst are cooked for a few minutes in boiling water or broth, then dipped into milk or cream and broiled or grilled. They are also panfried in butter. When you make a batch, be sure to make some patties to cook on the griddle.

TEXAS BRATWURST

The German immigrants around New Braunfels, Texas, take their sausage seriously, and thousands of pounds are grilled during annual festivals. Here's an excellent recipe that I have adapted from The Only Texas Cookbook, *by Linda West Eckhardt. Be sure to try this one, especially if you want to use lean pork.*

5 pounds lean pork (try loin)	3 cups ice water
5 pounds lean veal	hog casings
2 tablespoons salt	flour
4 teaspoons dried sage	butter
2 teaspoons white pepper	dry white wine
2 cups soft white bread crumbs	fried onions
1 cup milk	mashed potatoes

Cut the meats into chunks, mix, and spread out over your work surface. Sprinkle evenly with the salt, sage, and white pepper. Grind the meats twice with a ⅛- or ³⁄₁₆-inch plate. Soak the bread crumbs in milk, then, using your hands, mix them with the sausage meats. Mix in the ice water and beat until light and fluffy. Stuff into hog casings, tying off in 6-inch links. Either cook right away or freeze.

To cook the bratwurst Texas-style, place some links into a skillet with enough salted water to cover. (An electric skillet works fine.) Bring to a boil, lower the heat, and simmer for 10 minutes. Dry the sausages, then roll them in flour and sauté in butter. When the bratwurst is nicely browned, remove to a serving platter. Add a little dry white wine to the skillet, scraping up any pan drippings, and simmer until you have a nice gravy. Serve the bratwurst topped with fried onions, along with the gravy and mashed potatoes.

CREAMED BRATWURST

Here's a dish that I like to cook whenever I happen upon edible wild mushrooms. Puffballs will do, but morels or chanterelles are better. If you don't eat wild mushrooms, try store-bought shiitakes or sliced portobellos.

¾–1 pound bratwurst	¼ cup chopped fresh parsley
2 tablespoons butter	2 tablespoons flour
1 cup chopped onion	salt and white pepper to taste
1 cup sliced mushrooms	2 cups half-and-half

Heat some water in a pot and simmer the bratwurst links for about 15 minutes, until cooked through. Cool and slice the bratwurst into ½-inch wheels. Heat the butter in a skillet. Sauté the onion, mushrooms, and parsley for 5 to 6 minutes. Stir in the flour along with a little salt and white pepper to taste. Pour in the half-and-half and cook, stirring as you go, until the mixture is bubbly but not boiling. Stir in the bratwurst pieces and simmer for 2 to 3 minutes. Serve over toast.

BOCKWURST

This small delicate sausage is made from veal and pork, flavored with onion, clove, and parsley. The mix of meats can vary considerably, ranging from 9 parts veal to 1 part pork fat. I like it made with half veal and half fatty pork, as from the butt or shoulder. Traditionally, bockwurst is made in the spring, during bockbier *time, when the dark bock beer is ready.*

5 pounds pork butt or shoulder
5 pounds veal
2 large onions, chopped
¼ tablespoon minced dried sage
¼ tablespoon ground mace
2 tablespoons salt
2 tablespoons white pepper

2 tablespoons sugar
½ tablespoon ground clove
2 tablespoons minced dried parsley
5 cups milk
8 chicken eggs, lightly whisked
small hog or sheep casings

Cut the meat into chunks, mix with the onions, and spread it over your work surface. Sprinkle evenly with the sage, mace, salt, pepper, sugar, clove, and parsley. Grind with a ⅛-inch plate, or grind twice with a 3/16-inch plate. Mix in the milk and chicken eggs. Stuff in small hog casings or perhaps sheep casings, tying off in 3- or 4-inch links. Heat some water in a large pot. Simmer the bockwurst for 10 minutes. Dry the surface. Cook immediately, refrigerate for a day or two, or freeze. To cook, sauté the links in butter along with some chopped onions. Serve hot.

Variation: Add the juice of 3 to 4 lemons before stuffing the bockwurst into the casings.

BAVARIAN SALAD

Here's a recipe that I adapted from The New German Cookbook, *by Jean Anderson and Hedy Würz. The authors say that Bavarians make it with bockwurst, but that they substituted bologna because it is easier to obtain here in America. It's better, however, to make your own bockwurst. Also, the authors list corn oil in the ingredients, but I have changed this to olive oil.*

2 pounds bockwurst, simmered

2 medium onions, chopped

½ cup olive oil

¼ cup red wine vinegar

1 tablespoon brown mustard

salt and freshly ground black pepper to taste

2 tablespoons chopped fresh chives

2 tablespoons chopped fresh flat-leaf parsley

Cut the bockwurst into bite-size chunks. Mix with the onions in a large bowl. In a small bowl, mix the oil, wine vinegar, mustard, salt, and pepper. Whisk until creamy. Pour the oil mix over the bockwurst and onions, toss, cover, and marinate in the refrigerator for 2 hours. When you are ready to serve, toss in the chives and parsley.

KNOCKWURST

This hefty sausage can be stuffed into large hog casings or small beef rounds.

7 pounds beef	1 tablespoon ground mace
3 pounds fatty fresh pork	½ tablespoon ground coriander
6 tablespoons salt	10 cloves garlic, minced
5 tablespoons white pepper	2 cups ice water
4 tablespoons sugar	large hog casings or small beef rounds
2 tablespoons Hungarian paprika	

Cut the beef and pork into chunks, mix, and spread over your work surface. Mix all the dry ingredients, then sprinkle them evenly over the meat, along with the minced garlic. Grind the meat with a ⅛-inch plate, or grind twice with a ³⁄₁₆-inch plate. Mix in the ice water, working the mass with your hands. Stuff into large hog casings or small beef rounds. Dry the surface and cold-smoke for an hour or so. Cook immediately or freeze.

Knockwurst is usually baked or fried in a skillet. In the latter case, I usually simmer mine first before frying to make sure it is cooked thoroughly. Cooking times will vary with the thickness of the sausage. If in doubt, use a meat thermometer. The center of a representative link should read at least 152°F. Note that the sausage can be taken directly from the smoker and grilled over charcoal, or it can be cooked in the smoker by increasing the heat.

KNOCKWURST WITH BEER

I would like to say that I wrestled this recipe from a plump German chef during Oktoberfest, but in truth I have adapted it from The New York Times Cookbook, *put together by Craig Claiborne. I don't know what sort of beer Claiborne used, but I tried it with dark lager.*

1 pint German beer	2 tablespoons vinegar
8 knockwurst links	2 teaspoons sugar

Heat the beer in a saucepan, add the knockwurst, and simmer on very low heat for 15 minutes. (If the knockwurst are thick, perhaps stuffed in beef rounds, increase the cooking time to 20 minutes.) Place the cooked knockwurst onto a heated broiling pan. Preheat the broiler. Increase the heat under the saucepan, boiling and stirring until the beer stock is reduced to about ⅓ cup. Stir in the vinegar and sugar. Pour the resulting sauce over the knockwurst. Broil for a few minutes, turning to brown both sides. Serve hot.

METTWURST

This mild German sausage, made of fresh pork and pork liver, is similar to liverwurst. It makes a wonderful sandwich. Mettwurst recipes abound, however, and some of these do not call for liver or for cooking it. In my version, the fresh pork and liver are cooked before grinding and the whole sausage is simmered in salted water, then refrigerated. This sausage is difficult to slice because it tends to fall apart. I do, however, slice it when made in hog casings. With larger casings, I break the sausage apart with a fork and mix it with mayonnaise as a sandwich spread. Some recipes make a soft mettwurst (also called teewurst), which is used as a spread and is considered a tea sausage.

6 pounds fresh pork	2 tablespoons white pepper
4 pounds fresh pork liver	2 tablespoons ground coriander
lightly salted water	unsalted cold water
¼ cup salt	beef rounds or large hog casings

Cut the pork and liver into chunks. Simmer in lightly salted water for about 30 minutes, then drain. Cool the meat, then spread it out on your work surface and sprinkle evenly with salt, white pepper, and coriander. Grind and stuff into beef rounds or perhaps large hog casings. Simmer in lightly salted water for 30 minutes (20 minutes or less for hog casings, depending on size). Chill in cold water, dry the surface, and refrigerate for up to 2 weeks, using as needed as a sandwich filler or cracker spread. Freeze for longer storage.

GEHIRNWURST

Brains have always been one of my favorite meats, and I was therefore gustatorily aroused when I first ran across a cryptic version of this recipe in an old edition of Larousse Gastronomique.

5 pounds pork brains

3 pounds lean pork

2 pounds pork fat

2 tablespoons freshly ground black pepper

1 tablespoon ground mace

5 tablespoons salt

hog casings

Heat a pot of water and simmer the pork brains for about 10 minutes. Drain and cut the brains into chunks. Also cut the pork and fat into chunks. Mix the brains, fat, pork, pepper, mace, and salt on your work surface. Grind with a ³⁄₁₆-inch plate. Stuff into hog casings, tying off every 8 inches or so. To cook, poach in water for 5 minutes, then sauté, preferably in butter. Either cook or freeze gehirnwurst right away.

VIENNA SAUSAGE

This Austrian specialty is made from beef and pork, sometimes with veal added. Onion, mace, and coriander are the dominant seasonings. Stuffed into sheep casings, the Vienna sausage is similar to the frankfurter (see chapter 15, Deli Fare and Cold Cuts, page 227), but is a little shorter and not quite as fat.

4 pounds lean beef	1 tablespoon Hungarian paprika
6 pounds pork butt or shoulder	½ tablespoon cayenne pepper
2 tablespoons ground coriander	½ cup chopped onion
3 tablespoons salt	2 cups cold milk
1 tablespoon sugar	1 cup flour
1 tablespoon ground mace	sheep casings

Cut the beef and pork into chunks suitable for grinding. Mix these on your work surface and sprinkle evenly with the coriander, salt, sugar, mace, paprika, cayenne, and chopped onion. (The spices can be mixed before sprinkling over the meat.) Grind with a ³⁄₁₆-inch plate; then grind twice with a ⅛-inch plate. Thoroughly mix in the milk and flour. Stuff the mix into sheep casings, tying off every 4 inches. Place the links into a large pot and cover with water. Bring to a boil, then reduce the heat and simmer (do not allow it to boil again) for 45 minutes. Remove the links, cool, dry the surface, and refrigerate or freeze. (These can also be canned, but I don't recommend the practice.) Before eating, reheat the sausages in boiling water or, better, grill over charcoal or a wood fire.

CHAPTER 7

ITALIAN SAUSAGES

Italy is the home of some of the world's most popular sausages, including bologna, salami, and pepperoni. Since these three are popular as cold cuts and sandwich meats in America and other parts of the world, I have covered them in chapter 15, Deli Fare and Cold Cuts (page 227). Don't worry. There's still enough good eating left to distinguish Italy in the world of sausage. It all started long ago.

Ancient Roman Sausage

Apicius, the ancient culinary sport, gave us the work *Cookery and Dining in Imperial Rome*—our oldest extant cookbook. The Romans adopted the sausage from the ancient Greeks, who had a profound influence on the food and cookery of southern Italy and Sicily. In addition to making their own, the Romans also imported tons of cured sausage and ham from the Gauls. In any case, Apicius left us several sausages. By today's standards, the recipes are rather cryptic, lacking complete instructions and measurements. The recipes below are reconstructed as best I can make out. The inquisitive scholar might want to take a look at the Latin text or a translation. A translation of the whole work has been reprinted by Dover Publications, and other translations are no doubt available.

Meanwhile, notice that the sample recipes below are very close to a modern sausage. But none of the original recipes listed salt or any sort of cure. Beware. My guess is that it never occurred to Apicius to list salt as an ingredient, as any fool would know to add salt to fresh pork. Salt was very much in demand in the Roman Empire, and, in fact, our word *salary* came from the Roman word for salt allowance, or ration. It has even been argued that the word *sausage* is derived from *salt*.

LUCANIAN SAUSAGE

Mince some fresh pork. Add crushed pepper, cumin, savory, chopped parsley, and broth. Pound the mixture. Add some whole peppercorns and nuts. Stuff into casings and hang to smoke. The original recipe also called for rue, laurel berries, and "condiment." Since I don't know exactly what these are in modern culinary terms, I have left them out. The "nuts" could have been any of several, but my guess is that pine nuts were the favorite. In any case, if the recipe is made with reasonable amounts of meat and spices, it will be perfectly acceptable today. Try simmering the links for 15 minutes, then frying them.

Apicius has a recipe for sautéing sausage with the white part of chopped leeks and serving them with a wine sauce. I can't piece together the sauce recipe, but a translator's footnote speculates that the recipe came from Tarentum, a town of southern Italy noted for its wine and luxurious living. Anyhow, the sausage and chopped leeks is a very good sauté.

ANCIENT BRAIN SAUSAGE

Poach the brains in a little water until cooked. Mix with raw chicken eggs, pine nuts, pepper, broth, and a little laser. (Laser was a very popular ancient wild herb. It was in great demand and, being picked too frequently, may now be extinct.) Stuff the mixture into hog casings. Simmer in water for a few minutes, then sauté or fry.

Since brains and eggs (scrambled together) are one of my favorite foods, I have cooked this recipe several times, using various leafy herbs in lieu of laser. Ordinary parsley will do. This sausage is very good, and these days brains are one of the best nutritional values available at our supermarkets and meat shops.

SPELT SAUSAGE

Spelt is an ancient wheat-like grain that is still available today. (I purchase whole spelt berries from King Arthur Flour, listed in Sources of Materials and Supplies, page 373.) Any hard wheat berry will do. First, cook the spelt or wheat berries in stock until tender. (It helps to soak the berries overnight in water.) Chop some bacon, *hot* fat (from around the innards), and fresh pork. Mix with the cooked spelt berries, crushed pepper, lovage, chicken eggs, pine nuts, and broth. Pound with a mortar and pestle. Stuff the mixture into hog casings. Poach in water for 20 minutes, then serve hot. These sausages can also be poached and fried or grilled. The Apicius text is a little unclear, but notes from translators indicate that this sausage was served with pheasant gravy flavored with cumin.

In any case, I hope that this recipe will introduce a few readers to spelt and wheat berries. They can be used in soups and stews, adding a delightful change of texture as well as taste, and will boost the recipes' nutritional value tremendously. Why we Americans have neglected this healthful food is a cultural mystery to me.

SWEET ITALIAN SAUSAGE

Fennel dominates the seasonings in this mild sausage. I prefer to measure out the seeds, then crush them on a suitable surface with the flat side of a meat mallet. Most recipes, however, merely specify seeds. Suit yourself.

10 pounds pork butt or shoulder	1 tablespoon dried sage
2 tablespoons salt	10 cloves garlic, minced
2 tablespoons fennel seed	2 cups good red wine
1½ tablespoons white pepper	hog casings

Cut the meat into chunks suitable for grinding. Spread the meat out on your work surface. Sprinkle evenly with the dry seasonings and garlic. Grind with a ³⁄₁₆-inch plate. Work the wine into the ground meat. Stuff in hog casings or use as bulk sausage—or try half one way and half the other.

To cook, fry or bake. The stuffed sausages should be poached for about 15 minutes before frying in a little olive oil. This sausage can be refrigerated for several days, or frozen for longer storage.

A. D.'S EGGPLANT PARMIGIANA

This combination of tomato, eggplant, bulk Italian sausage, and Italian cheeses is one of my favorite dishes. Although the ingredient list below calls for flour, I sometimes dust the eggplant in fine stone-ground white cornmeal.

1 large eggplant	2 cups tomato sauce
salt	pepper to taste
olive oil	1 pound bulk Italian mild sausage
1 cup chopped onion	flour, for dusting
5 cloves garlic, minced	1 cup freshly grated mozzarella cheese
2 cups chopped Italian tomatoes	½ cup freshly grated Parmesan cheese

Preheat the oven to 375°F and grease a shallow 8- to 12-inch baking dish. Peel the eggplant and cut into ¼- to ½-inch slices. Sprinkle the slices on both sides with salt, then spread them out over absorbent paper. Heat a little olive oil in a skillet. Sauté the onion and garlic for 5 to 6 minutes. Add the tomatoes and tomato sauce, stirring and heating through, adding salt and pepper to taste. In another skillet or saucepan, heat a little olive oil and sauté the sausage for a few minutes. Drain and mix the sausage into the tomato and onions. If needed, heat a little more olive oil. Pat the eggplant slices dry and sprinkle on both sides with flour, shaking off the excess. Sauté the eggplant slices until they are golden on both sides. Spread a little of the tomato-sausage mixture over the bottom of the baking dish. Cover with eggplant slices and a layer of both cheeses. Add another layer of tomato sauce, eggplant, and cheeses. End with tomato sauce. Sprinkle lightly with olive oil. Cover the dish and bake for 30 minutes. Uncover and bake for another 15 minutes or so. Serve hot with plenty of crusty Italian bread, lots of fresh tossed salad, and vino.

LUGANEGA

I've seen several recipes for Sicilian or Italian sausage made with the aid of a grated dry cheese and wine. Some of these call for vermouth or chablis, but I say that a dry red wine is in order. I won't insist on chianti, but it is a good choice and is usually readily available in America. Suit yourself. In any case, this recipe (and the name of the sausage) has been adapted from The Sausage-Making Cookbook, *by Jerry Predika (who specifies dry vermouth). Rytek Kutas set forth a similar recipe in his* Great Sausage Recipes and Meat Curing, *listing Romano cheese and chablis wine; this, he said, is his favorite Italian sausage. In* Home Sausage Making, *Charles G. Reavis calls luganega unique because it is flavored with freshly grated lemon and orange zest. I might add that other sausages are flavored with orange or lemon peel, and in Catalonia, zest of the bitter Seville orange is used. In any case, I consider the wine and cheese to be the distinguishing ingredients.*

10 pounds pork butt

2 tablespoons salt

1 tablespoon freshly ground black pepper

1½ teaspoons ground coriander

1½ teaspoons ground nutmeg

2 cloves garlic, minced

1 teaspoon freshly grated orange zest

1 teaspoon freshly grated lemon zest

3 cups grated Parmesan cheese

2 cups dry vermouth

hog casings

Cut the meat into chunks suitable for grinding. Mix the salt, pepper, coriander, and nutmeg, sprinkling the mixture evenly over the meat. Grind it with a ³⁄₁₆-inch plate. Mix in the garlic, orange zest, lemon zest, cheese, and wine. Stuff into hog casings. Cook immediately or freeze. (Freezing will alter the flavor somewhat.) Use in soups and stews, or poach for 15 minutes and then fry or grill.

TUSCAN BEANS WITH SAUSAGE

Dean & Deluca, the New York mail-order outfit, specifies Jacob's cattle beans for this recipe. These are large, quick-cooking beans, and I highly recommend them not only for taste and texture but also for color. Substitute calypso beans if you have them on hand. In Italy, Tuscans are called mangiafagiole, *meaning "bean eaters." This recipe goes a long way toward justification of the predilection.*

½ pound Jacob's cattle beans	1 teaspoon chopped fresh sage
1 pound luganega	1 teaspoon chopped fresh rosemary
1 large onion, chopped	salt and freshly ground black pepper to taste
2 large tomatoes, chopped	

Rinse the beans. Simmer them in a pot, well covered with water, for 1 hour. Remove the pot from the heat but leave the beans in the hot water as you proceed. Place the sausage in a large skillet. Add enough water to measure 1 inch. Cook the sausage uncovered until almost all the water has evaporated, leaving the grease that will have cooked out of the sausage. Add the onion and cook for 5 minutes. Remove the sausage, slice into 1-inch pieces, and set aside. Add the tomatoes, sage, rosemary, salt, and pepper to the onions. Cover and simmer on low heat for 10 minutes. Add the sausage pieces and cooked beans. Cover and simmer for 5 minutes. Serve hot, along with crusty bread and red vino.

COTEGHINO

This excellent sausage, usually rather large, calls for pork and pork skin with the fat attached. It's easy to use a fresh ham, cutting the meat and skin as needed. Stuff the sausage into small beef rounds or large hog casings.

7 pounds pork	1 tablespoon cayenne pepper
3 pounds pork skin with fat	1 teaspoon ground clove
6 tablespoons salt	1 cup grated Parmesan cheese
3 tablespoons freshly ground black pepper	4 cloves garlic, minced
1 tablespoon ground nutmeg	2 cups cold water
1 tablespoon ground cinnamon	small beef rounds or large hog casings

Cut the pork and skin into chunks suitable for grinding. Spread the chunks over the work surface, mixing well. Sprinkle the spices evenly over the pork, then grind with a 3/16-inch plate. Mix in the Parmesan, garlic, and water, working with your hands. Stuff the mixture into beef rounds or hog casings, tying off with twine in 8-inch lengths, leaving a loop on one end. Hang the links in a cool, breezy place for 4 to 5 days before cooking. If you don't have a suitable place, clean out a section of your refrigerator and hang the links. To cook, simmer the links in water for 1½ hours. Prick the links with a fork while cooking. Traditionally, these sausages are served with lentils.

Note: Some coteghino recipes call for saltpeter. This ingredient will give the coteghino a reddish color, but I elect to leave it out. If you want it, use ⅓ teaspoon for the recipe, and be sure to mix it very evenly into the salt and other dry ingredients. Going the other way, another recipe calls for a greatly reduced quantity of salt, which I can't recommend. In any case, remember that the recipe above is not for a fully cured sausage. It should be treated as a fresh sausage. In other words, it should be either cooked right away, refrigerated for a few days, or frozen for longer storage.

CHAPTER 8

BRITISH ISLE SAUSAGES

The British Isles are noted more for meat pies than for sausages, and cows or sheep are probably more important than hogs. Still, sausage is popular for breakfast, especially bulk patties, and sometimes it is cooked in beans and other dishes.

BULK COUNTRY SAUSAGE WITH WATERCRESS

This recipe calls for lean pork butts, but the mix can be made with 80 percent lean pork, as from the loin, and 20 percent fat. If you start off with a butt that contains too much fat, trim it a little. Often country sausage is made with lots of fresh herbs, making it the ideal sausage for home gardeners.

10 pounds pork butt, on the lean side
4 cups minced fresh parsley
4 cups minced green onions with tops
4 cups minced watercress
¼ cup minced fresh marjoram
¼ cup minced fresh rosemary

¼ cup minced fresh tarragon
¼ cup minced fresh thyme
¼ cup rubbed dried sage
6 tablespoons sea salt or kosher salt
2 tablespoons caraway seed
1 tablespoon freshly ground black pepper

Cut the meat into chunks, spread it out on your work surface, and sprinkle it evenly with the herbs and spices. Grind with a ³⁄₁₆-inch plate. Mix again with your hands and shape into patties. Either cook the patties right away or wrap tightly in foil and freeze. Note that frozen patties can be pan-grilled successfully or sautéed without thawing.

BANGERS

Here's an old English sausage made with pork, seasonings, and crumbled stale biscuits; stale bread can be substituted. The recipe also calls for chilled pork stock. If this is a problem, use ice water, chilled beef broth, or perhaps chicken stock.

8 pounds lean pork

2 pounds pork fat

6 tablespoons salt

1 tablespoon white pepper

½ tablespoon ground mace

½ tablespoon ground ginger

¼ tablespoon dried sage

2½ pounds stale biscuits

7 cups chilled pork stock

hog casings

Cut the meat and fat into chunks suitable for grinding. Spread the meat on your work surface, mix well, and sprinkle evenly with the salt and spices. Grind the mix with a ³⁄₁₆-inch plate. Crumble the biscuits and soak them in a little of the stock. Mix the meat, biscuits, and stock. Stuff into hog casings, tying off in convenient lengths. Hang in a cool, airy place for 24 hours. Cook immediately, refrigerate for a day or two, or freeze. These sausages, popular for breakfast, can be simmered, broiled, grilled, baked, or fried.

OXFORD SAUSAGE

This delicious sausage is made with a mix of fatty pork, veal, and beef, seasoned with various spices and lemon zest. When grating the lemon, use a fine mesh and be careful to avoid the bitter white pith.

4 pounds fatty pork, such as butt or shoulder

4 pounds veal

2 pounds lean beef

3 tablespoons salt

1½ teaspoons freshly ground black pepper

2 teaspoons dried sage

2 teaspoons dried thyme

2 teaspoons dried rosemary

2 teaspoons grated nutmeg

2 teaspoons dried minced savory

zest of 3 lemons

crumbs from 1 loaf sourdough bread

8 chicken eggs, whisked

2 cups ice water

medium hog casings

Cut the meat into chunks suitable for grinding, mix, and sprinkle evenly with the salt and dry spices. Grind with a ³⁄₁₆-inch plate. Mix in the lemon zest, bread crumbs, chicken eggs, and ice water. Mix thoroughly. Stuff into medium hog casings. Cook, refrigerate for a day or two, or freeze. To cook, fry in a little cooking oil, broil, or grill. I like to simmer these for about 15 minutes in water, then dry and sauté or broil them. When frying, add a little water to the skillet so that the sausage is partially steamed.

BLACK PUDDING

This English blood sausage is distinguished by rice that has been cooked separately and mixed into the pork. Sometimes cooked barley or oatmeal is used instead of, or in addition to, the rice.

1½ pounds uncooked rice

2 pounds pork fat

2 cups chopped onion

1 quart very fresh pig or beef blood

4 chicken eggs

⅓ pint heavy cream

2 tablespoons salt

1 tablespoon freshly ground black pepper

1 tablespoon celery seed

1 tablespoon ground coriander

1 tablespoon dry mustard

½ tablespoon dried thyme

2 bay leaves, ground

beef rounds or muslin bags

Cook the rice according to the directions on the package. Chop the pork fat into ¼-inch dice. Heat the pork fat in a skillet until a little grease cooks out. Take up the pork fat, then sauté the onion in the grease for 5 to 6 minutes. Mix the blood, eggs, pork fat, rice, onion, cream, spices, and seasonings. Stuff the mixture loosely into beef rounds or muslin bags, tying off in 8-inch links. Simmer the sausage in very hot (but not boiling) water for 40 minutes. Maintain the water temperature at about 200°F so that the black pudding will cook through. Prick the skin of a sausage; if no blood oozes out, it is done. Keep an eye on the links while poaching. Prick those that rise to the surface, letting the air escape to prevent bursting. Cool the links. To cook, slice the links and grill over charcoal, or slice and fry. Serve hot with applesauce.

IRISH SAUSAGE

This pork sausage is traditionally stuffed into sheep casings. Substitute small hog casings if they are more convenient. The pork should contain about 30 percent fat; the typical pork butt or shoulder will do just fine.

10 pounds fatty pork	1 tablespoon dried rosemary
15–20 cloves garlic, minced	1 tablespoon dried marjoram
3 tablespoons salt	4 cups cold water
1 tablespoon freshly ground black pepper	8 chicken eggs, whisked
1 tablespoon dried thyme	10 cups bread crumbs
1 tablespoon dried basil	sheep casings

Cut the pork into chunks suitable for grinding, spread it out on your work surface, sprinkle it evenly with the garlic, salt, pepper, and herbs, and grind it with a ³⁄₁₆-inch plate. Mix the ground meat with the cold water, eggs, and bread crumbs, then stuff the mixture into sheep casings. Cook right away, refrigerate for a day or so, or freeze. These are best when sautéed in butter.

DUBLIN CODDLE

I found this recipe, and the name for it, in Traditional Irish Recipes, *a quaint little book by George L. Thomson. The format has been changed; the recipe, rewritten.*

THE STEW

8 slices ham (¼ inch thick)

8 links Irish pork sausage

1 quart water

4 pounds Irish potatoes, chopped

4 large onions, chopped

4 tablespoons chopped fresh parsley

salt and pepper to taste

Cut the ham slices into bite-size pieces. Simmer the ham pieces and sausage in 1 quart of water for 5 minutes. Drain the ham and sausage, saving the stock. Put the ham and sausage into a pot along with the potatoes, onions, parsley, salt, and pepper. Barely cover with the stock. Bring to a boil, then reduce the heat to very low. Cover with grease-proof paper, then cover with the lid and simmer for 1 hour. Serve hot with freshly made Irish soda bread and stout.

THE SODA BREAD

1 pound flour

½ teaspoon baking soda

½ teaspoon salt

½ pint buttermilk

Preheat the oven to 400°F. Sift the flour into a bowl, mixing in the soda and salt. Make a well in the middle of the flour, then add the buttermilk. Stir with a wooden spoon until you have a soft dough. Flour your hands and knead the dough lightly. Place the dough on a floured board, then flatten it into a circle about 1½ inches thick. Place on a cast-iron griddle. Using a knife, make a cross on top of the dough, centering it precisely. Bake for 40 minutes. Break the bread into four pieces (along the lines of the cross) and serve hot with the stew and stout.

SCOTCH-IRISH EGGS

Hard-boiled chicken eggs encased with breakfast sausage make a tasty lunch or brunch, especially suited for wayfarers and hikers. Because the recipe has been attributed to both Scotland and Ireland, I call them Scotch-Irish eggs.

oil for deep-frying	1 pound breakfast sausage (bulk)
6 large hard-boiled chicken eggs	2 raw chicken eggs
1 tablespoon flour	1 cup dried bread crumbs
salt and pepper, if needed	

Rig for deep-frying. Shell the hard-boiled eggs. Mix the flour, salt, and pepper into the sausage, then divide into sixths. Pat each part into a thin roundish patty, just wide enough to encase a hard-boiled egg. Carefully wrap each egg with a patty, distributing the sausage as evenly as possible. Beat the 2 raw eggs in a bowl and put the bread crumbs onto a plate. Dip each sausage-encased hard-boiled egg in the beaten egg, then roll it in the bread crumbs, coating evenly all around. Deep-fry the eggs in hot oil (350°F) for 3 to 4 minutes. Unless you have a very large deep-fryer, it's best to cook the eggs in batches. Remove the eggs with a large slotted spoon and drain them on a brown paper bag. Eat warm or cold. If properly wrapped, the eggs will keep half a day without refrigeration. These will freeze nicely.

HIGHLAND HAGGIS

Some recipes for haggis are just too long to be realistic, almost as if the authors of the recipes were trying to hide the essential ingredients. Here's a short version that is closer, I think, to the original Highland recipe.

1 sheep stomach

salted water for soaking stomach

1 sheep heart

1 set sheep kidneys

1 sheep liver

1 set sheep sweetbreads (if you can find them among the innards)

½ pound fat, diced

1 large onion, grated

1 cup oatmeal

salt and pepper to taste

water

milk

Clean and soak the stomach in salted water overnight. When you are ready to proceed, simmer the heart and kidneys for 1½ hours in a pot; cool and trim away the pipes and gristle. Cut the cooked heart and kidneys into chunks. Cut the liver and sweetbreads into chunks. Mix all the meats and fat, along with the grated onion, oatmeal, salt, and pepper. Run the mixture through a sausage mill, using a ¼- to ½-inch plate. Add a little water to the mixture, working it with your hands. Stuff the mixture into the stomach, leaving some room for the oatmeal to expand. Sew up the opening with cotton twine. Place the stuffed stomach into a pot of suitable size, add enough water and milk to almost cover it, and bring to a boil. Prick the stomach here and there as soon as it begins to swell. Simmer for 3 hours. Serve the haggis plain with straight Scotch whisky. Lots of whisky.

CHAPTER 9

FRENCH SAUSAGES

In ancient times, the region of Europe known as Gaul, with France as its heart, contained sprawling forests of oak and beech trees. Pigs foraged on the beechnuts and sweet acorns, with an occasional truffle going to the best sniffers. As soon as the word got out that these acorn-fed hogs were of excellent quality, the Gauls started exporting cured hams and sausages to the Romans in large quantities.

In time, the *charcuterie* trade became highly regulated under various governmental rules and restrictions, explaining, I think, the decline of the homemade French sausage. For whatever reason, modern French cookbooks may give a few recipes for cooking *with* a variety of sausages, but they offer no directions for actually making them, leaving this task to the professional *charcutiers*. My old edition of *The Escoffier Cook Book*, for example, sets forth fewer than ten recipes that I consider to be about sausages (or how to cook with them), whereas it contains—in telling contrast—well over one hundred recipes for sauces of one sort or another. Of the

sausage recipes, five are for "puddings," as Escoffier called blood sausages, or boudins. In addition to the puddings, he gives us two recipes for *crépinettes*—seasoned ground meat wrapped in caul fat and fried—which may or may not be a sausage, depending on your definition. Of the other three recipes, the first is merely a condescending statement, to wit, "The most known sausages of many nations are cooked like the French kind, and are often served at breakfasts as an accompaniment to bacon. . . . Their seasoning is often excessive." One of the remaining two Escoffier recipes tells us how to cook Frankfort and Strasburg sausages (poach for no longer than ten minutes and serve with grated horseradish, applesauce, or braised sauerkraut).

Predictably, Escoffier's final recipe tells us how to cook sausages with the aid of wine. Although the recipe is short enough at first glance, it calls for ⅙ pint of half-glaze, recipe 23. That's where the trouble starts. To make a half-glaze, Escoffier says, we'll need, along with some excellent sherry, 1 quart of

Espagnole sauce, recipe 22, page 18, and 1 quart of Brown Stock, recipe 7, pages 9 and 10. Astoundingly, recipe 7 for Brown Stock calls for the following: 4 pounds shin of beef, 4 pounds shin of veal, ½ pound raw ham, ½ pound fresh pork rind, blanched, ¾ pound minced carrots browned in butter, ¾ pound minced onion browned in butter, and 1 herb bunch containing a little parsley, a stalk of celery, a small sprig of thyme, and a bay leaf. I don't know what we need to make the Espagnole sauce proper, as I didn't get that far. All I wanted to do was cook a link or two of sausage!

Nonetheless, I have puzzled out a few French creations, starting with a spice mix that can be used in several recipes. Also, some modified French sausage recipes were set forth in chapter 5, Cajun and Creole American Sausages (page 156).

QUATRE ÉPICES

This French blend, sometimes available commercially, is often used in sausages and pâtés. You can mix your own easily enough.

5 teaspoons ground white pepper

1 teaspoon ground ginger

1 teaspoon freshly grated nutmeg

½ teaspoon ground clove

½ teaspoon ground cinnamon

Thoroughly mix all the spices. Store in a tightly closed jar in a cool, dark place. The measures set forth above can easily be doubled or increased tenfold.

CHIPOLATA

This recipe for this excellent French sausage has been adapted from Jack Ubaldi's Meat Book. *It is a small sausage and should be stuffed into sheep casings. Small hog casings will do as well.*

5 pounds pork butt or shoulder

2½ pounds fresh pork belly

2½ pounds boned veal neck

1¼ pounds chopped onion

3 cloves garlic, minced

3½ ounces salt

3 teaspoons coarsely ground pepper

1½ teaspoons quatre épices
(see previous recipe)

sheep casings

Cut the meat into chunks, spread it out on your work surface, and sprinkle evenly with the onion, garlic, and seasonings. Grind the mixture once with a ⅛-inch plate or twice with a ³⁄₁₆-inch plate. Stuff the mixture into sheep casings, tying off into 3- to 4-inch links. Panfry for breakfast or use in casseroles and other well-cooked dishes. Refrigerate for a day or two, or freeze.

Note: When you bone the veal neck, be sure to save the bones for soups or stock.

CHICKEN AND CHIPOLATA

The Australians are not generally credited with creative cookery, but they did adapt the British oxtail soup to kangaroo tail, and they stuffed a steak with oysters before grilling it, calling it carpetbag steak. In this creation, they stuff a roasting chicken with small whole French sausages. I adapted the recipe from Australia the Beautiful Cookbook, *by Elise Pasco and Cherry Ripe. Be sure to try it.*

1 Granny Smith apple

about ¾ pound chipolata sausage links

1 roasting chicken, about 4 pounds

salt and freshly ground black pepper to taste

1 teaspoon chopped fresh sage

1 medium onion, chopped

1–2 tablespoons melted butter

Preheat the oven to 350°F. Peel, core, and chop the apple. Bring some water to a boil in a pot. Simmer the sausages for a few minutes, drain, and cool. Trim the fat away from the chicken but do not skin it. Sprinkle the inside of the chicken with salt, freshly ground black pepper, and sage. Stuff the cavity loosely with 1 tablespoon of the chopped onion, one-fourth of the chopped apple, and 4 or 5 of the sausages. Set the rest of the onion, apple, and sausage aside. Baste the chicken heavily with butter, then sprinkle with salt and pepper. Place the chicken on a baking pan and position it in the upper third of the preheated oven. Bake for 1 hour and 40 minutes. Add the rest of the sausage, apple, and onion to the pan. Bake for another 20 minutes, or until the bird is done. Turn off the oven and let the chicken rest for 10 minutes. Place the chicken on a heated serving platter along with the sausage, apple, and onion. Serve hot.

DUCK SAUSAGE

Duck is one of my very favorite meats. Any kind can be used in this sausage, but the small wild ducks, such as teal, are difficult to bone and don't yield much meat. For starters, it's best to use the larger domestic ducks. You'll need 5 to 6 pounds of meat. Skin the ducks. (Be sure to render the fat, saving the cracklings for bread or to sprinkle over potatoes or salads. Also, save the bony parts for soup or stock.)

2 large Long Island ducks	1 teaspoon freshly ground black pepper
1½ pounds pork butt or shoulder	½ teaspoon dried marjoram
1½ pounds veal	½ teaspoon dried sage
1½ tablespoons salt	1½ cups cold water
2 teaspoons quatre épices	hog casings

Skin the ducks and fillet the breast. Cut the breast meat into ¼- to ½-inch cubes; set aside. Bone the rest of the ducks and cut the meat into chunks for grinding. Cut the pork and veal into chunks. Spread the veal, pork, and duck chunks (but not the breast meat) onto your work surface. Sprinkle evenly with the salt and spices. Grind once with a ⅛-inch plate, or twice with a ³⁄₁₆-inch plate. Mix the ground meat and diced duck breast. Stir in the cold water. Stuff into hog casings, tying off in 6-inch links. Cook or refrigerate immediately, or freeze. To cook, panfry the links in butter over low heat until done, or grill over a low charcoal or wood fire.

CRÉPINETTES

This tasty sausage is made by wrapping seasoned sausage meat in caul fat, then frying the roll until crisp. Caul fat is the sheetlike membrane extending from the stomach over the intestines; it can be purchased in some meat stores or might be available on special order. For making crépinettes, the sheet of fat should be soaked in warm water until it is pliable and then cut with kitchen shears into 4- to 6-inch squares or rectangles. Place a little sausage mix into each piece of caul fat, roll, and flatten slightly to about ½-inch thickness. (Some experts shape the meat into triangles, then wrap it accordingly, ending up with a sausage that resembles an arrowhead.) Fry until done. Enjoy.

Any good bulk sausage mix can be cooked by this method. If you want something special, try grinding 2 pounds of pork loin with 4 ounces of chopped truffles, all moistened with a good red wine.

CHAMPAGNE SAUSAGE

Here's an expensive sausage for special occasions. Be sure to sample the champagne while grinding the meat.

10 pounds pork butt or shoulder

3 tablespoons quatre épices

1½ tablespoons salt

12 ounces fresh mushrooms, finely chopped

1 dozen chicken eggs, whisked

2 bottles cold champagne

sheep casings

Cut the pork into chunks, spread them over your work surface, and sprinkle on the spice mix, salt, and chopped mushrooms. Grind the mix with a ⅛-inch plate (or grind it twice with a ³⁄₁₆-inch plate), then mix in the chicken eggs and champagne, saving a little champagne to sip while you stuff the meat into sheep casings, tying off every 6 inches or so. Bring some water to a boil in a large pot, add the sausage, and simmer for 15 minutes. Sauté the sausage in butter.

Variation: If you really want to spend lots of money, reduce the mushrooms and make up the bulk with chopped truffles.

SAUCISSES DE TOULOUSE

These plump sausages, made with chopped pork, are best stuffed into rather large hog casings.

10 pounds pork butt

4 tablespoons salt

4 tablespoons sugar

1 tablespoon quatre épices

1–2 cups water

large hog casings

Dice the meat and mix in the salt, sugar, and quatre épices. Place in a nonmetallic container, cover, and refrigerate overnight. Work in the water and stuff the mixture into hog casings, tying off in 6-inch links. Refrigerate for up to 2 days or freeze. To cook, simmer in water to make sure the pork is cooked through, then fry or grill. This sausage can also be used in soups and stews.

HERTER'S SOUP BOURBON

After claiming that bourbon whiskey was made from grape seeds in France during the Middle Ages, George Leonard Herter, coauthor of Bull Cook and Authentic Historical Recipes and Practices, *attributed this "authentic" soup to a cook employed by the Duke of Clermont. The Duke, Herter said, liked the soup so much that he ate it every Sunday, Tuesday, and Thursday. Being something of a fanatic about cauliflower as well as sausage, I was eager to test the recipe. But I couldn't in good conscience follow the directions. Herter starts off by boiling the cauliflower and celery for an hour before adding the sausage. This makes the cauliflower a little mushy, so I have cut back on the cooking times. Suit yourself.*

1 medium head cauliflower	¾ pound pork sausage
5 ribs celery with tops	salt and freshly ground pepper to taste
3 tablespoons fresh parsley	3 chicken eggs
2 green onions	

Heat 3 quarts of water in a large pot. Break up the head of cauliflower, cutting it into 2-inch pieces. Cut the celery into ½-inch slices, and mince the leaves. Mince the parsley. Cut the green onions and tops into ¼-inch pieces. Cut the sausages into ½- to ¾-inch wheels. As soon as the water starts boiling, add all the chopped ingredients as well as salt and pepper. Bring to a new boil, reduce the heat, cover, and simmer for 20 minutes. Whisk the eggs in a bowl with the aid of a fork. Then—here's the trick—add the eggs to the soup by dribbling them from the fork, then stirring them into the mixture, working with a small amount at a time. If all goes well, the egg will resemble noodles. Serve hot in soup bowls, along with buttered bread.

CHAPTER 10

SCANDINAVIAN SAUSAGES

The potato, which originated in the cool Andes region of South America, was not a big hit when the Spanish first took it to Europe. In fact, it became popular in Scandinavia long before it was generally accepted in many parts of the Continent. A major use of the potato was as an ingredient (possibly a filler) in sausages. Potato sausages are still popular; all the Scandinavian countries have at least one favorite recipe, usually made with beef, pork, and potatoes, and the same sausages pretty much can be found in strong Swedish, Danish, Norwegian, and Finnish communities in the United States and Canada. Some of the recipes call for cooked potatoes, some for raw potatoes.

The Vikings, I might add, brought the sausage idea to Scandinavia from the warmer parts of Europe. Because of the Scandinavian climate, the highly spiced and hard sausages didn't take hold as deeply as the softer kinds. On the other hand, the hard air-dried sausages, such as the Göteborg, were ideal for taking along on lengthy sea voyages and consequently did not go unnoticed by the Vikings.

POTATIS KORV

Here's a Swedish sausage made with cooked potatoes, pork, and beef. This recipe calls for only 4 pounds of meat, but note that it contains a large volume of potatoes.

10 pounds potatoes (peeled weight)

2 pounds lean beef

2 pounds fatty pork (such as butt)

2 large onions, chopped

10 cloves garlic, minced

2 tablespoons salt

1 tablespoon white pepper

½ tablespoon freshly ground black pepper

½ tablespoon ground allspice

½ teaspoon ground mace

½ teaspoon ground nutmeg

ham stock or chicken broth (or bouillon)

hog casings

Peel, dice, and boil the potatoes for about 10 minutes, or until they are done but not mushy. Cool and mash the potatoes, permitting a few small lumps. Cut the meat into chunks, mix in the onions, garlic, salt, and spices, and grind with a ³⁄₁₆-inch plate. Mix the potatoes and ground meat. Stuff into hog casings, tying off in 12-inch links. Tie the end of each link together, forming a ring. Heat some ham stock or chicken broth in a pot. Simmer the sausages for 45 minutes. Refrigerate. Serve hot or cold.

NORWEGIAN RAW POTATO SAUSAGE

Here's an excellent sausage that is seasoned, except for salt and pepper, during cooking. Be sure to try it.

5 pounds peeled potatoes

10 pounds pork butt or shoulder

1 large onion

1 tablespoon white pepper

salt

hog casings

6 cups chicken broth

3 bay leaves

1 tablespoon allspice

Dice the potatoes, meat, and onion. Mix on your work surface, sprinkling on the white pepper and 1 tablespoon of salt. Grind with a ³⁄₁₆-inch plate. Stuff into hog casings, tying off in 8-inch links. Sprinkle the links with salt and hang in a cool place overnight. To cook, bring the chicken broth to a boil, add the bay leaves, 1 teaspoon salt, and the allspice. Simmer the sausages for 1 hour. Serve hot.

PERUNAMAKKARA

According to The Complete Sausage Cookbook, *by Jack Sleight, this is the most popular of the Finnish homemade sausages. It is made with lean meats without the addition of animal fat.*

4 large potatoes	1 tablespoon ground ginger
7 pounds lean pork	1 teaspoon ground nutmeg
3 pounds lean beef	8 cups milk
salt	hog casings

Peel, boil, cool, and mash the potatoes. Cut the meats into chunks, mix, and spread out over your work surface. Sprinkle evenly with 1 tablespoon salt, the ground ginger, and nutmeg. Grind the mix with a ³⁄₁₆-inch plate. Mix in the mashed potatoes and milk. Stuff loosely into hog casings, tying off in 6-inch links. Sprinkle the links with salt and refrigerate overnight. For longer storage, freeze or soak in a brine made with 3 tablespoons salt per quart of water.

To cook, simmer the sausages for 15 minutes, pricking them here and there to keep them from bursting. Serve hot.

GÖTEBORG

This Swedish sausage, made of beef and pork, is stuffed into beef casings and air-dried.

6 pounds beef	2 tablespoons crushed peppercorns
4 pounds fatty pork butt (certified)	2 tablespoons minced fresh thyme
¾ cup salt	1 tablespoon ground cardamom
4 tablespoons ground mustard seed	2 cups dry sherry
4 tablespoons sugar	beef casings (middles)

Cut the meats into chunks suitable for grinding, sprinkle evenly with the salt, pack into a plastic tray, cover, and refrigerate for 48 hours. Spread the salty meats over your work surface, sprinkle with the spices and seasonings, and grind with a ³⁄₁₆-inch plate. Mix in the sherry and stuff into beef middle casings. Stuff the sausages tightly, trying to avoid any air bubbles. Hang the sausages to dry for 4 to 5 hours. Cold-smoke for 12 hours, then dry in a cool, airy place for 10 to 12 weeks, as discussed in chapter 3, Stuffing Sausages (page 121).

To cook, simmer the sausages in stews and soups.

MEDISTERPOLSE

This Danish pork sausage is made with finely ground pork that is stuffed into sheep casings. The recipe calls for beef stock, but it's okay to use canned broth or bouillon cubes with water.

10 pounds pork butt or shoulder

1 large onion, minced

3 tablespoons salt

1 tablespoon white pepper

1 teaspoon freshly ground black pepper

1 teaspoon ground cardamom

½ teaspoon ground allspice

½ teaspoon ground clove

2 cups beef stock

sheep casings

Cut the pork into chunks suitable for grinding, spread out on a work surface, sprinkle evenly with the onion and seasonings, grind with a ³⁄₁₆- or ¼-inch plate, and then grind twice more with a ⅛-inch plate. Work in the beef broth a little at a time. Stuff into sheep casings. To cook, fry or grill until well done, or simmer in broth for 10 minutes, then panfry. These can be refrigerated for a few days or frozen for longer storage.

CHAPTER 11

OTHER EUROPEAN SAUSAGES

Sausages are popular all over Europe, and many of the recipes are quite similar from one country to another. Indeed, the map of Europe tends to change faster than old cultural ties. Other recipes in remote regions are quite unique, as far as cookbooks go, and are not likely to have broad appeal for modern readers. On the island of Corsica, for example, one may find *tripa*—sheep casings stuffed with spinach, beets, herbs, and sheep's blood, cooked in salted water.

In any case, here are some European favorites to try, along with some classical recipes that call for sausage.

KIELBASA

The traditional Polish sausage, which is also popular in other European countries as well as in the United States, is called kielbasa. It is usually made with pork. Other meats can be added, but pork is the main ingredient. It is seasoned generously, and almost always contains garlic. The kielbasa sold in American markets is usually lightly smoked, but traditionally the sausage is consumed fresh. A middling to large sausage, it is sometimes stuffed in beef rounds. The larger hog casings will do. Kielbasa is about 12 inches long and 1½ inches in diameter. It is marketed in the shape of a horseshoe. The recipe below is rather basic.

10 pounds fatty fresh pork (butt will do), partially frozen

1 large onion, chopped

4 cloves garlic, minced

6 tablespoons salt

2 tablespoons Hungarian paprika

1 tablespoon coarsely ground black pepper

1 tablespoon red pepper flakes

1 teaspoon dried marjoram

2 cups ice water

beef casings or large hog casings

Cut the partially frozen meat into cubes. Spread the cubes out on your work surface, then sprinkle evenly with all the other ingredients except for the ice water and casings. Grind the meat with a ³⁄₁₆-inch plate, mix in the ice water thoroughly with your hands, and stuff in large hog casings or small beef rounds, tying off in 12-inch or longer lengths. Dry the sausages overnight in a cool, airy place or in your refrigerator. These sausages are best when simmered for an hour or so, or used in stews such as *bigos*, a Polish national stew. They are also delicious when baked at 425°F for 45 minutes, or when grilled slowly over charcoal.

These sausages can be cold-smoked for an hour or two for flavor, but they should not be considered cured. Note that most of the kielbasa sold in American supermarkets is lightly smoked and precooked.

Variations: Reduce the pork measure and add a little beef or veal. Also, vary the spices, adding, perhaps, a little allspice and summer savory.

BIGOS

This old stew was originally made with bear, venison, boar, and other game. These days, pork and beef are used, along with spicy sausage to flavor the whole.

¼ pound salt pork, diced

1 large onion, chopped

8–12 ounces fresh mushrooms, sliced

½ pound pork, cut into 1-inch cubes

½ pound beef, cut into 1-inch cubes

½ pound kielbasa, cut into 1-inch wheels

2 cups beef broth

½ cup white wine

1 tablespoon Hungarian paprika

1 teaspoon freshly ground black pepper

2 bay leaves

2 pounds sauerkraut

Fry the salt pork until crisp in a large stove-top dutch oven. Remove and drain the salt pork, leaving the drippings in the pot. Sauté the onion and mushrooms for 5 to 6 minutes. Brown the cubed pork and beef. Add the sausage, beef broth, wine, paprika, black pepper, and bay leaves. Bring to a boil, reduce the heat, cover, and simmer for 2 hours. Add the sauerkraut. Bring to a new boil, reduce the heat, and simmer for a few minutes. Serve hot, along with a hot crusty bread. Save the salt pork cracklings for salad or baked potatoes, or perhaps sprinkle them over each serving of bigos.

HUNTER'S POTATOES

Like bigos, this is an old hunter's dish, often made in camp. Leftovers are especially good, according to Jack Czarnecki, author of Joe's Book of Mushroom Cookery, *from which this recipe has been adapted. Like many good camp dishes, exact measurements of ingredients aren't necessary. The dish is best cooked in a large pot. I use a cast-iron, stove-top dutch oven.*

bacon strips

potatoes, sliced

carrots, sliced

fresh mushrooms, sliced

onions, sliced

kielbasa, sliced

salt and freshly ground black pepper

a few cabbage leaves (red or white)

Line the bottom of the pot with bacon strips. Add a layer of potatoes, carrots, mushrooms, onions, and sausage, in that order. Sprinkle with a little salt and pepper. Repeat the layers until the pot is full. Cover the layers with cabbage leaves and a tight lid. Place on low heat. Cook for 1 hour, or, if you prefer, bake in a 350°F oven for 1 hour.

BUCKWHEAT SAUSAGES

Buckwheat sausage of one sort or another is made in Russia and several other parts of Europe. Sometimes the sausage is made with the aid of blood, and sometimes with liver, trotters, or snouts, along with various other ingredients. I have added a little beef broth to the recipe below, just in case the buckwheat turns out a little on the dry side. Whole buckwheat groats can be purchased from King Arthur Flour (see Sources of Materials and Supplies, page 373) and possibly other outlets.

6 pounds fresh pork butt

3 tablespoons salt

2 tablespoons freshly ground black pepper

1 teaspoon ground dried marjoram

4 pounds cooked and cooled buckwheat groats

beef broth, if needed

hog casings

Cut the pork into chunks suitable for grinding, spread it over your work surface, and sprinkle evenly with the salt, pepper, and marjoram. Grind with a ¼- or ⅜-inch plate. Mix in buckwheat and some beef broth if needed. Stuff into hog casings. Cook by simmering the links in broth or by baking.

SMOKED HUNGARIAN SAUSAGE

The fresh pork used in this recipe should be about 25 percent fat. If in doubt, separate the lean meat and fat, using 6 pounds lean and 2 pounds fat.

8 pounds fresh Boston butt or picnic ham

2 pounds lean beef

¼ cup minced or crushed fresh garlic

¼ cup salt

1 tablespoon freshly ground black pepper

¼ cup Hungarian paprika, sweet or mild

2 teaspoons Prague Powder 1 (optional)

½ teaspoon ground clove

hog casings

Trim the meat, cut it into chunks, and spread out on your work surface, mixing it more or less equally. Sprinkle on the garlic. Thoroughly mix the salt, pepper, paprika, Prague Powder, and clove; sprinkle evenly on the meat.

Grind the meat using a ¼- or ⅜-inch plate. Stuff into hog casings, tying off in convenient lengths. Cold-smoke the meat for several hours at a temperature of less than 90°F. Or, if you have a small commercial unit, smoke it at 150°F or so for about an hour. If in doubt about the temperature, use a thermometer. (It's best to avoid the temperate range between 90°F and 150°F.) Air-dry the sausage in a cool, airy place for 2 days. Cook thoroughly before eating, remembering to punch a few holes in the casing. I like to cook these in a little oil in an electric skillet, tightly covered, so that the cooking process is a combination of frying and steaming.

The sausage will keep for several days in the refrigerator. Freeze for longer storage.

HURKA

In addition to paprikash recipes, the Hungarians also make an excellent sausage with cooked pork and rice.

5 pounds fatty pork (Boston butt or shoulder will do)
2 pounds pork heart
2 pounds pork jowl
1 pound pork liver
2 medium to large onions

lard
⅓ cup salt
1½ tablespoons freshly ground black pepper
¼ teaspoon ground dried marjoram
5 pounds cooked rice
medium hog casings

Cut the meats into chunks suitable for grinding, keeping the liver separate. Put the pork, heart, and jowl into a pot, cover with water, bring to a boil, reduce the heat, and simmer for 30 to 40 minutes; add the liver during the last 10 minutes. Drain, saving the stock. Chop and sauté the onions in a little lard. Spread the drained meats out on your work surface, mixing evenly. Sprinkle evenly with the salt, pepper, marjoram, and sautéed onions. Grind the meats with a ³⁄₁₆-inch plate. Using your hands, mix with the cooked rice and 1 cup of the stock from the boiled meats. Stuff into medium hog casings. Drop the links into boiling water for 1 to 2 minutes. Dry and refrigerate until needed. Freeze for longer storage.

Variations: Omit the liver if you prefer. If you like the liver, however, try a mix of 4 pounds butt, 2 pounds liver, 2 pounds lights (lungs), and 2 pounds heart. Also, use beef heart instead of pork if it is more readily available, and substitute pork belly for jowls if it is more convenient.

YUGOSLAVIAN BLOOD SAUSAGE

Several sausage recipes from the region once known as Yugoslavia call for pig's blood, along with the head, heart, lungs (or lights), and a pork butt. Unless you butcher your own hogs, it may be difficult to obtain all the ingredients. Here's a recipe, adapted from The Sausage-Making Cookbook, *by Jerry Predika, that is more easily managed. I find it interesting because it makes use of barley, one of my favorite groats.*

1½ cups dried pearl barley

4 pounds cooked pork butt

2 teaspoons vinegar

2 quarts fresh pork blood

1 cup sugar

1 teaspoon ground ginger

1 teaspoon ground allspice

2 tablespoons salt

hog casings

Soak the barley overnight in water. Cut the pork butt into chunks, cover with water, and simmer for 30 minutes. Drain, reserving the broth, and refrigerate the pork. Put 3 cups of the broth into a pot, bring to a boil, and add the barley. Simmer, covered, for 15 minutes. Add a little water if needed and simmer for another 5 minutes. Stir the vinegar into the pork blood. Grind the cooked pork with a ³⁄₁₆-inch plate. Mix in the other ingredients. Stuff into hog casings. Simmer the sausage for 15 minutes. Serve warm or chilled. Refrigerate for several days, or freeze for longer storage.

Note: For other interesting recipes for Yugoslavian blood sausages, see *The Sausage-Making Cookbook*, by Jerry Predika.

LITHUANIAN SAUSAGE

Here's an easy sausage recipe from Lithuania. Although heavy on onion, it is rather mild—and very good.

10 pounds pork butt

2 pounds minced onion

5 tablespoons salt

1 tablespoon coarse black pepper

1 tablespoon ground allspice

medium hog casings

Trim a little fat from the meat and heat it in a skillet until you fry out a little oil. Sauté the onion for a few minutes, until it turns transparent. Set aside. Cut the meat into chunks and sprinkle it with salt, pepper, and allspice. Grind with a ³⁄₁₆-inch plate. Mix in the cooked onion and any grease from the skillet. Stuff into medium hog casings, twisting into 5-inch connected lengths. Let dry to the touch. Heat some salted water in a large pot. Simmer (do not boil) the sausage links for about 20 minutes. Dry and refrigerate or freeze. To prepare for the table, brown the links nicely in a little oil or butter in a skillet.

MITITEI

Romanian sausages, of which there are several, tend to have some pleasant surprises in the ingredient list, such as dill seeds and lovage. Here's an all-beef recipe calling for baking soda, olive oil, and lots of parsley.

10 pounds beef (such as chuck roast)

¾ cup dried parsley

3 tablespoons salt

2 tablespoons baking soda

2 tablespoons freshly ground black pepper

15 cloves garlic, minced

2 cups water

1½ cups olive oil

medium hog casings

Cut the beef into chunks suitable for grinding, mix in the dry seasonings, and grind with a ³⁄₁₆-inch plate. Mix in the garlic, water, and olive oil. Stuff into hog casings. Dry and cook, refrigerate for a few days, or freeze. To cook, grill over charcoal, bake, or broil.

BULGARIAN VEAL OR LAMB SAUSAGES

I've seen several recipes for Bulgarian sausages, and all of them had one thing in common: a short list of ingredients. Here's one that is made from either beef or lamb. I tried it a couple of times, with great success, but I used 1 pound of meat (instead of 10) because I didn't want to store excess sausage that contained uncooked chicken eggs.

1 pound veal or lamb

1 medium onion, minced

1 large chicken egg

½ teaspoon salt

¼ teaspoon freshly ground black pepper

Cut the meat into chunks, then grind it twice with a ⅛- or ³⁄₁₆-inch plate. Mix in the other ingredients. Take out small portions with a tablespoon measure and roll into small sausages about 2 inches long. Fry, broil, or grill over charcoal. These require careful handling.

HOT-SMOKED SWISS SAUSAGE

Switzerland enjoys a number of sausages, mostly variations on German, French, and Italian themes, depending on the region and its influences. If there is a truly national Swiss sausage, it would probably be a farmer's recipe making good use of milk or cream, as in the following recipe, or some other dairy product. Because this sausage is hot-smoked, it's a good choice for backyard chefs. Note, however, that this sausage is very mild, which is typical of sausages from cold lands. Add a tablespoon of freshly ground black pepper if you long for it.

6 pounds beef chuck

4 pounds pork butt

salt

2 tablespoons caraway seed

1 tablespoon ground allspice

3 cups heavy cream

1 cup cold water

brown sugar to taste

medium hog casings

Cut the beef and pork into chunks suitable for grinding, spread the chunks out on your work surface, and sprinkle evenly with 4 tablespoons salt, the caraway seed, and allspice. Grind with a ³/₁₆-inch plate, then grind again with a ⅛-inch plate. Mix in the cream and water. Stuff into medium hog casings, tying off in 6-inch connected links. Sprinkle with salt and brown sugar. Refrigerate overnight. Also soak some hardwood chips in water. When you are ready to cook, build a charcoal fire on one side of a large grill. Place some wood chips on the fire. Hot-smoke the sausages for about 3 hours, or until done. (The lower the temperature, the longer the cooking time and the greater the smoke. Much depends on your fire, grill, draft settings, and so on.) If in doubt, check the internal temperature of the sausage before serving, making sure it is at least 150°F. This sausage can also be baked slowly in the oven.

GREEK SAUSAGE

Although sausage was mentioned in both The Iliad *and* The Odyssey, *as well as in other ancient writings, neither ancient nor modern Greece has left us a sausage of worldwide renown. I have read that the sausage originated in Greece, but this claim is difficult to prove. Who knows? The Greeks were very important in the history of the sausage, however, for they influenced the Silesians and Romans. Although several sausages are made in modern Greece, most of these are similar to European sausages. One exception, it seems to me, is the following, which uses orange zest.*

10 pounds pork butt

4 tablespoons salt

2 tablespoons dried coriander

1 tablespoon dried thyme

1 tablespoon dried marjoram

2 crushed bay leaves

2 cups red wine

3 tablespoons freshly grated orange zest

15 cloves garlic, minced

hog casings

Cut the pork into chunks suitable for grinding. Spread these out on your work surface, sprinkle evenly with the salt and dry ingredients, and grind with a 3/16-inch plate. Mix in the wine, orange zest, and garlic. Stuff into hog casings or shape into patties. Cook immediately, refrigerate for 2 days, or freeze. To cook, poach the sausage in a little simmering water for 10 minutes, dry, and grill or fry. These sausages can also be used in soups, stews, and casseroles. Try some in bulk form in a batch of Greek-style moussaka.

CHAPTER 12

MIDDLE EASTERN AND AFRICAN SAUSAGES

The vast area represented by the title of this chapter might suggest a long text, but the facts indicate that the sausage has not been very important in the culinary history of these lands. Indeed, we have to go all the way to South Africa to find a widespread passion for sausage, and even here the influence is probably more European (primarily Dutch) than African.

In the Middle East, the hog is not a very popular meat, owing mainly to religious and cultural traditions, and to the fact that the countryside is more suited to goats and sheep than to pigs. The region does not have the vast oak and beech forests that helped make the pig popular in Europe and, early on, in North America. Also, the Jews, Muslims, and Hindus forbid the use of pork in

any form, and there may be some resistance to blood and to the idea of stuffing meat into intestines. On the other hand, ground meat is very popular in the Middle East and North Africa. It is often shaped around flat skewers, and is sometimes made into little sausage shapes. Grilling over charcoal is a very popular way of cooking the meat, usually lamb, if we may trust modern Americanized cookbooks, but perhaps camel, goat, antelope, and other good meats as well. These ground meat fingers are very close to sausage without the casing, so I have included such a recipe from Algeria.

Lebanon bologna, I might explain before proceeding, is an American product, having been developed in Lebanon, Pennsylvania, and, as such, does not appear in this chapter.

214

ALGERIAN CASBAH SAUSAGES

Here's an excellent Algerian recipe for a sausage-shaped meat, adapted from The Grains Cookbook, *by Bert Greene.*

1 pound ground lamb

½ pound ground veal

1 tablespoon olive oil

¼ cup butter

1 medium to large onion, finely chopped

1 clove garlic, finely chopped

½ cup quick rolled oats

1 chicken egg, whisked

⅛ teaspoon ground allspice

¼ teaspoon ground cinnamon

2 tablespoons finely chopped fresh parsley

1 tablespoon fresh lemon juice

2 tablespoons water

salt and pepper to taste

hot pepper sauce to taste

Grind the meats with a ³⁄₁₆-inch plate. Heat the olive oil and about half the butter in a skillet, then sauté the onion and garlic for 4 to 5 minutes. Set aside. In a large bowl, mix the meats, oats, and egg. Add the sautéed onion and garlic, allspice, cinnamon, parsley, lemon juice, water, salt, pepper, and a little hot pepper sauce to taste. Mix thoroughly with your hands and shape into small sausage shapes. Heat the rest of the butter in the skillet. Add 5 or 6 of the sausages. Cook over medium heat until browned on all sides, which should take about 8 minutes for each batch. Serve hot.

ARMENIAN LAMB SAUSAGE

Here's an unusual sausage made of ground lamb and heavily flavored with fresh mint. Any good cut of lamb can be used. Try shoulder, which is usually available at meat shops. Be sure to make a lamb stew with the bones.

10 pounds boned lamb meat	15–20 cloves garlic, minced
3 tablespoons salt	1½ cups chopped fresh mint
1½ tablespoons freshly ground black pepper	2 cups water
2 cups finely chopped onion	sheep casings

Cut the meat into chunks, spread them out on your work surface, sprinkle with salt and black pepper, and grind with a ³⁄₁₆- or ⅛-inch plate. With your hands, mix in the onion, garlic, mint, and water. Stuff the mixture into sheep casings. These fresh sausages will keep in the refrigerator for several days, or they can be frozen for longer storage. To cook, grill over charcoal or broil in the oven. Try cutting them into chunks and grilling them on a skewer, along with suitable kebab vegetables; serve on rice.

MOROCCAN LAMB SAUSAGE

The North Africans make a lamb sausage similar to the Armenian recipe. In this Moroccan recipe, fresh chopped parsley takes the place of mint, and, predictably, more spices are added.

10 pounds boned lamb meat	1 tablespoon dried marjoram
3 tablespoons salt	1 teaspoon crushed cumin seed
1–2 tablespoons cayenne pepper	3 cups finely chopped onion
1 tablespoon freshly ground black pepper	3 cups finely chopped parsley
1 tablespoon dried oregano	2 cups water
1 tablespoon dried coriander	sheep casings

Cut the meat into chunks, spread them out on your work surface, sprinkle evenly with the dry spices, and grind with a ⅛- or ³⁄₁₆-inch plate. With your hands, mix in the onion, parsley, and water. Stuff the mixture into sheep casings. To cook, grill or broil. These sausages will keep for several days in the refrigerator, or they can be frozen for longer storage.

BOERISH SAUSAGE

Outdoor grilling is very popular in South Africa, where the cookout is known as braai. *These events call for freshly baked bread,* sosaties, *and a large round sausage called* boerewors. *The sosaties, of course, are lamb kebabs marinated with curry and other spices; the dish is of Malay origin, brought to southern Africa by Malaysian slaves of the Dutch settlers. The boerewors are of Dutch origin (possibly adapted for local South African meats such as aardvark). The bacon used in the recipe can, of course, be bacon ends and pieces, which are usually available at bargain prices.*

6 pounds lean beef	1 teaspoon ground nutmeg
2 pounds pork shoulder	1 teaspoon ground clove
2 pounds bacon	3 tablespoons salt
3 tablespoons ground coriander	2 cups vinegar
1 teaspoon freshly ground black pepper	hog casings

Cut the meats and bacon into chunks, mix together, and spread them out on a work surface. Sprinkle evenly with the dry spices and salt. Grind with a ¼- to ⅓-inch plate. Mix in the vinegar and refrigerate for 3 hours. Regrind with a ⅛-inch plate. Stuff into hog casings, tying off into 4- to 5-inch connected links. To cook, grill over charcoal or wood coals. Boerewors can also be baked in an oven or simmered for a few minutes in water or broth, then fried in a skillet.

CHAPTER 13

ASIAN SAUSAGES

Although the pig was first domesticated in China, the variety of sausages in that part of the world doesn't even begin to rival that of northern Europe. Typically, the Chinese sausage—called *lop chiang*—is hard, dry, strong, and on the sweet side. By contrast, the Thai like their sausage hot and spicy. The rest of Asia doesn't cook much sausage, and the island nations lean toward cooking the pig whole. Indonesians love pork sausages, but for the most part, these are made by recipes brought to the islands from Europe.

BASIC CHINESE SAUSAGE

Although the Chinese market a dried sausage made with only pork, pork fat, salt, and sugar, I consider soy sauce and rice wine to be essential to the real thing. Here's a standard recipe.

10 pounds fatty fresh pork	½ cup sugar
2 cups soy sauce	½ cup salt
2 cups rice wine	hog casings

Grind the meat with a ³⁄₁₆-inch plate. Mix in the rest of the ingredients and refrigerate for 2 days. Stuff the mixture into hog casings, tie off in 6-inch links, and dry in a cool, airy place for about 8 weeks. The links can also be cold-smoked for part of the curing period. After the drying period, I prefer to wrap them in plastic film and refrigerate or freeze them until needed. Being dry and hard, these sausages are best when steamed or simmered in stock, or used in various recipes. Typically, they are sliced diagonally before serving.

Variation: Note that the basic recipe doesn't contain any pepper. If you expect hot stuff in your sausage, try the Szechuan variety, made by adding ¼ cup crushed red pepper flakes and 1 tablespoon ground ginger to the above measures, along with 15 to 20 minced cloves of garlic. Cut the sugar measure in half.

HACKED CHICKEN AND CHINESE SAUSAGE

The Chinese sometimes cut a chicken into chunks, bones and all, before cooking it. It's a true hack job, like Kentucky Fried Chicken, but remember that the bones add to the flavor. To hack a bird, first disjoint it and then chop it into bite-size pieces with the aid of a meat cleaver. (If you prefer, first bone the chicken and then cut it into pieces with a regular knife. Then hack the bones and add them to the pot with the chicken.) For best results, use a barnyard or free-range chicken, plucked instead of skinned. If you use supermarket chicken with lots of fat, skin it. The recipe calls for dried Chinese forest mushrooms. These are available in Asian markets. They are very flavorful, but they are a little expensive. If you have dried morels or other dried mushrooms, use them.

1 ounce dried Chinese forest mushrooms	2 tablespoons soy sauce
1 chicken, about 3 pounds, cut into chunks	1 tablespoon rice wine, dry sherry, or vermouth
1 pound Chinese sausage, cut into chunks	1 tablespoon cornstarch

Soak the mushrooms in water for several hours, or overnight, then slice and drain them. Save the soaking liquid. Marinate the chicken, sausage, and sliced mushrooms for 2 to 3 hours in a nonmetallic container with a mixture of the soy sauce, wine, and cornstarch, along with 2 tablespoons of the liquid in which the mushrooms were soaked. Drain the chicken, discarding the marinade liquid.

Rig for steaming. If you don't have a steamer, pour a little water into a pot or wok, fit with a rack (which should be above the water level), and bring to a boil. Place the pieces of chicken onto the rack, cover with the sausage and mushrooms, and steam for about 45 minutes, or until the chicken is tender. Serve hot, along with rice, Chinese vegetables, and condiments of your choice, plus, perhaps, a dipping sauce.

CHINESE PILAN

Rice and sausage go together nicely, and the Chinese (before mechanical refrigeration became common) even stored dried sausages in the rice crock. They have an easy way of flavoring rice with sausage. Simply cook the rice as usual, but place some links of sausage on top. (There are many ways of cooking rice, but for this recipe, I use the more or less standard 2 cups of water for every 1 cup of rice, simmered without peeking for 20 minutes.) Be sure to prick the sausage links so that the juice will run down into the rice. When done, cut the sausages into thin slices and serve them along with the rice. Many peasant families serve only the sausage and rice for a meal, but, of course, they add steamed vegetables and other dishes for company.

Note that any good sausage can be cooked with rice by this method. If you don't have Chinese fare at hand, try dried chorizo for a Spanish touch or a pepperoni for Italian.

STEAMED CHINESE SAUSAGES AND CHICKEN EGGS

Sausages and chicken eggs go together nicely in most lands. The Chinese, however, are more likely to use duck eggs. Because duck eggs aren't readily available in most American markets, I have substituted chicken eggs in the ingredients. If you've got fresh duck eggs, use 4 instead of 6.

½ pound Chinese sausage, thinly sliced

½ pound fresh pork, chopped into ½-inch pieces

6 chicken eggs, whisked

1 small to medium onion, minced

2 green onions, minced with part of the green tops

½ cup chicken or duck stock

2 tablespoons light soy sauce

1 tablespoon peanut oil

1 teaspoon sugar

salt to taste

Rig for steaming and heat the water to a boil. Mix all the ingredients in a bowl of suitable size, which should allow at least 1 inch of space at the top for expansion. Carefully place the bowl on a rack in the steamer pot or wok. Cover tightly. Steam on medium-low heat for about 45 minutes. Serve hot. Conveniently, this dish can be cooked ahead of time, cooled, and resteamed.

SPICY THAI SAUSAGES

The Thai love sausages and have several sorts, all highly spiced. This version, adapted from the book True Thai, *by Victor Sodsook, is one of my favorite sausages because I love fish sauce. Although I have mixed feelings about most commercial curry powder, I do use canned red curry paste in this recipe. Sticklers for true Thai will choose to make their own curry paste.*

The recipe also calls for fresh kaffir lime leaves. If these are not available (fresh), substitute freshly grated lime zest. The fresh leaves are better, however, partly because they contribute green flecks to the sausages, as do the cilantro stems. (If you grow your own cilantro, as I do, you can also use some of the roots in this recipe. Also, the seeds of the cilantro plant, when ground, are the same as coriander.)

My version of the recipe also calls for only 1 pound of fatty meat (I usually use pork butt or shoulder), whereas True Thai, *I should point out, specified ¾ pound loin or tenderloin, which is very dry. Suit yourself. In either case, it's best to make a small batch of this sausage. Then, if you like the flavor, you can easily make a 10-pound batch simply by increasing the measures tenfold.*

1 pound fatty pork	1 tablespoon white pepper
12 fresh kaffir lime leaves or ½ teaspoon fresh lime zest	½ teaspoon crushed or ground coriander
½ cup chopped fresh garlic	½–1 tablespoon canned red curry paste
¼ cup finely chopped cilantro stems	1 tablespoon Thai fish sauce
	hog casings

Cut the meat into chunks and mix in the kaffir lime leaves, garlic, cilantro stems, white pepper, coriander, curry paste, and fish sauce. Grind the mixture with a ³⁄₁₆-inch plate. Mix again with your hands, then stuff it into medium hog casings, tying off every 4 inches. Refrigerate the links in a covered nonmetallic container overnight. Cook as needed, or freeze for longer storage.

Although these are rather spicy sausages, the Thai often serve them as an entree, along with suitable condiments, instead of using them to season other dishes in the Chinese manner.

BANGKOK FRY

The method of cooking these sausages is nothing new to connoisseurs, but the manner of serving them is likely to be unusual to culinary sports of the Western world. Having been raised on a peanut farm, I was especially interested in the recipe. (The Thai, by the way, are one of the few peoples who enjoy boiled green peanuts. I used to sell these around our town when I was a boy.)

1 lemon	fresh gingerroot
chili peppers	small lettuce or salad greens
cilantro	peanut oil
peanuts	Thai sausages
cucumber	

Prepare the condiments first, arranging them (unmixed) as you go on a serving platter. Cut off the ends of the lemon but do not peel it. Slice it into ½-inch wheels, then dice them. Seed and chop the chili peppers. Chop the cilantro. Chop the peanuts. Peel, seed, and slice the cucumber. Peel the gingerroot, then slice it very, very thinly. Select some small cup-shaped leaves of lettuce or other suitable salad greens. When the condiment platter is ready, quickly heat about 2 tablespoons of peanut oil in a heavy skillet. Cut the sausages into separate links, prick the links with a fork, and sauté them until nicely browned and cooked through, turning frequently. This should take about 10 minutes. Drain the sausages, cut them into 1-inch wheels, arrange them on a serving platter, and serve them with the condiments.

Each piece of sausage and a selection of condiments are wrapped in a lettuce leaf and eaten by hand, giving each diner a choice. This method permits me to pass on the cucumber, which doesn't agree with me, and will permit guests to vary the amount of chili or ginger. Serve with Thai beer.

GRILLED THAI SAUSAGE

Build a charcoal fire. Grill the sausage links slowly, turning from time to time, until they are nicely browned and cooked through. Cut the grilled sausages into 1-inch wheels, then serve with Thai condiments, as discussed in the Bangkok fry recipe.

Add some wood chips to the fire if you want some smoke. The Thai sometimes sprinkle the fire with dried coconut meat (left over from making coconut milk) to sweeten the smoke. They also wrap the sausage in banana leaves before grilling.

CHAPTER 14

AMERICAN AND CANADIAN SAUSAGES

I've seen hundreds of recipes for American and Canadian sausages, but the truth is that we are a nation of immigrant sausages. Not counting numerous local favorites and some brand names, only one American sausage has made a name for itself—Lebanon bologna. The real contribution that the New World made to sausage was the hot chili pepper. Another contribution (for better or worse) was even more basic, having to do with the nature of the meat.

Let me explain. In North America, the settlers found the hog to be highly adaptable, and, of course, the hog was easy for homesteaders to butcher compared to beef. The hog quickly became by far the main meat in North America and remained so until a network of railroads was built to haul cattle from western ranches to eastern markets.

At first, hogs were allowed to roam free in almost all areas. At homesteads on the barrier islands of North Carolina, for example, the inhabitants fenced in the houses and turned the hogs loose, usually with various notches cut in the ear for identification. Trained dogs were used to round up and catch the hogs in the fall of the year. One problem was that acorns usually made up a large part of the hogs' diet at that time of the year, and many of the American oaks produce very bitter acorns compared to European species. (There are exceptions, such as the white oak and live oak, which produce acorns with sweet meat and lots of usable oil.) The American acorns tended to cause the meat from the hogs to be bitter. So, the American settlers started penning up the hogs to fatten them for the slaughter. The pen, of course, also kept the hogs away from the acorns.

In Virginia, peanuts were used to fatten the hogs, and even today the famous Smithfield hams are made from hogs fattened on peanuts. As stated in the last chapter, I was born and raised on a peanut farm, so the idea has long been with me. At least in my neck of the woods, an entire peanut field (sometimes hundreds of acres) was fenced in and the hogs were loosed on it, free to root the nuts out of the ground. More likely, the peanuts were harvested and then the hogs were turned loose in the field to eat the nuts that were lost during the harvest. Corn was also "hogged off" in the same way, and I've known farmers to plant soybeans (runners) in corn just for forage. A few people even planted fields of chufas to fatten their hogs.

Also, many households in towns and country made use of just about anything edible, such as parsley and pigweeds, to feed a few pigs. In the Ozarks, an edible oak gall was fed to the hogs, along with table scraps. Slopping the hogs in troughs was an everyday household chore in some cases. Where I grew up, even cane skimmings (top scum and dredgings left from boiling cane juice down to syrup) were used to feed the hogs. Sometimes this stuff fermented, making the pigs tipsy.

I want to emphasize that hogs weren't only farm animals. Many small-town homes had a pigpen—and hogs were raised even in the cities. New York, I understand, permitted street hogs until well into the nineteenth century. The hogs helped control the garbage, just as they had done for centuries in European cities such as Rome and Paris. When a law forbidding the practice was passed in New York, the housewives, if we may believe food historian Waverley Root, armed themselves with broomsticks to fight off the hog carts. Of course, all the great cities of Europe used the hog as a garbage disposal.

In any case, the making of the great American no-name sausage—with thousands of variations—took place at the homestead. Most of these sausages were made of fatty scraps of meat at hog-killing time. While these sausages are very good and practical, some producers began to take pride in using whole shoulders and hams in their sausages instead of mere scraps. Some connoisseurs made what came to be known as whole-hog sausage.

But as a rule, the home sausage was kept on the simple side. Salt, black pepper, sage, and red pepper flakes were often the only seasonings used. I can tell you from personal experience that hog-killing time—usually at first frost in the fall of the year—was special in many areas, and these simple sausages were the best of all. Some of these recipes were set forth in chapter 1, Easy Sausages (page 99), but it would be impossible to cover them all.

To back up a little: Penning up the hogs so that they couldn't eat bitter acorns resulted in a fatter pig. This wasn't a bad trait at the time, since lard was a very, very important cooking medium. From a purely culinary viewpoint, lard is still very good for cooking purposes. During my boyhood, lard was still very important, and at our house, we had several 5-gallon containers called lard cans. These days, of course, animal fat is frowned upon by health experts, and we are seeing a trend toward leaner and leaner pigs.

In addition to the typical North American household sausages, many communities made sausages from Old World recipes. In addition, ethnic communities (such as

Chinatown) in various cities, often seaports, made traditional sausages, changing the recipes a little over a period of time. One other New World influence on sausages developed around French and Mexican sausages, modifying the recipes and also developing distinctive dishes making use of these sausages as an ingredient, for example, gumbo and menudo. These traditions and recipes were covered in previous chapters.

LEBANON BOLOGNA

This all-beef bologna has a distinctive sour flavor that is hard to duplicate at home because it, like a true Smithfield ham, goes through a highly controlled environmental process. One of the Lebanon bologna recipes I have seen calls for Prague Powder 2, corn syrup solids, powdered dextrose, and the starter culture Fermento. After being salted and cured for 5 to 6 days at 38°F to 40°F, it is mixed with spices and the additives, stuffed into large "protein-lined" casings, and hung to dry in three stages: 16 hours at 90°F with 90 percent humidity; 28 hours at 105°F with 85 percent humidity; and 6 hours at 110°F with 85 percent humidity. The sausage is said to develop its tangy flavor during these 50 hours of curing. It can then be heavily smoked for a day or two. For a fully cooked product, the smokehouse temperature is increased to 150°F. The sausage is then smoked until the internal temperature reaches 137°F, when it is removed from the smokehouse and allowed to cool down to 110°F. Finally, it is placed in a cooler and aged for 4 to 5 days.

I haven't tested the recipe because I don't have the facilities to control the temperature and humidity.

If you want to go the whole nine yards, check into Rytek Kutas's book Great Sausage Recipes and Meat Curing. *Meanwhile, you may want to hazard the following.*

10 pounds lean beef	¼ teaspoon sodium nitrate
2 ounces salt	1 teaspoon dried mustard
2 ounces sugar	1 teaspoon ground ginger
¼ teaspoon sodium nitrite	½ teaspoon ground mace
1 tablespoon white pepper	large casings (5-inch diameter)
1 tablespoon Hungarian paprika	

Cut the beef into ½- to ¾-inch chunks and place them in a large plastic tray. Mix a cure by combining the salt, sugar, and sodium nitrite. Sprinkle the cure evenly over the beef, tossing to coat all sides. Cover the tray and refrigerate for 8 days at about 35°F. Remove the tray and mix in the other ingredients. Grind with a ³⁄₁₆-inch plate. Regrind, preferably with a ⅛-inch plate. Stuff into the casings. Hang and cold-smoke for 5 or 6 days. After smoking, hang the links in the refrigerator until needed. For extended storage, you may prefer to freeze the links.

FARM SAUSAGE

As stated earlier, the great American sausage is a product of hog-killing time and is made from fatty scraps accumulated during the butchering process. These sausages are very good, although they are a little on the fatty side and tend to shrink up when cooked. If you don't have a fat pig to kill, the mix can be approximated by using 8 or 9 parts fatty pork butt or shoulder mixed with 1 or 2 parts pure fat, as from fresh fatback. Since the pork butt or shoulder is about 30 percent fat, the result is a sausage that is about half fat. Some country recipes call for red pepper flakes, and some don't. I like to use lots of mild red pepper flakes, but be warned that some commercial red pepper is very hot and some is not. The sage is also optional, but I recommend it.

8 pounds pork butt

2 pounds fatback or other pork fat

5 tablespoons salt

1 tablespoon coarsely ground black pepper

1 tablespoon red pepper flakes (optional)

½ tablespoon dried minced sage (optional)

hog casings

Cut the pork and fat into chunks suitable for grinding. Mix and spread the chunks out on your work surface. Combine all the seasonings, then sprinkle evenly over the meat. Grind a little of the meat with a ³⁄₁₆- or ⅛-inch plate. Shape a patty and fry it in a skillet. Taste and adjust the seasonings if required. Grind the meat and stuff into hog casings.

To cook these fresh pork sausages, simmer the links in a little water, covered tightly, for about 15 minutes. Dry the links with paper towels and fry them in a skillet until nicely browned. Many people will prefer the sausage merely fried, omitting the simmering. This sausage can also be used in recipes.

TOM BAXTER'S BEST

Mr. Tom Baxter, an old friend of my father's, managed some farms owned by a Ford tractor dealer at a time when small tractors were replacing mules and workhorses. The dealer, who also had other business interests as well as culinary yearnings, traveled frequently and sometimes took Mr. Tom with him for company and to help with the driving. Toward the end of his days, Mr. Tom was recounting his culinary experiences, describing the menus in fancy restaurants from New Orleans to New York. But the best thing he had ever eaten, he said, his mouth watering, was homemade sausage, biscuits, and syrup. He was talking about locally made cane syrup. His sausage, as I remember it, was hot with red pepper flakes. I, too, have eaten, albeit infrequently, in New Orleans and New York, and, for brute flavor, I'll have to agree with Mr. Tom.

CHAPTER 15

DELI FARE AND COLD CUTS

Be warned that the recipes in this chapter yield sausages and sandwich meats that are different from their modern supermarket counterparts. Most of the commercial franks, for example, have a spongy texture and a slick surface, and contain lots of emulsified fat. The recipes herein yield a firmer and more flavorful sausage or sandwich meat. The casings of the homemade kinds, however, along with the firmer stuffings, do make the sausages a little tougher. Or different. You may be able to make a closer approximation of the commercial fare by zapping the meat in a high-speed food processor, as explained in chapter 1, Easy Sausages (page 99), but remember that consistent results are difficult to achieve with home equipment. Besides, who wants to know how to do the wrong thing?

FRANKFURTER

Also known as hot dogs, wieners, wienerwurst, and franks, this is perhaps the world's most widely known sausage. Homemade hot dogs are so different from those sold in our supermarkets that we have to question the name. Countless recipes exist for franks, sometimes with a different ratio of beef to pork and always with a different set of spices. Try mine, below, then experiment.

6 pounds pork butt or shoulder	1 tablespoon ground coriander
4 pounds beef	2 teaspoons ground mace
4 tablespoons salt	8 cloves garlic, minced
1½ tablespoons white pepper	3 cups water
1 tablespoon Hungarian paprika	sheep casings

Cut the meat into chunks suitable for grinding, mix, and spread them over your work surface. Sprinkle evenly with the seasonings and garlic. Grind with a ³⁄₁₆-inch plate, then grind again with a ⅛-inch plate. Mix in the water and stuff into sheep casings, tying off in 6-inch lengths. Simmer them in hot water—do not boil, lest the links burst open—for 15 minutes or so, or until they float. Fat franks may require a longer simmering time before they float. Pat the franks dry with paper towels and refrigerate or freeze until needed. Although cooked, these are usually heated before making hot dogs, or they are reheated or cooked in another recipe.

Smoked Frankfurters: Proceed as above until the links have been stuffed. Air-dry, then cold-smoke (at 120°F or less) for about 2 hours, using any good hardwood. After smoking, proceed with the simmering.

HOT DOGS

The essential ingredients for hot dogs include the bun, the dog, and condiments like mustard and toppings such as chopped onion or sauerkraut. These are very good when made with simmered franks, but they can be improved simply by grilling or broiling.

If you use a plain steamed or boiled frank, it's best to have a soft bun, preferably steamed, and add a chili meat sauce (made with finely ground pork) and chopped onions.

WIENER ROAST AND GRILLED DOGS

Build a charcoal or wood fire and let it burn down to coals, or rake some coals aside from the main fire. Stick a dog onto the end of a skewer or pointed stick and hold it over the coals, turning as needed, until it is nicely browned or perhaps charred. Place it into a fresh hot-dog bun and, using the bun for a grip, pull it off the stick. Spread on a little mayonnaise, catsup, and mustard. Chopped onion, pickle relish, and other go-withs help, but if you are cooking around a campfire, it's best to keep things simple.

On the patio, the hot dogs can be grilled, in which case skewering isn't necessary for turning and handling. Use tongs.

In the kitchen, the hot dogs can be cooked on a stove-top grill and served at the table, along with a wide choice of condiments and go-withs.

GOOD OL' BOY WIENER ROAST

Build a hot charcoal fire in a large grill. Slit each wiener down the middle, insert a thin strip of cheese, and spiral a strip of thin bacon around the wiener. Secure the bacon with toothpicks or skewers. Grill over hot coals, turning as needed with tongs, until the bacon is ready to eat. Because these dogs drip lots of grease on the fire, they should be moved about on the grill to avoid flare-ups. It's best to have a large surface area. When the dogs are almost ready to eat, sprinkle lightly with Hungarian paprika. These can be eaten in a bun, but I like them on their own, served on a plate with lots of potato chips, baked beans, and other go-withs.

Variation: These dogs can also be baked or broiled. In either case, remember that the bacon will drip grease. I use a broiling pan as a grease catcher, fitted with a rack for holding the dogs.

CORN DOGS

At fairs and other jubilees, corn dogs are often served on sticks. If you are feeding children or if your good ol' boys have been drinking, it's best to use a skewer without a sharply pointed end. The large cookers and fish fryers heated by bottled gas make it easy to deep-fry these for outdoor events.

1 cup fine stone-ground yellow cornmeal

1 cup flour

2 tablespoons sugar

salt to taste

½ tablespoon baking powder

2 tablespoons lard or vegetable shortening

¾ cup milk

1 chicken egg, whisked

1 pound 6-inch hot dogs

cooking oil for deep-frying

Rig for deep-frying, heating the oil to 350°F. Mix the cornmeal, flour, sugar, salt, and baking powder in a bowl. Cut in the lard, mixing until the mixture forms crumbs. Stir in the milk and egg. Insert wooden skewers into the end of each hot dog and dip into the batter. Deep-fry the hot dogs, a few at a time, for 3 to 5 minutes, or until nicely browned. Drain. Serve with catsup and mustard.

TEXAS WIENERS

In The Only Texas Cookbook, *Linda West Eckhardt says that this sausage can be stuffed into ¾-inch casings (probably goat, she says) and be called wieners; or it can go into 1½-inch casings and be called knockwurst. The recipe below has been adapted from the book—but I choose to call them Texas Wieners.*

4 pounds lean beef

4 pounds lean pork

2 pounds fatty bacon ends

5 tablespoons salt

4 teaspoons sugar

2 tablespoons ground coriander

2 teaspoons ground mace

1 cup minced onion

10 cloves garlic, minced

2 cups cold water

sheep, goat, or hog casings

Chop the meats and fat into chunks suitable for grinding. Mix the chunks well and spread them out on your work surface. Mix the salt, sugar, coriander, and mace; sprinkle evenly over the meats. Grind with a ¼- or ³⁄₁₆-inch plate. Grind again with a ⅛-inch plate. Mix in the onion, garlic, and water. Stuff into sheep (or goat) casings for regular wieners or into hog casings for jumbos, tying off in 6-inch lengths. Place the stuffed sausages into a pot, cover with water, bring to a boil, and simmer for 10 minutes. Drain. Refrigerate until cooking time, or freeze. To cook, prick the sausages with a needle, then grill, broil, poach, steam, or bake. Be sure to try these on a grill, perhaps beside chicken, lamb chops, or beefsteaks.

ITALIAN SALAMI

Here's a recipe for a rather dry Italian-style salami, seasoned mostly with white pepper and a few red pepper flakes. It's my favorite for topping a cracker or, when thinly sliced, for helping fill a submarine or other sandwich. Note, however, that this sausage is not cooked. People who are bothered by this fact should know that jerky, gravlax, caviar, prosciutto, and ceviche are not cooked either. Anyone who prefers a fully cooked salami for noshing fare is encouraged to see the next recipe and Larry's Four-Day Venison Salami (page 253).

6 pounds pork butt (certified)	2 tablespoons ground white pepper
4 pounds beef	2 tablespoons whole white peppercorns
8 tablespoons salt	15 cloves garlic, minced
4 tablespoons sugar	2 cups dry red wine
1–2 tablespoons crushed red pepper	beef casings (middles)

Cut the meat into chunks suitable for grinding. Spread the chunks out in a plastic tray, sprinkle evenly with the salt, cover, and refrigerate for 3 days. Spread the cured meat out over your work surface and sprinkle evenly with the sugar, crushed red pepper, and ground white pepper. (Hold the peppercorns for now.) Grind the mix with a ³⁄₁₆-inch plate. Mix in the peppercorns, minced garlic, and wine. Stuff into beef casings, linking every 6 to 10 inches. Hang in a cool, dry place for 10 to 14 weeks, depending on the diameter of the salami. During the drying process, the salami will lose 30 to 40 percent of its weight. A few days of cold-smoking, if desired, should be considered part of the drying time. After drying, no mechanical refrigeration is required if the sausage can be hung in a cool, dry place. The links can, of course, be stored in the refrigerator or frozen.

If you want to cook the salami before eating, or use it in fully cooked recipes or for sandwiches and cracker snacks, simmer it in water for about 15 minutes per inch of thickness. Slices, of course, can be cooked quicker.

Variation: If you want to use a cure in addition to the salt, add 2 teaspoons of Prague Powder 1 or saltpeter mix, discussed in chapter 3, Stuffing Sausages (page 121), being certain to mix the cure thoroughly into the salt. The cure mixes using sodium nitrate, sodium nitrite, or saltpeter will give the salami a redder color.

SUBMARINE WITH SALAMI

Also called the poor boy, this great American sandwich was invented during the Great Depression at a wharf restaurant in New Orleans. Typically, it is made with slices of sandwich meats and cheeses. Although the original was probably made with sliced roast beef and ham, I can't imagine it without salami and thinly sliced tomato! The bread should be a whole small loaf, 8 inches or longer, and on the chewy side.

subway loaf	thinly sliced tomato
mayonnaise	thinly sliced onion
prepared mustard	thinly sliced red bell pepper
shredded lettuce	thinly sliced green bell pepper
sliced salami	sliced olives
sliced bologna	sliced pickled pepper (optional)
sliced ham or turkey	salt and freshly ground black pepper
sliced Swiss cheese	oil and vinegar (optional)
sliced American cheese	

Cut the bread loaf in half crosswise. Spread mayonnaise and mustard on the bottom. Sprinkle on a layer of lettuce. Add overlapping slices of salami and other sandwich meats. Overlap a layer of Swiss and American cheeses. Top with a layer of tomatoes, onions, bell peppers, olives, and, if desired, pickled hot peppers. Sprinkle with salt and freshly ground pepper, then drizzle on a little oil and vinegar, if desired. Replace the top half of the loaf. Enjoy. This is a complete meal.

HOT-SMOKED SALAMI

This salami is lightly smoked and fully cooked. Be sure to try it in sandwiches.

6 pounds beef

4 pounds pork butt

6 tablespoons salt

2 tablespoons whole white peppercorns

1 tablespoon freshly ground black pepper

1 tablespoon ground coriander

1 tablespoon ground cardamom

1 tablespoon ground mace

2 cups ice water

6 cloves garlic, minced

beef casings

Cut the meats into chunks suitable for grinding. Mix all the dried spices and seasonings; sprinkle evenly over the meats. Grind with a ³⁄₁₆-inch plate. Grind again with a ⅛-inch plate. Mix in the ice water and garlic. Stuff into beef casings. Cold-smoke for 1 to 2 hours, then increase the heat in the smokehouse to 170°F. Hot-smoke for several hours, or until the internal temperature of the salami reaches 150°F. Rinse in hot water, then dry and refrigerate for 12 hours or so before serving. This salami will keep for several days in the refrigerator. Freeze for longer storage.

BEEF SALAMI

This all-beef salami, lightly smoked, is not cured. It can be eaten without cooking, but see the introduction to Italian salami (page 232).

8 pounds lean beef

2 pounds beef fat

6 tablespoons salt

1 tablespoon ground white pepper

1 teaspoon freshly ground black pepper

1 tablespoon sugar

1 tablespoon ground coriander

2 tablespoons whole white peppercorns

6 cloves garlic, minced

1 cup dry red wine

beef casings (middles)

Cut the meat and fat into chunks suitable for grinding, sprinkle evenly with the salt (keeping the lean and fat separate), spread the chunks out in a plastic tray, cover, and refrigerate for 3 days. Spread the lean meat out over your work surface and sprinkle evenly with the ground white pepper, black pepper, sugar, and coriander. (Hold the peppercorns for now.) Grind the mix with a ⅛-inch plate. Then grind the fat with a ¼-inch plate. Combine the meat and fat, mixing in the white peppercorns, minced garlic, and wine. Stuff into beef casings, linking every 6 to 10 inches. Cold-smoke for several hours, then hang in a cool, dry place for 8 to 10 weeks, depending on the diameter of the salami.

Slice this salami thinly for cold cuts, snacks, and sandwiches, or use it in recipes that call for salami. It can be fully cooked by steaming or by simmering in water for about 15 minutes per inch of diameter.

Variation: Add 2 teaspoons of saltpeter cure and omit an equal amount of salt. Thoroughly mix the cure with the rest of the salt before curing the meat.

CALABRESE SALAMI

This highly spiced, hot salami is from the Calabria region of southern Italy. Be warned that the recipe is quite hot; you may want to cut back on the red pepper flakes or, better yet, use some mild red pepper flakes.

10 pounds pork butt (certified)

8 tablespoons salt

3–6 tablespoons hot red pepper flakes

2 tablespoons whole white peppercorns

1 tablespoon crushed dried fennel

10 cloves garlic, minced

1 cup brandy

1 cup vermouth

beef casings or large hog casings

Cut the meat into cubes suitable for grinding. Sprinkle with salt, put into a plastic tray, cover, and refrigerate for 48 hours. Spread the meat out, sprinkle with the dried seasonings, and grind with a ³⁄₁₆-inch plate. Mix in the garlic, brandy, and vermouth. Stuff into casings, dry, and hang in a cool place for 8 to 10 weeks.

Variation: Add 2 teaspoons of saltpeter cure and omit an equal amount of salt. Thoroughly mix the cure with the rest of the salt before curing the meat.

BOLOGNA

This old sausage originated during the fifteenth century in Bologna, Italy. Since then, it has spread over the world. Today, it is usually made with part pork and part beef mixed with ice or ice water. The water helps give it a fine texture. The texture of modern-day market bologna can be approximated at home more or less by emulsifying the meat in a food processor. But you may prefer bologna made the old-fashioned way. I do.

6 pounds lean beef	1 teaspoon ground coriander
6 tablespoons salt (divided in half)	1 teaspoon ground mace
4 pounds fatty pork (butt will do)	4 cups ice water
2 tablespoons white pepper	beef round casings or muslin bags

Cut the beef into cubes and grind it with a ½- or ⅜-inch plate. Sprinkle it with about half the salt and cure it in a cool place for 2 days. Cut, grind, and salt-cure the pork for 2 days. Mix the cured meats on your work surface. Thoroughly mix all the dried spices, then sprinkle the mix over the meats. Grind the meats with a ⅛-inch plate; if a ³⁄₁₆-inch plate is the smallest you have, grind it twice. Slowly add the ice water, working the mixture with your hands as you go. Continue to work the mixture until it becomes rather sticky to the touch. This may take 30 minutes. Stuff the mixture into beef rounds or muslin bags, making fat links about a foot long. Hang the links overnight in a cool place. In a large pot, heat some water to a boil. Simmer the links (do not boil) on low heat for 30 minutes, or until the internal temperature of the center of the sausage reaches 150°F to 160°F. (Some experts say to cook it until it squeaks when pressed and released with your finger. I think the thermometer is more reliable.) Immerse the links into ice-cold water, hang to dry, and refrigerate. This bologna will keep for a week in the refrigerator. Freeze it for longer storage. Being precooked, it can be sliced and used for sandwich meat, or it can be cooked again in recipes. I like to slice it thick and grill, broil, or panfry it.

Variations: If you want to add smoke flavor to the bologna, do so immediately after it is stuffed, using a cold smoke (less than 100°F). Then cook it in the simmering water, cool, dry, and refrigerate. For another variation, mix 1 to 2 cups of grated onion with the meat before stuffing.

SMOKED BEEF BOLOGNA

10 pounds good beef (such as chuck)

4 tablespoons salt

1 cup sugar

2 tablespoons white pepper

½ tablespoon freshly ground black pepper

1 tablespoon ground coriander

10 cloves garlic, minced

3 cups ice water

beef or large hog casings

Cut the beef into cubes, sprinkle with the salt and sugar, and refrigerate for 24 hours. Spread the beef out on your work surface and sprinkle evenly with the white pepper, black pepper, coriander, and minced garlic. Grind with a ⅜-inch plate. Grind again with a ⅛-inch plate. (Or grind twice with a 3/16-inch plate.) Mix in the ice water, working the mix with your hands. Stuff the mixture into beef rounds or large hog casings. Dry and cold-smoke for 2 to 3 hours. Plunge into a large pot of hot water. Simmer at about 200°F (do not boil) for an hour or longer, or until the internal temperature of the bologna reaches 150°F. Hang to dry the surface, then refrigerate or freeze.

LIVERWURST

This sausage should be more of a sandwich spread or cracker snack than a sliceable product. As such, it is packed into large casings and scooped out with a spoon or other utensil. There are many recipes, often calling for drastically different ratios of liver to pork. The measures below are about average. If you really like liver, add more and reduce the pork by an equal amount. If you don't like liver, maybe you're looking at the wrong recipe.

6 pounds pork butt	1 teaspoon ground sage
4 pounds hog liver	1 teaspoon ground nutmeg
salt	1 teaspoon ground ginger
2 tablespoons sugar	2 cups grated onion
1½ tablespoons ground white pepper	beef casings (middles)

Cut the pork into chunks, put it into a pot, cover with water, bring to a boil, and simmer for 30 minutes. Drain. Cut the liver into chunks and simmer it for 10 to 15 minutes. When cool, combine the pork and liver, mixing evenly on a work surface. Sprinkle evenly with 5 tablespoons salt, the sugar, spices, and onion. Grind with a ⅛-inch plate, or twice with a ³⁄₁₆-inch plate. Stuff into beef middles or large synthetic casings, tying off in 4-inch connected links. Put the links into some salted water in a large pot or oblong cooker. Bring to a boil, reduce the heat, and simmer for about 20 minutes. Put the links into cold water until they cool down, dry, and refrigerate until needed. It will keep for a week or so in the refrigerator. To freeze, separate the links and wrap in foil.

See also mettwurst in chapter 6, German and Austrian Sausages (page 174).

A. D.'S CRACKER SPREAD

Spoon out some liverwurst and mix in some mayonnaise, mashing them together with a fork. Taste and adjust. To eat, spread a little of the mix on a cracker, top with a thin slice of Vidalia onion, and enjoy.

PEPPERONI

One would think that this widely known sausage would have an ancient beginning. But the pepper *part of the name comes from capsicum sorts, unknown to the Old World until Columbus discovered the New. Pepperoni as we know it today is flavored with either flakes of dried red pepper or ground cayenne, or both, and is colored with another capsicum—mild paprika. Most pepperoni is rather small in diameter, partly because it is dried or semi-dried and partly because it is stuffed into rather small casings. Small hog casings are just right.*

6 pounds pork butt	1 tablespoon crushed anise seed
4 pounds beef	2 tablespoons sugar
6 tablespoons salt	4 cloves garlic, minced
1 tablespoon cayenne pepper	2 cups red wine
1–2 tablespoons crushed red pepper flakes	small hog casings

Cut the pork and beef into chunks suitable for grinding, sprinkle evenly with salt, and toss to coat all sides. Put the meats loosely in a plastic tray, cover, and refrigerate for 48 hours. Spread the meats, mixing them well, over a work surface. Sprinkle evenly with the dried seasonings and sugar. Grind the meats with a ³⁄₁₆-inch plate. Mix in the garlic and wine. Stuff into small hog casings, linking every 10 inches. Hang to dry in a cool place (34°F to 40°F) for 6 to 10 weeks. When dry, wrap each link in plastic film and keep refrigerated for 2 to 3 months. Freeze for longer storage.

Note: If you want to use a cure (see chapter 3, Stuffing Sausages, page 121), substitute 2 teaspoons of it for an equal amount of salt. Mix thoroughly with the salt before sprinkling the meat.

ALL-BEEF PEPPERONI

Follow the recipe above, using 10 pounds beef, 8 tablespoons salt, 3 tablespoons black pepper, 1 tablespoon crushed red pepper flakes, 1 tablespoon mustard seed, 1 tablespoon crushed fennel seed, 1 tablespoon anise seed, 10 minced cloves garlic, and 2 cups red wine. This recipe makes a very dry pepperoni, so you may want to shorten the drying period or substitute some beef fat for part of the meat.

CHAPTER 16

POULTRY AND WILDFOWL SAUSAGES

Ground turkey or chicken meat can be used in many of the recipes set forth in this book, with a few modifications. First, remember that chicken meat contains little fat marbled in the flesh. A sausage made with chicken that has been skinned and trimmed of fat will be on the dry side. You can add some pork fat or some fat and skin from the chicken.

Because of the salmonella problem with supermarket birds—birds raised, slaughtered, shipped, and stored in large batches—I believe it is best to raise and slaughter your own birds, or to hunt. I believe it strongly. Yet no one can deny the increasing popularity of chicken sausages and sandwich meats in our supermarkets and delis.

In addition to chicken and turkey, duck, goose, pheasant, ostrich, rhea, emu, and other birds can be used in sausage. Texture and content are usually more important than flavor, assuming, of course, that the

birds have been properly dressed. Here's a brief guide, followed by some recipes for more commonly available birds.

Pheasant. This is a lean and dry meat. When used with 20 to 30 percent pork fat or suet, they produce a good sausage.

Partridge. It's hard to find a large batch of partridge these days, but they do make good sausage, along with grouse, sage hens, and so on. Some of these birds can have a strong flavor; skinning will help. If you are lucky enough to have plenty of birds, make yourself some *königswürste,* a German creation composed of equal parts partridge and chicken, along with some chopped mushrooms and truffles, chicken eggs, salt, pepper, mace, and Rhine wine, all stuffed in large pork casings.

Ostrich. These large birds are now being raised in this country and other parts of the world. This good red meat is quite lean, although the bird contains lots of fat. Since these birds run instead of fly, the breast doesn't contain much meat, but the thighs do. Ostrich can be purchased in some meat markets and by mail order. Use it like beef in sausage recipes, or experiment with it in almost any recipe that calls for beef, pork, or veal. For texture, I recommend 80 percent lean meat and 20 percent fat.

I predict that sausages made with ostrich will become more common if the meat catches on with the American public. The bird yields lots of fat, and processors need a good way to use it.

Emu and Rhea. The Australian emu is similar to ostrich and is being raised commercially. Rhea, which is still hunted in Argentina, is also being raised, but it is smaller and may not be economically viable. Both have good red meat and should be used like ostrich.

Ducks and Geese. The rich, dark meat of the domestic duck is quite dry, although the skin is usually high in fat. Wild ducks and coot are also quite lean, and usually the skin doesn't contain as much fat. Wild and domestic ducks make excellent sausage. (Some of the wild birds, however, have a strong flavor if they have been feeding heavily on fish, in which case they should be skinned.) Geese have similar meat and can be used in the same way as duck. Since geese grow for a long time, some of them are quite old and tough, in which case sausage is a good way to use them.

CHICKEN SAUSAGE

The ingredient list below is for whole chicken, including the skin and fat. If you use lean breast meat, add some pork or beef fat.

10 pounds chicken with skin and natural fat (or 7 pounds lean chicken and 3 pounds pork fat)

2 tablespoons salt

1 tablespoon freshly ground black pepper

1 tablespoon red pepper flakes

1 tablespoon dried sage

1 tablespoon dried thyme

1 tablespoon ground allspice

hog or sheep casings

Cut the chicken and skin (or pork fat) into chunks suitable for grinding. Spread the chunks on your work surface, sprinkle evenly with the salt and spices, and grind with a ⅛- or ³⁄₁₆-inch plate. Shape a small amount into a patty, and fry it in a skillet to test for seasonings. Adjust the seasonings if necessary. Grind the whole batch and stuff into casings, linking every 4 inches or so. Cook right away or freeze. To cook, sauté in peanut or olive oil until cooked thoroughly and nicely browned. These can also be grilled, but make sure they are well done before serving. If in doubt, insert a meat thermometer into the center of the sausage. It should read at least 160°F.

Variation: Turkey can be used instead of chicken. If so, try 7 pounds of turkey and 3 pounds of pork fat unless you want a very dry sausage.

FRENCH CHICKEN SAUSAGE

The French make several sausages with chicken, and I find this one to be very easy because it uses cooked birds, which are simple to bone and grind. To make it, I normally use chicken quarters that are on sale. I also use bacon ends and fresh or fresh frozen livers. To cook the chicken, I put it into a large pot of boiling water (heated by my bottle gas outdoor cooker) and add a few bay leaves, chopped celery, carrots, and some red pepper flakes. Normally, I cook about 20 pounds of leg quarters, bone out enough to make 8 pounds for the sausage, and save the rest for sandwich meat or chicken salad. After boning all the meat, I crack the bones, put them back into the stock, and simmer, covered, for an hour or so. Strain the broth, measure out 2 cups for the sausage, and save the rest for any recipe that calls for chicken broth. I usually freeze it in 1-cup containers. To cook the bacon and livers, use a smaller pot and cook them in simmering water for about 20 minutes.

8 pounds boned chicken

2 pounds chicken livers

2 pounds bacon ends

3 tablespoons salt

1½ tablespoons white pepper

½ tablespoon ground clove

½ tablespoon ground nutmeg

12 large chicken eggs

2 cups bread crumbs

2 cups chicken broth

sheep casings

Cook the chicken, livers, and bacon by the directions given in the directions above. Chill the cooked meats, chop into pieces suitable for grinding, mix, and spread out over your work surface. Sprinkle the salt and spices evenly over the mixture. Grind with a ³⁄₁₆-inch plate. Using your hands, mix in the eggs, bread crumbs, and chicken broth. Stuff into sheep casings, tying off in 6-inch links. To cook, panfry in butter or olive oil. Or, baste with olive oil and grill or broil.

Variation: This recipe is an excellent way to deal with leftover turkey. I once tried it with about 6 pounds of leftover turkey, 2 pounds of leftover cooked fresh ham, 2 pounds of bacon ends, and 2 pounds of chicken livers purchased and boiled especially for the sausage recipe. Of course, the leftovers can be frozen and later thawed and made into sausage.

ITALIAN CHICKEN OR TURKEY SAUSAGE

Both chicken and turkey make excellent mild Italian sausages, lightly spiced. These can be used as patties or stuffed into small hog casings.

8 pounds lean chicken or turkey

2 pounds chicken fat, pork fat, or bacon

2 tablespoons salt

1 tablespoon cracked fennel seed

1 tablespoon freshly ground black pepper

5 cloves garlic, minced

small hog casings

Cut the meat and fat into chunks suitable for grinding. Mix and spread the chunks out on your work surface. Sprinkle evenly with the spices and garlic. Grind with a ³⁄₁₆-inch plate. Stuff into hog casings, linking every 4 or 5 inches, or shape into patties. Cook right away or freeze. To cook, sauté the patties or links in olive oil until well done and nicely browned.

HOT TURKEY SAUSAGE

Similar to a fresh pork chorizo, this turkey sausage is just the ticket to spice up soups and stews, or, when sautéed, to serve with a bland boiled pozole (whole hominy) and sliced vine-ripened tomatoes.

7 pounds lean turkey meat

3 pounds pork fat or bacon

3 tablespoons salt

1½ tablespoons coarsely ground black pepper

1 tablespoon crushed red pepper flakes

Spanish hot paprika to taste

¾ tablespoon crushed fennel seed

½ tablespoon ground coriander

½ tablespoon ground allspice

10 cloves garlic, minced

¼ cup dry red wine

½ cup brandy

¼ cup red wine vinegar

medium hog casings

Cut the turkey meat and pork fat into chunks suitable for grinding, mixing and spreading the chunks out on your work surface. Mix the salt, dry spices, and garlic, and sprinkle evenly over the meat. Grind with a ⅛-inch plate. With your hands, mix in the red wine, brandy, and red wine vinegar. Stuff into hog casings, linking every 4 inches or so. To cook, sauté in olive oil until nicely browned and cooked through. Also, prick the links with a fork and use whole in soups and stews. These should be cooked right away or frozen.

Note: Wild turkey can also be used. It is better, really, because the meat is not as dry.

FRESH OSTRICH SAUSAGE

Speculating on ostrich farms has received lots of media attention in recent years, but how well the meat will be accepted by the American people remains to be seen. Marketing, not farming, may be the big problem. In any case, the meat is excellent and can be used in sausages. I think that it, like beef, works best with a mixture of rather fatty pork.

5 pounds ostrich thigh meat	1 teaspoon dried sage
5 pounds pork butt	1 cup red wine
4 tablespoons salt	1 cup cold water
2 tablespoons freshly ground black pepper	hog casings

Cut the meats into chunks suitable for grinding, spread out over your work surface, and sprinkle evenly with the dry seasonings. Grind with a $\frac{3}{16}$-inch plate. Mix in the wine and cold water. Stuff into hog casings. Refrigerate for a day or two, cook, or freeze. To cook, simmer the sausage for 15 or 20 minutes. Then fry or grill over charcoal until nicely browned and cooked through.

Variations: Emu and rhea can be used instead of ostrich.

DUCK SAUSAGE

The domestic duck sold in most American meat markets is billed as duckling. It usually contains lots of fat in the skin or connected to it, and I recommend using it in this recipe. A mix of 20 to 25 percent pork fat to 80 to 75 percent lean duck will also work, but note that duck skin is very good. I like to make cracklings of the duck skin—and I use the rendered oil for stir-fries.

If you raise your own ducks, or have access to such birds, by all means use them. In any case, it's best to bone the easy parts of the meat—breast, thigh, and perhaps the leg—and save the rest for duck soup or stock.

10 pounds duck, with skin and fat	1 teaspoon dried minced sage
3 tablespoons salt	½ cup dry red wine
2 tablespoons white pepper	½ cup minced onion
2 teaspoons mustard seed	hog casings
1 teaspoon freshly ground black pepper	

Pluck the birds, bone out the meat with skin attached, cut into chunks, and spread out over your work surface. Mix all the dry ingredients and sprinkle evenly over the meat chunks. Grind with a ³⁄₁₆-inch plate. Mix in the wine and minced onion. Stuff into hog casings, linking every 6 inches or so. Hang in a cool, airy place just long enough to dry the surface of the casings, then cook, refrigerate, or freeze. To cook, prick the links with a fork and sauté in butter until nicely browned and cooked through. These can also be grilled over charcoal.

Wild Duck Variation: The meat from wild ducks can be used in the recipe above, adjusting for fat content. Some wild ducks have a strong fishy flavor, which is usually concentrated in the skin. For this reason, skin the ducks unless you are certain of their diet. When skinning the bird, look for shot holes, then remove any lead or steel shot. When cutting the meat into chunks prior to grinding, remove any shot or bloodshot areas. Once you get past the hemming and hawing, you'll find the wild duck one of the best meats. Be sure to save the bony pieces for soup or stock.

Note: If in doubt about using duck meat, try substituting it with an equal amount of veal, beef, or pork in your favorite sausage recipe. Also see the Duck Sausage recipe on page 196, which calls for duck, veal, and pork.

CHAPTER 17

VENISON AND GAME SAUSAGES

If you'll close your eyes and disengage any preconceived taste buds when sampling sausages made with various meats, it's the texture and fat content that make the difference. When making sausage, the tenderness of the meat isn't of prime importance; it's the leanness of the meat mixture that makes the sausage hard and tough. It follows that any good game or exotic meat can be used, along with some fat, to make good sausage.

There is, however, a big "if." The so-called gamy flavor of most wild meats comes about because the animal is improperly butchered, and the same taste will be found in a pig that is run all over the country with dogs, shot, and hauled back home on the hot hood of a pickup truck. Also, even prime game must be promptly gutted and cooled. The real reason for prompt field dressing is to remove the heat that the innards contain and open the body cavity to promote cooling.

Often meat from prime venison isn't fit to eat because of improper handling, and there is nothing you can do with it to make it tasty. Although sausage, usually being highly spiced, might seem to be a good way out, it really isn't. You simply can't make good sausage from bad meat, and, believe me, people have given me sausage that I couldn't eat. The unfortunate part here is that the characteristic taste has, over the ages, been termed *gamy*, partly tainting all game in some people's minds.

In any case, game meat is widely available these days. One of the best animals—the white-tailed deer—is a downright nuisance in some areas of town and country. More and more, venison, buffalo, ostrich, alligator, freshwater turtle, and so on are available in special markets and by mail order. All of these meats can be made into good sausage. Most of these meats are on the lean side and, consequently, are better with the addition of fat.

When buying game or exotic meat for sausage, I recommend that you look for large chunks. It's true that the meat is often available in stew or ground form, but it's really best to grind your own. Freshly ground meat is not only better but is also safer, as a rule. If you butcher your own game, I would suggest that you reduce the meat to chunks suitable for stew meat or for grinding, then freeze it in 1-pound packages. Then you can use the meat for stews or ground for sausage, burgers, and so on. The 1-pound units permit you to get out exactly what you'll need, and the smaller units will be easy (compared to a whole ham) to fit into the freezer and quicker to thaw. Remember that partially frozen meat is also easier to grind.

There are hundreds of good meats eaten in the modern world, and I have eaten more than my share, including musk ox and lion. The list below is only an appetizer.

Bear. An excellent source of sausage meat, the black bear is hunted in several states. Other bears are also good, but legal hunting may be a problem. The meat is sometimes fatty, and the fat can be used in the sausage. Bear can carry trichinosis and should be cooked well done, or "certified" by freezing, as discussed in chapter 1, Easy Sausages (page 99).

White-Tailed and Other Deer. All deer, or venison, is quite lean compared to beef. The fat in these animals—usually layered between the skin and the meat—is usually discarded, possibly because it is unpleasantly tallowy when cold or warm. Pure venison can be used for sausage, but I recommend a mixture of half venison and half fatty pork.

Elk. This large deer has dark meat similar to lean beef. It can be used instead of beef in many sausage recipes. In Siberia, a variety of elk is bred on farms and is an important source of meat.

Boar and Wild Pig. Unriled European boar, as well as feral hogs, can make excellent sausages, used as lean pork. Proper handling—a quick kill, prompt field dressing, and cooling of the meat—is essential. I've got at hand a book on how to dress game. In the case of boar, it says to scald the animal in hot water, scrape off the hairs, and then skin it! Obviously, you don't need to both scrape and skin the animal. The choice is yours, depending partly on your equipment and the circumstances.

As a rule, the meat from both European boar and feral pigs will be a little tougher than domestic hogs, and sometimes the flavor will be better, depending in part on what they have been eating. European boar and feral pig can carry trichinosis and should be cooked well done, or "certified" by freezing, as discussed in chapter 1, Easy Sausages (page 99).

I might add that the feral pig is, or can be, a great boon to American charcutiers and hunters. The hog was loosed in Florida and Mexico long ago and now grows wild, free for the taking, over most of the country. In Florida, these pigs are often called piney wood rooters, and in Arkansas, razorbacks. Although these feral pigs can develop mean tusks over the years, they should not be confused with European wild boars.

I have heard and read reports of a super hog, a cross between the boar and the feral pig, called hogzilla, developing in the wild. Some of these reports were supported by photographs. Well, I'll believe all this when I see a wild pig as big as a cow rooting in the woods. And, if my aim is true, I'll be eating lots of sausage.

In any case, remember that the world's most expensive hams come from Spain, where the pigs roam free in the forests to feed on acorns and other mast. From these come the famous Spanish ibérico cured hams, which are on a culinary par with Kobe beef and beluga caviar. Expensive Spanish hard-cured sausages, which are often sliced and served tapas style with cheeses, are also made from these pigs.

Free-roaming American pigs make some excellent hams and sausages. At one time, these were lured (often with the aid of ear-grabbing catch dogs) with peanuts, corn, and other feed. The idea behind this old tradition was not to improve the flavor of the meat; it was to increase the production of lard, which was often more important than the meat. These days we may be experiencing a reverse trend on the production of fat, and I think our hams and sausages will be the better for it. In any case, the hunter doesn't have to wait for the supermarkets to catch up.

Moose. Called elk in Europe, this large animal makes excellent sausage. Owing to its size and internal body heat, it should be gutted as soon as possible after the kill.

Caribou. Called reindeer in Europe, this excellent deer might have been man's first domesticated animal after the dog. The Lapps and some Siberians still herd reindeer on a more or less nomadic basis, and they are raised commercially in some parts. Try caribou meat in any sausage recipe that calls for beef.

Buffalo. Also called bison, this dark, rich meat makes wonderful sausage. Leaner than beef, it should be mixed with fatty pork or bacon for the best results. It is available in some markets and by mail order these days. The real buffalo—the African cape—the Asian water buffalo, and the various African buffalo also make good sausages, and they are being raised commercially in limited quantities.

Other Meats. Mountain lion, giraffes (the neck meat is highly prized), various antelopes, wild sheep and goats, alligators, aardvarks, and dozens of other large animals are either hunted in some areas or raised commercially. Called exotics, some of these meats are available from specialty markets and by mail order.

Horse is also an excellent sausage meat, but it is seldom eaten in the United States. The horse was at one time a very important source of meat to the steppe people of Eurasia.

ELK SAUSAGE

Elk is usually quite lean but full of flavor. Use stew meat, shoulder, or any other cut, being sure to trim out the sinew before grinding. I use beef fat (suet) instead of pork. Talk to your butcher, or save up some fat from your T-bones.

7 pounds elk meat	½ tablespoon anise seed, crushed
3 pounds beef fat	½ cup red wine
3 tablespoons salt	6 cloves garlic, minced
2 tablespoons coarsely ground black pepper	hog casings

Cut the meat and fat into chunks. Mix and spread the chunks out on your work surface, sprinkle evenly with the salt and dry spices, and grind with a ³/₁₆-inch plate. Mix in the wine and garlic, stuff into hog casings, and twist into 4- to 6-inch links. Refrigerate overnight, then cook or freeze. They are best when grilled over charcoal or wood coals, flavored with smoke from a few wood chips.

HERTER'S WYOMING POLISH SAUSAGE

I have seen this recipe in several publications. This version has been adapted from Bull Cook and Authentic Historical Recipes and Practices, *by George Leonard Herter and Berthe F. Herter. The recipe calls for 34 pounds of meat, but this isn't too much if you've got a mule deer or elk that needs reducing. Be sure to chill the meat before cutting and grinding it.*

17 pounds mule deer (or other venison)	1 ounce ground ginger
17 pounds lean fresh pork	½ ounce ground allspice
12 ounces salt	½ ounce Hungarian paprika
8 ounces dried milk	1 teaspoon garlic powder
1½ ounces freshly ground black pepper	4 ounces cold water
1½ ounces ground sage	hog casings
1½ ounces ground nutmeg	

Trim the meats, cut into chunks, mix, and spread out on your work surface. Mix all the dry ingredients, sprinkle evenly over the meats, and grind with a ³⁄₁₆-inch plate. Mix in the cold water with your hands. Stuff into hog casings, linking every 6 to 8 inches. Dry the casings and cold-smoke for 4 to 6 hours. (Herter says to use a low wood fire of maple, apple, mesquite, or hickory, and to smoke at about 120°F. Colder smoke is better, I think.) Cook, refrigerate for several days, or freeze.

To cook Herter's Wyoming Polish sausage, place the links in a skillet and add enough water to cover them by a third. Bring to a boil, lower the heat, cover, and simmer for 15 minutes. Pour the water out of the skillet, then increase the heat and fry until slightly browned on all sides. "Makes wonderful eating," Herter says. I agree.

These sausages can also be made into patties instead of links, seasoned with 2 teaspoons of liquid smoke. Try cooking the patties the same way as the link sausage, turning them carefully with a spatula.

TEXAS VENISON SAUSAGE

I have adapted this recipe from The Only Texas Cookbook, *by Linda West Eckhardt, who asked, "I have tried everything from deer salami, which was dry, tough, and so strong it practically walked off the plate, to breakfast sausage so mild it was like eating hamburger. One of the best compromises I've found is a German links recipe, smoked to give it added resonance and containing saltpeter to retain a nice rosy color. If you object to nitrate, just leave the saltpeter out. The color will then be grayish. Don't be shocked at the quantity in this recipe. It assumes you just shot a deer."*

14 pounds venison	⅓ cup coarsely ground black pepper
7 pounds pork (80 percent lean)	2 teaspoons saltpeter (optional)
1 cup non-iodized table salt	hog casings

In the Texas book, the author said to mix the seasonings, sprinkle them over the meat, and grind once using a coarse blade. Then stuff into 1½-by-10-inch casings. I have altered the procedure a little. First, cut the meat into small chunks and sprinkle with the seasonings, being sure that the saltpeter is evenly mixed in with the salt and pepper. Put the meat into a plastic tray, cover, and refrigerate for 48 hours to cure the meat. Then grind, stuff, and hot-smoke slowly until the internal meat temperature reaches 160°F. Cook right away or freeze until needed. To cook the sausage, place a link or two in a skillet with 3 tablespoons water, then "cover, cook, and turn until the water has evaporated and the sausage is an even brown color."

LARRY'S FOUR-DAY VENISON SALAMI

I have adapted this recipe from The Bounty of the Earth Cookbook, *an excellent work by Sylvia Bashline. In addition to doubling the measures, I have changed the procedure a little, mostly to fit my way of grinding the meats. The recipe calls for beef suet, which is beef fat; if you don't have any, talk to your local butcher. Also, the recipe calls for red pepper; I use mild red pepper flakes, not cayenne. Suit yourself.*

9 pounds venison	5 teaspoons freshly ground black pepper
1 pound beef suet	3 teaspoons mild red pepper flakes
12 teaspoons salt	4 teaspoons garlic powder
5 teaspoons whole mustard seed	5 teaspoons liquid smoke

Trim the venison, removing the sinew and fat. Cut the venison and suet into 1- to 2-inch chunks, mix them, and spread them out on a work surface. (Remember that partially frozen meat will be easier to cut and grind.) Mix the salt, mustard seed, black pepper, red pepper flakes, and garlic powder. Sprinkle the mixture evenly over the meats. Drizzle the liquid smoke over the mix. Grind the meats. Mix with your hands, place in a nonmetallic container, and refrigerate overnight. Mix the meats every day for 3 days. On the fourth day, mix again and divide the mixture into 10 equal parts. Shape the parts into logs about 12 inches long. Place the logs on cookie pans and bake at 155°F for a total of 10 hours. After about 5 hours, turn the logs over. Remove the salami and roll each log in a paper towel. Wrap in foil and refrigerate until needed, up to 3 weeks. For longer storage, wrap each log first in plastic film and then in freezer paper. It will keep in the freezer for up to a year.

For noshing fare, slice the salami thinly and serve on crackers. Also, cut into slices for pizza and sandwiches, or in chunks for spaghetti sauce.

A. D.'S EASY GAME BREAKFAST SAUSAGE

It's no secret that I am fond of unusual meats, such as the emu. Hoping to introduce family and friends to such fare, I find that a mild breakfast sausage helps pave the way for medium-rare steaks. The ingredient list calls for venison—which can be from moose, elk, white-tailed deer, mule deer, caribou, and so on—but any good fresh lean meat can be used. The ingredient list also calls for bacon ends. These are scraps left over from commercial bacon operations and as such are often sold in bulk quantities in supermarkets and meat markets at reduced prices. Regular bacon can be used. The list also calls for A. D.'s Basic Sausage Mix (page 113). Use any commercial mix that you choose, or, better, come up with your own, starting with salt, pepper, and, I insist, a little sage.

7 pounds venison (or other lean game meat)

3 pounds bacon ends

4 tablespoons A. D.'s Basic Sausage Mix

bacon grease or cooking oil

Cut the meat and bacon into pieces suitable for grinding. Spread out over your work surface, sprinkle with about three-fourths of the seasoning mix, and grind a little of it with a ³⁄₁₆- or ⅛-inch plate. Shape into a thin patty. Heat a little bacon grease or oil in a skillet, then fry the patty for a few minutes on each side, until just done and lightly browned. Taste and adjust seasonings if necessary. Grind the rest of the batch. Shape into patties and either cook or freeze. To freeze, I wrap each patty in plastic film. I find that it is not necessary to thaw the patties prior to frying, and that not much cooking oil will be needed. Thus, these patties make a quick and good breakfast when served with eggs or perhaps between biscuits—or both ways.

CHAPTER 18

FISH SAUSAGES

Don't make a face. Fish sausages can be very good and have been made by man since ancient times. Some of these were rather elaborate preparations. Madrilene sausages, for example, according to my old edition of *Larousse Gastronomique*, are made with a mixture of veal, pork fat, and sardine fillets packed in oil. Made in small beef casings, these sausages are poached for 10 minutes in veal stock, then fried in butter. Sounds good—at least to me. My guess is that fish sausages might well become the rave of the future or at least a staple in American cookery. My thinking is that ground or flaked fish meat is an ideal way to market "trash fish" and fish parts that are considered undesirable, just as ground beef makes use of scraps of beef left from the butchering process.

The American angler, of course, doesn't have to wait for the crowd to catch up. Here are some suggestions to try now.

BONY FISH SAUSAGE

Sausage is a very good way to use bony fish, most of which are really quite tasty. For this recipe, I use chain pickerel because I catch lots of 'em, but any good fish with mild white flesh will do. Suckers are especially good, which may be a surprise to many people. Many writers claim to be able to "gash" bony fish in such a way that the meat can be eaten bones and all. (Of course, I'm talking about the small Y-shaped intermuscular bones, not the backbone or rib cage.) I've never figured out whether the fish should be gashed crosswise, lengthwise, or diagonally. So, I came up with my own way of dealing with the bones: (1) Fillet the fish and cut out the rib bones; (2) cut the fish lengthwise into ¾-inch strips; (3) cut the strips into a ½-inch dice; and (4) grind the dice in a sausage mill with a ⅛-inch plate. By then, the bones are scarcely noticeable—except perhaps by someone looking for them.

Of course, you can use several kinds of fish in the same recipe in case you catch a mixed stringer.

10 slices white bread	1 teaspoon cayenne pepper
2 cups milk	1 teaspoon dried sage
10 pounds fish fillets	½ cup chopped fresh parsley
2 tablespoons salt	10 large chicken eggs
2 teaspoons freshly ground black pepper	sheep or small hog casings

Shred the bread, discarding the crusts, and soak in milk. Set aside. Dice the fillets as directed above. Mix in the salt, black pepper, cayenne, and sage. Grind with a ⅛- or ³⁄₁₆-inch plate. Mix in the milk, bread, parsley, and eggs. Shape a patty and fry it in a skillet. Taste for seasonings and for bones. If needed, grind the mix again. Stuff the mixture into sheep casings or small hog casings. Cook, refrigerate for a day or two, or freeze. To cook, sauté the sausage in butter until nicely browned.

Note: This recipe is a variation of *rabakozi halkolbasz*, a Hungarian fish sausage. I don't have documentation for my hunch, but it seems probable that carp are used in Europe, as they are popular as table fare as well as for sportfishing.

Variation: Vary the seasonings to suit your taste or fancy. The fish will pick up on most any theme. Try mixed seasonings, such as Italian, Greek, or Cajun.

A. D.'S SKATE SAUSAGE PATTIES WITH SALSA

One of the best ways to cook skates and rays, in my opinion, is to grind them in a sausage mill, shape the meat into patties, and cook them on a griddle or skillet, or perhaps stuff them into medium hog casings. The sausage patties can be eaten between buns, or they can be eaten on a plate along with vegetables, rice, salad, and other parts of a complete meal.

THE PATTIES

1 pound skate wings	salt and pepper to taste
bacon drippings	1 or 2 chicken eggs (if needed)
1 small to medium onion, chopped	flour (if needed)

Cut the skate into chunks and brush with bacon drippings. Mix the skate and onion, adding a little salt and pepper. Grind the mixture in a sausage mill, using a ⅛- or ³⁄₁₆-inch plate. Shape part of the mixture into a patty, handling it very carefully. Heat about 1 tablespoon of bacon drippings on a griddle or in a skillet, then cook the patty for about 5 minutes on each side, or until done, turning once. Do not overcook. If the patty has held together properly, proceed with the rest of the batch. But if the patty tears apart, you may need some binder to help hold things together. In this case, whisk a chicken egg or two and stir it into the sausage along with a little flour. When all of the patties have been cooked, top with salsa and serve hot.

THE SALSA

1 tablespoon olive oil	¾ cup chopped tomato
¾ cup finely chopped onion	¾ cup mango cubes (½-inch dice)
¼ cup red bell pepper	1 fresh jalapeño, seeded and minced
¼ cup green bell pepper	1 teaspoon fresh lemon juice
2 cloves garlic, minced	½ teaspoon salt
¼ cup chopped fresh cilantro	

Heat the oil in a skillet, then sauté the onion, peppers, garlic, and cilantro for 5 to 6 minutes. Stir in the rest of the salsa ingredients, then simmer for a few minutes. Keep hot until the sausage patties are cooked.

A. D.'S GEFILTE FISH SAUSAGE (NOT KOSHER)

According to The Jewish Festival Cookbook, *by Fannie Engle and Gertrude Blair, poached fish balls, like gefilte fish, are served up with dill pickles and a relish made of chopped beets and horseradish. When working on a magazine article a while back, I tried recipes for various mixes of ground fish shaped into balls and for gefilte, which is such a mixture stuffed into the skin of the fish. It didn't take much of a spark to expand on the theme. Hog casings may not be kosher, but using them is a good deal easier than skinning a fish (for me, the problem is how to keep the fish skin intact without making holes in it). I made the sausage with suckers and chain pickerel, a cousin to the northern pike, a fish often used in gefilte, along with carp. But any good fresh fish will do. You should, of course, make good use of the trimmings; that is, the head, fins, skin, and bony parts. These will be needed for the fish stock used to cook the sausage and as an ingredient in the sausage. Having an exact amount of fish isn't critical, but for best results I like to have about 4 pounds of undressed chain pickerel, suckers, or other good fish.*

THE SAUSAGE

fillets from 4 pounds pike	1 tablespoon olive oil
2 medium carrots, diced	1 teaspoon ground sea salt
2 medium onions, diced	1 teaspoon sugar
2 chicken eggs	hog casings or sheep casings
¼ cup matzo meal	

Fillet, gash, and dice the fish exactly like those in the Bony Fish Sausage recipe (page 256). Mix the diced vegetables with the fish. Grind the fish and vegetables in a sausage mill, using a ⅛-inch plate. Using your hands, mix in the chicken eggs, matzo meal, olive oil, sea salt, and sugar. Stuff the mixture into small hog casings or sheep casings, linking every 3 inches.

Heat the strained fish stock in a large electric skillet. Ideally, the stock should be just deep enough to cover the sausages. Add a little water if needed. Bring the stock to a boil, then reduce the heat. Add the sausages and simmer for 15 to 20 minutes. Serve these sausages directly from the electric skillet, which is used to keep them warm. Delicious.

Variations: If you have frozen fish fillets without the head and trimmings, use canned or homemade chicken stock instead of fish stock. Also, feel free to add more pepper and spices, or experiment with the vegetable ingredients. I want to point out, however, that the carrots give a nice color to this sausage.

THE FISH STOCK

heads and trimmings from 4 pounds pike

water

2 medium carrots, diced

2 medium onions, diced

2 stalks celery with tops, diced

½ teaspoon ground cinnamon

salt and pepper to taste

Put the fish parts into a pot, cover with water, and add the rest of the ingredients. Bring to a boil, cover, reduce the heat, and simmer for an hour or so. Strain the stock. Discard the remains, unless you want to gnaw on what's left of the fish heads, as I do.

PART THREE | COLD-SMOKING AND SALT-CURING MEAT

INTRODUCTION

I have written almost a dozen introductions for this part of the book. Some long, some short. Some direct, some oblique. All of these earlier drafts seemed too serious for the text, and maybe this one is, too. Curing and smoking meats, fish, and game at home ought to be fun, and the results ought to be culinary delights, or at least be a welcome change from supermarket fare. In order to cure and cold-smoke meat safely, however, salt is required. Lots of salt.

Unfortunately, *salt* has become a bad word in the culinary and health-food trade. The trend these days is for writers, TV reporters, and marketing experts to pussyfoot around the issue or to capitalize on it by treating salt in the negative. As a result, a lot of modern people suffer from what I call salphobia. I wrestle a round or two with this problem in chapter 1, The Salt Imperative (page 262), because I feel obliged to do so to the best of my ability. At this point, I want to say two things: In the short term, skimping on the salt used for home-cured and

-smoked meats and fish can be very dangerous to your health; indeed, an unsalted turkey put into an electric smoker during windy or cold weather, along with a pan of water to keep the moisture up, can be a veritable salmonella factory. In the long term, cutting out salt-cured and home-preserved meats has brought us to rely more and more on supermarket fare. Read the newspapers. People die of food poisoning. Chicken has become a toxic substance. We are told to cook everything until well done, even prime T-bone beefsteak. We are told to wash our hands thoroughly after handling meat. We are told to spray the countertop with antibacterial cleaners. The situation is so bad that we hear more and more about zapping supermarket foods with radiation. Safely, we are told. Our "cured" hams are already embalmed with water and chemicals. Safely, we are told.

But all this is heavy stuff. I don't want to clutter my mind with it, and I resent having to burden this book with it. Consequently,

I have decided to front the issue in chapter 1 and get it out of the way. Then I'll get on with some hopefully enjoyable information about curing and smoking meats at home, along with definitions and nuts-and-bolts how-to text on such topics as cold-smoking, hot-smoking, salt-curing, sugar-curing, and so on.

But what if I am wrong about salt? Well, in that case, I'll have to recall a spirited discussion that I once had with a fun-loving doctor who made some money and took it to Alaska. The gist of the conversation was that society simply can't afford to keep people alive forever, a matter that our politicians will have to face sooner or later. The good doctor's solution was that everybody should be issued a book of tickets. When all the tickets are gone, he said, that's it. Well, it seems to me an equitable way to run things, giving a break to people who die accidentally in their youth, or in war, and punishing those of us who tend to burn the candle at both ends. In any case, when the new deal goes into effect, I'll surely spend two tickets, if necessary, on a Virginia ham.

CHAPTER 1

THE SALT IMPERATIVE

When our daughter comes home for a visit, she watches me like a hawk while I am in the kitchen. The girl has a problem. On the one hand, she is starved for good home cooking and a return to the old ways; on the other hand, she lives in mortal fear of common table salt. It's a miserable dilemma, in that you simply can't have good cooking without a little salt. It's a gustatory necessity.

The trouble, I think, is that the girl fell in with the wrong crowd. Health-food freaks. Yuppies. Vegetarians. New Agers. Meditators. I tell you, some of our young people are too gaunt and thin and sickly. The worst of them eat no meat and run or exercise a lot—a highly dangerous combination simply because most vegetables contain very little salt and because sweating depletes the body's supply of the mineral. If these people feel weak and tired and crave dill pickles, they may very well need some salt instead of vitamins and herbs and zucchini and meditation. Why? Why else would the US Navy have advised me to take a large salt tablet daily when I worked in the hot engine room

of the USS *Donner*? Why else would the US Army have issued salt tablets to soldiers in Desert Shield and Desert Storm? Because the human body must have salt to function properly, that's why. It's biochemistry.

Is it possible that the American press—magazine articles, advertisements, popular health books, and TV shows—has greatly misled the public? I think so, and I have support from a modern British book called *Food in History*, written by Reay Tannahill. In addition to requiring salt to function, we humans may also be conditioned psychologically to salt. As Tannahill says, "Modern health advisors who would ban all salt from the diet are, in effect, recommending rejection of a substance that humanity has been genetically and socially programmed, over a period of tens of thousands of years, to desire and need." I can't repeat the whole argument here, but, from a historical viewpoint, salt has been man's best friend in the mineral world. Without salt, we might not have been able to domesticate grazing animals, which must have salt and which know this instinctively and travel long distances to salt licks. One theory has it that animals were first domesticated near the cave entrance, where human urine concentrated salt.

Without salt, and before mechanical refrigeration was invented, man could not have preserved meats, the lack of which would have greatly restricted travel and sea voyages. Also, salt was by far the most important item in early trade. Many of the desert trails still lead to sources of salt. The modern Via Salaria of Italy was first made by Roman carts carrying salt. The word *salary* came from the Roman word for salt allowance, or ration. Indeed, salt has been used as money from Abyssinia to Tibet, and it has been an important source of tax revenue even in modern times, as Mohandas Gandhi well knew.

In any case, I personally want and need some salt in my food, and I prefer to dine with people who feel the same way. Of course, I don't want to give advice in this matter, except to say that anyone who quits eating salt because of media medicine or new wives' tales really ought to consult a doctor of medicine. Even then, a second opinion may be in order. If the human body is functioning properly, any excess salt that may have been ingested through normal eating practices will be eliminated quite naturally in perspiration and urine. Naturally, there may be limits to how much salt one can safely eat, but the taste buds and common sense are usually safe guides in this matter. Of course, if your doctor tells you not to add any salt whatsoever to your daily food, then you are clearly reading the wrong book.

Meats and fish have been cured for many centuries with the aid of salt, and sometimes with both salt and smoke. From time to time, other ingredients were added. For a while, saltpeter (a term that usually means potassium nitrite) became popular, but it has been more or less replaced by sodium nitrite, sodium nitrate, and other compounds such as ascorbic acid. Some of these substances are used primarily to preserve the color of the meat, and the meat trade has even resorted to various dyestuffs.

If we look back at the folk cures of America, we see that there's more than one way to cure meats. The *Foxfire* books, which became something of a hit many years ago, contained an interesting collection of meat cures. The material for these books was gathered in the Appalachian Mountains of northern Georgia by students from a rural school at Rabun Gap. Unfortunately, most of the cures are set forth far too sketchily to be of much practical value. Even so, I find the material to be very interesting, and I hope that the summary below helps establish the fact that curing meat does not have to be an exact science and can be accomplished without pumping good meat full of water and chemicals and dyestuffs and liquid smoke.

At hog-killing time in *Foxfire* country— usually the first cold snap in the fall of the year—the meat to be cured was cooled down and salted as soon as possible. Some people would simply cover each piece of meat with salt and let it cure for a suitable length of time; usually, but not always, the salted meat was arranged on a wooden shelf or packed into a wooden box or barrel for curing. One man named Taylor Crockett used exactly 8 pounds of salt per 100 pounds of meat. He mixed the salt with 1 quart of molasses, 2 ounces of black pepper, and 2 ounces of red pepper; he smeared this mixture onto the meat and let it cure for 6 to 8 weeks, depending on the weather.

Valley John Carpenter used 5 pounds of plain salt for a 200-pound hog, and Ron Reid used 10 pounds of salt per 100 pounds of meat. Most of the *Foxfire* people left the salted meat on wooden shelves in the smokehouse to cure, although a few packed it into boxes or barrels. Lake Stiles took the meat down into his cellar and put it on the dirt floor, allowing the earth to "draw the animal taint out of the meat, keep it cool, and prevent souring or spoiling."

If the meat was not to be smoked, the *Foxfire* people usually left it in the curing mode for the winter, during which time they could simply take out what they needed and cook it. In the spring, the unused meat was washed and treated again. At this time, some people covered the meat with a mixture of black pepper and borax to keep the skipper fly larvae out. Bill Lamb put a mixture of borax and black pepper on the washed meat, then smoked it. Others used brown sugar and pepper, put the meat in a cloth bag, and hung it in the smokehouse. Lake Stiles washed the meat and then buried it in a box of hickory ashes, whereas his grandmother used cornmeal instead of ashes. Another fellow—who allowed no one to spit into the fireplace—sifted the ashes, put them onto the dirt floor of the smoke-house, and buried the meat in them. Lizzie

Carpenter put some freshly shelled white corn into the bottom of a wooden box, then added middling meat, another layer of corn, and so on until the box was full. She claimed that the corn draws the salt out and gives the meat a good flavor.

Of course, some of the *Foxfire* people smoked their meat after first putting it through a salt cure. This was usually accomplished in a walk-in smokehouse, which was considered to be an essential structure at most homesteads. The smokehouse usually had a dirt floor. More often than not, the fire was built on the dirt, or perhaps in a small trench, but sometimes an iron wash pot was used as a firebox. Although the *Foxfire* books indicated that the fire was made of small green chips of hickory or oak, pieces of hickory bark, or even corncobs, my guess—based on experience with old-timey home smoking—is that long-burning green limbs or logs of hickory were also used.

The early settlers on the barrier islands of North Carolina, called the Outer Banks, also made very good use of both pork and fish, and both were cured in the fall of the year. At first, hogs were allowed to roam free on the islands, gathering acorns and whatever they could find to eat—and the houses were fenced in to keep the hogs out of the yards. Of course, each settler marked his hogs with a coded series of notches in the ear. Hog-killing time was something of a social event, usually held at first frost or first freeze, at which time the neighbors gathered to help each other. Almost all of the hog was used, from snout to tail. The hams, shoulders, and bacon were salted and smoked, and the trimmings were made into sausage and smoked. The methods of curing pork are similar to those set forth in *Foxfire* and won't be repeated here.

Salted fish was a great staple of the Outer Banks until recent times, and the tradition lives on there simply because the taste for salt fish can't be satisfied by other means. A book called *Coastal Carolina Cooking* sets forth a few favorite methods:

Bill and Eloise Pigott of Gloucester corn their spot (a small member of the croaker family) in brine. They gut the fish but leave on the scales. The fish are placed in a light brine for several days in a barrel, then they are washed and placed in a heavier brine. The spot are taken out as needed—Eloise advises one to avoid using a metal spatula to remove fish from the brine, as metal will taint the whole batch. Before being cooked, the fish are freshened by soaking them for some time in fresh water.

Mitchell Morris of Smyrna uses a dry cure for spot, layering them with salt in a barrel. The fish stay in the salt until 24 hours before cooking, at which time they are placed in fresh water to soak. Mitchell also salts roe from mullet, which are ready in October and are best, he says, on a full moon. He salts the sacs and presses them between unpainted wooden boards in a sunny place for several days. He eats the roe fried, baked, scrambled, or plain, saying, "Old folks put roe in their pocket and eat it like candy."

I, too, am fond of mullet roe—or any good roe of small grain—salted in a similar manner (see *batarekh*, page 279).

Although the techniques are easy—requiring only salt, time, and a relatively low temperature—the authors of *Coastal Carolina Cooking*, who worked for the Sea Grant program, a federally funded project, felt obligated to say, in a sidebar, "Even though coastal residents still use these methods of preserving seafood, seafood specialists discourage their use unless you are experienced in the techniques, as improperly preserved fish could spoil. Experts recommend you freeze your catch instead."

The same sort of disclaimer was inserted into the *Foxfire* books. The chapter on curing hog, for example, starts off, condescendingly I think, with the following paragraph: "Meat was cured by the mountain families in several ways. Professional butchers today would probably shudder at the apparently haphazard measurements they used, but they often seemed to work." Well, I suspect that some of the old practitioners from the mountain families would shudder at the modern methods of pumping chemicals and water into good hams. Some of the old-timers might even marvel that the new methods "often seem to work," in spite of constant reports in the media these days about food poisoning and salmonella.

I could sketch in a hundred folk cures from other parts of the country, all with variations in method and ingredients. But the old cures all have three things in common: lots of salt, plenty of time, and relatively cool weather. And that's all you need to cure fish and meats at home. Smoke can be added to the process, as discussed later in this section, but it is more for flavor and is usually not a necessary part of the curing process. Other ingredients, such as sugar and spices and garlic, can be added to alter the flavor of the end product, and chemicals such as sodium nitrite or ascorbic acid are often added to preserve the color. But salt is the only ingredient that is really needed for curing the meat. Omit it at your peril.

CHAPTER 2

CURED FISH

As pointed out in the previous chapter, salt fish has been very important to the world's expanding population. During the Middle Ages and later, a great commerce developed. The nations of Europe rose and fell by their control of the herring fishery of the North Sea. Later, salt cod from Newfoundland and New England became very important.

In addition to preservation, another reason for salting fish was to reduce its weight. Fresh fish are mostly water, and the salting process draws out a good part of it. In fact, salting and drying reduces the overall weight of fish by as much as 80 percent. The volume is also reduced. This fact was important to anyone transporting fish by mule train, sailboat, or dogsled.

Even today, salting the catch will often help with storage and transport problems, since the salt cure requires no refrigeration or ice. But culinary considerations are perhaps more important for modern man. As the recipes in this chapter show, properly prepared salt fish have a unique flavor and have become part of the regional cuisine of some areas. Even the texture of a familiar fish can be altered by a salt cure. Soft fish such as crappie or spot, for example, can be made much firmer. Also, bony fish such as suckers, pickerel, and shad can be salted to advantage; the salt softens the bones, making these fish easier to eat.

There are some rather fierce regional salt-fish favorites, such as salt mullet along the Gulf of Mexico, salt cod along the northeastern seaboard, and salt herring in the North Sea countries, but the techniques for salting the various kinds of fish are pretty much the same from one area to another. There are, of course, a number of recipes for salting fish at home or in camp, and champions of this or that exacting technique will no doubt stand firm, regardless of what I say. But the plain truth is that if you leave the fish in contact with enough salt for a long enough period of time, it's hard to go wrong from a curing viewpoint.

How much salt? Lots of it. It's best to buy inexpensive salt by the bag—25-, 50-, or even 100-pound sizes. Almost any salt will do, even that used to de-ice roads and sidewalks.

Salting Techniques

Anyone who has a burning culinary or historical interest in salt fish should read *Fish Saving: A History of Fish Processing from Ancient to Modern Times*, by C. L. Cutting. In this tome are many salting techniques, mostly of commercial application. Since the advent of mechanical refrigeration and more speedy transportation, the commercial trend has been toward a lighter cure. Also, the cure is often combined with light smoking in modern times.

In spite of a wealth of historical and regional formulas, I feel that the modern practitioner, and certainly the novice, can get by nicely with the simple methods below.

A Basic Salt Cure

Catch lots of good fish, preferably in the 1- to 2-pound range. Low-fat, white-fleshed fish like large crappie, walleye, and black bass are good when salted, and so are the fatty fish like mullet and mackerel. Dressing the fish for salting is easy. Without scaling or skinning, merely cut a slab of fish off each side of the backbone, lengthwise, as when making a fillet cut. Of course, you will cut close to the bone, getting all the meat you can. That's it. No gutting or beheading. Leave the skin and scales on. Wash the fish in a solution of 1 cup of salt to a gallon of water. Then drain the fish.

Find a wooden, plastic, or other nonmetallic container of suitable size and shape. Wooden chests are traditional, but large plastic or Styrofoam ice chests are easy to use at home, in camp, or even in a boat. Put a layer of salt in the bottom. Also place some salt in a separate container such as a plastic dish or tray. Lay each fish on the salt in the tray, turn it, and pick it up by the tail, bringing out as much salt as sticks to it. (Also put some salt into the body cavity if the fish has been dressed in the round.) Place a layer of salted fish, skin side down, atop the salt on the bottom of the chest. Then add another layer of salt, a layer of fish, and so on. Place the last layer of fish skin side up, and cover it well with salt. Lots of salt. Cover the container, and put it in a cool place for a week. (A basement is ideal. I have also put them under the house.) A brine will develop as the salt draws the water out of the flesh. In short, the fish will shrink in size and become firmer.

After a week, remove the fish and discard the brine. Make a new brine by boiling some water and adding salt to it until the solution will float a raw egg. While the new brine is still hot, add a few peppercorns if you want. Cool the brine. Put the fish back into the container and pour the cooled brine over them. A weight of some sort, such as a glass platter or a block of wood, should be put on top so that the fish will not float and be exposed to the air. Never use a metallic weight. Cover the container with a cloth and leave it in a cool, dark place for 2 weeks. The fish can be stored for longer periods in the brine, or they can be removed, washed, packaged, labeled, and frozen until you are ready to use them.

OLD DOMINION PICKLED HERRINGS

Here's an interesting cure that provides a method of taking the fish out of the water and putting them into the brine without having to waste time gutting or cleaning them, which makes it a good technique for curing fish that are taken in large numbers. The method is quoted in full from Mary Randolph's *The Virginia Housewife*, first published in 1860. The words "brine left of your winter stock for beef" refer, of course, to the brine left over from salt-curing beef; if this sounds just too frugal, remember that salt was harder to come by in those days. Of course, the modern practitioner might prefer to use fresh brine. (If not, see the brine cure on page 342.)

> The best method for preserving herrings, and which may be followed with ease, for a small family, is to take the brine left of your winter stock for beef, to the fishing place, and when the seine is hauled, to pick out the largest herrings, and throw them alive into the brine; let them remain twenty-four hours, take them out and lay them on sloping planks, that the brine may drain off; have a tight barrel, put some coarse alum salt at the bottom, then put in a layer of herrings—take care not to bruise them; sprinkle over it alum salt and some saltpeter, then fish, salt, and saltpeter, till the barrel is full; keep a board over it. They should not make brine enough to cover them in a few weeks, you must add some, for they will be rusty if not kept under brine. The proper time to salt them is when they are quite fat: the scales will adhere closely to a lean herring, but will be loose on a fat one—the former is not fit to be eaten. Do not be sparing of salt when you put them up. When they are to be used, take a few out of brine, soak them an hour or two, scale them nicely, pull off the gills, and the only entrail they have will come with them; wash them clean and hang them up to dry. When to be broiled, take half a sheet of white paper, rub it over with butter, put the herring in, double the edges securely, and broil without burning it. The brine the herrings drink before they die has a wonderful effect in preserving their juices: when one or two years old, they are equal to anchovies.

A. D.'S WOODEN-PLANK CURE

I once salted down a batch of small fish—6- and 7-inch golden shiners—on a wooden plank. The fish were scaled, beheaded, washed, and drained. A layer of salt was sprinkled onto the plank. The fish were dredged in salt, then put down in a single layer without touching. Salt was piled on top, and the board was tilted a little in the deep sink in our laundry room so that the moisture could run off.

After a few days, some of these were freshened and fried. I found them to be quite tasty, and, as I hoped, they could be eaten bones and all. For the sake of gastronomic research, I washed the salt from the remaining shiners, put them back on the board, and placed them under an air-conditioning vent for drying. These were kept for several months without signs of rotting, but finally my wife claimed that they were starting to smell and she wanted them out of her laundry room. Since they were bone-dry by now (and really didn't smell), I put them into a plastic container and hid them under the counter in the kitchen. She ran across them one day about a year later and said, in gist, that she wanted them out of her house. The fact that the fish were still edible seemed to make no difference to her. Some women are just hard to live with. In any case, dried fish are covered later in this chapter.

After experimenting with the shiners, I used the same wooden-plank method to salt down some mullet fillets and again to salt a few sucker fillets. The method worked nicely, and I recommend it for salting a few small fish or fillets.

Recipes for Salt Fish

Ironically, some of the best recipes for salt fish were developed in West Africa, the West Indies, and eastern South America—far from the codfish banks of Newfoundland and the North Sea. Why? During the world's colonial period, salt fish was shipped by the ton to these parts from Europe, Newfoundland, and New England. The people developed recipes for cooking the hard salt fish, often with the aid of native ingredients, and developed a taste for them. Even today, in an age of mechanical refrigeration, salt fish are quite popular in many parts of the world. I like them, too, and I remember that my father was fond of eating fried salt fish for breakfast.

Before cooking, most of the salt is removed by soaking the fish overnight in several changes of cool water. This is called freshening. Still, anyone who objects to the salty taste should avoid the fried fish recipes and try those that contain other ingredients—especially potatoes, which absorb some of the salt. In any case, the recipes that follow should contain something for everybody. When serving, remember that salt fish is firm and rich and quite filling, so large portions aren't required.

SALT FISH MAURITIUS

One of my favorite salt-fish recipes comes from halfway around the world. In the Indian Ocean, 500 miles east of Madagascar, sits the small island of Mauritius. Over the years, its people developed a superb blend of flavors with salt fish and other ingredients.

1 pound salt fish	6 green onions with tops, chopped
¼ cup peanut oil	2 cups fresh cherry tomatoes, halved
1 medium onion, chopped	1 teaspoon finely grated fresh ginger
2 cloves garlic, minced	cooked rice
1 tablespoon chopped fresh parsley	

Wash the salt fish, remove the skin, and flake the meat from the bones in large chunks. Put the fish pieces into a glass or nonmetallic container, cover with water, and soak overnight in the refrigerator. Change the water a time or two if it is convenient to do so.

When you are ready to cook, drain the fish and pat dry. Heat the peanut oil in a large frying pan and sauté the fish chunks for 5 to 6 minutes. Then add the onion, garlic, parsley, chopped green onions, and halved cherry tomatoes to the frying pan with the fish. Heat and stir until the onion is soft. Add the ginger and stir. Cover and simmer for 15 to 20 minutes. Spoon the fish over fluffy rice. This dish is quite rich and will serve 4 people of ordinary appetite.

A. D.'S FRIED SALT SUCKERS

This technique works for most bony fish, but suckers are my favorite in spite of the bad press they have received over the years. These are salted by the method given in the first part of this chapter. Before salting, however, the suckers are filleted. Each fillet is "gashed" with a sharp knife on a diagonal, placing the cuts about ½ inch apart. Do not cut all the way through the fish, but do cut through the layer of Y-bones. With a little practice, you can feel the bones as you cut.

salt suckers or other bony fish	fine stone-ground white cornmeal
buttermilk	peanut oil
pepper	

Soak the salt fish in cool water all day or overnight, changing several times. Scale the fish and soak them in buttermilk for 4 hours. Drain the fish, sprinkle each piece lightly with pepper, and shake them in a bag with cornmeal. Heat at least ½ inch of peanut oil in a frying pan. (Or rig for deep-frying if you prefer.) The oil should be very hot, but not smoking. Fry the fish for a few minutes, until they are nicely brown on each side. Drain each piece well on brown grocery bags or other absorbent paper. Eat while hot.

SALT FISH HALIFAX

Here's a recipe from the Nova Scotia Department of Fisheries. The official version calls for salt cod, but any good salt fish will do.

1 pound salt cod	¼ cup grated cheddar cheese
2 cups mashed potatoes	1 teaspoon black pepper
¼ cup finely chopped onion	dry bread crumbs
¼ cup finely chopped fresh parsley	cooking oil

Freshen the fish by soaking it overnight in cold water. Change the water once or twice if convenient. Simmer the fish in a little water for 10 to 15 minutes, until it flakes easily when tested with a fork. Drain the fish and flake the flesh off the bones. Mix the fish flakes, mashed potatoes, chopped onion, parsley, cheese, and pepper. Form the mixture into patties. Roll each patty in bread crumbs. Heat about ¼ inch of oil in a skillet and fry the cakes for 2 to 3 minutes on each side, or until golden brown. There's enough here to serve 3 or 4 people.

Variation: For fish balls, add an egg to the mixture and shape it into small balls instead of patties. Deep-fry in very hot oil. Drain well on absorbent paper before serving.

SCANDINAVIAN SALT FISH

The Scandinavians developed a way of preparing salt fish with sour cream, and several other peoples, especially in the Middle East, cooked salt fish in cream or milk. Here's my version.

1 pound salt fish, boned and skinless	1 tablespoon chopped fresh parsley
1 tablespoon butter	1 tablespoon fresh lemon juice
¼ cup sour cream	⅛ teaspoon white pepper
¼ cup chopped onion	

Soak the salt fish in fresh water overnight or longer, changing the water several times. Flake or chop the fish and drain it well. Melt the butter in a frying pan and sauté the fish flakes for 6 to 7 minutes over high heat. Drain on brown paper. In a serving bowl, mix fish, sour cream, onion, parsley, lemon juice, and pepper. Serve cold on crackers. Feeds 3 or 4.

SOLOMON GUNDY

Here's an old recipe that calls for salt herring. Other salt fish can also be used.

2 salt herring	2 tablespoons brown sugar
2 large onions, sliced	½ teaspoon black pepper
2 or more cups hot vinegar	

Wash the salt herring. If they are whole, fillet and discard the backbone. Cut the meat into chunks and soak overnight in cool water, changing it a time or two. Drain and rinse the pieces. Layer the fish in a deep bowl, alternating with a layer of onions. Cover with water, then pour the water into a measuring bowl and note the amount. Discard the water and place an equal amount of vinegar into a saucepan, then stir in the brown sugar and black pepper. Bring the vinegar to a light boil, then pour it over the fish. Cover the container, then cool it in the refrigerator for several hours. Serve cold.

SALT COD WITH PARSNIPS AND EGG SAUCE

In The Country Kitchen, *a British cookbook, author Jocasta Innes says that this dish was a favorite in medieval times, when salt cod was a way of life. She says the sweet parsnips balance the salty fish. I agree. The measures in this recipe make up a good batch, and you may want to reduce everything by half.*

THE COD

2 pounds salt cod

¾ cup milk

¾ cup water

2 pounds parsnips, peeled and cut into strips

⅓ cup butter

pepper to taste

1 teaspoon ground coriander

Freshen the salt fish in several changes of cold water. Then put the fish into a large pan or stove-top dutch oven and cover with cold water. Bring to a boil, then drain off the water and discard it. Next, cover the fish with a mixture of the milk and ¾ cup water. Add the parsnips. Bring to a boil, reduce the heat to low, cover, and simmer for 45 minutes. Remove the fish carefully and place it in a slow oven to dry. Strain out the parsnips, being sure to retain the stock. Mash the parsnips with a potato masher, adding the butter, pepper, and coriander as you go. Stir in a little of the reserved stock until the parsnips are creamy. Serve the fish and mashed parsnips separately, along with the following egg sauce.

THE SAUCE

¼ cup butter

1 tablespoon flour

3 chicken egg yolks, well beaten

2 cups reserved fish stock

Melt the butter in a saucepan. Stir in the flour and then the egg yolks. Slowly add fish stock. Stir until the sauce is thick, then turn off the heat and let the sauce rest for a while. Serve the sauce hot over the fish.

SALT FISH BREAKFAST

My father was fond of eating salt fish for breakfast, and I, too, like them after nine o'clock, along with fresh sliced tomatoes. In rural Florida, it is traditional to serve this with grits. Exact measures aren't specified, but I like to have about half egg and half fish by volume.

salt fish, flaked	black pepper
chicken eggs	toast
green onions, finely chopped	vine-ripened tomatoes
butter	

Soak the fish in water overnight, changing the water a time or two. When you're ready to cook, drain the fish, bone the meat, chop it, and mix it with the eggs in a bowl. Stir in a little green onion, including part of the tops. Melt some butter in a frying pan. Scramble the egg-and-fish mixture until done. Add pepper to taste. Serve hot with toast and slices of homegrown tomatoes.

International Salt-Fish Specialties

A surprising number of specialty dishes, from Swedish gravlax to Indian Bombay duck, are made with salt fish. Some of these—mostly appetizers—are eaten without being cooked. On first thought, this fact may turn you off from these delicacies, but remember that caviar is not cooked either. I enjoy most of these dishes very much, but I want to make my own, starting with very fresh fish.

GRAVLAX

In Iceland and Sweden, Atlantic salmon are salted and eaten with a mustard dill sauce. I highly recommend the method for coho or any fresh salmon that you have caught yourself, or that you are certain are very fresh. (This recipe calls for a light salt treatment, which in my opinion should be used only with very fresh fish.) Some books recommend that you use salmon steaks, but boneless fillets work much better. Note also that the name for this delicacy is sometimes spelled gravad lax.

boneless fillets from a 5- to 6-pound salmon

3 tablespoons coarse sea salt

2 tablespoons sugar

2 teaspoons freshly ground black pepper

2 teaspoons crushed dried juniper berries

fresh dill

Pat the salmon fillets dry with a paper towel and place them, skin side down, on an unpainted board about 6 inches wide and long enough for the fish. (Cut two such boards and save one for the top.) Mix the salt, sugar, pepper, and juniper berries; sprinkle the mixture over the salmon fillets evenly from one end to the other. Place a few sprigs of dill over half of the fillets, then put the other fillets on top with the skin side up. (In other words, put the salmon halves back together, sandwiching the salt and dill sprigs.) Wrap and overlap the fillets first with wide plastic wrap and then with wide freezer paper. You'll need to seal the fish, remembering that it will be turned over a few times while curing.

Put a plank over the fish and press down on it a little, more or less seating the boards. Then weight the top board with several cans of vegetables (or some other suitable weight of about 5 pounds). Put the whole works in the refrigerator for at least 2 days, turning the planks and fish every 12 hours or so. Do not unwrap the fish; the idea is to contain the liquid in the package. The salmon should be eaten within 4 days.

To serve the gravlax, remove it from the wrap, drain it, and pat it dry. Put it skin side down and, with a thin, sharp knife, slice it crosswise into thin slices—no more than ⅛ inch thick. Cut down to the skin, then cut the slice away from the skin. This is easy once you get the hang of it. Keeping the salmon cold will make it easier to slice. Serve the salmon slices on a plate with the mustard dill sauce and fresh pumpernickel. Here's what you'll need for the sauce:

¼ cup Dijon or German prepared mustard

1 tablespoon sugar

½ teaspoon ground white pepper

3 tablespoons olive oil

2 tablespoons white wine vinegar

salt to taste

¼ cup minced fresh dill

Thoroughly mix the mustard, sugar, and pepper in a bowl with a whisk. Continue to whisk while adding a little oil in a thin stream. Stop. Whisk in 1 teaspoon of wine vinegar. Whisk, add more oil, whisk, and so on until the oil and vinegar have been used up. Stir in the salt to taste, then stir in the dill. Transfer the sauce to a serving bowl and refrigerate it until you are ready to eat. The sauce will keep for a few days, but it will need to be fluffed up with a whisk before serving. The same sauce can be used with the following recipe.

RAKØRRET

This Norwegian dish usually is made these days with farmed rainbow trout. Traditionally, the trout are processed in a wooden container that will hold about 4 gallons, but I have found a Styrofoam ice chest to be satisfactory.

Catch some trout of about 1 pound each and fillet them. In the bottom of the container, put a layer of coarse salt at least 2 inches deep. (You may want to use rock salt for this purpose because sea salt is so expensive these days.) Add a layer of trout, skin side up. Do not overlap the trout. Add a thin layer of salt, covering all the fish but not piling it on. Add another layer of trout, and so on, until you fill the box or run out of fish. Top with salt.

This dish is usually made in the fall, when the weather is cool, and the Norwegians merely sit the box outside in the sun for 3 to 4 weeks. If you live in a hot climate, turn the air conditioner down to 70°F and set the box in a picture window that catches the morning sun. Be warned that this stuff smells almost as loudly as *batarekh* (page 279), so keep the lid on tightly if your spouse is hard to live with.

Serve the trout (without cooking it) with thin bread and a little hot prepared mustard. If you have prepared a whole box of these trout only to find that you don't like them, or they are too strong or too salty for your taste, soak them in milk overnight to soften and sweeten them. Then dust them with flour and fry 'em in butter. Or flake off the meat and use it to make salt codfish balls, using any good New England recipe. In Boston, according to my copy of the *Old-Time New England Cookbook*, salt codfish balls, Boston brown bread, and Boston baked beans are traditionally served up for breakfast on Sunday morning. (Really good Boston baked beans, I might add, are always cooked in a cast-iron pot with a slab of salt pork.)

CAVIAR

If we may believe the critics (and I have no reason to disagree), the best caviar is made from the roe of various sturgeons. Usually, expensive caviar is made from roe with large berries. Part of the gustatory sensation occurs when these berries pop, releasing a burst of flavor. Although caviar can be made from good roe from most fish, such as salmon and carp, I suggest that roe with small berries (or grains) be made into another delicacy, as described in this recipe, or be used for pressed caviar instead. Like wine making, the processing of caviar can be as complicated and as highly technical as you choose to make it. For openers, try the simple recipe below.

2 cups very fresh roe with large berries	1 cup sea salt
4 cups very good water	

Keep the roe on ice until you are ready to proceed—preferably very soon after catching the fish. Find some nylon netting with the mesh a tad larger than the berries. (Netcraft and some mail-order houses carry netting.) Boil the netting to sterilize it, then stretch it over a clean nonmetallic bowl. Break the roe sacs and dump the berries onto the netting, carefully helping them along, and gently rub them about so that the berries drop through the netting. The idea is to separate the eggs from the membrane without breaking the eggs open.

When you have separated the eggs, mix the water and salt, then pour the brine into the bowl over the eggs. Stir gently with a clean wooden spoon, and with your free hand remove any membrane that rises to the top. After 20 minutes, scoop out the berries and place them in a strainer (preferably made of plastic) over another bowl. Put the strainer and its bowl into the refrigerator to drain for an hour or so.

Have ready a sterilized 2-cup jar (or several jars if you have landed a sturgeon). Using a sterilized wooden spoon, put the berries into the jar. The jar should be as full as possible to minimize the amount of air, but the berries should not be broken by packing too tightly. Cap the jar with an airtight lid, then store the caviar in the refrigerator. Note that caviar made by this method is not really cured and should be eaten within 3 to 4 weeks.

I like caviar on thin crackers with a little cheese, but more sophisticated folks have other ideas. In any case, this caviar can also be used in most recipes that call for caviar.

BATAREKH

Old salts in Florida and along the Atlantic Coast will be surprised to learn that salt-dried mullet roe was enjoyed by the ancient Egyptians. Ready-made *batarekh* is still marketed in Egypt, and possibly in some Paris outlets, where it is called *boutargue* or (I think) *bottarga*. European or Egyptian gourmets might argue for the roe of the gray mullet seined from the Mediterranean or perhaps caught with a hook baited with cooked macaroni, but the weathered folks along the Outer Banks of North Carolina will tell you that the roe of their coastal mullet is the best in the world—far surpassing the golden berries of even the rare sterlet sturgeon. Old crackers on Florida's Gulf Coast will champion their own mullet, some of which are a little different from those that run the Atlantic Coast. Once, I could buy fresh mullet roe and milt from my local fish markets, but in recent years, Japan and Taiwan have hogged the market for the sushi trade. They buy the roe by the ton, salt it, dry it, change the name to *karasumi*, and sell it back to us at $70 an ounce, or thereabouts. They also make a similar product, *tarako*, from salt-cured Pacific pollack.

In any case, the roe of cod is also excellent and can be used in this recipe. Menhaden, American shad, hickory shad, mooneye, and other good herring also yield excellent roe. My favorite batarekh, however, is made from the roe of bluegills, which is readily available to most Americans. Most of the farm ponds in this country are overstocked with bluegills, and these are fat with roe in summer. Catch some and try batarekh. True, it's an acquired taste, but before long you'll crave more—especially if you have been on a no-salt diet.

Start by carefully removing the roe from the fish, being careful not to puncture or divide the two sacs. Wash the sacs and dry them with a paper towel or soft cloth. Place them on a brown grocery bag and sprinkle them heavily with sea salt. (Ordinary table salt can be used, but sea salt has more minerals and more flavor.) Put the bag in a cool place. After about 2 hours, the salt will have drawn some of the moisture out of the roe and the brown bags will be wet in spots. Put the roe sacs on a new brown bag and sprinkle them again with salt. Change the bag after about 3 hours and resalt the roe. Then wait 4 to 5 hours. Repeat until the roe is dry and leaves no moisture on the bag, at which time it will be ready to eat. This will take about 3 days, but after the first 8 hours or so the bag won't have to be changed very often. Small roe won't take 3 days, however, to dry sufficiently. Be warned that batarekh smells up the house, so it is best to make it on the screened porch or in a well-ventilated place. After it is cured sufficiently, it can be stored for a while in the refrigerator, but it's best to wrap each roe sac separately in plastic wrap. For longer storage, dip each roe sac in melted paraffin.

Beginners should eat batarekh in thin slices with a drop of lemon juice and a thin little cracker or buttered toast. After the first 2 or 3 slices, omit the lemon and cut the slices a little thicker. Being salty, batarekh goes down nicely with cold beer. Don't throw out your batch of batarekh if it doesn't hit the spot, or if you've got squeamish guests scheduled for dinner or cocktails. (As I've often pointed out, one of my sons won't touch batarekh, pharaohs notwithstanding, because, he says, it looks like little mummies.) I like to use grated batarekh as a seasoning and topping for pastas and salads—and it really kicks up an ordinary supermarket pizza. Just grate some on the pizza atop the regular toppings. (I prefer pizza supreme with a little of everything.) Sprinkle shredded cheese over the batarekh and broil until the cheese begins to brown around the edges and the pizza is heated through. Have plenty of good red wine at hand if you are feeding bibulous guests.

This pizza is one of my favorite quick foods. The grated batarekh can, of course, also be used to advantage in pizza made from scratch if you are a purist.

Also, I find that grated batarekh can really pick up a piece of cheese toast for a quick snack. Here are some other ways to use batarekh—gourmet fare without the mummy image.

TARAMASALATA

This dish, popular in both Greece and Turkey, is often made these days with smoked cod roe. The original, however, calls for salt-dried roe of the mullet. It's made from tarama, *which is similar to* batarekh *(page 279) except that the roe is pressed. (The Russians also eat bricks of highly salted and pressed caviar that could be used in this recipe.) Most people won't know the difference.*

<table>
<tr><td>3 ounces batarekh</td><td>juice of 1 lemon</td></tr>
<tr><td>4 slices white bread</td><td>¼ cup olive oil</td></tr>
<tr><td>1 cup milk</td><td>Greek black olives</td></tr>
<tr><td>1 clove garlic, crushed</td><td></td></tr>
</table>

Crush the batarekh in a mortar and pestle until it has a smooth texture. Remove the crust from the bread and soak the bread in milk. Squeeze out the milk, then mix the bread into the batarekh, along with the garlic. Grind this mixture with the mortar and pestle until the mixture is smooth. Slowly stir in the lemon juice and then the olive oil, tasting as you go. Add more lemon or more garlic if needed to suit your taste. Serve with thin toast or crackers, along with the black olives. I like a little white feta cheese on the side.

FESSIH SALAD AND PITA BREAD

According to Claudia Roden's A Book of Middle Eastern Food, fessih *is a fish that has been salted and buried in the hot sand to ripen. When ready, it will be soft and salty. Ms. Roden allows that people in the West may want to use anchovy fillets in lieu of fessih. (Use canned anchovies, or make your own "anchovies"; see below.) Also, the recipe requires some tahini, a paste made of sesame seeds.*

½ cup tahini	½ teaspoon ground cumin
½ cup fresh lemon juice	2 (2-ounce) cans anchovy fillets
1 large mild onion, sliced	1 large, ripe tomato, thinly sliced
2 cloves garlic, crushed	pita bread
salt to taste	chopped fresh parsley

Put the tahini, lemon juice, onion, garlic, salt, and cumin in a blender or food processor. Zap it until you have a smooth paste, adding a little water if needed. Purists will want to adjust the amount of lemon juice, salt, and cumin until they have an exact flavor and texture. Mince the anchovies and stir them into the tahini cream. Serve in a bowl with large, thin slices of tomato and pita bread. Garnish with parsley.

ANCHOVIES

If you've got real anchovies, you're in business. Also, finger fish such as smelts, shiners, and sand lances will do. If the fish are 4 inches or less, behead and gut them. If they are larger, fillet them. Even small bluegills can be used if they are filleted and perhaps cut into strips to resemble canned anchovies.

Clean and wash the fish according to size. Pat the fish dry. Sterilize some jars with canning lids. Cover the bottom of each jar with a little salt. Add a layer of fish, sprinkling the body cavity of each one with salt as you go. Add a layer of salt, a layer of fish, and so on, packing lightly as you go and ending with a layer of salt. A top space of about ½ inch should be left in each jar. Weight the anchovies with a slightly smaller jar (or other suitable nonmetallic container) that has been filled with water. Put the packed jar (with the weighted jar in place) in a cool place for a week or so. When ready, remove the weighted jar or container. By now, a brine will completely cover the fish. (Fatty fish such as echelon may develop a layer of oil on the surface. Skim this off if you choose.) Seal the jars and store them in the refrigerator. They will keep for a year or longer.

Before serving these in Greek salads and other raw dishes that call for canned anchovies, I like to remove the fish from the brine, rinse them, pat them dry, and dip them in olive oil. Note that the salt will have softened the small bones in the fillets. Whole fish should be boned, which is easily accomplished by spreading the body cavity, pulling off one side, and lifting out the backbone.

SALT SALMON BIRDSEYE

According to George Leonard Herter, the late Clarence Birdseye, the father of frozen supermarket foods, came up with the following recipe for salmon and other fatty fish such as bullheads. Further (Herter says), the same dish was once called salmon fuma in New York City.

<table>
<tr><td>1 gallon water</td><td>$\frac{1}{32}$ ounce sodium nitrite</td></tr>
<tr><td>2½ cups salt</td><td>5 teaspoons liquid smoke</td></tr>
<tr><td>⅙ ounce sodium nitrate</td><td>3 pounds skinless fresh salmon fillets</td></tr>
</table>

Pour the gallon of water into a crock or other large nonmetallic container. Dissolve the salt in the water, along with the sodium nitrate and sodium nitrite. See whether a chicken egg will float in the solution. If not, add more salt until the egg rises. Then stir in the liquid smoke. Put the fillets into the solution and weight with a plate or some nonmetallic object of suitable size; the idea is to keep the fish fillets completely submerged at all times. Leave the fish in the solution for 4 days. (If you feel compelled to stir the fish a time or two, use a wooden spoon.)

Drain the fish. Before serving, slice the fillets into very thin slices. Partially freezing the fillets and slicing with a sharp, thin knife will help. Serve atop crackers.

Air-Dried Fish

Although air-dried fish—one of man's first preserved foods—is very important from a historical viewpoint, the method has not been popular in America in recent history and has not been widely practiced except by some native peoples in Alaska and Canada. Fish has often been dried for use as food for sled dogs, partly because drying reduces the weight by about 80 percent. In parts of Africa and no doubt other places, fish were dried with the aid of smoke. The smoke helped keep the blowflies away from the fresh fish, and was sometimes discontinued after a day or two.

Stockfish

In the recent past, very large quantities of dried fish were produced commercially in Scandinavia and Iceland, where the dry air and cool breeze made the process feasible on a large scale. Air-dried cod—called stockfish, from the Norwegian *stokkfisk* or Swedish *torrfisk*—provided the people of the Middle Ages with food and was later shipped in large quantities to parts of Africa, where dried fish were preferred to salt fish (and still are in some places). Although refrigeration has hurt the stockfish trade, tons of cod are still air-dried commercially in Scandinavia each fall; Norway alone exports 50 million to 55 million pounds of stockfish to Africa in a year, according to *The Encyclopedia of Fish Cookery,* by A. J. McClane.

Typically, those cod destined to be stockfish are merely gutted and hung out to dry on huge wooden racks. Of course, a few fish can be dried for home consumption without large racks; often, the gutted fish are hung under the eaves of the house. The drying will take from 2 to 6 weeks, or even longer, depending on the weather and the size of the fish.

The dried fish become very hard, and they require lengthy soaking in fresh water before they become suitable for human consumption. A medieval recipe calls for boiling dried fish in ale, then shredding them and mixing in chopped dates, pears, and almonds. The mixture is reduced to a paste in a mortar and pestle, then shaped into patties, dusted with flour, dipped in a batter, and fried in hot oil.

Modern practitioners may prefer the following recipe.

TRADITIONAL FINNISH CHRISTMAS FISH

Several weeks before Christmas, the dried fish are put into a solution of 1 gallon of water and 1 tablespoon of lye; then they are soaked for 2 weeks. For the next week, the fish are soaked in fresh water, changed daily, to leach out the lye. Then the fish are poached gently until the meat flakes easily. The flaked meat is put into a white cream sauce seasoned only with freshly ground black pepper, and served with boiled potatoes.

Racking

Racking is used to dry rather large fish with a low fat content, such as cod, hake, or even flounder. The fish are cut in half, then the backbone, rib bones, and head are removed, leaving the collarbone intact. The sides of the fish are cut into long strips about 1 inch wide; these are left joined together at the collarbone. After being washed, the fish are soaked for an hour in a saturated salt brine (that is, a brine with enough salt to float an egg). They are then hung by the collarbone in a dry place, out of direct sunlight. Drying takes from 1 to 2 weeks, after which the fish can be stored for future use.

The dried fish are soaked in fresh water to freshen the flesh, then creamed or flaked and used in recipes for chowders, fish loafs, or fish cakes. At one time, the dried strips were eaten without cooking, like jerky.

Fish hanging to dry under the overhanging roof of a house

MEXICAN SUN-DRIED SHARK

According to A. J. McClane's *The Encyclopedia of Fish Cookery*, a major shark fishery exists in Mexico's Sea of Cortés. In fact, the industry is centered on Isla Tiburón, or Shark Island. The sharks include the mako, brown, blacktip, hammerhead, tiger, bull, leopard, nurse, thresher, and horn. After processing, most of the meat, McClane says, is sold in Mexican markets as salt cod. The fins are dried and sold for Chinese shark-fin soup. The back meat is cut into fillets and soaked for 20 hours in a weak brine of 4 pounds of salt to 10 gallons of water. This soaking leaches out the uremic acid, which is present in most sharks and which gives the meat a strong smell of ammonia.

After brining, the shark fillets are dried in the sun. McClane says that careful drying is critical in preservation, and that the fillets must be evenly exposed to the sun on both sides and protected from damp night air.

DRIED SHRIMP

For this method of drying shrimp, I am indebted to Frank G. Ashbrook, author of *Butchering, Processing and Preservation of Meat*. Although shrimp of any size can be dried, the smaller ones work best and are less desirable for the market or other methods of home use. People who have tried to peel enough tiny shrimp to stay ahead of their appetite will see the advantage!

For best results, start with very fresh shrimp. Wash these and bring to a quick boil in salted water, using 1 cup per ½ gallon of water. (Do not try to boil too many shrimp at the same time because they will lower the temperature of the water.) Boil the shrimp for 5 to 10 minutes, depending on size. Drain the shrimp and spread them in the sun to dry. If bugs are a problem, rig a way to cover the shrimp with a fine-meshed screen. The shrimp can be rather crowded but should not form a layer more than 1 inch deep.

For the first day, the shrimp should be turned every half hour. At night or during a rain, remove them to a dry, well-ventilated place; do not merely cover the shrimp with a tarpaulin or other direct covering. If you are really into drying, it's best to build movable trays with wire or slat bottoms; then the whole tray can be taken inside at night or during a rain. In most areas, you'll also need a screen cover to keep the flies off the shrimp, or perhaps to keep the seagulls away.

Drying small shrimp will require 3 days in sunny weather, longer if the days are short of sun and wind. When the shrimp are dry and hard, place them in a cloth sack. Beat the sack with a board; this will break the shells. Then winnow the shrimp in a sifting box, made with a wooden frame and ¼-inch mesh. The bits of shell will fall through, leaving the dry shrimp meat on top. This will be much smaller and lighter than the original. In fact, 100 pounds of shrimp will shrink down to 12 pounds of meat. The dried shrimp can be put into jars and stored in a dry place.

The dried shrimp can be used in soups and stews that will be cooked for some time, or they can be freshened by soaking in water for several hours. Freshened shrimp can be dusted with flour and fried or sautéed in butter, or they can be eaten raw as appetizers.

Asian and regional Mexican cuisines make good use of dried shrimp, which can be purchased in some ethnic markets. Usually, the shrimp are dried with the aid of salt. In addition to shrimp, the Chinese also dry and market oysters, squid, sea cucumbers, and even jellyfish. Scallops are sometimes air-dried.

EASY DRIED SHRIMP

Here's a technique that I like to use for quick-drying 2 to 3 pounds of shrimp. Peel and devein the shrimp, place them in a shallow tray, and cover them with a cure made with 1 pound salt, 2 cups brown sugar, 1 tablespoon onion powder, and 1 teaspoon ground allspice. Place the tray in the refrigerator for 6 to 8 hours.

Wash the salt cure off the shrimp and pat them dry with paper towels. Place the shrimp on cookie sheets and dry in the oven for about 12 hours on low heat; use the lowest setting on your oven, and leave the door ajar. After drying the shrimp, pack them into airtight containers and refrigerate them for up to 3 months, or freeze them for longer storage. Use the shrimp in soups and stews, or in any Asian recipe that calls for dried shrimp.

AIR-DRIED SALT FISH

One purpose of adding lots of salt to fish is that it draws out the moisture, thereby speeding up the drying and curing processes. Usually, small fish to be salt-dried are gutted and beheaded; larger ones are filleted, leaving the collarbone intact to help hold the fish together while hanging.

After dressing, the fish are usually washed in salted water, made by adding 1 cup of salt to each gallon of water. The fish are drained, then dredged in a box of salt. Another box is lined on the bottom with salt, and the dredged fish are put down in a layer. Salt is scattered over the layer, then another layer of fish is put down, and so on. As a rule, the total amount of salt used in this process is 1 pound per 4 pounds of fish. Using too much salt will "burn," or discolor, the fish.

The fish are left in the salt for at least a day, or up to a week, depending on the size of the fish and the weather. Then the fish are rinsed and scrubbed to remove the brine. Next, they are drained for a few minutes and hung on racks or placed on drying trays. They are usually kept in a shady place with a good breeze.

CHAPTER 3

DRY-CURED MEATS

Meats cured with dry salt rather than brine are covered in this chapter; next, chapter 4 covers brine-pickled meats.

Although beef and other red meats can be dry-cured, in this country and in most other parts of the world, pork is by far the most popular salt-cured meat, as in salt pork, bacon, and ham. At one time, pigs were raised in towns and cities as well as on the farm; in fact, the pigs were allowed to roam the streets, thereby helping control the garbage problem instead of adding to it. I have raised a pig or two in a pen inside town limits, but these days you really need a place in the country to raise your own. If you buy fresh pork for curing from a local farmer or a meat processor, make sure that you get it very fresh and properly chilled.

SALT PORK

Salt pork is one of the world's great seasoning meats and is often used in such dishes as Boston baked beans and hoppin' John as well as in fish chowders. It can be made from side meat or from fatback. The jowls are also used, and these are traditionally eaten on New Year's Day in some areas. I prefer to use a good cut of side meat so that it will have a lot of lean meat along with the fat. In fact, I consider the whole side of pork to be salt pork if it is cured and not smoked; if smoked, it's bacon, I say. Usually, salt pork is the thickness of slab bacon and is prepared with the skin on. Slabs can be cut into convenient lengths and widths. I find that 6-by-12-inch pieces work just fine. You can salt-cure the whole side, then trim it for storage; of course, the trimmings can be used for seasoning meat.

½ side of hog meat, trimmed   lots of salt
and cut into sections

Rub the pieces of side meat on all sides with salt. Place each piece on a bed of salt, preferably on a wooden plank or in a shallow wooden box or tray, then cover it with salt. Place the meat in a cool place for 1 week. Resalt the pork and leave it in a cool place for another week; after that, it can be cooked as needed.

Although cured salt pork can be packed in boxes and barrels, it will sometimes become rancid, especially in warm weather. It's best to wrap each piece separately and store it in the refrigerator or freezer until needed.

Note: If you prefer, add some sodium nitrite to the salt that is rubbed onto the meat. Mix 1 ounce of sodium nitrite with each pound of salt. It is important that the sodium nitrite be mixed well with the salt so that it is distributed evenly.

SALT PORK BREAKFAST

These days we are constantly told that animal fat is not good for us. If you tend to eat too much of a good thing and have no self-control, or if you are under a doctor's orders, proceed at your own peril.

salt pork with lean streaks	2 cups milk
oil	black pepper
cornmeal	hot biscuits
2 tablespoons all-purpose flour	

Slice the salt pork to about ⅛ inch thick and cut off the rind. Allow at least 4 slices per person. Put the slices into a pan and cover them with water. Bring to a quick boil, cover, and simmer for 10 minutes. Drain the salt pork and discard the water. Heat about ⅛ inch of oil in a skillet. Coat the salt pork with cornmeal and fry it in hot fat until brown and crispy. Put the salt pork pieces on a brown paper bag to drain.

For gravy, pour all the grease out of the frying pan except for about 2 tablespoons. Heat this grease and then stir in the flour. Using a wooden spoon, stir well until the flour is brown. Slowly add the milk. Add a little black pepper to taste. Stir and simmer until the gravy has the consistency you want. Serve the gravy over hot biscuit halves and eat with the fried salt pork strips. Have plenty of hot coffee. This dish also goes nicely with cold slices of homegrown tomatoes.

YANKEE BAKED BEANS

Beans were raised by Native Americans and, along with corn, formed a big part of the early colonists' diet. Although there are hundreds of variations on baked bean dishes, often called Boston baked beans, here is one that I highly recommend. Most of the Boston recipes seem to call for molasses, which was shipped up from Jamaica for making rum; other recipes call for brown sugar. Purists might even hold out for maple sugar.

1 quart dried navy beans	½ teaspoon powdered mustard
water	½ tablespoon salt
1 medium onion	½ pound slab salt pork
½ cup molasses	

Put the beans into a nonmetallic container, cover them with water, and soak them overnight. Drain the beans and put them into a cast-iron pot. Cover with fresh water, bring to a boil, and simmer for 1 hour. Drain the beans.

Preheat the oven to 250°F and put on some water to boil. Chop the onion and put it into the bottom of a large cast-iron pot. Add the beans to the pot. Mix the molasses, mustard, and salt, then spread this mixture over the beans. Put the slab of salt pork on top of the beans so that the rind is facing up. Cover the beans and pork with boiling water. Put the lid on the pot and bake for 8 hours. Add a little water from time to time if needed, but do not stir, leaving the slab of pork on top.

Country Hams

A real country ham is salt-cured and aged. It may also be smoked, but not necessarily so, and it may have some sugar in the cure, in which case it can be called sugar-cured. Most modern curing recipes recommend that you add sodium nitrate or sodium nitrite, or both, and others recommend saltpeter, Prague Powder, and such formulas. Some texts even advise you to buy an injection pump and offer illustrations on how to use this device. Unless you're highly experienced, you'll need an X-ray machine to inject the ham in the right places. Moreover, if you are going to do all this and want to pump your ham full of liquid, you might as well buy one that an expert has "cured" for you.

If you want what I consider to be the real thing, forget the injection pumps and all the cures except salt. Then proceed with great care and caution, getting the various steps right. There is no shortcut. But before setting forth a ten-step recipe in detail, I would like to quote another man's recipe and comments. Although I might frown at his use of liquid smoke, I really can't argue with the results. What I really like is the man's spirit.

SAUNDERS'S CITY-CURED COUNTRY HAM

A culinary sport by the name of Madison Ames Saunders Jr. has formed some firm opinions about country hams, and his comments are in line with my experience and conclusions. The following excerpt is from A Man's Taste, *published by The Junior League of Memphis.*

You might think that it is difficult to cure a country ham while living in the city. Not so. When I became interested in curing a country ham, I read everything I could find including a Department of Agriculture pamphlet on the subject. This last was a mistake. True to form, the pamphlet only served to confuse. By this time, though, I realized that hams had been cured for hundreds of years, often by illiterate people, as a method of preserving pork. If illiterate people can do it, I thought, why can't I? Armed with all of my new-found knowledge, I then sought out my good and great friend, George F. Jackson. George spent a great deal of his youth following a pair of mules on small farms in northern Mississippi, northern Shelby County, Tennessee, and on one located on Centennial Island in the Mississippi River. He is incredibly wise in all things pertaining to the country, and I was to fill in the missing portions of information by questioning him.

By this time it was the middle of November, the traditional time to cure meat in this part of the country. First I built a plywood salt box. Size doesn't make too much difference, but mine is roughly 4 feet by 5 feet and is 1½ feet deep. I also drilled 8 or

10½-inch holes in the bottom and built a rather snug-fitting plywood top.

You must use non-iodized salt in the curing process, and this may require a trip out in the country. Any store that caters to the farm trade will have it, and at a very reasonable price. It comes in 25-, 50-, and 100-pound bags so don't stint. While you are there, also buy a quart of Liquid Smoke. It will save you a trip later on.

Now you are about to get into business. Go to a packing house or your friendly butcher and buy 4 20-pound fresh pork hams. I like 20-pound hams because they will lose 5 to 6 pounds in the curing process, and a 14-pound ham is about the best size. . . .

Put your salt box on the 4 concrete blocks in your garage or carport and cover the bottom of the box with 2½ to 3 inches of salt. Nestle the hams, skin side down, in the salt and then cover with salt so that no piece of ham is not in contact with it. Put the cover on the top and put 2 concrete blocks on the cover. This is to discourage city varmints such as cats, rats, dogs, raccoons, etc., that might, in the silence of the night, want to become silent partners. At least once a week remove the cover to the box and peer at the mounds of white salt. Don't disturb the salt or poke around. This weekly observation doesn't help the ham, but it increases your pride in accomplishment and anticipation.

In about 4 weeks the hams are ready to be removed from the salt. If the weather has been extremely cold, 15 degrees or below, cover the box with a blanket or an old rug to keep from freezing. If the weather remains extremely cold, leave the hams in the salt for 5 to 6 weeks, instead of the recommended 4. Remove the hams, brush the salt off, and paint with liquid smoke. Do this 3 nights in a row, returning the hams to the salt box for safe keeping but no longer covering them with salt.

Now they are ready to hang. Wrap each ham with about 3 layers of cotton cloth, old bed sheets, old undershirts, or anything that you think will keep insects from getting to the ham. I hang mine in my debugged basement. It's not a bad idea to hang a Shell No-Pest Strip close by.

Now we play the waiting game. The hams will be ready to eat in 6 months, but I believe that they really reach their peak when they have been hanging for 2 years. In the meantime, pinch, feel, fondle, and smell at regular intervals. Like other things I know of, anticipation is sometimes as good as realization.

At last comes the great day. When the hams have been hanging for 6 months, cook one using my recipe (page 298). After you have tasted it, invite your neighbors in for a drink. Put the whole ham out, with a very sharp knife for their enjoyment. Now comes the difficult part. You must be modest. As they rave about this culinary delight extraordinary, don't tell them that you both cooked and cured it. Let your wife tell them. When they stare at you in amazed disbelief that a mere mortal can do this, and start a barrage of questions, shyly admit that you have more aging in the basement, claiming all the while that it really wasn't so much.

A. D.'S 10-STEP GEORGIA HAM

As I hope has been made clear, there is far too much conflicting information about cured hams. One authority might advise you to use ascorbic acid instead of sodium nitrite or sodium nitrate, and another will tell you not to substitute. Others will say that neither ingredient is necessary for curing hams. One authority says to age the hams before smoking; another, after smoking. Some writers will say that country hams are best when they are aged for a year or longer; others say that they get too hard after 6 months. One authority says to sprinkle pepper over your hams after curing to prevent mold; another says that pepper causes mold. In short, writers and practitioners, along with booklets written in Federal Prose, have confounded the issue, and trade books on the subject have tried to treat cold-smoking and hot-smoking (i.e., cooking) in the same work, thereby causing even more confusion—and more margin for errors with serious consequence.

Guidance is needed, but not in the form of magic cures and gadgets. Those people who think that the problems can be solved with Prague Powder and brine injection pumps are wrong. For one thing, hams are more exacting to cure because they are large. Yet, owing to complicated enzymatic chemistry, they can be the most rewarding of the cured meats. Anyone who has sat down to eat a properly cured and expertly cooked country ham needs no further reason to proceed.

The process is really not difficult. Yet things can go wrong. My older brother, for example, once had a small farm on the Choctawhatchee River, where he let his hogs forage on acorns and rootables. Starting in late summer, he fattened some prime pigs on corn and peanuts; then, on first frost, he butchered a few for home use. One fall, he butchered four prime pigs and salt-cured the hams and shoulders, stacking them on a wooden shelf in his smokehouse. The shoulders worked out just right, but the larger hams soured and had to be thrown out. Why? He didn't know. He thought he had followed the exact procedure that he had always used, and the one that my father and grandfather had used before him.

In any case, I consider the following steps to a country ham to be more important than brine pumps and secret formulas.

1. Select a good hog—not too fat and not too lean. About 200 pounds on the hoof will be just right.

2. Scratch the hog down with a corncob until it starts to snore, then dispatch it quickly. (At least, don't chase the hog or otherwise rile it up before the slaughter.) Some people will want to bleed the hog, but remember that merely cutting its throat and jugular vein won't accomplish much except cut off the blood to the brain; for bleeding the meat, the hog should be "stuck" in order to sever the aorta artery.

3. Quickly gut the hog and scald it, then scrape off the hair in a vat full of boiling water. This process leaves the skin on the hams and other parts.

4. Chill the carcass as soon as possible. The carcass should cool down to at least 40°F through and through. If you have access to a mechanical cooler, use it. If not, you'll have to pick your time for killing hogs. On a cold day, perform step 3 in the afternoon and hang the hog in the night air to chill. A night with a light freeze is ideal.

5. When the meat has cooled down, reduce the carcass to hams, shoulders, and other cuts. (This can be done in step 4, but it's much easier if you chill the meat before cutting it; cold meat is simply easier to cut and handle.)

6. Trim the visible fat from your ham, but leave the skin intact.

7. Move the ham to a salting table or bench and apply the salt cure. Use at least 8 pounds of salt per 100 pounds of ham. Salt alone will cure the ham, but spices and other ingredients can also be mixed in for one purpose or another. Sodium nitrate, sodium nitrite, Prague Powder, and saltpeter preserve and enhance the bright red color of the ham, but they have little curing power. Sugar helps the flavor, the surface color, and the texture of a ham (helping prevent it from becoming too hard). Prague Powder is available in various formulas, some designed to give continuous aid to the curing process. Prague Powder 2, for example, is essentially a mixture of salt, sodium nitrite, and sodium nitrate. The thinking here is that the sodium nitrite is used up fast and the sodium nitrate is used up slowly, thereby giving continuous action. Both sodium nitrite and sodium nitrate are toxic when used in large amounts, and state and federal governments have set limits on its use in commercial hams. (I repeat that neither cure is necessary for home use; their purpose is primarily to give the cured ham a red color.) Saltpeter is used in some of the old cures; it may not be a safe chemical and should be used only in small amounts.

   If you want a good general cure for hams, I recommend the 10-1-2-1 formula—that is, 10 pounds salt, 1 pound sugar, 2 ounces sodium nitrite, and 1 ounce sodium nitrate. Dry spices and herbs can be added to the mix, but I don't think they are necessary. It's hard to beat the flavor of ham.

   It's best to apply the cure (or plain salt) at three different times during the curing process. Apply one-third on the first application; one-third after 7 days; and one-third after 17 days. For a 16-pound ham, use 8 ounces of cure per rub; for an 18-pound ham, 9 ounces; 20-pound, 10 ounces. (These figures are from *Curing Georgia Hams Country Style*, a booklet published by the University of Georgia College of Agriculture.) Rub the cure all over the ham, paying particular attention to the bones on either end. It's a good idea to pack a little salt or cure into any opening around the bone.

8. After the first rub, place the ham on a shelf in a cold place, preferably at about 36°F. (If the temperature is colder, increase the length of the cure a few days.) Do not cure the ham at temperatures above 40°F, because the "ham-souring" bacteria can multiply and cause the meat to spoil.

    After 7 days, rub the ham with the second application of the cure (one-third of the total). After 17 days, rub the ham with the final third of the cure. Then complete the curing period, the length of which depends on the thickness of the ham. These figures (which I consider to be about right) are given by the aforementioned Georgia publication: 4 to 5 inches of thickness, 28 to 35 days; 5 to 6 inches, 35 to 42 days; 6 to 7 inches, 42 to 49 days. The reason for the long curing time is that the salt penetration is slow; the thicker the ham, the longer it takes. (The idea behind brine pumps, of course, is to speed up the salt penetration. If used by a skilled operator, they might do that, but the danger is that all areas of the ham may not be injected properly. I don't recommend their use, partly because I don't want water and chemicals pumped into my ham.)

    Note that the ham will shrink considerably during the curing period.

9. At the end of the curing period, wash the excess salt off the ham, dry it, and put it in a cool place, or better, keep it under refrigeration at 40°F. Leave it for 20 days. Why? So that the salt will penetrate throughout the ham. After the curing period, most of the salt will be near the surface; after 20 days, it will be more evenly distributed (but not exactly even) throughout the ham.

    Called salt equalization, this process is essential for a properly cured ham. Most of the spoilage in country hams is caused by inadequate salt equalization and occurs during the aging process.

10. After salt equalization, hang the ham in a cool, airy place for aging. It can be hung by the shank end with cotton string, or it can be put into a stocking made of net material. (These are available from supply houses.) Wrapping the ham in clean sheeting will be fine. Air circulation is important during aging; consequently, the ham should never be wrapped in airtight material.

If all these steps have been duly observed, the temperature of the aging environment isn't as critical as for curing and salt equalization. According to the Georgia booklet, "When no controlled conditions are available, hams age best during the summer months as the inherent enzymes that produce the aged flavor are more active." The aging temperature should not exceed 95°F, however. During aging, the ham will lose more of its weight and shrink in size.

For how long should the ham be aged? Six months is a reasonable minimum figure, but many country hams are kept and treasured for generations. I worked with a student of nuclear physics at Oak Ridge, Tennessee, who boasted that his old eastern Tennessee family had treasured hams that were a hundred years old.

In any case, a country ham may develop mold on the surface during aging. This is completely normal, and the mold is easily washed off before cooking; for this purpose, it's best to use a stiff brush and warm water. Remember that salt-cured hams are much firmer than today's supermarket "cured" hams. They require soaking in water and longer cooking times. Often, they are simmered in water before being baked.

SMITHFIELD (OR VIRGINIA) HAM

I once tuned in on a TV documentary about Smithfield hams, in which they showed huge buildings, like barns, full of curing hams. Although I didn't learn any trade secrets, I saw enough to know that this is a highly controlled and exacting process that, like making a certain wine, cannot be duplicated easily at home; part of the problem, it seems to me, is making a product that is consistent from ham to ham, batch to batch, year to year. Sometimes, these Smithfield hams are touted as being fed or fattened on peanuts, but I think the secret is in the curing. Also, the name *Smithfield* is probably exploited commercially. In any case, my information on the cure is based almost entirely on Frank G. Ashbrook's *Butchering, Processing and Preservation of Meat*:

> These hams are cut with the long shank attached. They are cured in a dry mixture for 5 to 7 days, depending on their weight. They are then overhauled, resalted, and held in cure from 25 to 30 days (1½ days per pound). After this dry cure is completed, the hams are washed in warm water, dried, sprinkled with pepper, and cold-smoked (at 70 to 90 degrees) for 10 to 15 days, after which they are aged and mellowed by hanging in a dry room. These hams improve with age and are in perfect condition when 1 year old.

Note that the hams are cold-smoked for 10 to 15 days according to Ashbrook, and are then aged. The Georgia booklet says to smoke the hams *after* the aging process. From a safety viewpoint, it probably doesn't matter as long as both the salting and the salt equalization steps have been successful.

Cooking a Dry-Cured Country Ham

Most people don't know how to cook a country ham. Some of the old cookbooks don't go into much detail; no doubt those authors assumed that any fool would know to freshen the salty ham before cooking it. In any case, some country hams end up being not only too salty for human consumption but also too hard and too tough to eat. Of course, a cured country ham is supposed to be firmer than a modern embalmed ham, and as a rule, it should be carved in thin slices. In fact, some of the world's more famous cured hams are eaten raw, and part of the secret is very thin slices.

In Tennessee, I once ate in a restaurant that had quite a local reputation for country hams. The ham was simply machine sliced and panfried. Well, it was edible, but it was too hard and too salty to suit me. The redeye gravy, however, was just right for sopping with biscuits. The owner of the restaurant told me, on my next visit, that I had to buy ham in order to get the gravy. I did so.

SAUNDERS'S BOILED COUNTRY HAM

Weigh the cured ham, then place it skin side down in a large, deep pot. Add enough water to cover the ham. Then add 1 cup vinegar, 1 quart molasses or sorghum, 1 cup powdered instant coffee, and 6 to 7 dozen whole cloves. Bring the liquid to a boil, cover the pot, reduce the heat, and simmer for 20 minutes for each pound of meat. Turn off the heat and allow the ham to cool overnight in the liquid. Remove the cooled ham from the liquid and place it skin side down on a thick section of newspaper. Refrigerate the ham for 24 hours. Trim off most of the skin and fat. Now you're ready to slice and eat the ham.

A. D.'S WHOLE-HAM FAVORITE

Here's an old three-step method of cooking a country ham that combines soaking, boiling, and baking. It's hard to beat, making a beautiful ham as well as a tasty one without too much salt. This recipe can be used for a whole ham or just a butt or shank portion. Before proceeding, make sure you have large enough containers for holding and cooking the meat.

STEP 1

cured country ham   a little baking soda

Scour the ham with water and a brush dipped into baking soda. Put the ham into a large container, such as an ice chest, and cover it well with cool water. Let it soak all night, changing the water a time or two.

STEP 2

soaked ham   1 stick cinnamon

1 cup wine vinegar   20 black peppercorns

The next day, put the soaked ham into a large pot or container and cover it with fresh water. (If you are cooking a whole ham and don't have a container large enough or deep enough, consider using one of the large patio fish fryers that fit in a rack over a bottle gas cooker with double burners; a tall stockpot can also be used.) Bring the water to a boil, add vinegar, cinnamon, and peppercorns, then quickly reduce the heat and simmer (or poach) the ham for 30 minutes per pound. Add a little more water from time to time if needed. Remove the ham and let it cool in the pan liquid.

STEP 3

1 soaked, poached, and cooled ham   1 cup brown sugar

1 cup prepared mustard   whole cloves

1 cup fine bread crumbs

Preheat the oven to 325°F. Skin the ham, leaving the fat on the meat, and score the top surface with a small knife; a 1-inch diamond pattern is ideal. Put the ham into a roaster or onto a suitable baking pan. Combine the mustard, bread crumbs, and brown sugar, then cover the ham with this mixture. Stick a whole clove in the center of each diamond. Put the ham in the oven and cook for 30 minutes, or until nicely browned. Small hams and portions of hams may take less time to brown; large whole hams may take a little longer.

FRIED COUNTRY HAM AND REDEYE GRAVY

Here's a hearty breakfast dish that can be made with leftover baked country ham or with center-cut slices of country ham. Some people make the dish without freshening the meat, resulting in a piece of ham that is too tough and salty for good eating. The gravy, however, will be good. Many southerners insist on serving redeye gravy with grits, but it is even better over fluffy white biscuit halves.

lard or bacon drippings	black pepper
ham slices, about ¼ inch thick	hot biscuits
½ cup black coffee	

Heat a little lard or some bacon drippings in a cast-iron skillet. Fry the ham slices for 5 to 6 minutes on each side, then place the slices on a serving platter. With a wooden spoon, scrape up the pan dredgings. Add the coffee, increase the heat, and simmer for 5 minutes. Season with pepper. Serve the gravy over the ham and biscuit halves.

Note: This recipe makes a thin gravy. It can be thickened with flour or perhaps with cream, and it will be very good, but it won't be redeye gravy.

European Dry-Cured Hams

I like to think that the perfect ham—salt-cured and hickory-smoked—was developed in the Americas, but this may not be the case. According to my old edition of *Larousse Gastronomique*, it was the Gauls who developed the technique of curing hams. After salting the hams, the Gauls smoked them for 2 days with "certain selected woods." Then they rubbed them with oil and vinegar and hung them to age. The Gauls are said to have exported these hams in large numbers to Rome and to the whole of Italy. But I'm sure that champions of Italy's Parma ham, which is fed on the whey left from making Parmesan cheese and fattened on parsnips, would have a few words to say about the origin of cured hams, so I won't pursue the matter further.

PROSCIUTTO

This delicious Italian ham is salted and air-dried. It is often served raw, thinly sliced, as an appetizer.

4 pounds coarse salt	2 tablespoons minced garlic
1 pound sugar	¼ pound fresh pork fat
1 teaspoon saltpeter	1 tablespoon flour
1 fresh ham with skin	salt and freshly ground pepper
2 cups red wine	water

Mix a dry cure with the coarse salt, sugar, and saltpeter. Weigh the ham, then put it onto a wooden worktable or countertop. Rub it well with the salt cure, packing the cure around the bone at either end. Place the ham in a wooden box and store it in a cool place (between 36°F and 40°F) for 2 days for each pound of ham. Check the ham every 7 days. If the salt has melted and run off, resalt the ham.

At the end of the curing time, remove the ham. Rinse it under running cold water, then rinse it with wine. Tie a cord to the shank end and hang the ham in a cool place for 2 days.

After 2 days, mash some garlic into a paste and rub the exposed meat of the ham. Dice the pork fat, put it into a skillet, and fry until fat is rendered. (Save the residue for crackling bread, or eat the bits on the spot.) Make a paste of the pork fat, flour, salt, pepper, and about 3 tablespoons water. Cover the ham with this paste. Wrap a sheet of cheesecloth around the ham, then place it in a large brown paper bag. Tie the paper bag loosely and hang the ham in a cool, airy place for at least 3 months.

Ibérico Ham

Jamón ibérico is a favorite noshing food in Spain, home of tapas, or "little dishes." There are several of these hams, all quite expensive. The key to gourmet Spanish hams is in range-fed pigs, free to roam the forests in search of acorns and other wild edibles. The hams from these pigs are salted and cured in cool mountain air.

The Spanish gourmets usually eat these hams raw, thinly sliced, along with various cheeses, olives stuffed with anchovies, beautiful roasted red piquillo peppers, green guindilla finger peppers, white asparagus spears, tiny artichoke hearts, almonds, dry-cured chorizo sausages (made from the same forest-fed pigs), and other finger foods. I like to add a log or two of palm hearts, some pork cracklings, melon balls, and quail eggs.

I go on at some length about these Spanish goodies because the feral pig in North America, which has roamed free since the Spanish introduced the hog to Florida and Mexico, enjoys pretty much the same diet as the Spanish free-range pig. The feral American pig, sometimes called the razorback or piney woods rooter, now grows in the wild across the country and is considered a nuisance in some areas. This affords a rare culinary opportunity for American hunters who are also culinary sports. The successful pig hunter should butcher the pig as soon as possible, being sure to scald the carcass and scrape off the hairs instead of skinning it. Salt and cure the two hams and two sides of bacon. Grind the rest of the meat and make chorizo or other sausage (for how-to details, see part two, Sausage, page 98).

Other Salt-Cured Meats

Although pork is the most popular meat for salting, other meats can also be used. In Russia, bear hams are cured exactly like pork hams. In many parts of the world, salt mutton is popular. In almost all cases, it's best to get the meat dressed and chilled as soon as possible, then apply salt once the meat is chilled.

Although opossums, rabbits, and other small animals and game can be salt-cured, it is usually larger animals and larger cuts of meat that are preserved.

MISSOURI VENISON CURE

The cure mix recipe I found in Cy Littlebee's Guide to Cooking Fish & Game *not only works well for Deer Jerky (see page 52), but also here for salt-curing venison. I found it to be very good with buffalo as well.*

A hunter from St. Louis sent this recipe to the Missouri Conservationist *in 1954. It eventually found its way into Cy Littlebee's* Guide to Cooking Fish & Game, *published by the Missouri Department of Conservation, on which this account was based. The curing mix is made ahead of the hunt and will be enough to jerk a hindquarter.*

THE CURE MIX

½ cup black peppercorns

¼ cup whole allspice berries

3 pounds salt

As soon after killing as possible, dissect the thigh, muscle by muscle. Skin off all membranes so the mixture will contact the raw, moist flesh. Best size for the pieces is not over 1 foot long by 6 to 8 inches wide and 4 inches thick.

Combine the ingredients and rub on the meat thoroughly. Then hang up each piece of meat by a string in the small end, and let them dry in the wind. If the sun is hot, keep the meat in the shade. (In the north, the sun helps the process.) Never let the meat get wet. If the weather is rainy, hang the meat rack by the heat of the campfire. Don't let it get any more smoke than necessary, and cover with canvas at night.

Meat prepared like this is not at its best until it's about a month old. After that, no hunter or trapper can get enough.

PUEBLO VENISON CURE

This recipe contains some ingredients brought to the Southwest by the Spanish, and the original probably contained red pepper instead of black. The allspice is, however, a New World ingredient.

fresh venison

3 pounds salt

5 tablespoons black pepper

4 tablespoons ground cinnamon

4 tablespoons ground allspice

Cut the meat into strips 12 inches long, 4 inches wide, and 2 inches thick. Remove all membrane from the surface of the meat so that the cure sticks to the moist meat. Mix the curing ingredients and rub the meat on all sides. Then dust on a little more. Thread each strip on a string and hang in a dry, cool place out of the sun. Do not use artificial heat. The venison should hang for a month. After that, it is ready to be eaten even without cooking.

CARIBBEAN DRY CURE

Many Caribbean cure recipes call for a brine flavored with allspice and other ingredients. Although this dry cure is not as spicy as the typical island brine cure, the salt does the job, and the brown sugar adds a distinctive flavor.

3 cups sea salt, or more as needed

1 teaspoon saltpeter

2 teaspoons brown sugar

3 pounds boneless meat (beef, venison, pork, etc.), in 1 piece

Mix the salt, saltpeter, and brown sugar. Put the meat into a glass container or crock and rub it well with some of the salt mix. Sprinkle the top with a little more of the salt mix, then put in a cool place. After a day, pour off any liquid that has accumulated, turn the meat, and sprinkle on a little more salt mix. Repeat the procedure for a total of 3 days. Then refrigerate the meat for 7 to 10 days.

Before using, freshen this meat by washing it thoroughly and then simmering it for 20 minutes per pound.

EASY DRY-CURED BRISKET

I used to think that all corned beef was prepared in brine. But maybe not. Here's a dry-cure recipe from the Morton Salt company, which they call deli-style corned beef, made with a commercial cure called Morton Tender Quick, which is available in some supermarkets. (If you don't find it with the salts, look in the canning section.) I can't argue with the results—or with the simplicity of this method. Personally, I prefer to find a fresh brisket that is on the lean side, if possible. The recipe calls for ground bay leaves and ground allspice. If you normally keep these ingredients whole, they can be ground with a mortar and pestle.

1 beef brisket, 4–5 pounds	1 teaspoon paprika
5 tablespoons Morton Tender Quick cure mix	1 teaspoon ground bay leaves
2 tablespoons brown sugar	1 teaspoon ground allspice
1 tablespoon black pepper	½ teaspoon garlic powder

Trim the brisket and measure its thickness. Combine the cure mix with the brown sugar, pepper, paprika, bay leaves, allspice, and garlic powder. Rub this mixture into the sides of the brisket, covering the surface. Place the brisket in a plastic bag and tie it closed. (I sometimes use large ziplock bags, if the meat will fit nicely.) Refrigerate for 5 days per inch of thickness.

When you are ready to cook, place the brisket in a stove-top dutch oven and add enough water to cover. Bring to a boil, then reduce the heat and simmer for 3 to 4 hours, or until the meat is very tender.

Note: You can also use this dry-cured brisket with the corned beef recipes in chapter 4, Corned Beef and Other Brine-Pickled Meats (page 307).

MORTON'S CANADIAN BACON

The very lean Canadian bacons are often smoked, but not necessarily so. Here's an easy recipe made with the loin instead of the tenderloin. (If you look at a T-bone pork chop, you'll see 2 rounds of meat. The smaller one, on the bottom, is the tenderloin; the larger one, on top, is the loin.) You can often purchase a whole pork loin at the supermarket, or talk to a local meat processor. It should be very fresh and properly chilled.

This recipe is designed to make use of such conveniences as the plastic bag, the modern refrigerator, and Morton Tender Quick, a commercial cure.

1 tablespoon Morton Tender Quick cure
mix per pound of pork

1 teaspoon sugar per pound of pork

1 boneless fresh pork loin

cooking oil

Thoroughly mix the cure and the sugar. Trim the pork loin. Rub the cure and sugar mixture into the meat, covering all exposed areas. Put the loin in a plastic bag, tie it shut, and put it into the refrigerator for 3 to 5 days. Remove the loin from the bag and soak it in cool water for 30 minutes. Pat the loin dry, then refrigerate it uncovered to allow it to dry slightly before cooking.

To cook the Canadian bacon, cut it into ⅛-inch slices and fry it in a little oil over low heat, turning to brown both sides. The cooking should take 8 to 10 minutes.

Variations: Use brown sugar instead of regular sugar. After the cure, remove the loin from the bag and smoke it for several hours.

If you want "pea meal" bacon, dry the loin as directed and rub it with a mixture of stone-ground cornmeal, black pepper, and cayenne. Cover the loin with plastic wrap and refrigerate. When you are ready to cook the bacon, slice it ⅛ inch thick, sprinkle with fine stone-ground cornmeal, and fry as directed.

CHAPTER 4

CORNED BEEF AND OTHER BRINE-PICKLED MEATS

One of my favorite recipes for corned beef, and for corned venison, comes from George Leonard Herter's rather outlandish *Bull Cook and Authentic Historical Recipes and Practices*. Herter seems to think that the name *corned beef* stems from a mistaken link to corn whiskey. Many Americans also tentatively associate the term with corn whiskey, usually without knowing why. By way of explanation, Herter says that corned beef originated in London in 1725. During World War II, he goes on, South American beef was shipped to the US forces fighting in Europe. The troops gave it the name *corned Willie*, meaning goat meat cured by soaking it in corn whiskey. But, Herter says, corn whiskey was not and is not used for corning beef. He's right about the corn whiskey, and maybe about London, but the rest of his derivation is questionable.

I think the confusion comes from the different meanings of the word *corn*. In England, the word originally meant "grain," which would include wheat and oats and barley. The term was in widespread use long before the discovery of American corn, or maize. In fact, the term was so common that it was also used to denote anything in small pieces, just as we now say a grain of sand. The salt used in early times was usually in the form of grains, much like rock salt today, and meat cured with the aid of these grains of salt was said to be corned. So there you have it.

Before proceeding, however, I must point out that water is a very important ingredient in corned meats. It doesn't have to be distilled, but it should have a clean taste. I've seen water in towns that has too much stuff added to it, whereas spring water in the area was excellent. Also, in parts of Florida and no doubt some other areas, the water tastes of sulfur. Soaking a piece of meat in this stuff doesn't help the flavor.

CORNED BEEF ACCORDING TO HERTER

Here's the "authentic historical" recipe for corned beef, which Herter claims to have published for the first time. To make the full measure of corning liquid, you'll need a container that will hold 6 gallons. It's best to pour in 6 gallons of water, then mark the level. In Herter's recipe, you'll end up with 6 gallons of corning liquid, including the water and other ingredients. This liquid is used to completely cover the meat. Reduce the measures if you don't need 6 gallons. Before dismissing the 6-gallon figure, however, remember that it's easy to corn venison as well as beef. Corning is an excellent way to solve a temporary storage problem with a fresh-killed elk or moose, and, of course, large chunks of beef can be purchased from meat processors. Beef briskets are popular for corning, but better and leaner cuts of beef can be used to advantage. I like sirloin tips cut into 4- to 8-pound chunks.

The container for the pickling liquid must be nonmetallic. Try a pickling crock or an old churn. Even a plastic or Styrofoam ice chest will work.

3 pounds salt	1 teaspoon ground cloves
1 large onion, minced	6 bay leaves
4 cloves garlic, minced	2 ounces sodium nitrate
1½ cups sugar	½ ounce sodium nitrite
4 tablespoons mixed pickling spice	1 chunk of beef, 4–8 pounds
1 tablespoon black pepper	

Place all the ingredients except the meat into the crock. Add enough water to make a total of 6 gallons. Add the meat, making sure that it is completely covered. Place a plate or wooden plank over the meat and, if necessary, weight it with a stone (or something nonmetallic) to keep the meat submerged. Corn the meat for a total of 15 days. On the 5th and 10th days, remove the meat, stir the corning liquid with a wooden paddle, and repack the meat. After the 15th day, remove the meat. Use some of the meat immediately, if needed, and store the rest in the refrigerator or freezer.

Ideally, the meat should be corned at a temperature of about 38°F. It can be corned at a higher temperature, but, Herter says, more salt should be added. For every 15°F increase in temperature, increase the salt measure by one-third.

To cook the corned beef, cover it with water, bring it to a boil, skim the surface, reduce the heat, and simmer for 5 hours or so, until the meat is fork-tender. Or use the meat in one of the "Recipes for Corned Beef."

A. D.'S CORNED MEAT

I have a tendency to go back to the basics on many traditional dishes. Here's my authentic historical recipe. The sea salt gives the meat a distinctive flavor.

1 (5-pound) chunk lean beef or venison	1 gallon water
3 cups sea salt	

Wash the meat and fit it into a nonmetallic container just large enough to hold it, but not too tightly. Mix the sea salt into the water, then pour the brine over the meat. Place a plate or saucer over the meat, then weight it down with a jar of water so that the meat will be completely submerged. Cover the container with a cloth and put it in a cool place or into the refrigerator for 10 days.

Rinse the corned meat and boil it in fresh water (without spices) until it is tender. Use the meat as a roast or slice it for sandwiches.

CARIBBEAN PICKLE

This salt-pickle recipe has been adapted from The Complete Book of Caribbean Cooking, *by Elisabeth Lambert Ortiz. Note that the brine contains allspice, a native West Indian ingredient. The popular jerked meats of Jamaica also contain lots of allspice, but these depend more on pepper than on salt.*

This recipe can be used for beef, pork, or venison—even mutton, for that matter. The measures are just right for 4 to 5 pounds of meat, and I suggest that you try a lean roast for making this Caribbean version of corned beef.

1 gallon water	3 cups sea salt
1 tablespoon powdered mustard	2 teaspoons saltpeter
1 tablespoon allspice berries	1 piece of fresh lean meat, 4–5 pounds
4-inch stick cinnamon	1 tablespoon minced fresh thyme
½ cup dark brown sugar (from the islands, if available)	1 medium onion, sliced
	1 or 2 hot red chili peppers

Put the water into a large saucepan. Mix in the mustard, allspice, cinnamon, brown sugar, salt, and saltpeter. Boil for a few minutes, then let cool and skim the surface. Put the meat into a stoneware crock or other nonmetallic container. (Try a large crockpot.) Pour the pickling solution over the meat, then add the thyme, onion slices, and chili peppers. Place a plate, saucer, or block of wood over the meat so that it is completely submerged in the brine. Leave the crock in a cool place for 10 days, turning the meat once a day. Remove the meat from the solution and refrigerate it until needed.

Simmer the meat in water for several hours, or until it is very tender. Use the meat as a roast or slice it for sandwiches.

Recipes for Corned Beef

Corned beef is rich enough that a quarter pound will be a sufficient serving for a person of normal appetite. Most of these recipes call for cooking a 4- to 6-pound chunk of meat, which is more than enough for the average family of today. Leftovers can be sliced for sandwiches or used in hash.

CORNED BEEF AND CABBAGE

I don't know where this dish originated, but Ireland is my guess. In any case, the combination of corned beef and cabbage is a happy one, at least to my taste.

4–5 pounds corned beef brisket	10 black peppercorns
1 tablespoon chopped fresh parsley	4 whole cloves
1 teaspoon powdered mustard	10–12 small onions, about 1 inch in diameter
2 bay leaves	1 large head green cabbage

Wash the corned beef and put it into a dutch oven or other container suitable for long, slow cooking. Cover the meat with water, then add the parsley, mustard, bay leaves, peppercorns, and cloves. Bring to a quick boil, reduce the heat, cover, and simmer for 3 hours. Skim off any fat that has come to the top, and pour off some of the water, so that the corned beef is only half covered. (The idea is to steam the cabbage instead of boiling it.) Peel the onions and put them around the sides of the meat. Wash and cut the cabbage into wedges, allowing at least 1 piece for each person, and put them on top of the meat. Cover tightly and simmer for 30 minutes, or until the cabbage is tender.

Leftovers can be refrigerated and heated later. If I have plenty of good bread, preferably corn pone, I can make a complete meal of leftover corned beef and cabbage. The stock from the corned beef and cabbage can be saved and used in soups and stews.

NEW ENGLAND BOILED DINNER

This is a pretty dish as well as a tasty one, and I like to serve it on a family platter about 20 inches long. The cooked corned beef is placed in the center with the other vegetables arranged all around.

4 pounds corned beef or venison

4 ounces salt pork, cubed

2 bay leaves

6–8 medium onions (golf-ball size)

1 teaspoon freshly ground black pepper

1 tablespoon chopped fresh basil

6 medium potatoes

6 carrots, scraped

2 medium turnip roots

2 small heads green cabbage, quartered

3 or 4 beets, cooked separately and sliced

Rinse the corned meat, put it in a pot along with the salt pork, cover with water, and boil for 10 minutes. Pour off the water, cover again with cold water, and bring to a new boil. Add the bay leaves, onions, pepper, and basil. Cover tightly and simmer (but do not boil) for 5 to 6 hours, or until fork-tender. Add the potatoes, carrots, and turnips; cover and cook until the potatoes are done. Add the cabbage, cover tightly, and simmer for 10 minutes. Note that it is not necessary to cover the cabbage with liquid; if you cover the pot tightly, the steam will cook it.

Center the corned beef on a large platter and arrange the vegetables, including the sliced beets, around it in groups. Serve hot with corn bread.

Note: There are many variations in vegetables and mixes. Try rutabagas, peeled and cubed, instead of turnips. Also try parsnips. A corned beef dish of old Virginia called for pumpkin cut into wedges. I have cooked the dish with corn on the cob and with Jerusalem artichokes. Also, brussels sprouts can be used if you cut back on the cabbage.

BOILED DINNER, THE MAINE WAY

People in Maine have firm opinions and often back them up. Once, for example, the Maine legislature passed a law prohibiting the use of tomatoes in anything called clam chowder. Maine people also have opinions about corned beef. A book titled *Good Maine Food* says that many families on the Maine coast corn their own beef, and "according to those Maine cooks whose reputations have gone farthest," it is best made from the thick rib or from a piece of flank next to the loin instead of from the brisket. The meat is salted down, then immersed in a brine. Some people pickle the meat for as long as a month; others pickle it overnight.

After pickling, the meat is boiled until tender, about 2 hours. Then the meat is removed from the brine, drained, and chilled. It will be served cold. The brine is saved until time to cook the dinner. To prepare dinners, start a countdown for a 2-hour period. Bring the liquid from the corned beef pot to a boil. After ½ hour, scrape 2 carrots, cut them into pieces, and add them to the pot. After 1 hour, add 1 sliced turnip and 1 small green cabbage cut into as many pieces as there are persons to be served. After 1½ hours, add 8 peeled potatoes, halved, and a sliced summer squash. At the end of 2 hours, remove all the vegetables. Put the cold corned beef on a platter and arrange the vegetables all around. Add 2 cups of sliced beets, which have been cooked separately so that they won't discolor the other vegetables. Serve with tomato catsup or vinegar.

MAINE CORNED BEEF HASH

For this fine dish, I also owe Good Maine Food. *The recipe is preceded by a dialogue from a Mrs. Ivy Gandy to a Mr. Roberts:*

"But how, my dear Mr. Roberts, can we have corned beef hash unless we first have real Maine corned beef? Didn't you know that nowhere in all the world do they know how to corn beef as it is done in Maine? All up and down the length of Long Island I have sought a meat market that has real corned beef, but all I can find is a tough length of reddened fibres, salty and bitter. My corned beef hash is made from meat that I corn myself by the old Maine recipe."

The hash is best when cooked in a large cast-iron skillet.

6 medium potatoes	½ cup boiling water
4 cups chopped cooked corn beef	salt and pepper to taste
¼ cup butter	catsup

Boil the potatoes in their skins until tender. Cool, peel, and dice. In a large wooden bowl, mix the diced potatoes with the corned beef and chop everything again until very fine. Melt the butter in a large skillet, then add the boiling water and corned beef mixture, stirring as you go. Add a little salt and pepper. Cook on low heat until a crust forms on the bottom. Fold the mixture over like an omelette. Serve hot with catsup.

Brine-Cured Pork Hams and Shoulders

Although large hams can be cured in a pickle instead of being dry-cured, the process really works best for the small hams and shoulders. One advantage of a pickle over a dry cure is that it allows the use of liquids such as honey and wine. Wine is used in some Italian cures and in the Spanish serrano hams. And the Suffolk hams of England are pickled in stout.

One problem with curing large hams, and large numbers of hams, in a pickle is that salt penetration is slow and the liquid drawn out of the ham tends to dilute the pickle. Large hams are best dry-cured at first, then transferred to a pickle. Shoulders and small hams (under 10 pounds) can be put directly into the pickle, which is what I recommend. (In other words, with small hams and shoulders you can omit steps 2 and 4 below.)

My favorite recipe is of Italian origin, but for it I am indebted to *The Country Kitchen*, a British cookbook by Jocasta Innes. The steps below can be completed with ordinary kitchen equipment, making this recipe ideal for curing a single shoulder. The recipe can also be used for large batches of pork, provided the pickle is kept up to strength. In any case, this is a good recipe for beginners as well as gourmets. Ms. Innes seems to be fond of scalding things, and I have left these instructions in the procedure, partly to appease my mother-in-law, a kindred spirit who scalds at every opportunity and who is still mad at me over my comments in my *Cast-Iron Cooking* book about her scalding and scrubbing my favorite skillet, thereby ruining the seasoning.

1. Rub sea salt into the surface of the ham, using 1½ pounds of salt for a 12-pound piece. Mash the salt into the cavity around the bone on either end.

2. Scald a nonmetallic container of suitable size. Scald also a wooden lid, or plank of suitable size, and scald a stone for weight.

3. Put the ham into the container, place the plank on it, and weight the plank with the stone. Leave the container in a cool, clean place overnight. (If you can make room, use the refrigerator, as I do.) If you have a large ham, say 18 to 20 pounds or so, salt it down for an extra day or two, rubbing in more salt after the first day.

4. Mix a pickle by boiling 4 pints of good water and adding 2 pounds salt, 1 tablespoon baking soda, and 2 tablespoons saltpeter or sodium nitrate. Turn off the heat and add 4 pints white wine, 1 tablespoon allspice, and ½ tablespoon black peppercorns. Set aside to cool.

5. Remove the ham from the container and drain off any liquid drawn out by the salt cure. Wipe the ham and put it back into the container. It's best to have the ham slightly cooler than the pickle. (If the pickle were colder, Ms. Innes says, it would continue the extracting process rather than the permeating one.) Pour the pickle

over the ham, straining it through a muslin bag. The pickle should completely cover the ham. If not, use a smaller container or make more pickle.

6. Place the wooden lid on the ham and weight it down with the stone. Leave it in a cool place for a total of 28 days.

7. After each 7 days, test the pickle for strength. Do this by putting a fresh egg into the solution. If it half sinks, the pickle needs more salt. Boil about one-fifth the total amount of fresh water with three times as much salt as the original pickle. Cool this mixture before adding it to the container.

8. Every 4 to 5 days, remove the ham and scald a wooden spoon. Stir the brine with the wooden spoon and replace the ham. Scald the wooden lid and scald the stone, then replace both.

9. Remove the ham after 28 days and scrub off the surface salt with a brush.

10. Hang the ham to dry in a cool, airy place for 7 days.

11. To cook the ham, put it in a pot of plain water, bring it to a boil, reduce the heat to very low, and simmer it for 2 hours. Then simmer it for 1 hour in clean water, along with chopped celery, carrots, onions, and so on for flavor.

Note: I highly recommend that you try this procedure with 2 shoulders, or with a single shoulder divided into a picnic and a butt cut. (Also, you can cut a whole ham into a butt and a shank portion.) By having more than one piece of meat, you can cook one as soon as it is ready and hang one for a month or so.

I might add that similar brine-cured hams are eaten in other parts of the world, often at Christmas dinner. (In other countries, turkey isn't as important as it is in America for Christmas and Thanksgiving.) In Finland and Sweden, the *grilijerad shinke* is put in brine weeks ahead of Christmas. It is served hot on Christmas Eve and cold on the following days. Finns serve baked rutabaga or turnip roots with the ham, whereas Swedes prefer to serve the ham with boiled red cabbage and mashed potatoes.

SWEET PICKLE FOR PORK

Here's an old Wyoming recipe. The measures are for 100 pounds of pork, but they can be scaled down for smaller amounts. Before applying the pickle, the meat is rubbed with dry salt and packed in wooden barrels or wooden boxes.

7 gallons water

salt

3 pounds sugar

2 ounces saltpeter

1 ounce ground red pepper

Put the water in a large pot and dissolve salt in it until it will float an egg. Stir in the remaining ingredients and bring to a boil. Let the brine cool, then pour it over the salted pork. Let stand for 10 days. Drain off the brine, bring it to a boil, let it cool, and pour it over the pork again. Cook the pork as needed.

CHAPTER 5

SMOKEHOUSES AND RIGS

On the family farm where I was raised, we had a smokehouse of the old-timey sort. My grandfather (Jeff Livingston) built it from rough, unfinished lumber hewn from the tall pines that he had cleared from the land. During my lifetime, the smokehouse has had a tin roof put on with lead-capped nails, but I am certain that the original roof, like that of the main house, was made of wooden shingles. Believe it or not, Grandpa put the family tub in the smokehouse. The main house didn't have a bathroom because there was no electricity or running water. The smokehouse was beside the well, making it more convenient for the tub. Later, when an electric pump and running water became available, the tub was moved into the main house.

The fire for the smokehouse was built in a shallow trench in the dirt floor. First, we built a hot fire with cured oak or hickory, burning it down to red-hot coals. These coals were concentrated in the trench; then two green hickory logs about 6 to 8 inches in diameter, as I remember them, were laid on top of the coals. Of course, the logs were the length of the trench. I emphasize that the limbs were green, freshly cut especially for smoking. Gradually the green limbs themselves became coals and had to be replaced by new green limbs to provide smoke.

The idea, when laying such a fire, is to produce lots of smoke without having to constantly add more wood. The fire should not blaze up and burn, producing too much heat for cold-smoking and using up too much wood, nor go completely out. Much depended on how close the green limbs were to each other and on the sloping sides of the trench. My father was an expert at laying such a fire. He was, it seemed to me, quite fussy about the details—and with good reason. On the one hand, he didn't like to go outside in freezing weather after nine o'clock at night to tend the fire. On the other hand, he wanted to see smoke when the new day dawned. Whether or not we had smoke all the time was a matter of great importance to us back then, although in more recent years, I have decided that letting the smoke expire for several hours won't hurt a thing in cold weather. Just don't tell Pa.

Our smokehouse was about 12 feet wide and 14 feet long. I doubt that Grandpa followed a set of plans or exact dimensions. He just built it. (He built the fourteen-room main house the same way, framing it on 14-inch sills, and there wasn't a square corner in it, as I found out when trying to remodel it.) The sides of the smokehouse were made of 12- or 14-inch rough-hewn pine boards, nailed to the frame with square nails. The boards had a crack between them. This crack wasn't there because Grandpa didn't fit the boards properly before nailing them; they were spaced by design so that the smoke could get out. The smokehouse had exposed rafters, and the meat was hung from cross timbers well above a strapping boy's head. I don't remember Grandpa's technique, but to tie the hams, Pa used thin strips (withes) of green hickory or white oak. My wife tells me that her father, on a similar farm in a contiguous county, used strips from the bladelike leaves of the yucca, which they called bear grass.

Another very important feature of our smokehouse was a wooden workbench built into one side. Just as the walls contained cracks for smoke to escape, the worktable contained cracks between the boards to drain the salty juices that seep out of the curing meat. (In time, the dirt inside the smokehouse became quite salty and would quickly rust hoe blades and axes if they were left there.) After being properly salted, the meat was grouped on the boards according to size and kind, then left on the boards to cure.

A similar smokehouse can be built today, and I have seen them converted from existing structures. (I know one fellow who inherited the family farm and converted an old two-seater outhouse for smoking. He said it worked pretty well, but somehow the sausages didn't come out quite as good as planned. He allowed that part of the problem might have been in his head.) Most modern families, rigged with mechanical refrigerators and freezers and supermarkets, won't require a large log-burning smokehouse and might therefore consider making a smaller structure. Instead of burning logs, you can heat chunks of hickory on electric hot plates or perhaps on a couple of charcoal-burning hibachi grills.

In any case, I am setting forth several suggestions for smokehouses. Some of these are obviously temporary, but some are compatible with modern houses and even suburban landscapes. I suggest that the beginner start with an inexpensive, temporary structure and use it until he gains some smokehouse experience. Then he can customize one of my ideas, or, better, design a smokehouse from scratch. Note that other uses of a smokehouse are possible. The modern practitioner probably won't have to put the family bathtub in the smokehouse, but the deer hunter or the farmer who butchers a goat might want to consider the structure as a place to hang a whitetail or goat for aging. In this case, it would be very important to cover all vents and openings with screening to keep the flies away.

The sketches in this chapter are merely suggestions, not detailed plans. I assume that any local builder or competent do-it-your-selfer can provide the construction details to suit local building codes, individual preferences, and landscape compatibility as well as available materials and funds. It is much more important to consider the function of a smokehouse and what it must do to accomplish cold-smoking—and what it must *not* do.

1. The smokehouse must *not* be an oven. That is, it must not get hot enough to cook the fish or meat in its normal operating environment. For cold-smoking, the smokehouse should remain below 100°F and preferably between 70°F and 80°F. This requirement of enough heat to produce smoke but not enough to raise the temperature to cooking levels can be accomplished in several ways, usually involving either a large smokehouse with a small fire or some scheme to generate the smoke outside the smokehouse and pipe it in.

2. The smokehouse must be a smoke chamber; that is, it must hold the smoke densely. On the other hand, the smoke must escape somewhere. It's best to have the exhaust openings at the apex, or in the top of the structure, or near the top, so that there is a slow flow of smoke from bottom to top. The fish or meats to be smoked should, of course, be hung or racked in the flow of smoke.

3. The smokehouse must have some means of holding the meat, either on racks or suspended from poles or rafters. Obviously, this requirement will be of great importance to those who smoke meat commercially, in which case the smokehouse should be designed to accommodate the maximum amount of meat.

4. For cold-smoking, the smokehouse must function safely for extended periods of time.

A. D.'s Walk-In Smoker

My favorite design is somewhat different from Grandpa's. The drawings here show the shape better than I can describe it. Note that the low side has a wooden workbench (best with cracks between the boards for drainage). The high side has a pole (or poles) in the top for hanging hams and whole fish. It can also be fitted with racks, but access is not as convenient.

This smokehouse can be made as long or as short as you wish, but I recommend *at least* 8 feet for smoking so that you'll have room to move about. If you want a storage shed, consider making the structure 16 feet or longer and then dividing it in half, with a door on either end. The structure can be framed with 2-by-4s. On the roof, wooden shingles would be great. I also like the sides made with overlapping wooden boards. All of the wood can be left unpainted, if that decor jibes with your landscape. The inside walls of a smokehouse are usually bare, and the rafters are exposed.

Modern conveniences can include electric wiring. Also, vents can be built in at ground level using standard units made for venting boxed-in houses. These usually have screening. Similar vents can be placed around the top of the smokehouse, under the roof overhang, but I really prefer to use a ridge vent along the top. (Ridge vents are available at building supply houses. They are a sort of vented cap that is placed over the apex of the roof, as shown in the sketch.)

If you prefer to make such a structure with a standard roof, consider an overhang design. This can be used for a woodshed or for storing garden tools.

If you plan to use wood or charcoal for fuel, consider putting the structure on the ground, with a dirt floor. A concrete footing can be used for a foundation.

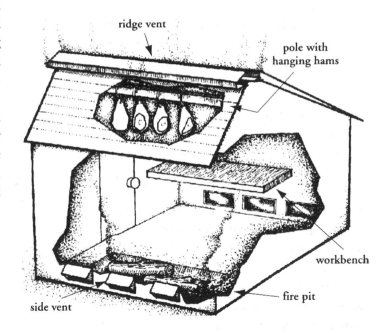

A walk-in smoker

Chimney Smoking

According to my copy of *Larousse Gastronomique*, cold-smoking is (or was) used almost exclusively in France for herring, which are first pickled in salt for a certain length of time, depending on how they are to be used. Bloaters, for example, are only lightly salted and will keep for only a few days. Pickled smoked herring, on the other hand, are salted for at least 8 days. After pickling, the herring are strung up on rods and placed in a chimney. A fire of beech wood is lit, which causes a rush of hot air up the chimney. This draught dries the herring quickly. Then the fire is dampened with beech sawdust and chips, which creates a dense smoke to flavor and color the herring.

I've never seen a commercial smoking chimney, but reading the French text gave me some ideas for home application. As it happens, I have a fireplace in my den, and the large chimney emerges on a rather flat roof with easy access. In short, I have hung fish on rods and suspended them into my chimney from the top. Usually, I first build a fire with oak or pecan wood and let it burn down before I load the fish. Then I dampen the fire with green wood. For true and safe cold-smoking, the temperature of the air that exits the chimney during smoking should not exceed 100°F. It's easy enough to hang a thermometer and check it.

In hot weather, you may have to forget the fire, turn on the air conditioner, and put a two-burner electric hot plate into the fireplace. Put a cast-iron skillet on each burner and fill it with green wood chips or partly fill it with hardwood sawdust that has been soaked in water. Adjust the heat on the hot plate to make smoke without burning the wood.

Try this method with small fish of about 1 pound. Larger fish should be filleted and smoked on a rack instead of being hung from a rod. In any case, be certain that your fish won't drop into the chimney.

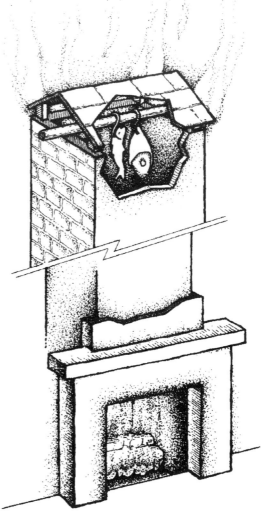

Chimney smoking

Note that you can also smoke sausages and other meats by this method. But don't allow too much grease to drip into your chimney. If you do, you may be setting the stage for a roaring and dangerous fire.

Backyard Barbecue Smokers

Some time ago, agricultural engineers with the US Department of Agriculture published some drawings of various smokehouses, most of which look quite like a typical country outhouse. Some of these plans, such as the one depicted here, were then reprinted in a book called *Butchering, Processing and Preservation of Meat*, by Frank G. Ashbrook. While all of the schemes will no doubt work, I am especially attracted to a design for combining a smokehouse and an outdoor grill. This could be a practical unit for the backyard, especially if old bricks or stones are used in the construction. The details here show the firebox and grill, with a flue leading back to the smokehouse.

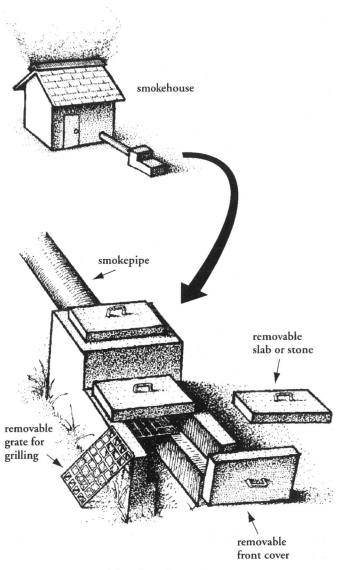

A backyard smoker

Tepee and Wigwam Smokers

The more or less conical shape of the tepee used by the nomadic Plains Indians has a hole in the top to allow smoke to escape. This same shape can be used for smoking meat and fish, and it's a good design for smoking a single ham or a few fish. It is not a good design for smoking a large batch of fish or meat, however. A wigwam structure popular with the Algonquian people can also be used.

With a tepee, three main poles are joined at the top and spread at the bottom like a tripod, and more poles are spaced to round out the structure. Then the poles are covered with hides or some other material, leaving a hole at the top. (A real tepee doesn't have the hole at the very top; rather, it is off-center, allowing for a flap to cover the hole.) A smoke fire is built on the ground, and the meat is suspended from the top. The covering for a temporary tepee can be made from canvas. Even plastic sheeting can be used if the tepee is large and the fire small and confined to the center.

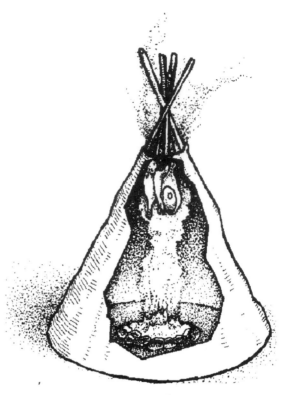

A tepee smoker

Note that a tepee is a portable, breakdown structure. The wigwam, on the other hand, is built with poles inserted into holes in the ground, or from sapling trees that can be bent over. This produces more of a dome shape, but it can still be used for smoking, simply by hanging the meat or fish near the vent hole in the top.

A-frame Smokers

An A-frame structure is relatively easy to make and can be permanent, temporary, or collapsible and portable. In the latter construction, the triangular ends would be removable and the two sides hinged at the top; thus, it can be partly disassembled and folded for storage. It must, of course, have a vent or vents at the top, which is easy to accomplish at the apex where the two sides join together. If the structure is permanent, it should be topped with a ridge vent. You can make a walk-in smoker 8 feet long with five sheets of plywood and a few 2-by-4s. For a permanent structure, of course, the outside plywood should be covered with shingles or some weatherproof material. For a really nice structure, consider using natural wood siding instead of plywood. Note that you can build a worktable and shelves at one end of the structure.

The fire is built on the ground. If you prefer, install a floor (or use a concrete slab) and generate the smoke with two or three electric heating elements properly spaced on either end, or perhaps with gas or charcoal heating elements.

The basic A-frame is good for smoking meat and fish on either one, two, or three longitudinal rods, but it is not so good for smoking on racks because access and top-of-the-structure space are limited.

Commercial Smokers

You may find commercial smoking units suitable for cold-smoking, rigged with a thermostatically controlled heating element, but they will be rather expensive. Most of the small home smokers, rigged with an electric heating pad, may or may not work for cold-smoking, depending partly on the outside temperature and wind. I've never had a problem with these units for hot-smoking a few fish, but a whole turkey is another matter. So, proceed carefully—and beware the gray area between 80°F and 140°F.

Although my old Outer's electric smoker has served me well for over thirty years, it is not ideal for cold-smoking, simply because it is difficult to attain enough heat to generate the smoke while at the same time keeping the smoke chamber cool. It's a big problem.

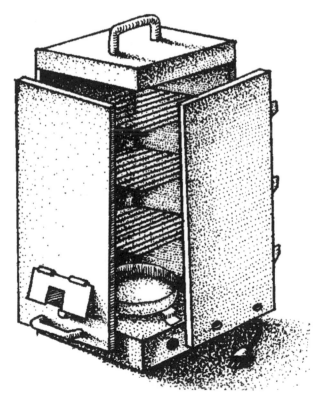

A portable electric smoker

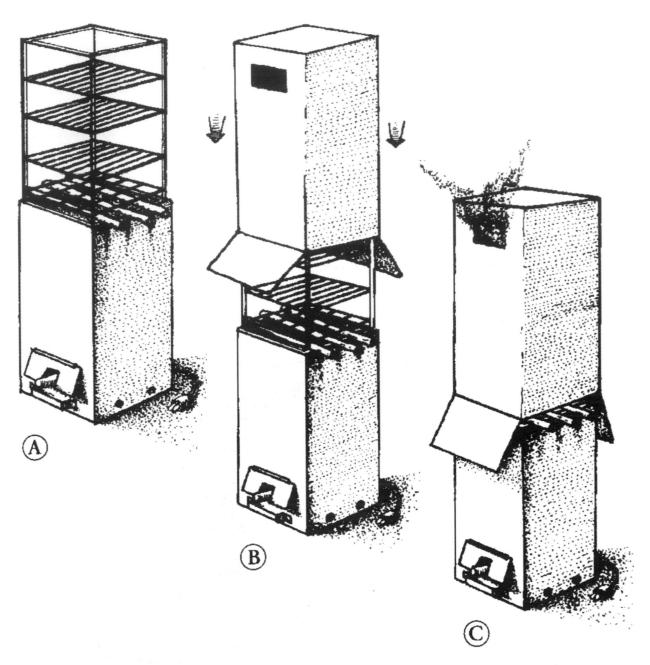

**(A) By removing the lid, putting wooden sticks across the top, placing the racks
on top of the sticks and (B) fitting the cardboard packing box over the racks,
(C) you can make a portable smoker taller, and thereby cool the smoke.**

One manufacturer, Luhr-Jensen, suggests that you can cool the smoke somewhat by making the portable smoker taller. This trick can be accomplished with top-loading units simply by removing the lid entirely, then putting two wooden sticks across the top of the unit. The rack fits atop the sticks, and the cardboard packing box fits over the racks. The same idea can be used to rig an extension compartment made with wood or tin. Tin would be better for cold-smoking because it conducts heat more readily. Also, you can rig a round extension for the silo cooker/smoker. Thus, you can have a neat rig for hot-smoking as well as for cold-smoking.

Obviously, any top-loading unit will be easier to extend. Further, the extension doesn't necessarily have to go straight up. It can dogleg or make two elbow turns. Just make sure that the smoker draws properly and doesn't get too hot for cold-smoking.

There are some expensive electric smokers on the market with automatic temperature control, and some of these work much better than the smaller units. In my view, however, the culinary sport will want to devise his own smoker. With it, he can brag that his smoked meats and fish are better than any other, and the smoker itself becomes part of the secret recipe or at least part of the reason for success. Truly, the improvised cold-smoker, however ugly, is a thing of inner beauty and self-fulfillment—and a walk-in rig can be the pride and joy of the patio chef's repertory.

Storage-Shed Smokers

There are lots of inexpensive sheet-metal storage sheds on the market, and custom units are also available. Some of these are attractive, but most of them are merely functional. In any case, these sheds can be used for smoking or be easily modified to do so. Most people want to put the sheds on concrete slabs, but this is not a good choice if you plan to generate smoke from a wood fire. Put the shed either directly on the ground or perhaps on concrete footers, leaving dirt in the center. If these units are too tightly constructed to allow

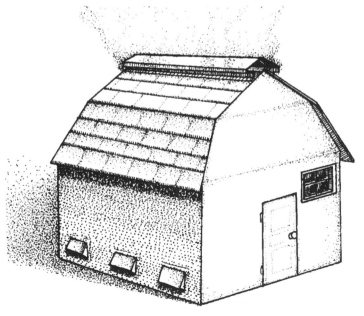

My favorite barn-shaped shed smoker

the smoke to escape properly, drill holes in the walls just under the overhang, if there is an overhang. You can also install adjustable vents and possibly even ridge vents on some units.

Although you can use such a shed for both storage and smoking, I really don't recommend that practice because the smoke covers everything and the salt will rust tools and equipment. Instead of using the space for storage, build in a wooden bench for salting and otherwise working with the meat.

While working on this book, I started looking at various storage sheds for sale in my area. The roofs of most of these don't have much slope. My favorite design is shaped like a barn—it has a good high point for the smoke to exit, and the shed I priced even had ridge venting. Perfect. It was attractive and might well fit into a country setting.

Old Refrigerator and Freezer Smokers

Converting an old refrigerator into a smoker is relatively easy if you've got all the racks. Such a smoker is also convenient to use. Many people put a hot plate in the bottom of the refrigerator and cut a vent hole in the top. This rig may or may not be satisfactory for cold-smoking, depending on how much heat it generates. It's best to check out the unit by leaving a thermometer on one of the shelves, or drilling a hole and installing a more or less permanent thermometer that can be read from the outside.

For cold-smoking in most climates, the source of the heat should be removed from the refrigerator. The heat can be charcoal or electric, or even gas of some sort. The length of the smoke pipe should be great enough to allow the smoke to cool properly, and the slope of the pipe should be great enough for the rig to draw the smoke properly. The rig really works best on a hillside.

If you want to use the heat inside the refrigerator for cold-smoking, remember that the size of the box and the intensity of the heat have a bearing on the temperature. Remember also that these boxes are

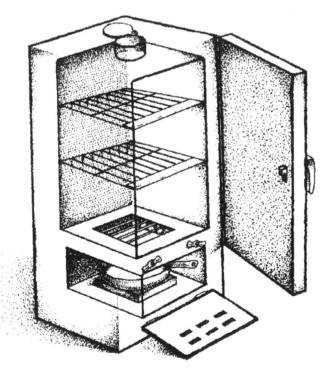

An old refrigerator turned smoker

well insulated, so the outside temperature won't be as important as when using one of the small aluminum smokers that conduct heat rapidly.

In addition to old refrigerators, old top-loading home freezers can be rigged for smoking. These can be fitted with racks and hanging rods.

Be warned that old refrigerators and freezers can be dangerous around small children, and most of them can't be opened from inside. Consequently, the locking handles should be removed or modified so that anyone playing hide-and-seek can get out.

Box Smokers

In Florida, smokers built of wooden boxes with several closely spaced removable trays are popular for smoking mullet and other fish. The trays are made with wooden frames fitted around hardware cloth. These trays slide in and out, and can be rotated from top to bottom during the smoking period.

Some of these boxes sit over the source of heat and smoke, and some have the firebox at some distance from the smoker. The latter is usually necessary for cold-smoking. In either case, the design is great for smoking butterflied fish or such small items as shrimp or oysters. Sausages can also be smoked on the trays.

In addition to the trays, you can also install a pole across the top for hanging hams, or perhaps screw metal hooks into the top.

A box smoker with trays

Barrel and Drum Smokers

Convenient cold-smokers can be made from wooden barrels and metal drums, provided that the fire or heating element is external. Metal drums conduct heat better than wooden barrels and therefore run cooler, but they are not as quaint as, for example, a used Jack Daniel's whiskey barrel.

If a vertical smoker is desired, cut a hole in the bottom to accommodate a stovepipe or other smoke conduit from the heat source. Then remove the top of the barrel and install racks or bars for holding or hanging fish or meat. Next, fashion a lid for the barrel and drill or cut holes for the smoke to escape. (A smokestack is not necessary, but it will look better if you are setting up a more or less permanent smoker.) Usually, a piece of plywood cut a little larger than the top of the barrel will make a satisfactory lid, and vent holes can be drilled directly into the plywood. Drill only a few holes at first, then add more if needed.

Some people have hot-smokers and hot-cookers made from old metal drums or barrels cut in half lengthwise, hinged, and fitted with a rack. These can also be used for cold-smoking if you put a vent on the top of one end and run a stovepipe or other heat conduit to the bottom of the other end. More and more, we see large barrel-shaped cookers with small barrel-shaped fireboxes attached to the bottom. Some of these may work for cold-smoking in cool weather. You can sometimes rig an electric hot plate and a sawdust or wood-chip pan in the firebox or a large offset unit, making a cold-smoker from a cooker/ smoker. In any experiment of this sort, it's best to make a trial run with a thermometer instead of meat or fish.

A drum or barrel smoker

So, there you have it. As stated earlier, I suggest that you start cold-smoking with a simple, disposable unit. Then you can expand later, after you determine your individual needs. Much might depend on the design of your house and landscaping. In any case, give some careful thought to the details before building something permanent. Be especially suspicious of the length dimensions given for chimneys and smoke conduits running from the fire to the smoke chamber. When planning smoke conduits, remember that aluminum piping will conduct heat much faster than concrete or plastic pipes. This fact should have a bearing on the required length. I do recommend that you build your own cold-smoker—but proceed cautiously.

Beware the Gray Zone

Be warned—again—**that a smoker designed for cold-smoking should not act as an oven and should not function in what I call the gray area.** For cold-smoking, it's best to keep the temperature below 100°F and preferably at 80°F or less. At higher temperatures, salmonella and other bacteria can multiply rapidly until a temperature of about 140°F is reached. Thus cold-smoking should be accomplished at temperatures below 100°F and preferably at 80°F or lower. Hot-smoking should be accomplished at temperatures higher than 140°F. *Avoid the gray area in between.* Note also that cooking and smoking at 140°F may not be safe in all cases. The US Department of Agriculture is now recommending that your Thanksgiving turkey be cooked to an internal temperature of 180°F—a figure impossible to attain in a 140°F smoker.

Note also that cold-smoked fish and meat is not cooked. It may or may not be safe to eat, but it is simply not cooked. A good salt cure and proper handling prior to smoking will make the meat safer to eat without cooking, but fully cooking the meat is the safest way to go. Recipes for smoked meats are included in the following chapters. I also recommend using a salt cure for meats that are hot-smoked at low temperatures, and especially in smoker-cookers that may dip below the 140°F mark in cold or windy weather.

CHAPTER 6

WOODS AND FUELS FOR SMOKING

Backyard chefs accustomed to heating with a few wood chips placed on charcoal or gas-heated lava rocks can get by with a small bag of chips purchased at the supermarket, where they are available in such flavors as hickory or mesquite or Jack Daniel's whiskey barrels. For cold-smoking in a large smokehouse, however, the practitioner must be concerned with quantity as well as quality and should have a large supply of suitable wood at hand. It's best and certainly cheaper to cut your own, using whatever good hardwood is readily available to you—pecan, oak, hickory, alder, and so on. It is also important to consider the size of the wood pieces, depending on availability and on your cold-smoking rig.

Sawdust

The sawdust from hardwood makes a dense smoke for a long period of time if used properly. Ideally, it should be smoldered in a pan instead of being put in direct contact with the fire. A cast-iron skillet over an electric burner is ideal. Of course, sawdust can also be piled over hot coals or charcoal. It can be used dry or damp. My favorite is fresh sawdust from green wood. A good supply can be caught in a strategically placed wide-open pan while you are sawing your winter firewood.

If you don't cut your firewood, you might visit a sawmill, cabinetmaker, or some tradesman who deals in wood. Many small sawmills simply throw sawdust away, blowing it out onto a pile that will eventually have to be burned or hauled off. But these days more and more sawdust is being used as a by-product, so that you may have to pay for it.

Sawdust from any good hardwood will work, provided that it has not been treated with chemicals.

If you have a walk-in smokehouse, you should consider building a small wood fire on the dirt floor. When this fire burns down to red-hot coals, cover them with sawdust. In about 30 minutes, you'll have a dense smoke. You may have to add more sawdust from time to time. If your wood burns out, you may be able to start it again with kindling, but it's probably best to start a new fire outside the smoker, then bring in some hot coals with a scoop. Cover the new hot coals with sawdust, and you're in business again.

You can also combine sawdust with chips and chunks.

Wood Chips and Chunks

Various sizes of chips and chunks can be used for smoking, but they are really better suited for use in hot-smoking applications. Buying packaged chips from barbecue supply houses can be quite expensive, but you may be able to find some at a bargain price from large wood-chip operations. In my part of the country, hardwood chips are being hauled out by the trainload.

Dry, soaked, or green chunks can be used in a pan over electric heat, or they can be piled over charcoal or another heat source.

Green or soaked wood chunks can also be used for cold-smoking. These can be piled over hot coals, but green chunks don't work too well in a pan. Again, buying wood chunks from a barbecue supply house gets expensive. It's best to saw off an inch or two of a good log, then chop the wheels into chunks with a hatchet.

You can also cut green limbs into small wheels.

Logs and Limbs

If you have a large walk-in smokehouse with a dirt floor and a talent for maintaining a fire, you can use green logs for both the smoke and the heat. This is the old-timey way. It's hard to get green logs just right, but once hot, they will smolder for a long time without making a blaze. A preliminary fire is built in a trench with dry wood and kindling, and sometimes it's helped along with charcoal. Then the green logs are placed on either side of the trench. As the logs burn, they can be inched closer and closer together. Also, if the trench is properly sloped, the logs will tend to settle down automatically as they burn. With luck, two new logs can be put down and consumed without having to build another fire. Thus, four green logs properly arranged will smolder for days, producing lots of smoke and not too much heat. Almost always, a freshly cut green log will not burn as hot as a dry log; part of the reason is that the heat is used up in vaporizing the moisture in the wood. Technically, this is called the latent heat of vaporization and explains why boiling water at sea level doesn't get hotter than 212°F.

Smaller logs, cut from limbs or saplings, can be placed directly atop a source of controlled heat, such as an electric burner. A rectangular cast-iron griddle or fish cooker heated over two stove burners can be used to heat green limbs or sticks of stove wood.

Again, green wood is my favorite, but dry pieces can also be used if they are merely heated instead of being part of the fuel.

Where There's Smoke . . .

In cold-smoking, you'll need enough heat to produce smoke—but not enough to overly heat the smokehouse or smoke chamber. Obviously, much will depend on the size of the smoke chamber, the location and intensity of the fire, and the outside temperature.

- *Electric Heat.* The familiar hot plate, usually with one or two coil-type rheostatically controlled heating elements, is by far the easiest way to go for most small-scale cold-smoking operations. They are quite efficient because a wood-chip or sawdust pan can sit directly on the coils; in short, they can easily heat the wood to the smoke point without heating up the smoke chamber too much. Some of these can be purchased from sausage and smoking equipment suppliers, but these are often expensive. You should be able to rig your own, using an old hot plate or a new one from a discount store. I recommend a cast-iron skillet to hold the chips or sawdust. Some of the small commercial "smokers" have a tin pan with a wooden handle.

  A single or double heating element will generate enough smoke for most chambers, but a walk-in unit may require two or three hot plates. An old electric kitchen stove or stove top will also work if it is properly installed (these usually require 220 to 240 volts, whereas most hot plates operate on 110 to 120 volts).

- *Gas Heat.* Any small gas burner can be used much like an electric hot plate, and portable units with gas cylinders will work where electricity isn't available. The larger refillable tanks are better (and cheaper in the long run) than small gas cylinders. Also, natural gas can be used if you have it. Of course, the burner should have a valve to adjust the flame. It's best to use a cast-iron skillet to hold the wood chips or sawdust for these units.

- *Other Burners.* Any sort of camp stove can be used for generating smoke in a skillet or wood pan. You'll need a long-burning stove for cold-smoking, unless you can be at hand to add new fuel as needed.

- *Coals.* You can heat sawdust and wood chips with hot coals, produced by burning wood, charcoal, or hard coal. Usually, the sawdust is piled onto and around the coals. The danger is that the sawdust or chips will become fuel for the fire, quickly burning up and raising the temperature in the smoke chamber.

- *Wood.* It is possible to combine wood for fuel and wood for smoke in large smokehouses with a dirt floor or, sometimes, in units that have the fire a good ways from the smoke chamber. For this purpose, I prefer to start the fire with dry wood, then add some freshly cut green wood for smoke. As the green wood burns into coals, more green wood can be added, thereby keeping the fire going and the smoke coming, if all goes according to plan. Parallel logs can be used in walk-in smokehouses, as pointed out earlier in this chapter. Be warned that this method requires lots of attention, but also remember that letting the fire go out from time to time isn't disastrous, except possibly early in the process when blowflies or other insects are a problem.

Personally, I find this method the most satisfying way to cold-smoke meat and fish. I believe that the quality of the smoke is better than smoke generated in a pan, but I have no explanation for the difference, be it real or imaginary.

- *Combinations.* You can combine the methods above, using, for example, green wood logs during the day and electric hot plates during the night.

The Best Woods for Smoking

Although some people champion one wood or another for smoking meats, fish, and game—often saying to use one wood for red meat and another for fish—I don't put too much stock in their claims, and I wouldn't hesitate to use any good hardwood that is readily available. For either hot-smoking or cold-smoking, I almost always prefer freshly cut wood to seasoned wood, but again, there are opinions on this matter. If you prefer green wood, you'll have to cut your own or make a deal with a local woodcutter. The little bags of wood sold by barbecue supply houses are dry. I think that cutting your own wood is part of the fun. A chain saw is handy, but a good bow saw will also cut lots of good wood in short order.

In most parts of the country, suitable woods can be gathered easily from woods and fencerows. Here are a few favorites:

- *Hickory.* Most of the country people in my neck of the woods use hickory for cold-smoking. That's what my father and grandfather used. Hickory does indeed make very good smoke, but I think its reputation was built on the long-burning qualities of the green wood. What the old-timers wanted was a wood that would smolder all night.

  A friend of mine asked me how to identify a hickory tree. Look for remnants of nuts that squirrels have gnawed scattered around base of the tree. I have been told that the nuts can also be used for smoking, but, it seems to me, these would be better for hot-smoking, where only a few would be used during the cooking process.

- *Alder.* This wood is quite popular for smoking fish in the Pacific Northwest and some other areas, and alder chips and chunks are packaged and sold all over the nation. Some practitioners who prefer alder go so far as to say that it's the only smoke to use for fish and poultry.

I'll allow that some of the best salmon I've eaten was smoked with alder, but it was smoked with freshly cut green alder. If you have plenty of alder free for the cutting, fine. If not, use some other good hardwood and lie about it.

- *Guava and Other Fruit Woods.* The guava tree grows in southern Florida and other tropical or subtropical regions. It is especially popular as a smoking agent in Hawaii. Citrus, plum, cherry, pear, and other fruit woods can also be used.

- *Pecans.* These are my personal favorite for both cold- and hot-smoking, partly because I grew up in pecan country. The nuts fill out in the fall of the year, and the tree limbs get heavy. A high wind, and sometimes ice, can cause large tree limbs to break off, especially if they are heavy with green nuts. These limbs are ideal for smoking, and most grove owners are glad to let you to haul them off. Of course, wild pecan trees also make excellent wood for smoking. If you live near a large pecan sheller, consider trying pecan shells instead of sawdust in a smoke pan over an electric burner. The shells are sometimes marketed for this purpose in expensive little bags, but you may be able to get shells free from a sheller.

- *Sassafras.* This tree often grows quite abundantly on fencerows in my part of the country. The small trees, from 4 to 6 inches in diameter, are easily felled and easily handled, and they make good logs for burning in a walk-in smokehouse. Sassafras wood is easy to cut when green, but when it seasons, it becomes very hard. It was once used for railroad cross ties and in making chicken coops. When you cut some sassafras saplings for smoking purposes (or when you pull some roots for herb tea), also pick a few green leaves. Dry these, crush them in a mortar, sift, and use the powder (very sparingly) to thicken soups and gumbos. Powdered sassafras leaves are a Native American seasoning and thickening agent, marketed at high prices under the name of *filé powder* in Cajun markets and in the spice sections of most large supermarkets.

- *Beech.* Wood of the beech tree is used for smoking in some areas, and at one time, it was popular in France for cold-smoking herrings.

- *Mesquite.* This tree has always been popular in parts of the Southwest, where it grows in very dry areas. It is highly regarded as fuel when other trees are scarce. Owing to its demand on the patio, mesquite is now bagged and shipped to Florida, Maine, Alaska, and points in between. The smoke is good, but the wood's early reputation was earned as a fuel, not as a smoking agent. It makes a hot fire with long-burning coals, which is great for camping and chuck-wagon cookery. Unless you have a ready supply of mesquite free for the cutting, I wouldn't recommend buying it in large quantities for cold-smoking. But I wouldn't make that statement in Texas, west of the Pecos.

- *Mangrove.* Wood of the mangrove tree is very good for smoking. Its high reputation for smoking mullet in Florida became an environmental concern. It is now illegal, at least in some areas, to cut or otherwise harm mangroves.

- *Roots.* Palmetto roots are highly touted in parts of Florida. Recently my wife ate some ham from a feral hog bagged near Sopchoppy, Florida, and smoked locally with a combination of palmetto and hickory. She says it was the best she has ever tasted. Out West, manzanita roots are highly touted.

- *Maple.* This good wood is popular in some quarters. According to A. J. McClane, maple or apple is "the only wood" to use for smoking clams or oysters. He doesn't say why.

- *Oak.* Although it is used to flavor some expensive Scottish smoked salmon, which I understand is eaten in Buckingham Palace, as well as for smoking hams in England, oak is really not very popular in America as a smoking agent. Ideal for a campfire, oak produces good hot coals but not much smoke as compared to other hardwoods. In any case, oak can be gathered freely in most parts of the country, and I recommend it highly when it is green, when it is easy to cut and split. Green oak doesn't burn quickly, which makes it a good choice for walk-in smokehouses, where parallel oak logs can be helped along, if necessary, with charcoal or a little dry wood.

- *Pimento, Myrtle, and Juniper.* The wood of the allspice tree, called pimento, is used for smoking jerk in Jamaica. The tree is a kind of myrtle—and evergreen—which is generally considered to be a no-no in smoke cookery. But remember that myrtle is also used to smoke meat on the island of Sardinia. I also understand that juniper has been mixed with other woods to smoke salmon on a large scale.

- *Driftwood.* I have read that driftwood makes a good smoking agent, but I don't understand how it could be consistent unless you can distinguish oak driftwood from that of hickory or eucalyptus. Maybe it doesn't matter.

- *Other Wood and Combinations.* Hardwoods such as walnut, chestnut, sweet bay, ash, or birch can be used to advantage for making smoke. Of course, some culinary sports and advertising specialists will hold out for local favorites, and some discriminating practitioners will say that a combination of certain woods is the best way to go. A fellow from South Carolina, for example, has said, "I prefer smoking with one-third hickory, one-third oak, and one-third fruit tree (plum)." Who could argue with that?

Dr. Eph Wilkinson notwithstanding, I'll have to add here that my father would have let out a belly laugh if somebody had suggested that he mix sassafras with his beloved hickory.

- *Corncobs.* Back when local gristmills and home (or farm) corn shellers were everyday equipment, cobs were often used for fuel as well as for smoking meats—and for other activities conducted in small outdoor structures. I'm sure that purists will have opinions on whether the white cob or the red is better for smoking. In any case, cobs tend to blaze up and should be watched carefully.

- *Peat and Organic Smokes.* Peat is used as a smoking agent on some of the British islands. Of course, one sort of peat is not as good as another for smoking purposes. Also, remember that in some barren lands such as Iceland, sheep chips are used for smoking.

CHAPTER 7

COLD-SMOKED FISH

Be warned once again that salt, not smoke, is the curative agent in cold-smoked fish. In addition to inhibiting the growth of harmful bacteria, the salt draws out moisture—and moisture is necessary for bacteria to thrive. How much salt and for how long depends on the size of the fish and other factors, and how long the fish is to be preserved. As a rule, the more salt, the drier the fish and the longer its shelf life. In modern times, the trend has been toward less and less salt combined with refrigerated storage, and this chapter tends to reflect this change. (If you want completely cured smoked fish, begin with a hard salt cure as described in chapter 2, Cured Fish, page 267, and cold-smoke the fish in the smokehouse for a week or longer.) The trouble with a light cure/light smoke approach is that the practitioner has no hard and fast rules to follow. In any case, I can only hope that I can shed enough light on the subject to keep the novice from proceeding in the dark.

Dressing and Hanging the Fish

It's best to start with very fresh fish. If you catch your own, gut and ice them as soon as possible. Better, gut them and put them into a slush of ice and brine; this will start the salting process right away. Before gutting and cleaning the fish, however, consider how they will be handled for salting, drying, and smoking.

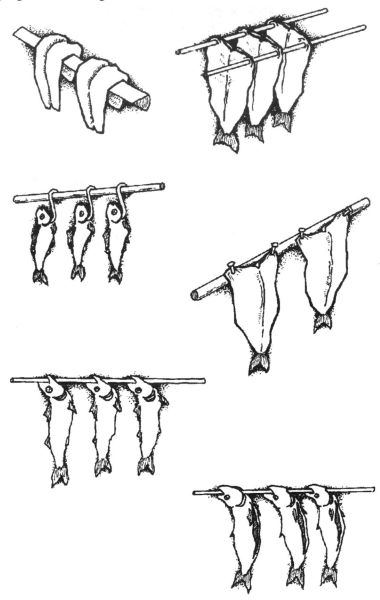

Common ways to hang fish for smoking

Fish to be smoked can be suspended vertically in several ways. They can also be placed horizontally on a rack. How they are to be hung depends partly on practical considerations, such as your facilities and the size of the fish. Here are some basic techniques to consider.

Gibbing

This is a method of dressing small fish without slitting the belly open. Instead, a small cut is made across the bottom of the fish, close to and behind the gills. The gills and innards are pulled out and the body cavity is washed thoroughly with cold water. (A hose with an adjustable, pistol-grip nozzle helps do a good job.) After gibbing, the fish can be hung on a rod, running it through the mouth and out the gill, or vice versa. They can also be hung by pushing the rod through the eye sockets. In either method, it's best to leave a little space between the fish.

Gutting

Small whole fish are usually dressed by cutting a slit in the belly and removing the innards. I prefer this method to gibbing. Gutting may or may not take a little longer, depending on how thoroughly you want to wash out the cavity. The fish can be hung by the methods described under gibbing.

Butterflying

This method of dressing a fish leaves the two halves hinged at the belly. First, the fish is beheaded. During beheading, the collarbone is left in if the fish is to be hung; it can be removed if the fish is to be placed on a rack. After beheading, the fish is cut from the head to the tail from the top. Cut as close as possible to the backbone and through the rib cage. (With large fish, you may prefer to work the knife around the rib cage, leaving the ribs attached to the backbone.) It is important that the knife not cut all the way through the belly flesh. Turn the fish and cut it in a similar manner on the other side. Next, the backbone and tail can be lifted out, along with the innards. Finally the fish is opened like a butterfly. It can be hung or placed on racks.

Filleting

Large fish should be filleted for both curing and smoking. In most cases, a slab of fish is cut off either side of the backbone. Of course, the process should waste as little meat as possible. In my opinion, it's best to start the cut from the tail, then cut through the ribs as you approach the head; this will leave the rib bones intact. For completely boneless fillets, you can cut out the rib section or remove the bones one at the time. There are other methods of filleting, and some people may prefer to work the knife in at the head and toward the tail. In either case, leaving the skin on the fillet will help hold it together during curing, smoking, and handling.

For smoking, fillets are usually placed skin side down on suitable racks. They can also be draped across a rod, skin down.

Tailing

Small whole fish, such as smelts, can be gibbed or gutted and tied at the tail in pairs. These can be hung over rods for smoking. One pair should not be allowed to touch another.

The Salt Cure

As a rule, it's best to dry-cure fish with a low fat content, such as cod, and brine-cure fish with a high fat content, such as mackerel. But the methods are usually interchangeable, especially if you are after a rather light cure to be followed by refrigeration or freezing. Unfortunately, there are infinite variations on the basic methods of salt-curing fish in preparation for smoking; instead of rhyme and reason, we have purely personal and regional variations, which are often staunchly defended. I'll try to keep it simple.

THE BRINE CURE

Although many ingredients are sometimes used in the cure to flavor or preserve the fish, most of these are not necessary and may be counterproductive. I do, however, insist on either brown sugar in a dry cure or molasses in a brine cure. The sugar or molasses helps the color as well as the flavor of smoked fish. The measures can be increased or decreased proportionally. Note that these proportions yield a relatively weak brine, as fresh water will dissolve well over 2 pounds of salt per gallon. Note also that water is a major ingredient in the brine cure and should have a good, clean, fresh taste. Distilled water isn't usually necessary, but some water tastes of natural elements, such as sulfur, and sometimes of added chemicals, such as chlorine. If in doubt, use distilled water or perhaps bottled mineral water. Water from a good spring is hard to beat.

| 1 pound salt | 1 cup dark molasses |
| 1 gallon good water | |

Dress the fish and place them in a nonmetallic container, then cover with the brine, following the proportions above. Place a plank or plate over the fish and weight it with a bowl, stone, or some such nonmetallic object. The idea is to completely submerge the fish. Leave the fish in the brine for 12 hours or longer. (For a hard cure, more time is recommended, as was discussed in chapter 2, Cured Fish, page 267.) Remove the fish from the brine, but do not wash. Dry the fish and smoke them, as described later in the chapter.

THE DRY CURE

The dry cure should be started by first soaking the dressed fish in a light brine made with 1 cup salt dissolved in 1 gallon water for a period of about 1 hour. (You can actually start this initial brining as you dress the fish, timing the process after dropping in the last one; if I have a choice, I dress the larger fish first simply because they should have more time in the brine.) After soaking the fish, drain them but do not fully dry them. Have a dry cure ready, using the following 8-to-1 formula:

8 pounds salt	**1 pound dark brown sugar**

Mix the salt and sugar. Place part of this cure (about ½ inch) into the bottom of a curing box, then put the rest into a handy container. Place each fish in the cure, coating both sides, and pick it up with as much cure as will adhere to it. Place the fish on top of the layer of cure in the box. Layer the fish if necessary, sprinkling extra cure between each layer. Leave the fish in the curing box for about 12 hours, or longer for whole fish that weigh more than 1 pound.

Wash the salt cure off of the fish, and then dry the fish as described next.

Forming a Pellicle

After the fish are treated with either a brine or a salt cure, they should be washed and dried before putting them into the smoker. The drying helps in a number of ways, but basically it forms a pellicle, or glazed film, on the surface. This film helps give the fish a better and a more uniform color, and it may also aid in preservation.

After washing the salt from each fish, pat each one dry with paper towels and place it on a rack (or hang it) in a cool, breezy place. If you don't have a natural breeze, a fan will help. Usually the pellicle will form within 3 hours or less, depending on the size of the fish. After the pellicle forms, proceed with the cold-smoking operation.

Cold-Smoking

The first requirement for cold-smoking is to keep the temperature in the smokehouse or smoke chamber cool. Usually, this requires having the fish a good distance from the fire or source of heat, as discussed in chapter 5, Smokehouses and Rigs (page 318) and chapter 6, Woods and Fuels for Smoking (page 332). It's best to keep the temperature below 90°F, and certainly below 100°F. I consider 70°F to 80°F ideal.

If the salt cure was sufficient to be on the safe side, you can cold-smoke the fish for a few hours, a few days, or a few weeks. As a general rule, the longer the fish is smoked, the more smoky the flavor; but at some point, the law of diminishing returns sets in and the smoking, if done in a dry atmosphere, becomes more of a drying period than a flavor-enhancing period.

For the modern practitioner, I recommend that the fish be smoked until the surface of the flesh is a good mahogany color and the texture is firm but still pliable to the touch. Drying out the fish is unnecessary if you are going to cook them right away. They can be refrigerated for a week or so, or wrapped and frozen for several months. If you do dry the fish, remember that they should be freshened overnight in cool water before they are cooked.

It is best (but not necessary) to start cold-smoking fish with a light or moderate smoke, then increase the density. It's also best to keep the smoke coming continuously, but all is not lost if your fire goes out for an hour or so or the fuel gets low in a chip pan over electric heat. Merely resume smoking as soon as you can.

How long should the fish be smoked? A day or two with whole fish of about 1 pound will be about right, but this statement has to be qualified with a bunch of "ifs," "ands," and "buts." The real concern in my conscience is that the fish not be salt-cured properly and then be exposed to a temperature high enough to promote rapid growth of harmful bacteria (higher than 80°F)—but not high enough to cook or retard the bacteria (140°F). Again, beware the gray zone.

How long? If the fish is to be cooked right away, they should be smoked at least long enough to give them flavor—at least several hours, preferably 12 hours or longer for whole fish of 1 pound or more. If the fish are to be preserved for 2 weeks, they should be properly salt-cured and smoked for at least 24 hours; 4 weeks, 48 hours. If the fish are to be preserved indefinitely, they should receive a *heavy* salt cure and be smoked for several weeks.

In short, if you first salt-cure your fish, cold-smoking is easy if you have a suitable smoke-house. It may be hard to duplicate a particularly good batch exactly (unless you measure all the variables scientifically and keep meticulous notes), but this isn't an overriding concern unless you are smoking fish commercially.

My best advice is to salt-cure your fish, then cold-smoke more or less at your convenience, give or take an hour or two either way, until the fish have a good color and texture. Then either cook the fish right away, refrigerate them for several days, or freeze them for several weeks. Simple enough? If not, you may want to follow the more specific recipes below, some of which reflect the philosophy of smoking mainly to add flavor instead of preservation.

Modern Cold-Smoking Methods

Although thoroughly cured fish are normally smoked for a long period of time, partly to dry the flesh, you can cut back on the time if the product is to be cooked right away. The shelf life of partially smoked fish can be extended by refrigeration or by freezing. Here are some suggestions for cutting back on the salt or on the smoke, or both.

2-DAY SMOKED SALMON

This salmon method calls for a relatively short cure and short smoking time. After smoking, the fish should be cooked by some method of your choice, or used in the recipes set forth later in this chapter.

1 very fresh salmon, about 10 pounds	1 cup light brown sugar
2 cups Morton Tender Quick cure mix	1 gallon good water

Fillet the salmon and rinse it. Mix the Tender Quick and brown sugar into the water. Put the salmon fillets into a nonmetallic container and cover them with the curing mixture. Place a plate on top so that the salmon fillets are completely submerged, then place the container in the refrigerator for about 24 hours. Remove the salmon fillets and air-dry them. Then arrange the fillets on your smoker racks, skin side down, or drape them over a cross beam, skin side down. (Do not attempt to hang the fillets by the end. If you use the rack in a small smoker, you may have to cut the fillets in half.) Cold-smoke for 24 hours or so.

Then cook the salmon as described below, or use a recipe such as kedgeree (page 350). I like to freeze one fillet for later use, and steam the other fillet for 15 to 20 minutes, or until it flakes easily when tested with a fork. To steam the fillet, cut it in half and place it on a plate, skin side down. Put the plate in a steamer for 15 minutes, or until it flakes easily when tested with a fork. Serve the steamed salmon, skin side down, with rice and vegetables of your choice.

To bake the smoked salmon fillets, simply put them skin side down on a suitable flat cookie pan and bake in a preheated 300°F oven for 25 minutes, or until they flake easily when tested with a fork. Baste once or twice with butter or bacon drippings while baking. Do not overcook.

Cold-Smoked Shrimp

Here's a method for cold-smoking precooked shrimp. It will add flavor, but the shrimp should be refrigerated after smoking and should be eaten within a week. For best results, you'll need a large pot that won't crowd the shrimp during boiling. Add some salt—about 1 cup per gallon. Remove the heads of the shrimp and devein them, but leave the tails on. Bring the water to a boil, add the shrimp, bring back to a boil, and cook for 3 minutes for medium shrimp. (Large shrimp require another minute; smaller shrimp, less time. The shrimp are ready when they turn pink.) Drain the shrimp and arrange them on racks. Cold-smoke for 30 to 60 minutes, depending on size. Eat the smoked shrimp cold, or put them into shrimp salad or other dishes. I like a few chopped shrimp scrambled with chicken eggs and a spring onion or two chopped with half the green tops.

Note: Many people add all manner of Cajun spices and court bouillon vegetables to a shrimp boil. I think that plain salt or sea salt is better, but suit yourself.

Smoked Oysters

Freshly shucked oysters can be smoked successfully, but I really can't recommend the pre-shucked "bucket oysters" for sale in supermarkets. Most of these have been washed, or otherwise lack the flavor of their natural juices. An oyster should never be washed, George Leonard Herter notwithstanding, even if it is to be cooked in a stew.

For smoking oysters, you'll need fine-meshed racks so that they won't fall through. Grease the racks and build up a head of smoke. Shuck the oysters and place them on the racks without touching them. (Any oyster that is not alive should be thrown out. Also throw out any oyster that has opened, and any oyster that seems a little dry as compared to the others.) Smoke the oysters for 1 hour, or until they have taken on a nice golden color. Place the smoked oysters in a container and coat them with olive oil. Refrigerate and eat within a few days.

If you are squeamish about eating raw oysters, try steaming them on a grill over a hot fire until they pop open. Then shuck them and smoke for 30 or 40 minutes.

A. D.'S 1-DAY WONDER

Early in the morning, catch some good fish of about 2 pounds each. Fillet the fish. Soak the fillets for a couple of hours in a brine made of 2 cups salt per gallon of water. Dry the fish in a breezy place for 2 to 3 hours, or until a nice pellicle forms. Cold-smoke the fish for about 6 hours.

Fry some smoked bacon in a large skillet. Remove the bacon and save it to eat with the fish. Reduce the heat to the lowest setting and sauté the smoked fillets in the bacon grease, turning them from time to time. If your skillet is large enough, also sauté some sliced portobello mushrooms. If necessary, use a separate skillet for the mushrooms. For a complete meal, serve with white rice and steamed vegetables.

Of course, this technique also provides a recipe for cooking the fish after smoking. Here are some other recipes to try using smoked fish.

SCRAMBLED SMOKED FISH

This dish is one of my favorite ways of using a small amount of smoked fish. It's also one of my very favorite breakfast dishes. Be sure to try it with either cold- or hot-smoked fish. I use scallions. For this recipe, I use about half the green tops along with the small bulbs. First, I cut off the root ends and the tips of the green parts. Then I peel off a layer and chop what's left. I also use wild onions with green tops, but be warned that some of these are quite strong.

1 cup flaked smoked fish	2 or 3 scallions, finely chopped
6 large chicken eggs	2 tablespoons butter or margarine
1 tablespoon milk	salt and freshly ground black pepper to taste

Break the fish into small pieces, or chop it with a chef's knife. Beat the eggs with a little milk, then mix in the fish flakes and chopped green onions. Heat the butter in a skillet, add the egg mixture, and scramble until the eggs are set. Sprinkle with salt and pepper.

This makes a wonderful breakfast, especially when served with slices of luscious red homegrown tomatoes and fresh toast.

RUSSIAN SALMON AND NEW POTATOES

Here's a recipe that I adapted from Kira Petrovskaya's Russian Cookbook. *Although billed as a salad, it makes a nice lunch for two people on a hot day. The olives can be either green or black, or a mixture. Black ones, however, make a more attractive salad.*

1 tablespoon minced onion	½ pound smoked salmon
1 tablespoon minced green onion, with some tops	1 tablespoon wine vinegar
1 tablespoon drained capers	2 tablespoons olive oil
½ cup sliced pitted olives	1 teaspoon prepared mustard
4 or 5 boiled small new potatoes, diced	salt and pepper

Mix the onion, green onion, capers, olives, and potatoes in a bowl. Cut the salmon into fingers and mix very carefully into the potato mixture. Chill.

Prepare a dressing by combining the vinegar, oil, and mustard; season with a little salt and pepper to taste. When you are ready to serve, pour the dressing over the salmon, but do not stir it in. Eat immediately with crackers or toast.

SMOKED FISH PATTIES

Here's a dish that I like to cook on a cast-iron griddle. The fish patties can be eaten as part of a meal or used in a sandwich. For the latter, all you'll need in addition to the patties is some mayonnaise generously spread onto each slice of bread.

2 cups flaked smoked fish

1 cup fine cracker crumbs

3 green onions, minced with about half the tops

½ red bell pepper, seeded and minced

1 clove garlic, minced

2 medium chicken eggs, whisked

salt and pepper to taste

flour

butter

Mix the fish, cracker crumbs, green onions, red pepper, garlic, eggs, salt, and pepper in a bowl. Shape the mixture into patties, then dredge each patty lightly in flour. Heat a little butter on your griddle or in a skillet. Over medium heat, sauté the patties for a few minutes or until nicely browned on the bottom, then turn carefully with a spatula and brown the other sides. If the patties tend to tear apart, use two spatulas, one on top and one on bottom, for turning.

This makes 4 large patties. I need 2 for a full meal, but can get by with 1 for lunch or in a sandwich. I like to sprinkle the patties with Asian fish sauce (*nam pla* or *nuoc mam*), which can be put on the table as a condiment. Oyster sauce is also good.

IRISH HERRING

According to my old edition of *Larousse Gastronomique*, the Irish once had a simple but unusual method of preparing smoked herring. The fish were beheaded and split in half lengthwise, spread flat in a suitable container, covered with whiskey, and flamed. When all the whiskey had burned away, the herring were ready to eat. I recently ran across the same technique in a book on British country cooking, in which the author used the term *Rob Roy* for cold-smoked fish prepared by this method.

One day I intend to try the method with real Irish whiskey and smoked herring, but to date, I have not had the opportunity. I did, however, prepare some at a smoked mullet fest in the north of Florida, where the tradition is to butterfly the mullet before smoking it. I selected some smaller smoked mullet and poured some sour-mash bourbon over them and burned it off. The fish were delicious. The idea got some attention in the area, and the northern Florida good ol' boys may have picked it up.

AVOCADO STUFFED WITH SMOKED FISH

The best avocados I have ever eaten were grown on a large tree near Tampa Bay, an area also noted for its smoked mullet. The two ingredients fit nicely together in a recipe from Ghana, which I have adapted here. Any good smoked fish will do, but those that have been cold-smoked should first be steamed or poached for about 15 minutes, or until they flake easily when tested with a fork.

4 chicken eggs, hard-boiled

¼ cup milk

½ teaspoon salt

¼ teaspoon sugar

2 limes

¼ cup peanut oil

¼ cup olive oil

1 heaping cup flaked, cooked, smoked fish

2 large avocados, quite ripe

Peel the whites from the hard-boiled eggs. In a bowl, mash the yolks with the milk until you have a paste. Add salt, sugar, and the juice of 1 lime. Stir in the peanut oil a little at a time, then stir in the olive oil. Chop the egg whites and add them to the bowl. Stir in the fish. (This stuffing can be refrigerated for later use, or served at room temperature.)

When you are ready to eat, cut the avocados in half, remove the pits, and fill the cavities with the stuffing. Squeeze on a little lime juice and enjoy.

In Ghana, the dish is served with strips of red bell pepper or pimiento as a garnish. This is a nice touch. I also like it sprinkled with paprika and served on lettuce, along with wedges of lime so that each person can squeeze some juice onto his serving.

Note: This stuffing is a good spread for crackers, especially when made with garlic oil (olive oil in which garlic cloves have steeped for several months; I preserve garlic in this way, then use the oil for cooking purposes).

SMOKED FISH WITH CREAM

Here's a dish that I like to cook in a large cast-iron skillet. A large electric skillet will also work.

2 tablespoons butter

2 pounds smoked fish

salt and freshly ground black pepper

½ cup half-and-half or light cream

chopped fresh parsley or green onion tops

Melt the butter in a skillet and sauté the fish for 1 minute on each side. Sprinkle on a little salt and black pepper, then pour in the cream. Simmer (do not boil) for 5 minutes. Turn the fish and simmer for another 5 minutes. Place the fish on a serving platter and pour the pan liquid over it. Garnish with parsley or green onion tops. Serve with boiled new potatoes, steamed vegetables, and hot bread.

KEDGEREE

This dish from Britain takes its name from the Indian khichri, *but one English writer suggests that the only thing Indian about it these days is the curry powder. In America, even that ingredient is sometimes omitted, thank god.*

2 cups water

1 cup long-grain rice

½ pound smoked fish, cooked and flaked

½ cup butter or margarine

2 large onions, chopped

1 teaspoon curry powder (optional)

salt (if needed) and black pepper to taste

1 hard-boiled chicken egg, sliced

½ lemon

4 tablespoons light cream or half-and-half

Bring 2 cups of water to a hard boil, add the rice, return to a boil, reduce the heat, cover tightly, and simmer for 20 minutes without peeking.

If the smoked fish has not been cooked, steam or poach it until it flakes easily, about 10 minutes. Heat half the butter in a large skillet and sauté the onions for 5 minutes. Add the fish, stirring about, and mix in the curry powder, salt, if the latter is needed (depending on the salt content of the fish), and pepper. Add the sliced egg.

Melt the rest of the butter and mix it into the rice, which should be fully cooked by now. Stir the rice into the fish mixture. Squeeze the juice of half a lemon over the kedgeree, then spoon the cream over all. Serve hot. Feeds 3 or 4.

SMOKED FISH CHOWDER

I've never cooked a chowder that wasn't good (at least to me), but I'll have to admit that I am partial to one made with smoked fish. Here's an old recipe from Maine. Any good smoked fish can be used, hard- or light-cured, but fish with large scales should be scaled before being boiled.

1 whole smoked fish, about 1–1½ pounds	3 or 4 medium to large potatoes, diced
¼ pound salt pork, diced	black pepper to taste
1 cup diced onion	2–3 cups whole milk

Put the fish in a pot, cover it with water, bring to a boil, reduce the heat, and simmer until the fish is tender. (The time will depend on how hard it was cured and how long it was smoked.)

While simmering the fish, sauté the salt pork in a skillet until the pieces begin to brown. (Some cooks may want to put the salt pork in with the fish instead of browning it; suit yourself.) Drain the salt pork and sauté the onion in the skillet for 5 minutes.

When the fish is tender, remove it from the pot, and flake the meat, discarding the bones. Add the potatoes, salt pork, and pepper to the pot. Cover and simmer for 10 minutes. Then add the onion and simmer for another 10 minutes or so, or until the potatoes are done. Stir in the fish flakes. Slowly add from 2 to 3 cups of milk, stirring and tasting as you go. Ladle the chowder into bowls and serve with plenty of hot bread. A loaf of chewy-crusted French or Italian bread suits me better, but hot biscuits or even bannock will do. I like to grind some more black pepper onto my serving. Feeds 4.

CHAPTER 8

COLD-SMOKED MEATS

Most meats that have been properly cured can also be smoked. It is so simple, once you have the facilities and the skill to maintain the smoke at about 80°F. Since the meat will be fully cooked after it is smoked, you can cold-smoke it for as long as you choose, within reason. Ideally, it should be smoked just long enough to get a good flavor but not long enough to dry out the meat. If you are smoking the meat for long or unrefrigerated storage, however, it will be necessary to dry it out somewhat. If you plan to cook the meat soon after smoking, color is a good indication of readiness. Most nicely smoked meats and fish take on a mahogany brown color. But color alone is not a foolproof measure of the quality of smoked meat, since many commercial operators use dye in or on the meat.

The first step in cold-smoking meat is to cure it with salt by either the dry-salt or the brine method. These subjects were treated at length in chapters 1 through 4 of this part (part three). At the risk of boring the reader, I repeat some of the cures or variations I've

discussed previously in the recipes below. My fear is that some no-salt freak will omit this important step, or cut back on the cure, thereby making the smoked meat dangerous. Even with plenty of salt, most cold-smoked meats should be thoroughly cooked before you eat them, although raw smoked meats, usually thinly sliced, are considered to be delicacies in some quarters. I have eaten uncooked meats from time to time, and I have no objection to the practice if I am certain that the meat was handled properly before and after curing and smoking. I have even eaten Middle Eastern kibbeh, made with raw ground meat, but I can't recommend the practice to others—and certainly not with supermarket fare these days.

Cold-Smoked Hams

If you have salt- or sugar-cured a ham successfully, the smoking part is easy. It can be aged and then smoked, or it can be smoked first and then aged. I prefer the latter method. (The smoking period can be considered part of the total aging time.) After the salt equalization period, wash the ham with warm water, then hang it in the smokehouse by the shank to dry for several hours or, better, overnight. Since the ham is (or should be) completely cured, the temperature is not as critical as for some other smoking operations.

The cured ham can be cold-smoked for 2 days or several weeks, depending on your schedule and on how hungry you are. I recommend a minimum of 2 weeks for cold-smoking. If the smokehouse is screened, it is not necessary to keep the smoke going for the entire 2 weeks. If the fire goes out for a few hours, no harm will be done.

It's best to hang the hams by the shank end, using strong cotton string. My father used withes of green hickory for tying the hams; my wife's father used strips of yucca leaves, called bear grass in her neck of the woods.

The smoked and aged ham will be quite hard and should be cooked pretty much like the salt-cured hams described previously (or by one of the recipes below). If you don't want to cook a whole ham, have it sliced into steaks, saving the smoked hocks for such dishes as hoppin' John. The steaks should be soaked overnight in water before cooking, unless they are going into a stew.

Smoked hams to be aged can be put into muslin bags and hung with a string tied around the bag at the shank end of the ham. For security, it's best to fold over the top of the bag before wrapping the string around it. Some people paint the bag with a wash made with various materials, including lime, clay, and flour. Others dust the surface of the ham with a mixture of finely ground red and black pepper. Unless insects are a problem, I think the open-air method is best, provided the ham can be hung freely and in a cool place. If you don't have a bag, a clean, well-used cotton sheet will do. Tear out a square, center the butt of the ham on it, bring the corners together over the shank, and tie off tightly.

Cooking a Cold-Smoked Ham

A home-smoked, cured ham is vastly different from—and better than—a supermarket cured ham. At least to my taste. But it *must* be freshened and cooked differently. Usually, the result will be much firmer than a supermarket ham, some of which even have a spongy texture. In most cases, a cured ham should be sliced very thin before it is served.

In addition to the recipes below, those set forth for salt-cured hams can also be used for smoked hams.

DR. EPH'S LAMENT

Before setting forth his recipe in A Man's Taste, *published by The Junior League of Memphis, Dr. Eph Wilkinson said, "The quality of the ham makes all the difference in any country ham recipe. I grew up on a farm in East Tennessee where we killed hogs every fall. The hams were sugar-cured and smoked with hickory and sassafras. I sure wish I could get just one of these hams!" I, too, would like to have one of those hams, but I tested Dr. Eph's recipe with an ordinary salt-cured and smoked ham of my own devising, and I found it to be a very good one. I'm not sure what the Coca-Cola does, but it certainly doesn't hurt anything.*

THE SIMMERING

1 whole country ham, smoked	6 allspice berries
1 quart Coca-Cola	6 black peppercorns
1 teaspoon whole cloves	cool spring water

Scrub the ham and soak it overnight in cool water. Weigh the ham. Cut off the ham hock with a hacksaw, if necessary, to fit the ham in your pot or roaster. (When choosing a utensil, remember that the ham should be completely covered with liquid.) Put the ham into the pot, then add the Coca-Cola, cloves, allspice, peppercorns, and enough spring water to cover. Bring to a boil and simmer for 25 minutes per pound of ham. Let the ham cool in the liquid.

THE BAKING

1 cup Coca-Cola	lots of whole cloves
1 cup water	lots of dark brown sugar
Simmered ham	

Preheat the oven to 350°F. Select a baking pan or roaster large enough to hold the ham. Put a mixture of the Coca-Cola and 1 cup water into the bottom of the pan. Trim all the skin from the ham, leaving about ½ inch of fat. Stud the ham with whole cloves spaced ¼ inch apart. Cover the ham (and cloves) with a ½-inch layer of dark brown sugar. Bake for 1 hour. Turn the heat down to 250°F and bake for 30 minutes more. The sugar should caramelize and appear dark brown or almost black. Cool and slice thinly.

A BRITISH BAKED HAM

In Great Britain, a baked ham is traditionally served at Christmas. (Baked ham is also traditional Christmas fare in Sweden and Finland.) The typical British ham is a little sweeter than most European hams. It is sugar-cured, and before sugar was widely available, honey was used in the cure; molasses is also used at times. British hams are lightly smoked with oak wood.

1 whole cold-smoked ham	1½ cups dark molasses
3 cooking apples, peeled and chopped	1 cup chopped fresh parsley
3 ribs celery with leafy tops, chopped	12 black peppercorns
2 medium onions, chopped	whole cloves
2 medium carrots, chopped	dark brown sugar
2½ cups hard cider	

Put the ham in a large container of cold water. Soak it for at least a day, preferably longer, changing the water several times.

When you are ready to cook, scrub the ham and put it into a container large enough to hold it and add enough water to cover it. Add all the ingredients except the cloves and brown sugar. Bring to a boil, reduce the heat, and simmer for 5 hours, adding more water if needed. Turn off the heat and let the ham cool overnight in the liquid.

Preheat the oven to 450°F. Skin the ham, leaving much of the fat on the meat. (The skinning should be done with the aid of a small, sharp knife.) Make crisscross cuts over the fat and insert a clove in the center of each diamond. Sprinkle the brown sugar over the ham and put it into the hot oven for 5 or 10 minutes. Check it a time or two after 5 minutes—and don't let the crust burn.

Leftover Ham Recipes
Ideally, a whole ham, cooked as above, should be put on the table at a festive dinner, such as Thanksgiving or Christmas. What's left over can be eaten in various ways, such as in sandwiches or casseroles and stews. Here are a few of my favorite recipes.

SCOTCH MESS

My mother made this dish frequently (by request) and called it ham pie. Almost always, it was made with the trimmings taken from around the bone of what was left of a baked country ham. Mother never did measure the ingredients—and I don't, either.

chicken eggs

ham bits and pieces

dumpling strips cut from rolled pastry

salt and pepper

whole milk

Hard-boil the eggs, peel them, and cut them into slices. Preheat the oven to 350°F. Trim off some ham, and with it, line the bottom of a baking dish or pan about 9 by 13 inches, and about 2 inches deep. (I use a Pyrex dish.) Put a sparse layer of dumpling strips atop the ham, then add a layer of egg slices. Add another layer of ham, dumpling strips, and eggs. Add a layer of ham. Sprinkle with salt and pepper. Add a crisscrossed layer of dumpling strips, then cover it all with the milk.

Bake the pie for about 30 minutes. Then turn on the broiler and lightly brown the top. Serve hot.

Although I don't offer exact measurements for this recipe, the dish benefits from lots of ham and sparse use of dumplings—but, of course, a good deal depends on how much meat you've got and on how many folks you've got to feed. If you don't have a recipe for dumpling strips, try this:

2 cups all-purpose flour

2 teaspoons baking powder

1 teaspoon salt

¼ cup vegetable oil

about ½ cup cold milk

In a medium bowl, mix the flour, baking powder, and salt. Cut in the vegetable oil. Slowly stir in the milk, using just enough to make a rather stiff dough. Put the dough on a well-floured surface and roll it out about ⅛ inch thick. Cut the dough into strips 1 inch wide and use as directed.

PINTO BEANS AND HAM BONE

While writing this book, I looked at a number of books about the chuck-wagon cooks of the Old West, looking for recipes and ways of cooking salt pork, cured bacon, and so on. I didn't find much information of culinary value, but I did find some good stories. Just the titles of the books were interesting, such as Shoot Me a Biscuit. *On the trail, of course, the cowboys ate mostly beans, coffee, biscuits, fresh beef, and cured meats. Beans were always available, partly because they traveled well, stored compactly, and didn't spoil.*

In one of the books, a cowboy fresh off the trail went into a swanky restaurant in St. Louis or somewhere. He couldn't read the menu, so, after some hemming and hawing, he asked the waiter to identify all the entries that contained beans. The waiter spoke, but the words didn't help.

"Put your finger on them that contains beans," the cowboy said. Somewhat impatiently, the waiter put his finger on a single entry, knowing that he wasn't going to get much of an order or tip from anyone looking for beans. "That's the only one?" the cowboy asked. The waiter assured him that it was the only bean dish available at the establishment. "Well, you hold this one," the cowboy said, putting his left index finger on the entry and sweeping his right hand over the entire menu, "and bring me an order of all the rest of this stuff."

I don't claim that my pinto bean recipe would have sold that cowboy on the idea of eating another spoonful of beans, but I do recommend it to anyone who has been eating pinto beans that have been soaked all night in water and boiled without a good ham bone.

1 ham bone, with some meat on it	½ teaspoon hot red pepper flakes
1 pound dried pinto beans	salt, if needed

Put the ham bone into a large pot or dutch oven. Pour in the beans and cover with water. Add the red pepper flakes. Bring to a boil, reduce the heat to a simmer, cover tightly, and cook for 6 to 7 hours, adding more water from time to time if needed. Season with salt, if needed.

Serve hot with sliced Vidalia or Texas onions and corn pone made from stone-ground meal. If the ham bone has lots of meat left on it (as well it should), I can make a whole meal of this dish. Leftover beans can be mashed, shaped into patties, and fried on a griddle.

HAM AND SWISS CHEESE ON RYE

At our house, most leftover ham is used in sandwiches. Usually, these are made as needed or as wanted, and require nothing more than white sandwich bread and mayonnaise. For a light meal, my wife and I make a sandwich of swiss cheese, rye bread, Dijon or Creole mustard, lots and lots of thinly sliced ham, and maybe a little lettuce. The thinner the ham, the better your sandwich will be. Cut the sandwiches in half and serve with thick potato chips and huge dill pickles.

After the first edition of this work came out, a critic asked why anyone would spend good money on a book that contained instructions for making a ham sandwich.

Well . . . after much hemming and hawing, turning and tossing, I have left the sandwich suggestions in the revised edition of this modest work, simply because some people (never mind who) really do need some help, not only with a deli-type rye-bread sandwich, but even with an ordinary white-bread ham sandwich.

Here's my advice. Use very fresh white sandwich bread. Smear 2 slices quite liberally with a good mayonnaise. Then sandwich a dozen or so pieces of thinly sliced ham. No lettuce.

It's that simple. Try it. Cut the sandwich in half diagonally. Pick up a half in your right hand and look at it. Go ahead. Take a bite right out of the middle. This one bite will be worth more than the small price of this little book.

Cold-Smoked Bacon

The procedure in chapter 3, Dry-Cured Meats (page 288), for making salt pork can be extended for cold-smoked bacon. After the cure, wash the belly slab, dry it, hang it in a smokehouse, and cold-smoke it for at least a full day, or up to a week. Some people like honey and pepper on their bacon. I think it's best to add these ingredients after the smoking is completed.

SUGAR CURE FOR BACON

If you want a good sugar cure, especially for bacon, try this old British formula, adapted from The Country Kitchen.

1 pound salt	1 ounce saltpeter
1 pound brown sugar	approximately 12 pounds bacon
2 tablespoons black peppercorns	1¾ pints wine vinegar

Mix the salt, brown sugar, peppercorns, and saltpeter, then divide the mixture in half. Rub half the cure into the meat, covering all surfaces nicely. Leave the meat on a wooden shelf or table in a cool place, turning daily. After 5 days, mix the rest of the cure ingredients with the wine vinegar. Rub the bacon with part of this mixture. Turn daily, rubbing again with part of the liquid, for 5 days or so, or until the cure has been used up.

Punch holes in two corners of the bacon, then insert cotton string or hickory withe. Hang the bacon in a smokehouse or cold-smoker for at least 24 hours, preferably for a week or so. This bacon will keep for several weeks at room temperature, and longer in the refrigerator. It can also be frozen.

PIONEER BACON

Here's an old recipe adapted from Cooking in Wyoming, *which contains a chapter or two on pioneer cooking.*

2 ounces saltpeter	80 pounds side meat for bacon
½ cup brown sugar	black pepper
plenty of salt	starch
water	cayenne pepper

Pulverize the saltpeter, then mix it with the brown sugar and 4 cups of salt. Dampen the mix slightly with a little water and rub it all over the meat. Lay the meat skin side down on boards for 9 days. Then rub thoroughly with more salt; use all the salt that will adhere to the meat. Let lie for 3 days.

Hang the side meat in the smokehouse and cold-smoke it for 3 days. Sprinkle each piece with black pepper. Have ready a cloth sack for each slab of bacon. Mix a solution of starch and water, adding a little red pepper to prevent mold and keep the flies away. Wet the sacks with the starch solution, making them stiff. Put each piece of meat in a cloth sack, tie the end, and hang in a cool place. (In warm climates, it's best to refrigerate the bacon if it is to be kept very long. Bacon, being fatty, tends to go rancid if kept too long after curing and smoking.)

Cold-Smoked Sausage

Be warned that smoked sausage can be dangerous, leading even to deadly botulism. The problem, as I see it, is that (1) the meat is not normally given a proper salt cure, and (2) the meat-grinding process tends to spread any bacteria that might be present on the surface. With pork sausage, the inherent fat may work to your advantage because lard is a known preservative. In other words, fatty sausage may be safer than lean sausage. Also, the hog casing somewhat protects the surface of the sausage. But there may be other opinions on this matter. My best advice on smoked sausage is that it be cooked thoroughly and refrigerated or frozen as soon as the smoking period is over. If you want to keep the sausage without refrigeration, it's best to cook it, layer the cooked links in a clean crock or other suitable container, and cover it with lard. This is an old-timey method of preserving sausage.

COLD-SMOKED SAUSAGE

I don't remember how my father preserved our sausage, but I do remember that (1) it wasn't left in the smokehouse for very long, and (2) it was very, very good.

I agree that good sausage is hard to beat for brute flavor. Here's my recipe, made with rather lean meat. Traditionally, pork sausage is made from all the trimmings, but some of the better sausage is made with the whole hog and is called whole-hog sausage. Some farmers of my acquaintance boast of putting a whole ham or two in with the sausage.

¼ cup finely ground sea salt

2 tablespoons black pepper

2½ tablespoons dried sage

1–2 tablespoons red pepper flakes

10 pounds pork with about 20 percent fat

Mix all the seasonings. Chill the pork, cut it into small chunks, and sprinkle it with the seasonings. Run the pork through a sterilized sausage grinder, using a fine wheel. Stuff the ground meat into pork casings, hang the links in a smokehouse, and cold-smoke for 2 to 3 days. Cook the sausage thoroughly before eating it.

Cold-Smoked Birds

As a rule, the larger the bird, the more time it takes to cure and smoke it properly. In all cases, cold-smoked birds should be cooked before they are eaten. In most cases, it's best to pluck the birds instead of skinning them.

Pheasant and Chickens

Although the meat is on the dry side, pheasant can be salt-cured and cold-smoked successfully. Start by plucking the birds and removing the heads, feet, and innards. Mix a brine in the proportions of 2 cups salt, 1 cup sugar, and ¼ cup crushed allspice berries per gallon of water. Put the birds into a crock or other suitable nonmetallic container. Pour the brine over the birds, covering them. Then weight the birds with a wooden block or some such object so that they are completely submerged. Leave the birds in the brine for 10 days.

Remove the birds, wash them with clean water, and hang them to dry for several hours. Then cold-smoke the birds for at least 2 hours. The longer they smoke (up to a point), the better the color and flavor will be—and the dryer the flesh. Birds to be baked can be smoked for a couple of hours, barded with bacon, wrapped in aluminum foil, and baked until done. Birds to be used in stews and soups, or cooked by any wet method, can be smoked longer for more flavor.

Chickens can be smoked by this method, but I personally don't want to start out with supermarket birds or birds that have been raised in compartments, cleaned in a mass operation, and run through a salmonella bath. My concern is freshness and salmonella, plus the fact that most commercial birds are too fat. I eat the birds purchased at the supermarket, but it's best to cook them as soon as possible. I don't even want them in my refrigerator these days. There are surely other feelings about this matter; some people can't bear the thought of eating game birds or barnyard chickens that aren't inspected by the US Department of Agriculture.

Quail and Small Birds

Quail are very good when cold-smoked, and they are easy to prepare. Simply soak them in a brine (the one for pheasant will do) for a couple of hours, dry them, cold-smoke them for 3 to 4 hours, and cook them by a recipe of your choice. I especially like quail baked with mushroom soup and rice. I am fond of wild quail, but I also like the pen-raised quail for smoking. If you don't grow your own quail, look for someone in your area who does. I have also been successful with frozen quail from the supermarket.

Other small game birds, such as doves and snipe, can be cold-smoked before cooking. (Personally, however, I prefer to smoke game birds with white meat.) Grouse and Cornish game hens can be smoked, but you'll need to extend the curing and smoking times.

Turkey

I much prefer wild birds (which, contrary to much opinion, are not as dry, at least before cooking, as domestic birds) or birds that have been raised on the ground (with plenty of room to scratch) instead of in a compartment. A happy bird makes better eating.

More and more these days, people are raising their own turkeys, so it shouldn't be too difficult to find a local grower who will sell you a live bird or two. After you chop off its head, draw and pluck it as soon as possible. Wash the bird quickly with salted water, then weigh it and record the figure. Place the bird in a crock or other suitable container and cover it with brine. (The brine formula used for pheasant will do.) Weight the bird with a block of wood or other suitable nonmetallic object so that it stays completely submerged. If the bird weighs less than 10 pounds dressed, leave it in the brine for 1 day per pound; if it weighs between 10 and 15 pounds, 1¼ days per pound; over 15 pounds, 1½ days per pound. It is important also that the bird be cured in a cool place, preferably at 38°F. Every 7 days or so, remove the bird (or birds), stir the brine about, and put the bird back into the brine.

After completing the cure, wash the bird inside and out in fresh water, then hang it to dry. I hang it with a cord tied to each foot, but some people tie a cord around each wing and suspend the bird with the breast down; still others prefer to put the bird in a net bag for hanging. After the bird dries, hang it in the smokehouse and cold-smoke it for at least 2 days, until the skin is a mahogany color. The longer it is cold-smoked, the stronger the flavor—and the dryer the meat will be. After being cold-smoked, the bird should be aged in a cool place for a week or so.

Of course, a turkey smoked by this method should be thoroughly cooked before it is eaten. For baking, preheat the oven to 350°F, wrap the bird with strips of bacon, insert a meat thermometer into the thickest part of the thigh (without touching bone) or the breast, and bake the bird until the internal temperature reaches 180°F. If I know that I have a good bird, I'll turn off the oven heat when the thermometer reads 160°F, then let the bird coast for an hour or so as the oven cools down. Turkey is best, at least culinarily, when it is cooked to only 145°F or 150°F, but the US Department of Agriculture recommends 180°F, a figure that I feel obligated to report here.

It is possible, of course, to cold-smoke a turkey for a couple of hours and then put it in the oven to cook. The results may be quite tasty, but the deep, rich smoke flavor may not be present in the meat except on the surface.

Wild Ducks and Geese

These days, smoked wild ducks are usually hot-smoked during the cooking process. It is possible, however, to cold-smoke ducks, getting a more intense flavor. Here's a report by Dr. Andrew Longley from Cundy's Harbor, Maine, as published in *The Maine Way*:

Prepare ducks by plucking and dressing as one normally would for baking. Soak the ducks overnight in salted water. Smoke in smokehouse for 36 to 48 hours. (For optimum results, smokehouse should be maintained at 80 degrees.) After smoking is completed, ducks are baked as one would normally prepare ducks. Whistlers, buffle-heads, and black ducks have been smoked with good results.

I recommend that the ducks be drawn, plucked, and salted as soon as possible after the kill. For the brine soak, I recommend at least 2 cups of salt per gallon of water.

The above method also works for wild geese. (It's best to proceed with a young bird unless you are going to cook it by long stewing.) Soak the bird in brine for 2 days, smoke it for 3 to 4 days, and then cook it with your favorite recipe. I am especially fond of a slowly cooked gumbo made with smoked goose.

Cold-Smoked Small Game

Rabbits and other small game can be cured and smoked quite successfully. Opossum is especially good for smoking. For animals of cottontail size, wash and soak them in a light brine for several hours, put them in a pickle for 5 to 6 hours, then cold-smoke them for a day or so. Whole hares and larger domestic rabbits should be pickled for about 10 hours, or dressed and pickled the same as cottontails.

Cold-Smoked Venison and Large Game

Most game tends to be on the dry side as compared to pork and feedlot cattle. Even so, it can be pickled and cold-smoked. In Russia, for example, bear hams are salt-cured and smoked exactly like pork. The hams, shoulders, and saddle of deer smoke nicely, if you first use a sweetened pickle in the proportions of 1 pound salt, ½ pound brown sugar, 2 tablespoons sodium nitrite (optional), and ½ cup juniper berries per gallon of water. If you have a whole deer and a large pickling container, put the hams on the bottom, the saddle in the middle, and the shoulders on top. (Some people recommend that the deer be aged for a week or so before starting the pickle, but I don't think this is necessary if you have a good deer that was cleanly killed and promptly field-dressed.) You can also add the ribs and perhaps the tenderloin along with the ribs, but I like to start eating on these right away. Be sure to keep the meat completely submerged in the pickle. After 3 days, remove the top layer or two, dry the meat, and start cold-smoking. Turn the other meats and stir the pickle. After another 3 days, remove the shoulders, dry them, and start cold-smoking. After another 3 days or longer, remove the hams, dry them, and start cold-smoking. The shoulders should be smoked for 1 week, the saddle for 1½ weeks, and the hams for 2 weeks or thereabouts. During cold-smoking, it's best to rub the venison from time to time with bacon drippings.

Note that the curing and smoking times do not have to be exact if the meat is cooked or frozen shortly after cold-smoking. Note also that large game such as elk and moose can be cured and smoked, but I think it better to separate the rear leg into several roasts instead of trying to cure the whole thing.

Cold-Smoked Mutton Ham

At one time, this dish was quite popular in northern Europe, and it is still eaten in some countries, especially Norway. This recipe has been adapted from *The Country Kitchen*, a delightfully British book. Mutton has a stronger flavor than lamb, and is not often marketed in the United States. This is a pity, but lamb can also be used. It's best, of course, to proceed with very fresh meat. Anyone who has a few acres should look into raising lamb and mutton for food. They are relatively easy to butcher as compared to beef, and they don't have to be scalded and scraped like hogs.

SMOKED MUTTON HAM

½ pound sea salt

½ cup dark brown sugar

2 teaspoons saltpeter

1 tablespoon crushed coriander seeds

1 tablespoon crushed allspice

1 tablespoon crushed black peppercorns

1 fresh leg of lamb or mutton

wine

chopped celery

chopped onions

chopped garlic

Thoroughly mix the salt, brown sugar, saltpeter, coriander, allspice, and peppercorns. Rub the fresh leg of lamb all over with the salt mixture, pushing it in around the exposed bone. Place the leg of lamb on a nonmetallic surface and put it in a cool place for 10 to 14 days. Turn the leg daily and rub the top side with the liquid that accumulates on the bottom. After 10 to 14 days, dry the ham and cold-smoke it for a day or two.

When you are ready to cook, place the ham in a large container and cover it with a stock made of 4 parts water to 1 part wine, along with some chopped celery, onions, and garlic. Bring the liquid to a boil, reduce the heat, and simmer for 4 hours, adding more liquid from time to time if needed. Let the ham cool in the liquid. Then remove the ham, cover it with a clean cloth, lay a wooden board on top, and weight it overnight with a flat iron or two.

Cold-Smoked Tongue

Cured and smoked beef tongue is one of my favorite delicacies. It's best to cure several of these at a time, and they should be purchased fresh at a meat processing plant. Wash the tongues in salted water, then pack them loosely in a nonmetallic container. Cover them with brine (at least 2 cups of salt per gallon of water) and weight them down with a plate, board, or some nonmetallic object. Leave the beef tongues in the brine for 3 to 4 weeks, repacking and stirring the brine every week or so. Dry the tongues and cold-smoke them for a day or longer.

To cook, cover the smoked tongue with water, then add a few juniper berries, peppercorns, and celery tops; boil the tongue for 6 to 7 hours, or longer, until the meat is very tender. Let the tongue cool, peel it, and slice it crosswise.

I can make a meal of smoked tongue, but it is more often served as an appetizer. It is good with stone-ground brown mustard and thin slices of party bread. Sliced tongue also makes a tasty sandwich. If your guests tend to be on the squeamish side, always slice the tongue crosswise and arrange it in a nonsuggestive manner. Otherwise, it might not be an appetizer.

Tongues from sheep, deer, and other mammals can also be cured and smoked to advantage. Tongues from elk and moose should be about the same size as beef tongues, and should be cured and smoked accordingly. For smaller tongues from deer and sheep, reduce the curing and smoking times by about 70 percent. Whale tongue—an old Basque delicacy—should be cured and smoked considerably longer.

METRIC CONVERSION TABLES

US Measurements and Metric Equivalents

LIQUID INGREDIENTS

Metric	US Measures	Metric	US Measures
1.23 ML	¼ TSP.	29.57 ML	2 TBSP.
2.36 ML	½ TSP.	44.36 ML	3 TBSP.
3.70 ML	¾ TSP.	59.15 ML	¼ CUP
4.93 ML	1 TSP.	118.30 ML	½ CUP
6.16 ML	1¼ TSP.	236.59 ML	1 CUP
7.39 ML	1½ TSP.	473.18 ML	2 CUPS OR 1 PT.
8.63 ML	1¾ TSP.	709.77 ML	3 CUPS
9.86 ML	2 TSP.	946.36 ML	4 CUPS OR 1 QT.
14.79 ML	1 TBSP.	3.79 L	4 QTS. OR 1 GAL.

DRY INGREDIENTS

Metric	US Measures	Metric		US Measures
2 (1.8) G	1⁄16 OZ.	80 G		2⅘ OZ.
3½ (3.5) G	⅛ OZ.	85 (84.9) G		3 OZ.
7 (7.1) G	¼ OZ.	100 G		3½ OZ.
15 (14.2) G	½ OZ.	115 (113.2) G		4 OZ.
21 (21.3) G	¾ OZ.	125 G		4½ OZ.
25 G	⅞ OZ.	150 G		5¼ OZ.
30 (28.3) G	1 OZ.	250 G		8⅞ OZ.
50 G	1¾ OZ.	454 G	1 LB.	16 OZ.
60 (56.6) G	2 OZ.	500 G	1 LIVRE	17⅗ OZ.

GLOSSARY

Age. To hang meat in a dry place after curing. If the meat has been properly cured, the temperature at which the meat is aged is not critical. Proper aging gives a distinct flavor to country hams and other meats, and sometimes to sausages.

Ascorbic acid. A form of vitamin C used in canning to preserve the color of fruits and vegetables. It is sometimes added to a meat cure to help retain the color of the meat or sausage. Some authorities plug this stuff for use in sausages; others don't.

Botulism. A deadly food poisoning that is usually caused by improper canning of meat, fish, and vegetables. It can develop in sausages. In order to reach dangerous levels, the spores, which produce a toxin, require moisture and a lack of oxygen. It may, however, occur in some cased sausages (made with meat that hasn't been salt-cured) and possibly in other moist meats. Some authorities say that the use of sodium nitrate, sodium nitrite, and saltpeter help prevent botulism in sausages and other meats.

Brine. Salty water used for curing meats and fish. Ordinary salt is the major element, but other ingredients may be added for flavor or color. An egg will float in a strong brine, and this fact is often used to measure the strength of a brine. A salinometer can also be used. Note that the salt in a brine draws moisture from meats, so that the brine can become diluted during the curing process unless more salt is added. Brines used to cure meats should be stirred from time to time, which may require the meat to be removed and repacked; this process is called overhauling. For culinary purposes, the water used in the brine should be of good flavor.

Casings. Cleaned sheep, hog, or cow intestines used to stuff sausages. When properly cleaned and salted, these can be kept for months and months in the refrigerator or longer in the freezer. They can be purchased, already salted, from sausage and meat supply houses. Artificial casings are also used these days. See also part two, chapter 3, Stuffing Sausages (page 121).

Certified pork. Uncured pork that has been frozen at a low temperature for a long time in order to negate any trichina—a microscopic worm found in hogs (and bears). When ingested, it can cause serious illness. Fully cooking the meat kills trichina. See also part two, chapter 1, Easy Sausages (page 99).

Clostridium perfringens. Bacteria that can form a toxin if they are allowed to multiply in foods. These are inactive at temperatures below 40°F and above 140°F. Once the toxin develops, it cannot be destroyed by ordinary cooking. The toxin can, however, be avoided by properly handling the meat before, during, and after grinding. The bacteria are inhibited by salt, alcohol, acid, sugar, lack of moisture, and low temperatures.

Cold-smoking. Smoking meats or fish at a low temperature for a long period of time. The temperature should be below 100°F, and preferably between 70°F and 80°F. Bacteria multiply rapidly at temperatures between 80°F and 140°F. Smoke itself does little to cure meat or prevent bacterial growth. The absence of moisture that goes along with many smoking operations retards the growth of moisture—a point that you should remember before using the water pan provided with some types of smokers. (Hot-smoking is really cooking with the addition of smoke for flavor. It should be accomplished at temperatures higher than 140°F.) See *Hot-smoking.*

Country sausage. This popular term has no precise meaning, and I take it to mean the old-time sausages made on hog-killing days, usually in the fall of the year. There are thousands of recipes, but usually they are made with only a few ingredients, and in America are likely to contain flaked red pepper and sage.

Cure. A brine or a dry mixture containing salt and sodium nitrite and possibly other ingredients. Salt is the critical element. The word *cure* is sometimes used to denote sodium nitrite, sodium nitrate, potassium nitrite, or potassium nitrate. As a verb, *cure* means simply "to cure." *Aging* has a separate meaning. Cured meats can be aged, in which case temperature is not as important as in curing. See *Age.*

Curing salt. This mix is ordinary salt with a small amount of sodium nitrate, saltpeter, or some such compound mixed in.

Dry. To dry sausage by hanging in a cool, dry place for several weeks. Before drying, the sausage meat must be cured. See also part two, chapter 3, Stuffing Sausages (page 121).

Dry cure. A meat cure consisting of dry ingredients, mostly salt. As a verb, *dry-cure* means "to cure with dry ingredients." In home sausage making, the meat is usually cut into chunks, put into a plastic tray, sprinkled with the cure (or plain salt), covered, and placed in the refrigerator for about 2 days. (Note that cutting the meat into chunks reduces the time required to cure the meat. With larger chunks of meat, such as a whole ham, salt penetration and salt equalization may take months.) After stuffing in casings, the sausage may or may not be dried.

Hot-smoking. Flavoring meats or other foods with the aid of smoke during the cooking process. Most hot-smokers will attain a temperature of 200°F or higher. Hot-smoked sausages can be eaten immediately after the simultaneous cooking and smoking is over, but they are not cured or preserved. The process is not used extensively in jerky making. See *Cold-smoking.*

Honey. A natural preservative, honey is sometimes used instead of sugar in a sugar cure. It is also applied to the surface of some meats, especially bacon.

Hygrometer. A device used to measure the humidity inside a meat-curing chamber. It can be important for commercial applications, where exactness is important to duplicate results from one batch to another. As a rule, ham curing and salt equalization should be accomplished at a relative humidity of 75 to 90 percent; ham aging, on the other hand, is best at 50 to 60 percent.

Injection pump. A syringe designed for injecting liquid cures into large pieces of meat.

Kosher salt. A coarse salt that can be used for pickling and sausage making.

Liquid smoke. A liquid ingredient, readily available in supermarkets, that has been flavored by smoke. It's available in hickory and other flavors. Some practitioners consider it safer than real smoke because the tar, resin, and soot are removed in the manufacturing process. It may have some value as a meat preservative. In any case, use this stuff carefully and in small amounts lest you overpower the good flavor of the meat. It can be added to many of the recipes in this book. When mixing with sausage, add 2 teaspoons per 10 pounds of meat.

Monosodium glutamate. A crystalline salt that enhances the flavor of meat and other food; especially common in some Asian cuisines. It had a flurry of popularity in the United States, then dropped out of the culinary picture when it was deemed unsafe to eat. It does, however, remain as an ingredient in many old recipes. A little from time to time won't hurt anything, except possibly for people who are allergic to the stuff. Also called MSG, it is a major ingredient in Ac'cent.

Nitric oxide. When sodium nitrite is applied to meat, it breaks down into a chemical called nitric oxide, which is really the stuff that does the work.

Overhauling. Removing meat from a brine, stirring the brine, and putting the meat back into it. Sometimes more salt is added to the brine at this point.

Pellicle. The thin, shiny layer that forms on the surface of fish that has been soaked in brine and then dried for several hours in a breeze. A good pellicle improves the appearance of the final product, and may aid in preserving the fish.

Pickling salt. A refined salt that contains no iodine (non-iodized). It is used in pickling, canning, and meat curing. It can be used for making jerky, but ordinary salt will also do.

Potassium nitrate. Saltpeter. In the past, saltpeter was widely used in meat cures and in gunpowder. At the time of this writing, it has been banned for use in commercially cured meats. Saltpeter may be available in local pharmacies, and it can be purchased over the Internet, where it is sometimes spelled *saltpetre*.

Prague Powder. A trade name for a curing mixture of salt and chemicals. Prague Powder 1 contains salt and sodium nitrite. Prague Powder 2 contains salt, sodium nitrite, and sodium nitrate.

Salinometer. A device for measuring the salinity of a liquid. It can be used to determine the salt content of a brine used in meat curing.

Salmonella. Bacteria that can cause food poisoning. To reach dangerous levels in meats, they require moisture and the right temperature window. Salmonella is a problem especially with modern mass-produced poultry, although the bacteria can also multiply in other meat and fish, as well as in eggs. It is not a problem with sausages that have been properly cured and fully cooked. If in doubt about cooking fresh sausages, it's best to simmer the links in water for about 20 minutes. Then they can be dried to the touch and sautéed or grilled.

Salt. Sodium chloride. The term *curing salt* is sometimes applied to sodium nitrite and other chemicals. There are several kinds of salt, depending on how it is mined or processed. Of course, most salts are not pure sodium chloride. Any natural salt can be used for curing meats or making sausages.

It has been noted that man did not use sodium nitrite and other minerals in his cured meats until quite recently. This is not the whole story. Until recently, these minerals were not removed from natural sea salt before it was used for curing meats. Modern man is, in short, taking sodium nitrite and potassium nitrate and other minerals out of salt—and then putting them back into the salt used to cure meats.

In any case, my favorite salt for curing and table use is unrefined sea salt simply because it has a good flavor. Sea salt is, however, too expensive these days to use for large-scale meat curing.

Salt also comes in various grains, from fine to large chunks commonly known as ice cream salt. Any of the forms can be used in a brine, provided it is well mixed, but salts for dry cures work best in a fine grain. Regular table salt works just fine for making sausages.

Salt equalization. When a piece of meat is salted, at least two things happen: Moisture is drawn out of the meat, and salt penetrates into it. At first, only the outside of the meat will be salty. In time, the salt will penetrate deeper and deeper into the meat, tending to equalize the salt content. Salt equalization in a large ham may require 2 months, which includes a curing period of about 40 days and a salt equalization period of about 20 days. Salt equalization is a very important step in curing country hams.

Saltpeter. Potassium nitrate, NO_3, a naturally occurring mineral that was once used in meat curing and the manufacture of gunpowder. Today it is banned for commercial meat-curing use, having been replaced by sodium nitrate and sodium nitrite, both used in limited quantities. Saltpeter is, however, safe to use in small amounts—but I wouldn't want to eat it every day. Many of the old-time recipes for cured meats and sausage call for saltpeter, and some of the recipes in this book reflect this practice. It can, however, be omitted in recipes that call for lots of ordinary salt. Although saltpeter is a meat preservative, its main purpose is to help retain a reddish color in the meat. I once thought that the sale of saltpeter had been banned, or highly restricted, but while working on this book, I purchased a bottle off the shelf in my local pharmacy.

Seasoning salt. Regular salt flavored with herbs, spices, and other ingredients. Several kinds are available in spice departments at supermarkets, such as lemon-pepper and hickory-smoked.

Smoking. See *Cold-smoking* and *Hot-smoking*.

Sodium nitrate. A sodium salt that is used in meat curing as well as in fertilizers and explosives. It is toxic and should be used in small amounts, usually thoroughly mixed with ordinary salt. Although some experts, some of whom sell curing mixes, say it is necessary in meat curing, its use is primarily to preserve color in sausage, corned beef, and so on.

Sodium nitrite. A compound used in curing meats. It is toxic and should be used in small amounts. See *Sodium nitrate*.

Soy sauce. A wonderful Chinese condiment and standard ingredient made with soy, salt, barley, and other ingredients. Low-salt or "lite" soy sauces are marketed, but these are not recommended for jerky unless the recipe also calls for salt. Note, however, that a "light" soy sauce refers to the color and may indeed contain more salt than "dark."

Staphylococcus aureus. Bacteria that can form a toxin if allowed to multiply in foods. These are inactive at temperatures below 40°F and above 140°F. Once the toxin develops, it cannot be destroyed by ordinary cooking. The toxin can, however, be avoided by properly handling the meat before, during, and after grinding. The bacteria are inhibited by salt, alcohol, acid, sugar, lack of moisture, and low temperatures.

Sugar cure. A mixture of salt and sugar for meat or fish, although salt is the essential ingredient. Up to a point, sugar gives the ham a better flavor and a good color, but too much sugar makes the meat slimy.

Summer sausage. This term is loosely used. I use it to mean any sausage that is made in cold weather and intended to last into or perhaps through the summer. Usually, summer sausage is cured and dried.

Trichina. A microscopic worm found in hogs and bears. When ingested, it can cause serious illness (trichinosis). Fully cooking the meat kills trichina. Freezing will also kill the worm, as discussed in part two, chapter 1, Easy Sausages (page 99).

SOURCES OF MATERIALS AND SUPPLIES

Allied Kenco Sales, 26 Lyerly Street, Houston, TX 77022. Jerky-making equipment, spices, cures, and supplies. Telephone: (800) 356-5189. Website: www.alliedkenco.com.

Billabong Jerky. Outback jerky of several sorts, including emu, kangaroo, and crocodile. The early Aussie cowboys were especially fond of beef jerky—and still are. Website: www.jerky.com.au.

Cumberland Mountain General Store, 6807 South York Highway, Clarkrange, TN 38553. This mail-order firm publishes an interesting catalog, chock-full of hard-to-find old-time items. They carry several hand-cranked sausage mills and stuffers, along with a complete line of spare parts and attachments. Spices, cures, and seasonings are also available, as are books, knives, etc. Telephone: (931) 863-3880. Website: cumberlandmountaingeneralstore.net/Index.

Eldon's Sausage and Jerky Supply Catalog, HC 75, Box 113A2, Kooski, ID 63539. Meat grinders and other equipment and supplies for making sausage and jerky. Telephone: (509) 926-4949.

Excalibur, 8250 Ferguson Avenue, Sacramento, CA 95828. Excalibur brand dehydrators and accessories. These have up to nine (depending on the model) square trays. Telephone: (800) 875-4254. Website: www.excaliburdehydrator.com.

Grandma LaMure's Spice 'n' Slice, 436 North Washington Avenue, Prescott, AZ 86301. If you want to make 2-pound batches of sausages without using a stuffer, try this firm's inexpensive no-fuss mixes. At present they offer packages for salami, bologna, pepperoni, jerky, country sausage, "southern sausage," and jerky. I have tried all the mixes with excellent results. Telephone: (800) 310-4094. Website: www.spiceandslice.com.

King Arthur Flour, 135 US Route 5 South, Norwich, VT 05055. Whole grains, buckwheat, and other ingredients. Website: www.kingarthurflour.com.

L.E.M. Products, Inc. Jerky and sausage seasonings, curing salts, and spices, as well as dehydrators, jerky shooters, and vacuum-pack systems. Telephone: (877) 336-5895. Website: www.lemproducts.com. E-mail: info@lemproducts.com.

Myron's Fine Foods, 131 West Main Street, Suite 320, Orange, MA 01364. Myron's 20-Gauge, a wild-game and fish sauce, and other fine sauces. Telephone: (978) 673-8031. Website: www.chefmyrons.com.

Nesco American Harvest, PO Box 237, Two Rivers, WI 54241. This firm manufactures several round dehydrators with stackable trays—up to twelve—along with jerky guns and other accessories. Telephone: (800) 288-4545. Website: www.nesco.com.

Pendery's, 1221 Manufacturing Street, Dallas, TX 75207. Seasonings and spices for sausage and jerky, chili peppers, cookbooks, and other items of interest. Telephone: (800) 533-1870. Website: www.penderys.com.

Penzeys Spices, 12001 West Capitol Drive, Wauwatosa, WI 53222. An excellent mail-order source for spices and seasonings. In addition to peppers, spices, and herbs, Penzey's also offers various sausage seasonings, including mixes for bratwurst, Italian sausage, venison sausage, Polish sausage, Russian sausage, and a breakfast sausage. Telephone: (800) 741-7787. Website: www.penzeys.com.

Pleasant Hill Grain, 210 South 1st Street, Hampton, NE 68843-0007. This firm sells the L'Equip 528 dehydrator, featuring trays that are basically rectangular with rounded corners. The trays are stackable, up to six high.

Professional Marketing Group, Inc., 16817 188th Avenue SE, Renton, WA 98058. This firm markets the PressAIREizer dehydrators, along with a jerky press, mesh screens, spices, and so on. The unit features round trays in which the air is said to move up an outside ring and flow horizontally across each tray. Stackable to a whopping thirty-five trays. Telephone: (425) 264-0195.

Ronco Holdings, Inc., 15505 Long Vista Drive, Suite 250, Austin, TX 78728. This outfit markets a dehydrator with round trays, expandable to five. The air flows upward by convection, without a fan. Telephone: (855) 857-6626. Website: www.ronco.com.

The Sausage Maker, Inc., 1500 Clinton Street, Building 123, Buffalo, NY 14206. Bulk spices, sausage spice mixes, meat cure mixes, sausage additives, and equipment for grinding, stuffing, drying, and smoking sausage. Some of the equipment is designed for the small manufacturer. I find the firm to be a reliable mail-order source for natural and artificial casings, including several sizes of salted hog, sheep, and cow gut. Telephone: (888) 490-8525. Website: www .sausagemaker.com.

Waring, Waring makes a circular dehydrator with clear trays, giving a good view of the contents during the drying process. Telephone: (800) 492-7464. Website: www.waringpro.com.

FURTHER READING

Ashbrook, Frank G. *Butchering, Processing and Preservation of Meat*. Van Nostrand Reinhold Company, New York, 1955.

Kutas, Rytek. *Great Sausage Recipes and Meat Curing*. The Sausage Maker, Inc., Buffalo, NY, 1984.

Predika, Jerry. *The Sausage-Making Cookbook*. Stackpole Books, Mechanicsburg, PA, 1983.

Reavis, Charles G. *Home Sausage Making*. Storey Communications, Inc., Pownal, VT, 1987.

Ruhlman, Michael, and Brian Polcyn. *Charcuterie*. W. W. Norton & Company, New York, 2005.

Savic, I. V. *Small-Scale Sausage Production*. Food and Agriculture Organization of the United Nations, Rome, 1985.

Sleight, Jack. *The Complete Sausage Cookbook*. Stackpole Books, Mechanicsburg, PA, 1995.

Ubaldi, Jack, and Elizabeth Crossman. *Meat Book*. Macmillan Publishing Company, New York, 1987. This book has some excellent recipes for sausage, along with some strong opinions on the use of saltpeter, but its main focus is on the meat itself, especially pork, beef, lamb, veal, and poultry.

INDEX

ABOUT THE AUTHOR

A. D. Livingston claimed to have hopscotched through life. Navy at seventeen. Mechanical engineering at Auburn. Atomic bombs at Oak Ridge. Creative writing at University of Alabama. Missiles and rockets at Huntsville. Published a novel and played a little poker. Travel editor at *Southern Living* magazine. Freelance writing and outdoor photography. Word man for fishing rods and bait-casting reels with Lew Childre, the genius of modern fishing tackle. Bought the family farm. Lost the back forty publishing *Bass Fishing News*. Lost the rest of the farm manufacturing fishing lures. Back to freelancing. Published twenty-some books. Food columnist for *Gray's Sporting Journal*. All his life he loved to hunt and fish and to cook and eat the bounty. And he loved to write about it his way.